*Psychic Bisexuality: A British-French Dialogue* clarifies and develops the Freudian conception according to which sexual identity is not reduced to the anatomical difference between the sexes, but is constructed as a psychic bisexuality that is inherent to all human beings.

The book takes the Freudian project into new grounds of clinical practice and theoretical formulations and contributes to a profound psychoanalytic understanding of sexuality. The object of psychoanalysis is psychosexuality, which is not, in the final analysis, determined by having a male or a female body, but by the unconscious phantasies that are reached *après coup* through tracing the nuanced interplay of identifications as they are projected, enacted and experienced in the transference and the countertransference in the analytic encounter.

Drawing on British and French Freudian and post-Freudian traditions, the book explores questions of love, transference and countertransference, sexual identity and gender to set out the latest clinical understanding of bisexuality, and includes chapters from influential French analysts available in English for the first time. *Psychic Bisexuality: A British-French Dialogue* will appeal to psychoanalysts and psychoanalytic psychotherapists as well as gender studies scholars.

**Rosine Jozef Perelberg** is a Fellow of the British Psychoanalytic Society, Visiting Professor in the Psychoanalysis Unit at University College London and Corresponding Member of the Paris Psychoanalytical Society. Her books include *Psychoanalytic Understanding of Violence and Suicide* and *Female Experience: Four Generations of British Women Psychoanalysts on Work with Women* (with Joan Raphael-Leff). She is the author of *Time, Space and Phantasy* and *Murdered Father, Dead Father: Revisiting the Oedipus Complex*. In 2007, she was named one of the ten women of the year by the Brazilian National Council of Women.

THE NEW LIBRARY OF PSYCHOANALYSIS
General Editor: Alessandra Lemma

The New Library of Psychoanalysis was launched in 1987 in association with the Institute of Psychoanalysis, London. It took over from the International Psychoanalytical Library which published many of the early translations of the works of Freud and the writings of most of the leading British and Continental psychoanalysts.

The purpose of the New Library of Psychoanalysis is to facilitate a greater and more widespread appreciation of psychoanalysis and to provide a forum for increasing mutual understanding between psychoanalysts and those working in other disciplines such as the social sciences, medicine, philosophy, history, linguistics, literature and the arts. It aims to represent different trends both in British psychoanalysis and in psychoanalysis generally. The New Library of Psychoanalysis is well placed to make available to the English-speaking world psychoanalytic writings from other European countries and to increase the interchange of ideas between British and American psychoanalysts. Through the *Teaching Series*, the New Library of Psychoanalysis now also publishes books that provide comprehensive, yet accessible, overviews of selected subject areas aimed at those studying psychoanalysis and related fields such as the social sciences, philosophy, literature and the arts.

The Institute, together with the British Psychoanalytical Society, runs a low-fee psychoanalytic clinic, organizes lectures and scientific events concerned with psychoanalysis and publishes the *International Journal of Psychoanalysis*. It runs a training course in psychoanalysis which leads to membership of the International Psychoanalytical Association – the body which preserves internationally agreed standards of training, of professional entry, and of professional ethics and practice for psychoanalysis as initiated and developed by Sigmund Freud. Distinguished members of the Institute have included Michael Balint, Wilfred Bion, Ronald Fairbairn, Anna Freud, Ernest Jones, Melanie Klein, John Rickman and Donald Winnicott.

Previous general editors have included David Tuckett, who played a very active role in the establishment of the New Library. He was followed as general editor by Elizabeth Bott Spillius, who was in turn

# THE NEW LIBRARY OF PSYCHOANALYSIS

General Editor: Alessandra Lemma

# Psychic Bisexuality

## A British–French Dialogue

Edited by
Rosine Jozef Perelberg

Routledge
Taylor & Francis Group

LONDON AND NEW YORK

First published 2018
by Routledge
2 Park Square, Milton Park, Abingdon, Oxon OX14 4RN

and by Routledge
711 Third Avenue, New York, NY 10017

*Routledge is an imprint of the Taylor & Francis Group, an informa business*

*British Library Cataloguing in Publication Data*
A catalogue record for this book is available from the British Library

*Library of Congress Cataloging in Publication Data*
Names: Perelberg, Rosine Jozef, editor.
Title: Psychic bisexuality : a British-French dialogue / edited by
Rosine Perelberg.
Description: Abingdon, Oxon ; New York, NY : Routledge, 2018. |
Series: New library of psychoanalysis | Includes bibliographical
references and index.
Identifiers: LCCN 2017041460 (print) | LCCN 2017048491 (ebook) |
ISBN 9781351262965 (Master) | ISBN 9781351262958 (Web PDF) |
ISBN 9781351262941 (ePub) | ISBN 9781351262934 (Mobipocket/Kindle)
| ISBN 9781138579026 (hardback : alk. paper)
Subjects: LCSH: Sex (Psychology) | Bisexuality.
Classification: LCC BF175.5.S48 (ebook) | LCC BF175.5.S48 P7925
2018 (print) | DDC 155.3–dc23
LC record available at https://lccn.loc.gov/2017041460

ISBN: 978-1-138-57902-6 (hbk)
ISBN: 978-1-138-57903-3 (pbk)
ISBN: 978-1-351-26296-5 (ebk)

Typeset in Bembo
by Wearset Ltd, Boldon, Tyne and Wear

MIX
Paper from
responsible sources
FSC
www.fsc.org   FSC™ C013985

Printed in the United Kingdom
by Henry Ling Limited

# Contents

# Contents

**In Memory of**
Marion Burgner, Mervin Glasser, André Green, Pearl King, Dinora Pines, Joseph Sandler and Harold Stewart,
*who paved my way towards a psychoanalytic understanding of psychic bisexuality.*

# Contributors

**Marilia Aisenstein** is a Training Analyst of the Hellenic Psycho-analytical Society and the Paris Psychoanalytical Society and Past president of the Paris Psychoanalytical Society and of the Paris Psychosomatic Institute. She is a member of the editorial board of the *Revue Française de Psychanalyse*, co-founder and editor of the *Revue Française de Psychosomatique*. She has been chair of the IPA's International New Groups, and the European representative to the IPA's Executive Committee. She presently works in private practice, gives seminars in both the Hellenic and the Paris Societies, and is the President of the Executive Board of the Paris Psychoanalytical Society's Clinic. She has written 130 chapters and papers on psychosomatics and hypochondria. She received the Maurice Bouvet Prize in 1992.

**Donald Campbell** is a Training and Supervising Analyst for children, adolescents and adults at the British Psychoanalytical Society and is a past President of the Society. He is also a former Secretary General of the International Psychoanalytical Association. For thirty years he worked at the Portman Clinic, a National Health Service outpatient facility in London, assessing and treating in psychoanalytic psychotherapy children, adolescents and adults who were violent or delinquent or suffered from a perversion. His published work includes the subjects of child sexual abuse, perversion, suicide, violence, self-analysis, adolescence and horror film monsters. His most recent publication is *Working in the Dark: Understanding the Pre-suicide State of Mind* (2017), which he co-authored with Rob Hale.

**Catherine Chabert** is a Training Analyst, a Member of the Association Psychanalytique de France and Professor in Psychopathology and Clinical Psychology at Paris–Sorbonne (Paris–Descartes University), France. She has published widely in French and international psychoanalytic journals and was co-editor with Jean-Claude Rolland of the *Libres Cahiers pour la Psychanalyse* (2000–2015). She edited several collections at Dunod Editions, in particular, *Psychoanalysis and Psychopathology*, and many contributed books (with Jacques André) in the Petite Bibliothèque de Psychanalyse. She is the author of *Féminin mélancolique* (2003) and *L'amour de la différence* (2011). Her latest book is entitled *La jeune fille et le psychanalyste* (2015).

**Rachel Chaplin** is a psychoanalyst and a Fellow of the British Psychoanalytical Society. She is an Honorary Senior Lecturer at University College London, with particular interests in French psychoanalytic thinking and in the relationship between literature and psychoanalysis.

**Monique Cournut-Janin** is a Training Analyst of the Paris Psychoanalytic Society. She was Director of the Jean Favreau Centre of Consultations and Treatment. With Rosine Perelberg, she was co-chair for COWAP for Europe. In 1993, with Jean Cournut, she presented her work to the Congrès des Psychanalystes de Langue Française (CPLF). She has many publications in the *Revue Française de Psychanalyse* and *International Journal of Psychoanalysis*. She published *Féminin et féminité* (1998), contributed to the book *Incestes* and, in 2002, to the *Monographie de la RFP* with her paper "Clés pour le féminin: femme, mère, amante et fille". She contributed a paper on Dora for *Freud: A Modern Reader* (2005).

**Christian David** was a philosopher, poet, artist, medical practitioner and psychoanalyst; he became a full member of the Paris Psychoanalytical Society in 1965. Co-editor of the *Revue Française de Psychanalyse* and of the Fil Rouge series (PUF), he was one of the founders in 1972 of the Paris Psychosomatic Institute. His innovative work has dealt with being in love, representation of affects, psychic bisexuality, emotional perversion and mourning the loss of one's self. He contributed to several books, wrote articles and poetry, and his paintings have been exhibited. Among his major works are: *L'état amoureux* [Being in Love] (1992) and *La bisexualité psychique* [Psychic Bisexuality] (1992).

**Rosemary Davies** is a Training and Supervising Analyst; she works in private practice in London. She is an Honorary Senior Lecturer at University College London, where she has taught Freud, and a series on Contemporary Clinical Theory. She has delivered papers in the UK and abroad, most recently "Rivalry, Benign or Belligerent Sibling of Envy?" and "The Setting, Whose Frame is it Anyway?" She edited and has contributed to various psychoanalytic books: "Regression, Curiosity and the Discovery of the Object" and "Treatment of a Violent Young Adult". She has published in the "Analyst at Work" (2007) series and wrote a paper on "Anxiety, the Importunate Companion" (2012) for the *International Journal of Psychoanalysis*.

**Jacqueline Godfrind** is a Training Analyst and Supervisor, and Past President of the Belgian Psychoanalytic Society, where she is currently the Chair of the Education Committee. She is a former lecturer at the Université Libre de Bruxelles. She has written numerous papers for international journals and chapters for books. She has written *Les deux courants du transfert* (1993) and *Comment la féminité vient aux femmes* (2001), and she co-authored *Ce qui est opérant dans la cure* (2008).

**André Green** was a Training Analyst and Supervisor and was a Past President of the Société Psychanalytique de Paris. He was a Freud Memorial Professor at the University of London from 1979 to 1980. A prolific writer, several of his books have been translated into English, including *On Private Madness, Life Narcissism, Death Narcissism, The Work of the Negative, Key Ideas for a Contemporary Psychoanalysis, Time in Psychoanalysis*, and *The Diachrony in Psychoanalysis*. A biography of André Green, written by François Duparc, appeared in the Psychanalystes d'aujourd'hui series. A book of the conference held in memory of André Green in the British Psychoanalytical Society, entitled *The Greening of Psychoanalysis: André Green's New Paradigm in Contemporary Theory and Practice*, edited by Rosine Perelberg and Gregorio Kohon, was published in 2017.

**Denis Hirsch** is an adult and adolescent psychiatrist and psychoanalyst. He is an Associate Member of the Belgian Psychoanalytical Society and of the International Psychoanalytical Association. He is the Director of Consultation in Child and Adolescent Psychiatry, of the Mental Health Service of the City of Brussels (Service de Santé

Mentale de la Ville de Bruxelles). He has also trained in group analysis and psychodrama and is a member of CEFFRAP (Cercle d'Études Françaises pour la Formation et la Recherche: Institute for Research and Training in Group Analysis and Psychodrama), created by Didier Anzieu and René Kaës. He has published widely in the area of risk in adolescence, the psychic transmission of psychic bisexuality, transmission of collective traumas, religious radicalism, contemporary malaise and destructivity in postmodern civilization.

**Gregorio Kohon** is a Training Analyst of the British Psychoanalytical Society and works in London in private practice. He edited *The British School of Psychoanalysis: The Independent Tradition* (1986), and *The Dead Mother: The Work of André Green* (1999). He also published *No Lost Certainties to Be Recovered* (1999), *Love and Its Vicissitudes* (co-authored with André Green, 2005), and *Reflections on the Aesthetic Experience: Psychoanalysis and the Uncanny* (2015). He edited *The Greening of Psychoanalysis* (with Rosine Perelberg, 2017). His novel *Papagayo Rojo, Pata de Palo* [*Red Parrot, Wooden Leg*] (2007, 2008) was a finalist in the 2001 Fernando Lara Prize. He has also published, in Spanish, four books of poetry and a collection of short stories, *Truco Gallo* (co-authored with Mario Flecha and Viqui Rosenberg). He has two new books in preparation: *British Psychoanalysis: An Independent Tradition*, and *Symbolic Impoverishment*.

**Rosine Jozef Perelberg** is a Fellow and Training Analyst of the British Psychoanalytical Society, Visiting Professor in the Psychoanalysis Unit at University College London, and Corresponding Member of the Paris Psychoanalytical Society. She has published widely, especially in the *International Journal of Psychoanalysis* and *Revue Française de Psychanalyse*. She edited *Gender and Power in Families* (with Ann Miller, 1990), *Psychoanalytic Understanding of Violence and Suicide* (1997), *Female Experience: Four Generations of British Women Psychoanalysts on Work with Women* (with Joan Raphael-Leff, 1997, 2008), *Freud: A Modern Reader* (2006), *Time and Memory* (2007), *Dreaming and Thinking* (2000) and *The Greening of Psychoanalysis* (with Gregorio Kohon, 2017). She is the author of *Time, Space and Phantasy* (2008) and *Murdered Father, Dead Father: Revisiting the Oedipus Complex* (2015). In 1991, at the IPA Congress in Buenos Aires, she was the co-winner of the Cesare Sacerdoti Prize. In 2007, she was named one of the ten Women of the Year by the Brazilian National Council of Women.

**Harvey Rich** resides in Paris, France, and Washington, DC, USA, where he works in clinical practice in psychotherapy and psychoanalysis. He is a Member of the American Psychoanalytic Association and a Corresponding Member of the Paris Psychoanalytical Society. He retired as Training and Supervising Analyst of the Washington Psychoanalytic Society when he moved to Paris. He is the author of *In the Moment: Celebrating the Everyday* (2000). He has served as a consultant to the World Bank in post-conflict civil reconstruction.

**Nathalie Zilkha** is a Training and Supervising Psychoanalyst of the Swiss Psychoanalytical Society. She first trained as a child and adolescent psychiatrist and psychotherapist, and now she works in private practice in Geneva. She has published numerous papers, most of them in the *Revue Française de Psychanalyse* and the *Monographies de la Revue Française de Psychanalyse*. She is the co-author of *Les scénarios narcissiques de la parentalité* (with Juan Manzano and Francisco Palacio-Espasa, 1999). She was awarded two prizes in French psychoanalysis: the Prix Pierre Mâle in 2008 (co-laureate) and the Prix Maurice Bouvet in 2013.

# Foreword

*Juliet Mitchell*

This is a beautifully orchestrated and rich collection of essays without a weak moment. Its appearance is timely – timely both because there is still much to explore and because currently "transgender", in challenging the binary, is claiming to replace the bisexual *subjectivity*, whose importance I will be arguing for here. Wandering through my mind, like wine through water, is the example of great artists whose art is in bringing the unconscious to consciousness and for whom, therefore, "bisexuality" is a *sine qua non* for an art practice. As André Green says here on behalf of psychoanalysis, bisexuality "relates to the theory as a whole". Of her father, Maya Picasso wrote: "In my opinion my father was, in a sense, 'bisexual' from his birth, or rather since his debut as an artist..."[1] The sculptor and painter Louise Bourgeois' many works and sayings about bisexuality can, for our purposes here, be reduced to her knowledge that "we are all male–female".[2]

"Bisexuality" is a complicated subject; in an exemplary way, this collection does justice to its importance and its expression as it plays out in clinical encounters and in its historical and theoretical significance, so well described in the comprehensive and excellent Introduction written by Rosine Perelberg.

Bisexuality as a concept makes us ask questions of the theory (or theories) of psychoanalysis. In a recent exchange on the "death drive" between the psychoanalyst Michael Parsons and the sociologist Michael Rustin, Parsons speaks for both when he says that nowadays all of psychoanalysis would disagree with the primary need of "drive satisfaction". They claim that Freud's undying insistence on drive theory has been superseded by the understanding that psychic growth only takes place in a context of relationships to others.[3] I believe that repudiating drive theory presents a major problem for the concept of bisexuality. If such a compulsively heterosexual man as Picasso, as an artist, is notably bisexual, we might want to set our enquiry into his bisexual "objects" within the framework of his bisexual subjectivity. I am not sure we could do so only within "object relations" theory if it has discarded the theory of the conflictual and amalgamating drives. Freud lamented that: "The theory of bisexuality is still surrounded by many obscurities and we cannot but feel it as a serious impediment in psychoanalysis that it has not yet found any link with the theory of the instincts."[4] The task remains.

A theory of object relations is very different from the metapsychology for which Freud strove. Put reductively, the theory of object relations *reflects* the practice on which all theories must be based; Freud's "metapsychology", on the other hand, endeavours to *shift* it into another intellectual dimension – one in which one can talk about the key ideas of psychoanalysis without having to offer examples from the empirical specificities that must underpin them and to which they always refer. A pay-off of a metapsychology is that it aims to be for everything, everywhere, within its *limited and identifiable* field of enquiry, which I still take to be "unconscious processes" and "primary-process thinking".[5] "Object relations", on the contrary, aspires to universality through an accumulation of instances based on their inevitable availability/unavailability, like parents or the self. Einstein claimed that any theory must start in the absurd. A reflective theory such as ego psychology or object relations elucidates the unabsurd. The "witch metapsychology" tries to represent absurdity.

Thinking here with "drive theory", I would argue that for "bisexuality", we are all, always, "bisexual *subjects*", who will satisfy our conflicting and coinciding drives for life and death through some sort of object, perverse or not. In other words, bisexuality is a condition of our sexuality within our drives, but – and here's the rub – it therefore must not only relate to sexuality and life but also be a condition of our drive towards inorganic death or outward-bound destruction. Klein's object relations theory made the death drive her own. Where Freud's different concept is accepted, there has been no satisfactory metapsychological term to equal "libido" – the energy that transforms the sexual drive. "Nirvana" aims at one feature – the desire for the inorganic – and "destrudo" – the wish to destroy – at another, but, as they cannot be together as one word, neither will do. Although the importance of the issue of the death drive as Freud hypothesized is underexplored, it will be crucial for thinking further about "bisexuality" within drive theory.

So, to go for the moment with Freud's oft-dashed hopes for the link between bisexuality and drive theory: what "bisexuality" needs, if it is to be part of the metapsychology, is an understanding comparable to the revolutionary breakthrough that is, to this day – and beyond – *The Three Essays on Sexuality*. It is in these essays that Freud argues that sexuality has no object other than a "satisfaction" that is never finally achieved, and all the crucial mental tasks and hard work that such a pursuit entails. The sexual drive will use an object – but the object may be an animal or a fetish as well as a mother or a lover. Along with Freud's discovery of the partially known infantile sexuality and its unknown psychic elucidation, the understanding of a continuity between perversion and "normality" was, and remains, a break-through. Everyday understanding into which psychoanalysis is inevitably in danger of falling is transformed.

The concept of bisexuality has been one of the main fall-guys of this invariable collapse into the commonplace. Common understanding of "bisexuality" is that it indicates the choice of both a homosexual and a heterosexual object; object relations' understanding follows suit. So, too, does Freud when referring to object relations; however, taking a wider viewpoint than this, he also always maintained that we have a bisexual "tendency" that must be our stance as subjects. This is crucial, that we acknowledge with Freud that bisexuality is *innate* – that the child is "originally" bisexual. I suggest it is with this recognition that bisexuality could have a position within the drive postulates of the metapsychology. Independently of any identifications or object choices, subjectively our sexuality is always bisexual. As with the sexuality, the bisexuality will come into conflict with key prohibitions.

There is one libido for both sexes, the unconscious is generic – our dreaming is not gendered, psychic defences, pathologies and the making of art are the same, bisexuality as a state of being is a universal condition of both sexes. Yet the universal undifferentiated experiences are pursued in a way that results in a gender distinction and a sexual difference. There is a puzzle here. Green sees the "neuter gender" as sounding the death-knell of sexuality as *difference* and, with it, bisexuality. However, transgender's opposition to the binary of sexual difference could be on behalf of a social seriality.

So far, the question of any distinction only arises with the sexuality of the life drive. Even though women and men have different experiences of death and destructiveness, these are nowhere made to affect the unisex psychosocial processes – the compulsion to repeat and the negative therapeutic reactions, the pathology of melancholia. The death drive could here be a model for the life drive. We need to recall that within the concept of sexual difference, girls and boys are subject to the *same* castration complex. Freud was rightly resistant to any effort – such as that of Karl Abraham – wherein it was proposed that the threat of castration *in itself in any way* differed for the sexes. Boys and girls may differ in the way they go through universal prohibitions – but the prohibitions are the same. The prohibitions are on certain sexual relations that go under the generic title of incest and certain forms of killing that are specified as murder. Girls and boys may (castration's sexual difference) or may not (lateral gender distinction) negotiate the prohibitions differently – but that is all.

Psychoanalysis is (*pace* post-modernism) knowledge about the universal psychosocial; hence the presence of *male* hysteria was its foundation. How would we live together in love and in hate if unconsciously we were from Venus *and* Mars? The unconscious, psychoanalysis, bisexuality are all "both/and" formations. We are all girl *and* boy; boy *and* girl. Unconscious processes are not in themselves gendered.

Freud charted the "more bisexual" outcome of the Oedipus complex for the girl. For me – after two decades during which I have been concerned with sibling processes as the starting point of a horizontal axis of lateral relations – the theoretical question has always been: do they, as Freud proposed, become only a part of the vertical "family complex", on a par with the parents? Or do they contribute an autonomous set of unconscious processes to the vertical axis (with which they are muddled and interactive)? A clinical experience in Chapter 10 (in this volume) takes us in this latter direction for "bisexuality": Rachel Chaplin movingly describes the effect of her analyst's assumption of post-oedipal "sexual difference" invading her patient's bisexuality, which, being psychically earlier, precedes "analytic metaphorization". This interests me greatly. The infant-becoming-a-child speaks, often fluently, but is still thinking in a literal manner through its body. This child is usually described as "pre-oedipal" – and so it is, on the vertical axis. On the horizontal, it is pre-*social* – "expelled" from the family to find and make groups of friends and enemies at school, on the street, in the fields or on bomb sites.

Although I think the same child will be amalgamated to the vertical axis of the oedipal, it has long been my argument that there is also a social horizontal axis, and, on this, siblings contribute to unconscious processes autonomously. They do so with earlier narcissistic–psychotic defences (as does Chaplin's patient), privileging these for the social world with widespread implications. To support this thesis, my suggestion is of a "sibling trauma" and its effects, which elicit an absolute prohibition from the ever-reality-inducing mother on the horizontal axis. This "mother's law" only prohibits incest and murder *between* her children.

Psychically, despite being described as "girl" or "boy", the baby – conceived, carried in pregnancy and born – is bisexual. However, *meaning* is only given to the primal naming of "girl" and "boy" when a sibling arrives (or is expected) by the toddler: it will be a sister or a brother, but not neither nor both. By the same token, the toddler can only be one or the other, so either girl or boy. This is a major curtailment of omnipotence and a different one from not being able to be mother or father, which has yet to come.

The defences against the mother's prohibition on killing the new baby who has occupied the place of existence of the old "baby" (murder) and against loving it too much, as though it really were one and the same (incest), are not repression to unconsciousness, but the earlier ones of splitting, reversal into the opposite, dissociation, and so on. This is what happens to the gender – on the acquisition of a sister or a brother, the bisexual child is no more: the child should no longer be bisexual. But the establishment of sibling gender distinction is always on the basis of the continued availability of bisexual subjecthood. Bisexuality has a special place here, where siblings equally find the "same" and the "other" across the sister–brother gender distinction.

However, in all of us, this child will remain bisexual unconsciously throughout life. Its second gender is partially unconscious – but over there, somewhere else, not deep down, but in another place. The defences along the "narcissistic–psychotic" axis are not neurotic. These are unconscious effects produced by a generic, *necessary* universal trauma – the "sibling trauma", in which archetypally the toddler feels annihilated by its "replacement". It is a trauma as trauma is understood both by object relations thinkers exemplified by D. W. Winnicott but also by drive theory, which emphasizes the psycho-economic effects of the excess of the traumatic invasion from without and within.

Based on this traumatic experience, for the toddler this is a rite of passage from infancy to childhood. The child needs help. The immense importance of stories for the 2-year-old has been taken up therapeutically as "narratives" of object relations in treatments for the later victim of subsequent trauma, which have inevitably evoked the universal "sibling trauma". But the child wants this story, with the drive theory's compulsive correctness of every tiny detail, over and over again – a "compulsion to repeat" that belongs to the "death drive". It is here, in the identical desire of girl and boy, that Freud might have sought a place for bisexuality in his metapsychology.

Before the variously defined notions of the "intersubjective" origins of subjectivity gained popularity, Charlotte Bleuler's understanding of "transitivism" described the operation of an intersubjective context for the sibling toddler and the child it becomes. One child falls over, and the other one cries; one hits the right eye of the other and claims it has *been* hit, clutching its matching left eye to prove the point. This is another type of mirroring, which provides the foundational subjectivity of lateral individuals and collectivities of sisterhoods and brotherhoods, affines, partners and enemies.

From our bisexual subject-hood we will all make conscious or unconscious object choices. However, if we neglect this primal bisexuality and its initial setback for siblings who, while obeying (or not) the same prohibitions in the same way, should nevertheless become gender-distinct as sisters and brothers, we will be liable to miss bisexuality's creativity. Picasso could only capture in art the women he adored and loathed on the basis of his bisexual subjectivity, whose unconsciousness he strove relentlessly to bring to consciousness. In his prolific series, "the painter and his model", the two characters shift gender places. It remained for Louise Bourgeois, outstandingly conscious of the psychoanalytic understanding of unconscious factors in general, and here specifically in her complex experience of her younger brother and of her own three boys, to become subjective bisexuality's most profound portraitist.[6] Of *Janus Fleuri*, Bourgeois wrote: "It is perhaps a self-portrait – one of

*Figure 0.1* Louise Bourgeois's *Janus Fleuri* (1968) installed above Freud's couch during "Louise Bourgeois: The Return of the Repressed" at the Freud Museum in London in 2012. © The Easton Foundation/VAGA, New York/ DACS, London, 2017.

many." The sculpture that, in one exhibition of her work, hung above Freud's couch, is an exemplary study in bisexuality as a subject position rather than an object choice. The subject position is clearly not singular: ambivalently both ponderous and flowery, this is herself as a girl *and* a boy – boy and girl, looking both ways, Janus-like.[7]

Cambridge, July 2017

## Notes

1 Maya Picasso, in W. Spies (Ed.), *Picasso's World of Children* (Munich: Prestel Verlag, 1996), p. 57.

2 Louise Bourgeois, in M.-L. Bernadac & H.-U. Obrist (Eds.), *Louise Bourgeois. Destruction of the Father. Reconstruction of the Father: Writings and Interviews 1923–1997* (Cambridge, MA: MIT Press, 1998), p. 101.

3 M. Parsons & M. Rustin, M. Rustin quoting M. Parsons in "Why the idea of the death instinct is mistaken", *British Society Bulletin*, 53 (55), June, 2017, p. 6.

4 S. Freud, *Civilization and Its Discontents, S.E.* 21 (1930), p. 106, fn 3.

5 See S. Freud, *The Question of Lay Analysis, S.E.* 20 (1926), pp. 230–231. The statements in this essay are crucial.

6 Describing *Janus Fleuri*, I wrote:

> In this piece are two clitorises or flaccid penises: comforting sex rather than phallic dominance. In the centre are the female genitals experienced as if from inside – if touched they would respond with pleasure. Stasis and movement are captured in bronze – a hard material made to represent softness. Its title recalls that flowers contain both male and female elements.
>
> (J. Mitchell, "Love and Hate, Girl and Boy". *London Review of Books*, *36* (21, 6 November 2014), pp. 11–14)

7 L. Bourgeois, *The Return of the Repressed*, ed. P. Larratt-Smith (Buenos Aires, 2011); subsequently at The Freud Museum, London. As for all my work on Louise Bourgeois, my grateful acknowledgement is to the opportunities and support given to me by the generosity of the Easton Foundation and Louise Bourgeois Trust.

# Acknowledgements

Monique Cournut-Janin and first I met in Brighton in 1998, at the first of the Anglo-French Colloquia organized by Anne-Marie Sandler and Haydée Faimberg. The book I had edited with Joan Raphael-Leff, *Female Experience: Three Generations of Women Psychoanalysts on Work with Women* (1997), had just been published. Monique approached me and expressed her appreciation of the book. I was familiar with her work on femininity and female sexuality that she had written with Jean Cournut and presented for the Congrès des Psychanalystes de Langue Française, in 1993, *La castration et le féminin dans les deux sexes* (Paris: PUF), and was delighted that she had enjoyed our book. We decided to organize a series of meetings between French and British analysts, focused on the theme of sexuality, which would also be open to candidates. The first theme, femininity, was chosen on the spot, as this had been the topic that we had both been writing about. Another idea that emerged at the time was that we would lead preparatory seminars on both sides of the Channel, where we would read the same bibliographic works as a background to our discussions. This was the beginning of a fruitful and productive series of encounters that enabled cross-fertilization between our ideas and practices. Chantal Lechartier-Atlan and Danielle Kaswin Bonneford joined Monique Cournut-Janin in the organization of the Colloquia on the French side.

Several factors forced us to cancel in 2014 and then again in 2016: the terrorist attack in Paris, and then the SPP's move from Rue St Jacques to Rue Daviel. We had already decided on a theme

– masochism – which I started to discuss with a group of colleagues and candidates in the British Psychoanalytical Society. Thirty-five members and candidates came to the seminar on masochism that I led in May 2016 and again in June 2017. Perhaps other encounters will follow.

The following themes were the focus of our joint encounters, which alternated between London and Paris:

June 1999,  London: Femininity;
June 2001,  Paris: Femininity, anality, psychic space;
June 2003,  London: Femininity in men;
June 2006,  Paris: Countertransference and masochism;
June 2008,  London: The place of infantile sexuality in the formulation of an interpretation;
May 2010,  Paris: Unconscious phantasies and the actualization of infantile sexuality in the analytic process;
June 2012,  London: Bisexuality.

One cannot underestimate the importance that these encounters have had for all of us who attended them. A rewarding dialogue emerged over the years, and it has had an impact on both our ways of thinking about theoretical psychoanalysis and our clinical practice. This book is a testimony to that.

After the 2012 Colloquium on bisexuality, I thought that it was time to produce a book. Most of the chapters included here have been especially commissioned. The exceptions are Christian David's and André Green's: as they are both seminal papers, I decided to include them. I am grateful to Sophie Leighton and Andrew Weller, who translated them into English, for their permission to reproduce them. My own chapter was written quite a few years ago and has now found a home in this book.

I am grateful to all my students and colleagues who have participated in the Colloquia and preparatory seminars since 1999, and particularly to all those who have contributed with their chapters; to the *International Journal of Psychoanalysis* for permission to reprint Chapter 4, "Love and melancholia in the analysis of women by women"; to Routledge for permission to reprint Chapter 1, Christian David's "The Beautiful Differences", published in D. Birksted-Breen, S. Flanders, and A. Gilbeault (2010) *Reading French Psychoanalysis*, pp. 649–676; to Karnac for permission to reprint

Chapter 6 by Marilia Aisenstein, which has now been published in her book, *An Analytic Journey: From the Art of Archery to the Art of Psychoanalysis*, pp. 158–173; to Free Association Books for kind permission to reprint Chapter 12 which was first published as, "Life Narcissism, Death Narcissism" (London: Free Association Books, 2001, pp. 15–169); and to Klara and Eric King for their thorough copyediting of the manuscript.

# INTRODUCTION

## A psychoanalytic understanding of bisexuality

*Rosine Jozef Perelberg*

Although, for psychoanalysis, *difference* is sexual, the question of bisexuality is related to psychoanalytic theory as a whole.

(Green, p. 243 in Chapter 12, in this volume)

### Introduction

In a letter to Fliess in 1896, Freud used the word bisexuality for the first time:

In order to account for why the outcome [of premature sexual experience (see above)] is sometimes perversion and sometimes neurosis, I avail myself of the bisexuality of all human beings. In a purely male being there would be a surplus of male release at the two sexual barriers as well – that is, pleasure would be generated and consequently perversion; in purely female beings there would be a surplus of unpleasurable substance at these times. In the first phases the releases would be parallel: that is, they would produce a normal surplus of pleasure.

(1950 [1892–99], p. 238)

Freud was to use the term "bisexuality" forty-four times throughout his work. In the initial phase, at the time of his correspondence with Fliess, Freud was still concerned with matching his ideas on bisexuality to the anatomical–biological substratum proposed by Fliess, to whom he attributed the discovery of bisexuality. It is only progressively that bisexuality acquired a more fundamental psychological meaning in his work. In time Freud was to regard bisexuality as an inherent characteristic of all human beings. Indeed, as I develop below, every single one of his clinical cases may be understood in terms of the interplay between masculine and feminine identifications. In a letter to Fliess on 7 August 1901, he was to write:

> And now, the main thing! As far as I can see, my next work will be called "Human Bisexuality". It will go to the root of the problem and say the last word it may be granted me to say – the last and the most profound. ... So perhaps I must borrow even more from you; perhaps my sense of honesty will force me to ask you to co-author the work with me.
>
> (in Masson, 1985, p. 448)

He adds:

> thereby the anatomical–biological part would gain in scope, the part which, if I did it alone, would be meagre. I would concentrate on the psychic aspect of bisexuality and the explanation of the neurotic.
>
> (p. 448)

Freud continued to think about the crucial relevance of bisexuality in his understandings of hysteria. By then he had moved some distance from the ideas that he had discussed with Fliess.

Freud thought that bisexuality and repression were linked to each other. In a letter to Fliess of 19 September 1901:

> I do not comprehend your answer concerning bisexuality. It is obviously very difficult to understand each other. I certainly had no intention of doing anything but working on my contribution to the theory of bisexuality, elaborating the thesis that repression and the neuroses, and thus the independence of the unconscious, presuppose bisexuality.
>
> (in Masson, 1985, p. 450)

He still wavered, nevertheless, between a physiological and a psychological explanation. The *Three Essays on the Theory of Sexuality* is an example of going back to some kind of physiological explanation:

BISEXUALITY A fresh contradiction of popular views is involved in the considerations put forward by Lydston [1889], Kiernan [1888] and Chevalier [1893] in an endeavour to account for the possibility of sexual inversion. It is popularly believed that a human being is either a man or a woman. Science, however, knows of cases in which the sexual characters are obscured, and in which it is consequently difficult to determine the sex. This arises in the first instance in the field of anatomy. The genitals of the individuals concerned combine male and female characteristics. (This condition is known as hermaphroditism.) In rare cases both kinds of sexual apparatus are found side by side fully developed (true hermaphroditism); but far more frequently both sets of organs are found in an atrophied condition.

(Freud, 1905d, p. 141)

And yet the following quotation expresses the tension between a physiological and a psychological explanation:

The theory of bisexuality has been expressed in its crudest form by a spokesman of the male inverts: "a feminine brain in a masculine body". But we are ignorant of what characterizes a feminine brain. There is neither need nor justification for replacing the psychological problem by the anatomical one. Krafft-Ebing's attempted explanation seems to be more exactly framed than that of Ulrichs but does not differ from it in essentials.

(p. 142)

## Hysteria and bisexuality*

Hysteria and bisexuality have an essential link for Freud, who suggested that hysterical attacks express an experience of rape in which the hysteric plays both roles.[1]

In one case I observed, for instance, the patient pressed her dress up against her body with one hand (as a woman), while she tried to tear it off with the other (as a man).

(Freud, 1908a, p. 166)

It was in the discussion of the case of Katharina in 1896 that Freud himself first related hysteria with the primal scene (Letter 52, in

3

Freud, 1950 [1892–99]). Freud mentioned at least three further cases linking anxiety to the primal scene – in a letter to Fliess, in his paper on anxiety neurosis (1895b), and in his analysis of Dora (1905e) – although throughout his work he oscillated between regarding this as a "real event" and a "phantasy":

> I maintained years ago that the dyspnoea and palpitations that occur in hysteria and anxiety neurosis are only detached fragments of the act of copulation.
>
> (1905e, p. 80)

Later, in 1909, in a letter to Jung on 21 November, Freud wrote about Anna O's term "chimney sweeping":

> The reason why a chimney sweep is supposed to bring good luck is that sweeping a chimney is an unconscious symbol of coitus, which is something of which Breuer certainly never dreamed.
>
> (in McGuire, 1974, p. 267)

The famous accounts of hysterical patients – Anna O, Lucy R, Elizabeth Von R, Dora – indicate that they had all been disappointed by their fathers through illness, impotence, weakness or death. Coupled with this picture of disappointment with the father is the longing for another woman, who becomes the personification of unattainable femininity, like Dora's longing for Mrs K. Is it the case that with the father's weakness, illness, impotence or death, the daughter becomes frightened of being at the mercy of an internal imago of the mother?

In the years between 1920 and 1925, a new dimension appears in Freud's writings in relation to his understanding of female sexuality. The daughter's love for her father is an attempt to re-find a more fundamental and older love, related to the mother. In a letter to Stefan Zweig on 2 June 1932, Freud wrote about Breuer's flight from Anna O when he heard about her hysterical pregnancy: "At this moment he held in his hand the key that would have opened the doors to the 'Mothers', but he let it drop" (in E. L. Freud, 1960, p. 413). The reference to the "Mothers" is an allusion to Faust's mysterious searches (in Goethe's *Faust*, Part II, Act I). Is this Freud's intuitive view of what the death of Anna O's father left her grappling with, her unconscious feelings towards her *mother*? Breuer

4

himself made this reference at the end of the first section of the theoretical chapter of the book he wrote with Freud (Freud, 1895d). The mysterious mothers are goddesses who dwell below, in an internal *void, without space, place or time* (in Pollock, 1968). Are these not markedly similar to what Green describes as the expressions of the negative? Does this not, therefore, suggest a link between the negative and femininity?

One can link these ideas about the world of the "mothers" to the episodes of depersonalization, mutism, paralysis, "time-missing" and gaps in memory that followed Anna O's hallucination of the snake. They are interruptions in the domain of a reality that is being disavowed, indicating perhaps what Britton has designated in his book as a "suspension of belief" (1998, p. 15): when something is both known and not known at the same time. What is fundamentally known and not known is the fact of the division between the sexes (Chasseguet-Smirgel, 1964c; Freud, 1927e, 1940e; Kohon, 1987; Perelberg, 1990a, 1990b, 2015b). Sexuality is created through division and discontinuity (see Lacan, 1958; Mitchell, 1982; Perelberg, 1981; Rose, 1982), and these symptoms seem, paradoxically, to represent Anna O's identificatory struggles.

The hysteric is the feminine in the neurotic representation (Schaeffer, 1986); it is also the very repudiation of the feminine. Kohon has suggested that the hysteric stage, within the context of the oedipal drama, is

> a specific moment in which the subject – caught up between the need to change object from mother to father – is unable to make the necessary choice.
>
> (1999, p. 18)

> In fact, stuck in her divalent stage, the hysteric … cannot define herself as a man or as a woman because she cannot finally choose between her father and her mother.
>
> (p. 19)

Schaeffer (using an expression coined by Michel Cachoux: see Schaeffer, 1997) suggests that the hysteric, like the ruby, displays what it is in fact rejecting: "The ruby is a stone that has a horror of red. It absorbs and retains all the other colours, but rejects and expels red" (1986, p. 925). Thus the hysteric has a horror of the colour red, of sexuality, while at the same time displaying it. In her hysterical pregnancy, paradoxically, Anna O was rejecting a feminine identification, the woman who would produce babies as a result of intercourse.

Some aspects of Bertha Pappenheim's later life represent transformations of Anna O's question, "Am I a man or a woman?" (see Kohon, 1986a; Lacan, 1993; Leclaire, 1980), albeit in a sublimated way. In her social work, she designated the social workers she trained as her daughters – products of an imaginary intercourse without a father or mother. The orphanage she built was known as "Papahome" – the house of the father – in which she would fulfil the two parental roles.

Hysteria becomes, fundamentally, a mode of thinking about sexuality and the sexual object (Schaeffer, 1986).[2] Hysteria works by imitation; the difference between identification and imitation is that between "being like the object" and "being the object". Through her symptoms, Anna O seems to be *imitating* the sexual act. *Her symptoms become like a theatre of the sexual act in an attempt to both deny and represent the primal scene and deny the mourning of her incestuous sexual desires.* It is also displaying a body that cannot be experienced as sexual and feminine, but only as bits and pieces that ache. The fracture of the mind (the Humpty Dumpty song she recited at her father's bedside) is mirrored in the fragmentation of the body through her symptoms.

## Bisexuality in dreams

In *The Interpretation of Dreams* (1900a), Freud establishes a link between bisexuality and repression:

> The theory of the psychoneuroses asserts as an indisputable and invariable fact that only sexual wishful impulses from infancy, which have undergone repression (i.e. a transformation of their affect) during the developmental period of childhood, are capable of being revived during *later* developmental periods (whether as a result of the subject's sexual constitution, which is derived from an initial bisexuality, or as a result of unfavourable influences acting upon the course of his sexual life) and are thus able to furnish the motive force for the formation of psychoneurotic symptoms of every kind.
>
> (pp. 605–606)

I will demonstrate that the impact of the sexual wishful impulses from childhood on later life is present in each of Freud's clinical studies. The interplay of masculine and feminine identifications in relation to the primal scene is implicit or explicit in each of Freud's case studies, from Dora (1905e), to Little Hans (1909b), the Rat Man (1909d), Schreber (1911c), the Wolf Man (1918b), and "The Psychogenesis of a Case of Homosexuality in a Woman" (1920a). I have suggested previously (Perelberg, 2015b, Chapter 5) that this was linked to Freud's theories on innate bisexuality.

## Case studies

### a. Dora (Freud, 1905e)

The theme of hysteria and its relationship with sexuality continues in the discussion of Dora's analysis, which expresses Freud's interest in the sexual origins of hysterical symptoms, as well as in the role of dreams as expressing unconscious conflicts. The hysterical symptom "enacts a fantasy with a sexual content" (Cournut-Janin, 2005), even if a single unconscious phantasy is generally not sufficient to engender a symptom.

In this analysis Freud is still interested in the reconstruction of the trauma that had led to the appearance of the symptom, through the analysis of dreams and free associations. This clinical emphasis would change in later years, when Freud started to see the analytic process more in terms of a process of construction. At the time of the analysis itself, Freud emphasized the paternal transference and the role of the father's impotence in the structuring of the symptom. Dora's aphonia and cough are understood as manifestations of the unconscious phantasy of having oral sex with a woman, Mrs K, in identification with her impotent father. In Freud's formulations, a symptom establishes a link between unconscious phantasy and sexuality: "a symptom signifies the representation – the realization of a phantasy with a sexual content, that is to say, it signifies a sexual situation" (1905e, p. 47).

There is a link between the current phantasy and a childhood memory as Dora tells Freud that as a child she had been a thumb-sucker. She remembers an occasion when she would be thumb-sucking at the same time as she would be tugging at her brother's ear lobe (p. 51). Freud believes that these are new versions of a "pre-historic impression of sucking at the mother's or nurse's breast" (p. 52).

It is only retrospectively, after Dora broke off the analysis, that Freud identified the relevance of the maternal transference.

In one of several footnotes added to the text of the analysis of Dora, Freud indicated his mistake in underestimating Dora's love for Frau K:

I failed to discover in time and to inform the patient that her homosexual (gynaecophilic) love for Frau K. was the strongest unconscious current in her mental life.

(Freud, 1905e, p. 120)

Yet, quite a few years were to pass before Freud discovered the pre-oedipal passion for the mother expressed by children of both sexes. The homosexual love for Frau K will then be seen as the "strongest unconscious current" in the mental life of all individuals. It is always the mother, in the words of Kristeva (see Perelberg, Chapter 4, in this volume). Bisexuality was at the core of Freud's understanding of hysteria.

Cournut-Janin (2005) has suggested that

in the longing for Frau K it is her own femininity that Dora – still an adolescent – also loves the woman she herself will be in the person of the lovely Frau K., who is desirable, as her father has clearly indicated to her.

(p. 58)

Frau K, from this perspective, becomes the ideal of unattainable femininity.

More recently, Mitchell has suggested that the identification with the mother is also present in this analysis. Freud himself says that

[Dora] identified with her mother by means of slight symptoms and peculiarities of manner, which gave her an opportunity for some really remarkable achievements in the direction of intolerable behaviour. ... The persistence with which she held to this identification with her mother almost forced me to ask whether she too was suffering from a venereal disease.

(Mitchell, 2000, pp. 75–76)

8

At the time, it was believed that syphilis could lead to madness. In her analysis of the case, Mitchell suggests that Freud is both the father and the mother in the transference. She also convincingly emphasizes the importance of Dora's identification with her older brother, Otto Bauer, in the development of Dora's symptoms. "She had wanted to be positioned as a child in the family like her brother, only to discover that she was not like him in gender and that (probably) he, first-born and male, had their mother's love" (p. 104). Her hysteria emanated from childhood and a "breakdown of her identification *with her brother*" (p. 105).

### b. Little Hans (Freud, 1909b)

This was an analysis carried out by Little Hans's father, Max Graf, who sent Freud extensive notes about his son. When he was 4 years old, Herbert witnessed a cart horse that was pulling a heavy load collapse. The little boy became fearful of horses: Freud understood Hans's phobia as being related to the anxiety caused by the arrival of his younger sister and the lies that the adults were offering him about the origin of babies.

Hans's material offered Freud evidence about his theories on infantile sexuality, castration anxiety and the Oedipus complex. Progressively, Freud understood Hans's fear that his father would bite him (castrate him) for his desires towards the mother. As Hans's father was acting as analyst, Freud conjectured that this fear was impeding the progress of the treatment, so Freud invited Hans to see him so that he could explain his symptoms to him.

Hans also expressed jealousy towards his father and a desire to give his mother babies, thus revealing himself as a "little Oedipus" (Freud, 1909b, p. 11). At the same time, however, his homosexual attachment to his father is recognized. His father described the boy's loving feelings towards boy companions, as well his loving responses to girls. Freud referred to these "accesses of homosexuality" in Hans as one of the many polymorphous libidinal strands that flourished before the effects of repression became evident.

> Hans was a homosexual (as all children may well be), quite consist-ently with the fact, which must always be kept in mind, that *he was acquainted with one kind of genital organ* – a genital organ like his own.
>
> (p. 110)

Little Hans is an example of the infantile theory of phallic monism that is impermeable to observation. He believed that girls and boys had "widdlers", in spite of the evidence against it through his observation of his sister. This is again an expression of the force of phantasy life and the anxiety provoked by the threat of castration (a fuller discussion of this is to be found later in this Introduction).

The account of the case gives plenty of evidence of Hans's identification with his mother and the wish to give birth to babies, although this is not explored by Freud in the paper and would only be discussed in 1926. As Temperley (2005) indicates, it is only in *Inhibitions, Symptoms and Anxiety* (Freud, 1926d) that Freud linked Hans with the Wolf Man and stated that in both cases the animal phobia derived from tender, passive homosexual desires towards the father, which have been distorted by regression to the oral phase, as well as by repression:

> The process of repression had attacked almost all the components of his Oedipus complex – both his hostile and his tender impulses toward his father and his tender impulses toward his mother.
>
> (Freud, 1926d, p. 107)

In the next paragraph, however, he writes:

> A tender feeling for his father was undoubtedly there too and played a part in repressing the opposite feeling: but we can prove neither that it was strong enough to draw repression on itself nor that it disappeared afterwards. Hans seems in fact to have been a normal boy with what is called a "positive" Oedipus complex.
>
> (p. 107)

The interplay of different desires co-existing within each individual was, throughout his work, identified by Freud. "The emotional life of man is in general made up of pairs of contraries such as this" (Freud, 1909b, p. 113).

### c. The Rat Man (Freud, 1909d)

In the Rat Man Freud describes a bright young man whose emotional, sexual and social development had been severely stunted by obsessional thinking, the roots of which seemed to stretch back into his infancy. He also describes a precocious sexual life: at the age of 4, the Rat Man had undertaken exploration of his governess's genitals.

Freud gives a vivid description of the patient's conflict of identifications, which was reached only "through the painful road of the transference" (Freud, 1909d, p. 209). While Freud had met a polite man, with a polite demeanour, on the couch, in his dreams the patient shouted the "grossest and filthiest abuse upon me and my family", expressing his utter fury towards Freud as his father. At times the disjunction between the conscious behaviour and unconscious expressions led the patient to despair, as he paced the consulting room. He could not lie in a comfortable position, he would say, while feeling so uncomfortable with what was going on. Further analysis indicated that he was also afraid that Freud would give him a beating, although in light of the later text, "A Child is Being Beaten" (1919e), one could also understand his longing for it.

There is indeed an account of Lorenz's masturbatory fantasies, where Freud indicates Lorenz's longing for his father and his battles with him – especially over his choice of a girl – and a complex story of a beating by the father in which Lorenz had flown into a fury and following which, he told Freud, he had "become a coward", fearing physical violence. The father had made a comment about the son, that "The child will be either a great man or a great criminal" (1909d, p. 205).

Freud emphasizes Lorenz's disavowed hostile feelings towards his father as having greatly intensified his obsessional illness. It was not only a conflict between love and hate that drove Lorenz's illness: it was made particularly complex by pleasure, shame and disgust at the feelings and ideas associated with the conflict.

There can be no question that there was something in the sphere of sexuality that stood between the father and son, and that the father had come into some sort of opposition to the son's prematurely developed erotic life. Several years after his father's death, the first time he experienced the pleasurable sensations of copulation, an idea sprang into his mind: "This is glorious! One might murder one's father for this!" This was at once an echo and an elucidation of the obsessional ideas of his childhood. Moreover, his father, shortly before his death, had

11

directly opposed what later became our patient's dominating passion. He had noticed that his son was always in the lady's company, and had advised him to keep away from her, saying that it was imprudent of him and that he would only make a fool of himself.

(p. 201)

Lorenz's episodes of masturbation took place when thinking about his father. Freud understood these as acts of defiance towards this father, who had interfered with the patient's sexual enjoyment, although one cannot avoid thinking about the homosexual excitement that is also present.

Freud's linking of obsessional thinking to anal eroticism in the understanding of the case is a clinical insight that should not be underestimated, especially as knowledge of the connection between obsessive–compulsive neurosis and anal regression emerges only in 1926 – twenty years after Lorenz's analysis (Williams, 2005). As Catherine Chabert suggests, the Rat Man can be regarded as "the very example of the tortures inflicted by object choice and the vicissitudes of psychic bisexuality" (Chabert, p. 84, Chapter 2, in this volume).

Ignès Sodré has contributed to the understanding of obsessionality, suggesting that it may be understood as a defence against triangularity. Splitting mechanisms are used in the service of preserving an exclusive two-person relationship with the object. Sodré (1994) suggests a differentiation between two modes of obsessional thinking: in the first, the oedipal situation is avoided, and thoughts connected to it are forbidden; the second indicates a configuration on the threshold of the depressive position, whereby the oedipal situation is omnipresent, and thoughts constantly engage in rivalrous battles with each other (p. 380).

In connection with bisexuality, the Rat Man had become frozen at the threshold of the oedipal configuration, unable to elaborate his feelings – both positive and negative – towards his father. Like Freud's other clinical accounts, all written before his discovery of the pre-oedipal phase, one has very little information about the patient's mother, although one can understand his inability to decide between the two ladies in terms of his hesitation about making a sexual choice away from his mother.

## d. The Schreber case (Freud, 1911c)

In the discussion of the Schreber case, the theme of repressed homosexual desire by a man towards his father is again discussed. Freud hypothesizes that persecutory anxiety and paranoid delusions are the result of a defence against repressed homosexual desire. Paranoia is the transformation of love into hate, which is then projected onto an external persecutor. The person whom I now hate was at one time loved (Freud, 1911c, p. 41). "I love him" is transformed into "I hate him", which through the mechanism of projection becomes "he hates me". "The person he longed for now became his persecutor, and the content of his wishful phantasy became the content of his persecution" (p. 47). At the centre of the paranoid persecution lies an emasculation phantasy, coupled with the idea of a transsexual phantasy that he would be transformed into a woman in the act of copulation (see also the discussion of this case by Steiner, 2005).

> The exciting cause of his illness, then was an outburst of homosexual libido; the object of this libido was probably from the very first his doctor, Flechsig; and his struggles against the libidinal impulse produced the conflict which gave rise to the symptom.
> (Freud, 1911c, p. 43)

In the following phase, Schreber thought he would be impregnated by divine rays in order to produce a new race of human beings (pp. 20–21). Schreber also refers to a state of bliss, "uninterrupted enjoyment", an "uninterrupted feeling of voluptuousness" (p. 29), achieved through the contemplation of God. In his analysis, Freud establishes a connection between Dr Flechsig, Schreber's physician, God and his father, and concludes that the sun is itself a sublimated symbol for the father. "The father's most dreaded threat, castration, actually provided the material for his wishful phantasy ... of being transformed into a woman" (p. 56). Yet, at the same time, Freud himself indicates in a footnote that the sun is feminine in German (p. 54), offering the comment that in most languages the sun is masculine. The feminine of the German sun would nevertheless also offer the interpretation of a bisexual, phallic element, before any division between masculine and feminine.

Freud related Schreber's psychosis to what he suggests is the "father-complex". One should bear in mind that the concept of the Oedipus complex had not yet been suggested:

> Thus in the case of Schreber we find ourselves once again on the familiar ground of the father-complex. The patient's struggle with Flechsig became revealed to him as a conflict with God, and we must therefore construe it as an infantile conflict with the father whom he loved. ... His father's most dreaded threat, castration, actually provided the material for his wishful phantasy (at first resisted but later accepted) of being transformed into a woman.
>
> (Freud, 1911c, pp. 55–56)

Towards the end of his work, Freud developed the concept of the splitting of the ego, which allowed him to deepen his views on psychosis from those he had developed in the case of Schreber. The psychotic individual disavows reality and puts aside the role of the symbolic, dead father. Lacan has understood psychosis as the foreclosure of the Name of the Father.

Freud in this text once again underlines his views on bisexuality: "Generally speaking, every human being oscillates all through his life between heterosexual and homosexual feelings, and any frustration or disappointment in the one direction is apt to drive him over into the other" (p. 46).

## e. The Wolf Man (Freud, 1918b)

In a letter to Ferenczi written in 1913 (quoted in Jones, 1974), Freud reported that the Wolf Man initiated his first session with him by offering to have rectal intercourse with Freud, and then to defecate on his head (see Jones, 1974, vol. II, p. 308).

> A rich young Russian, whom I took on because of compulsive tendencies, admitted the following transferences to me after the first session: Jewish swindler, he would like to use me from behind and shit on my head. At the age of six years he experienced as his first symptom cursing against God: pig, dog, etc. When he saw three piles of faeces on the street he became uncomfortable because of the Holy Trinity and anxiously sought a fourth in order to destroy the association.
>
> (p. 308)

This scene dramatizes a homosexual relationship characterized by anality and the threat of castration: it expresses the patient's state of mind at the beginning of his treatment (see also Perelberg, 2005). There is a repetition at the beginning of the analysis of a trauma which is analogous to that which had activated the anxiety linked to the obsessive symptoms. In his analysis of the statement in that first session, Bokanowski (2010) suggests the experience of a feminine that is not well internalized in the Wolf Man. He also suggests that the phantasies of seduction, castration and primal scene are present.

Freud indicated the anal–sadistic regression and cruelty that followed the prohibition of masturbation by his Nanya (1918b, p. 25). The Wolf Man tormented insects and people, had beating fantasies and enjoyed mistreating horses. In his disappointment with his Nanya, he turned to his father as a sexual object (p. 27). Freud had identified serious sadomasochistic trends in the Wolf Man, in his identification with the suffering Christ, and in his beating phantasies and depressive and masochistic self-reproach. This obsessionality appears to have continued until the age of 10. Freud understood the Wolf Man's terror of being eaten by the wolves in the famous dream of the wolves at the age of 4 as referring to his conflicting wishes in relation to the father: fear of him, on the one hand, and unconscious longing for homosexual gratification, on the other.

Freud also referred to the Wolf Man in the paper "A Child Is Being Beaten" (1919e). In his sadistic attitudes the Wolf Man identified with his father, but in his masochism, "he chose him as a sexual object" (1918b, p. 63). In this period of ruminations, The Wolf Man wondered if Christ had a behind, and Freud understands this as his question as to whether he, himself, could be used by his father as a woman (which reminds us of the very first offer at his first consultation with Freud).

There are three further dreams in this analysis that seem to contain the same conflicts in relation to his wish to submit erotically to his father. I find it very interesting that the dreams are narrated in a reverse order in the account of the case history: the later dream first, and then, in reverse order, the two others.

When he was about 7 or 8 years old, the Wolf Man was told that on the following day a private teacher would come to give him a lesson:

15

That night he dreamt of *his tutor in the shape of a lion that came towards his bed, roaring loudly and in the posture of a wolf, like one he had seen in a children's picture book*: he woke up in a state of anxiety.

(1918b, p. 39, italics added)

Analysis of the dream led to an understanding of his longing to take a passive sexual position in relation to his father.

In a second dream, *"he saw himself riding a horse and pursued by a gigantic caterpillar. He recognized in this dream an allusion to an earlier one from the period before the tutor"* (p. 69, italics added).

In this earlier dream *"he saw the Devil dressed in black and in the upright posture with which the wolf and the lion had terrified him so much in their day. He was pointing with his outstretched finger at a gigantic snail"* (p. 69, italics added).

He associated the Devil with the demon of a well-known poem; the dream itself was a version of a very popular picture representing the demon in a love scene with a girl. The snail was in the woman's place.

The patient remembered a particular event that had occurred a short time before the dream. He had one day passed by a peasant who was lying, asleep, with his little boy beside him. The latter woke his father. There was also a second recollection, that on the same estate there were trees that were quite white, spun all over by caterpillars. Freud suggests that the patient

> took flight from the realization of the phantasy of the son lying with his father, and that he brought in the white trees in order to make an allusion to the anxiety-dream of the white wolves on the walnut tree.
>
> (p. 70)

Freud understood the dream as a expressing the "dread of the feminine attitude towards men against which he had at first protected himself by his religious sublimation and was soon to protect himself still more effectively by the military one [p. 69]" (p. 70).

In his remarks to the text, Strachey underlines the "primary feminine impulses" of the Wolf Man:

> The very marked degree of his bisexuality was only a confirmation of views which had long been held by Freud and which

16

dated back to the time of his friendship with Fliess. But in his subsequent writings Freud laid greater stress than before on the fact of the *universal* occurrence of bisexuality and on the existence of an "inverted" or "negative" Oedipus complex. This thesis was given its clearest expression in the passage on the "complete" Oedipus complex in Chapter III of *The Ego and the Id* (1923b). On the other hand, a tempting theoretical inference to the effect that motives related to bisexuality are the invariable determinants of repression is strongly resisted (p. 110 f.) – a point to which Freud returned at greater length soon afterwards in "A Child is Being Beaten".

(Strachey, in Freud, 1918b, p. 6)

In the Wolf Man, Freud understands the phobia ultimately as linked to the fear of castration:

But it was from fear of being castrated, too, that the little Russian relinquished his wish to be loved by his father, for he thought that a relation of that sort presupposed a sacrifice of his genitals – of the organ which distinguished him from a female. As we see, both forms of the Oedipus complex, the normal, active form and the inverted one, came to grief through the castration complex.

(Freud, 1926d, p. 108)

I have suggested throughout this Introduction that the contrasts between passivity/activity, femininity/masculinity and sadism/masochism are indeed central to Freud's understanding of the structuring of psychic reality in each individual, male or female. They are the axes around which Freud thought about most of his patients, whether hysterics, obsessional neurotics, perverse or psychotic.

### f. "The Psychogenesis of a Case of Homosexuality in a Woman" (Freud, 1920a)

Freud's 1920 paper, the last of his published clinical studies, is a brief analysis of how an 18-year-old woman came to be homosexual. We are told that she "had aroused displeasure and concern in her parents by the devoted adoration with which she pursued a certain 'society lady' who was about ten years older than herself" (Freud, 1920a, p. 147). The parents claimed that this woman had a

17

notorious reputation and was known to be flagrantly carrying on affairs with both women and men (see also Budd, 2005).

When she was 16, the young girl had developed a maternal inclination and was bitterly disappointed when it was her own mother who gave birth to another brother. Freud believed that the birth of the new baby brother fatally disrupted her own attempts to identify with her mother. Prior to her being brought to Freud by her mother, she had attempted suicide by throwing herself over a guard wall beside the railway line (*niederkommen*). Lacan has shown the ambiguity of the word which, in German, also means "to give birth". The young woman had dreams of becoming a mother, at the same time as her mother had herself given birth to a child by the father.

Several authors have suggested that the interest that the young homosexual girl had in the lady perhaps expressed her identification much more than any sexual desire (e.g. Harris, 1991; Magid, 1993).

In this paper Freud thought that there is no simple distinction between homosexuals and heterosexuals: "a masculine man, masculine in his erotic life, may nonetheless love only men"; a feminine man, who loves like a woman, may be wholly heterosexual. Similarly for women: physical sexual characteristics, masculinity or femininity, and type of object choice vary independently. All human beings, in addition to their manifest heterosexuality, contain "a very considerable measure of latent or unconscious homosexuality". Human sexual differentiation is multi-factorial; there is not a separate homosexual "third sex".

In many ways, this paper can be seen as the precursor to the papers that were to follow on female sexuality as Freud tackles the passionate, consuming, idealized love that the little girl has towards the lady as a transferential object standing in for her mother. Lacan (1994, p. 102) thought the paper was one of the most brilliant of Freud's texts. He pointed out that the young girl desired nothing from the woman, a relationship of no satisfaction that established the relation of lack to this feminine object. She desired in the woman she loved precisely what she did not have (p. 110): what she did not have was the phallus.

Freud makes a crucial distinction between sexuality and object choice:

The literature of homosexuality usually fails to distinguish clearly enough between the questions of the choice of object on the one hand, and of the sexual characteristics and sexual attitude of the subject on the other, as though the answer to the former necessarily involved the answers to the latter. ... The mystery of homosexuality is therefore by no means so simple as it is commonly depicted in popular expositions – "a feminine mind, bound therefore to love a man, but unhappily attached to a masculine body; a masculine mind, irresistibly attracted by women, but, alas! imprisoned in a feminine body". It is instead a question of three sets of characteristics, namely –

- Physical sexual characteristics (physical hermaphroditism)
- Mental sexual characteristics (masculine or feminine attitude)
- Kind of object-choice.

(Freud, 1920a, p. 170)

Freud's distinctions in this paper are crucially relevant to current discussions in the psychoanalytic literature on the relationship between sexuality (as unconscious desire) and gender.

The paper concludes with this well-known reflection:

[P]sycho-analysis cannot elucidate the intrinsic nature of what in conventional or in biological phraseology is termed "masculine" and "feminine": it simply takes over the two concepts and makes them the foundation of its work. When we attempt to reduce them further, we find masculinity vanishing into activity and femininity into passivity, and that does not tell us enough.

(p. 171)

### *"A Child Is Being Beaten" (1919e)*

"A Child Is Being Beaten: A Contribution to the Study of the Genesis of Sexual Perversion" contains an important discussion in relation to bisexuality. If bisexuality is inherent to all human beings, what is it that is repressed in the course of development?

The text appeared in 1919, in a period of transition between Freud's models of the mind. As Catherine Chabert (2005) indicates, the text's intention was to consider the phantasy of "a child is being beaten" as one of the seduction fantasies and, in addition, describe the paradigmatic developments involved in the production of this phantasy. At the same time, it featured the "infantile" representations of masochism, heralding works still to come before the publication of *Beyond the Pleasure Principle* (1920g) and "The Economic Problem of Masochism" (1924c), thus anticipating the link between love and punishment, excitation and pain.

The phantasy "a child is being beaten" is composed of three phases. The scene of the first phase appears as *"My father is beating the child"* (a child is being beaten). The second phase, Freud indicates, is unconscious, and is a construction of the transference. It appears as *"I* [girl] *am being beaten by my father"*, where the author occupies the place of the beaten child of the first scene. The third phase (which is the one that appears first in the analysis) resembles the first. The author of the phantasy again occupies the place of spectator. However, two notable elements differentiate it. The partners have changed: the beaten child of the first phase has been replaced by a multitude of unknown children and the father (the beater) by more distant substitutes. This shift between the scenes, Chabert (2005) suggests, is a fundamental movement of the analysis, "a way of opening up positions of identification in movement" between activity and passivity, sadism and masochism, representations and actions.

This text suggests a link between masochism, femininity, and the guilt feelings engendered by incestuous desires towards the father – desires that are repressed and re-constructed in the analytic process.

Is this seduction by the father, however, not a second one, following a first seduction by the mother? The paper was written before Freud's reformulation of his theory of femininity and the discovery of the pre-oedipal phase. The mother is, according to Freud himself, the first seductress. "The first sexual and sexually coloured experiences which a child has in relation to its mother are naturally of a passive character" (Freud, 1931b, p. 236).

If bisexuality is characteristic of both sexes, what is it, then, that is repressed in the oedipal phase? Freud examines the idea that it is the opposite of each sex that is repressed. But he considers that such a view would be a return to a biologically determined view on sexuality. He thus considers the following:

Such a theory as this can only have an intelligible meaning if we assume that a person's sex is to be determined by the formation of his genitals; for otherwise it would not be certain which is a person's stronger sex and we should run the risk of reaching from the results of our enquiry the very fact which has to serve as its point of departure. To put the theory briefly: with men, what is unconscious and repressed can be brought down to feminine instinctual impulses; and conversely with women.

(Freud, 1919e, p. 201)

His second possibility refers to Alfred Adler's "masculine protest" in that

every individual makes efforts not to remain on the inferior "feminine line [of development]" and struggles towards the "masculine line", from which satisfaction can alone be derived.

(p. 201)

Freud raises questions about this theory, as it would mean that the repressing agency would always be masculine and the repressed element feminine. He considers that the theory of the masculine protest seems to maintain its ground very much better on being tested with regard to the beating phantasies, as in "both boys and girls the beating-phantasy corresponds with a feminine attitude – one, that is, in which the individual is lingering on the 'feminine line' – and both sexes hasten to get free from this attitude by repressing the phantasy" (pp. 202–203).

Freud's reflections turn, however, to his studies on infantile sexuality in order to indicate how active elements are present. He finalizes this text by suggesting that it is infantile sexuality that is the motive force in the formation of symptoms; the Oedipus complex is the nuclear complex of neuroses.

## The repudiation of femininity

The question of what it is that is then repressed remains a source of discussion. It is only in 1937 that Freud concludes that both sexes "repudiate femininity" – a phenomenon that is an essential element of the asymmetry between the sexes. This repudiation is, Freud suggests, the bedrock of psychoanalysis and part of the great riddle of sex (1937c, p. 252). It is part of the domain of what is unanalysable for Freud:

the resistance prevents any change from taking place ... everything stays as it was. We often have the impression that with the wish for a penis and the masculine protest we have penetrated through all the psychological strata and have reached bedrock, and that thus our activities are at an end. This is probably true, since for the psychical field, the biological field does in fact play the part of the underlying bedrock. The repudiation of femininity can be nothing else than a biological fact, a part of the great riddle of sex.

(p. 252)

This is a mysterious statement that has been a source of many debates, especially in France. What did Freud mean? Some authors have suggested that the repudiation of femininity is the repudiation of the child's position of passivity in relation to the mother when the infant is so dependent on her. André Green has suggested a distinction between passivity and passivation. The latter represents a position of receptivity in relation to maternal care; he sees it as a crucial requirement in an analytic process: "Now the psychoanalytic cure is not possible without this confident passivation, where the analysand gives himself to the analyst's care" (Green, 1986b, p. 248),[3] in a transformation of the way the baby trusts the mother's care.

In the *Ego and the Id* (1923b) and until *An Outline of Psycho-Analysis* (1940a), Freud considers the universality of bisexuality and the notion that in each individual, one should be able to find both the positive and the negative Oedipus complex.

We have seen that the concept of bisexuality followed a long trajectory in Freud's work. Starting with his allegiance to Fliess and his attempts to adapt his concepts to Fliess's ideas, Freud progressively gave a fundamental status to the concept, at the origin of the structuralization of the psychic apparatus itself. In the first edition of the *Three Essays on the Theory of Sexuality* (1905d), for instance, he had already written:

Without taking bisexuality into account I think it would scarcely be possible to arrive at an understanding of the sexual manifestations that are actually to be observed in men and women.

(p. 220)

In 1929, he still struggled with the idea of bisexuality, surrounded "by many obscurities". He maintained that we needed to link it to the theory of drives and its vicissitudes (1930a, p. 64).

Freud's revolutionary vision on sexuality was to maintain the inherent, unconscious, infantile, psychic bisexuality in both men and women. A fluidity was also postulated as existing between the two.

## Key concepts in the understanding of psychosexuality

Certain key concepts constitute building blocks towards an understanding of a psychoanalytic understanding of psychic bisexuality.[4]

### a  The mirror stage

This refers to the imaginary aspect present in the constitution of the subject's identity.

Lacan has highlighted the crucial moment at which the infant can recognize himself in the mirror as structuring the ego, which may take place from six months onwards. The child's identification with his own image leads to an end to the fantasy of a fragmented body:

> The mirror stage is a drama whose internal pressure pushes precipitously from insufficiency to anticipation – and, for the subject caught up in the lure of spatial identification, turns out fantasies that proceed from a fragmented image of the body to what I will call an "orthopaedic" form of its totality – and to finally donned armour of an alienating identity that will mark his entire mental development with its rigid structure.
>
> (Lacan, 2006b, p. 78)

There are several stages in the process. Initially the child believes that he sees a real human being. This leads Lacan to the notion that it is through the other that the child experiences himself. Following from this, the child finds out that the other in the mirror is an image, until finally the child discovers that the image in the mirror is his own. A third term needs to be present, for example, the mother saying to the baby: "this is you, in the mirror".

The whole process takes place in an imaginary dimension: the recognition of the self takes place through an optical image and a subjective alienation. As Joël Dor describes:

> Although the mirror phase symbolizes the "preformation" of the "I" it presupposes by its fundamental nature the destiny of the "I"

23

as alienated in the imaginary dimension. The re-cognition of the self in the mirror image is accomplished – for optical reasons – through indications that are exterior and symmetrically inserted. ... This implies the re-cognition of the alienation and the "beginnings of the chronic misrecognition that will characterize all his future relations with himself".

(1998, p. 97)

The mirror stage expresses the function of misrecognition that characterizes the ego in its relationship with itself and with others from then on.

As Lionel Bailly states:

The Mirror Stage points up the fundamental place of narcissism in the creation of identity/Subject – the seeing oneself *as* an image, and the love of the image that *is* oneself.

(2009, p. 31, italics in original)

What follows is the progressive identification of difference. These formulations are crucial to an understanding that in psychoanalysis, processes of identifications are of the order of the imaginary and include the messages that come from the adult other. (See below for more about this idea in the works of Laplanche, Braunschweig and Fain.)

### b  The structuring function of the phallus

The distinction between penis and phallus is an important reference to the understanding of a psychoanalytic understanding of bisexuality and sexual differentiation. It refers to the differentiation between biological and psychic reality. Penis designates the anatomical and physiological reality (Laplanche & Pontalis, 1967, p. 56); phallus, on the other hand, exists outside anatomical reality. Lacan suggests that it is the signifier of the mother's desire. The central question of the Oedipus complex thus becomes to be or not to be the phallus – that is, to be or not to be the object of the mother's desire (Dor, 1985, p. 102). The role of the father also becomes symbolic: he represents the impossibility of being the object of mother's desire.

Freud also defines patriarchy, however, as the law of the *dead* father. In *Totem and Taboo* (1912–13), he describes the primal

24

patricide committed by the original horde, which killed and devoured their father. This was followed by remorse and guilt (as they both hated and loved their father), and the dead father became more powerful than he had been while alive. This is Freud's myth of the beginnings of society. Gallop has pointed out that if this myth is internalized, then the living male has no better chance of achieving the sovereign position than the living female (1982, p. 14). However, Gallop also explores the ambiguity of this distinction. The phallus, unlike the penis, is possessed by nobody (male or female), and *it represents the combination of both sexes, where neither is given up.* The phallus has a structuring function, instituting the distinction between the sexes, where both have to come to terms with the impossibility of being the object of the mother's desire. There is an intrinsic link in Freud's formulations between the primacy of the phallus, the castration complex and the Oedipus complex (see Kohon, 1986a; Mitchell, 1974; Mitchell & Rose, 1982; Perelberg, 1990b). The phallus represents an impossibility of completeness; it is the signifier of *jouissance* for both sexes.

Why the penis? Kristeva (2000) points out that it is because it is visible. Its erection brings with it the representation that it may be detachable. It thus becomes the signifier of a lack and thus of everything that has a meaning. The phallus "subsumes other lacks already experienced", which include the thought that in itself refers to that which is lacking (p. 73). For Freud, in the beginning there is an infantile phantasy of phallic monism, organizer of sexual difference.

The phallus is an organ that becomes narcissistically and erotically invested, signifier of a lack. The image of the phallus that is most common is that of a penis cut off at the base and permanently erect (Morel, 2011, p. 19). The opposite that it evokes is castration. The statement that one is a man or a woman refers, thus, to imaginary identifications.

In Mitchell's words: "The selection of the phallus as the mark around which subjectivity and sexuality are constructed reveals, precisely, that they are constructed, in a division which is both arbitrary and alienating" (1982, p. 7). Yet sexuality only exists within this division, structured around the castration complex.

Freud makes it clear that he is referring to the primacy of the phallus and not the penis:

the main characteristic of this "infantile genital organization" is its difference from the final genital organization of the adult. This consists in the fact that, for both sexes, only one genital, namely the male one, comes into account. What is present, therefore, is not a primacy of the genitals, but a primacy of the *phallus*.

(1923e, p. 143)

Kristeva summarizes the relevance of this phallic organization:

it is the central organiser (as it is Oedipus); it is illusory (peculiar to infantile phallic organisation); and it shatters under the threat of castration and when the individual is effaced in favour of the race.

(2000, p. 98)

The differentiation between man and woman is thus the result of a long process that is never complete in that pure masculinity or pure femininity are never to be found.

Joyce McDougall started her book *The Many Faces of Eros* (1995) by stressing the intrinsically traumatic nature of human sexuality. For her, this traumatic dimension is connected with the recognition of otherness and the discovery of the difference between the sexes. In both the homosexual and heterosexual dimensions, the oedipal configuration confronts the child with not being able to have both sexes, and not being able to possess either of his parents.

McDougall wrote about her first session after the summer holidays with a 5-year-old boy:

He rushes into the consulting room in a state of evident excitement to announce an unusual event: "During the holidays we were in a camp where all the kids bathed together, naked!" "You mean boys and girls together?" Looking startled, he shouted: "Don't be stupid! How could I tell? I've already told you, they didn't have their clothes on!"

(1989, p. 205)

In terms of the conceptualization that I am developing here, the differences between the sexes is disavowed and the child's emphasis is on gender, as ascribed by the social group in terms of a multitude of symbols here related to the clothes that boys and girls wear.

26

### c Castration complex

The castration complex becomes the fundamental organizer of sexual difference. An important step in Freud's formulations was the analysis of Little Hans, who thought that his mother and his sister had penises and that both boys and girls could have babies. Of course nowadays one can feel upset at the fact that his mother and father were not answering his questions truthfully, and one can also hypothesize that Little Hans both knew and did not know about the differences that he was asking about. Freud indicated that Little Hans's phobia had arisen from his castration anxiety. This becomes a cornerstone of Freud's theory of the Oedipus complex. As Juliet Mitchell indicates:

> The Oedipus complex, then, is not the trinity it is so often envisaged as – mother, father, child – but a relationship between four terms of which the fourth and the determinant one is castration.
>
> (1974, p. 79)

It is castration that inserts the individual in a specific position in the oedipal triangle (Mitchell, 1999). One must not lose sight of the eminently symbolic nature of this division, and that the phallus can only be seen as missing in the girl in terms of a "pre-existing hierarchy of values" (Rose, 1982, p. 43), as "there is nothing missing in the real" (Lacan, 1968, p. 113).

According to Perelberg:

> what is there in contrast with the phallus is a lack, an impossibility, an absence, a gap – everything that is not there and is not possible, a fundamental renunciation which is the basis of the human order ... Both masculinity and femininity ... contrast with the phallus, both expressing a lack.
>
> (1997b, pp. 220–221)

Castration becomes the signifier of a dialectic relationship in sexuality; it requires the renunciation of the incestuous desires and the inauguration of culture. In the structural model of the mind, this threat is internalized, and the fear of the father becomes the fear of one's own superego.

Morel[5] has distinguished between the certainty of perception and doubt (2011, p. 7); a child may discover that a woman does not have a penis and yet continue to assume that the mother possesses a phallus. The observation of the anatomical difference is not enough for the registration of this difference (also Mitchell, 1982). Another aspect will need to be added, which is the threat of castration (Freud, 1924d, p. 252).

Morel provides the following example of a child's resistance to acknowledging the differentiation between the sexes:

> Sara, aged six, a little girl who was in analysis, knew perfectly well, and had evidence to prove it, that boys have a "willy" and girls do not. But she was reticent about it, and immediately afterwards would draw three types of human beings: boys, girls and witches. The last were wearing very tall hats. … Alongside "scientific" knowledge with respect to anatomical difference, the unconscious belief in the mother's phallic power remained unaltered.
>
> (2011, pp. 77–78)

From my own practice, another example:

> Sam, aged three, made the following statement: "When I grow up, I want to be a Daddy. Then I will grow up and I will be a Mummy."

The horror of castration is expressed in the notion of the uncanny: something that is at once familiar and yet disturbing. *Unheimlich* (the uncanny) has been interpreted with reference to the maternal body, to the female maternal organ that has been repressed (Perelberg, 2013a):

> Whenever a man dreams of a place or a country and says to himself, whilst he is still dreaming: "this place is familiar to me, I've been here before" one may interpret the place as being his mother's genitals or her body. In this case too, then the *Unheimlich* is what was once *heimisch*, familiar; the prefix "un" is the token of repression.
>
> (Freud, 1919h, p. 245)

Something that is known and not known at the same time, a sense of "déjà vu", and yet repressed.

Sexual difference is assigned in relation to the phallus and castration.

## d *Jouissance*

The concept of *jouissance* occupies a central role in Freud's writings.

In the topographic model of the mind, the pleasure principle is linked to the discharge of tensions. The essential function of mental activity consists of reducing to as low a level as possible the tensions induced by either instinctual or external excitations. The prototypical example of this would be hunger and the pleasure that the baby achieves through feeding at the breast. This brings with it the first experience of satisfaction. Once the first experience of satisfaction has been introduced to the baby, however, then the next time the baby is hungry, he will expect a fulfilment that repeats that first experience. There is now an intrinsic link between hunger and the psychic representation of satisfaction that will be experienced through hallucinatory wish-fulfilment. There is a wish to "re-find" that very first experience that is characterized by impossibility, as it can never be repeated. Fundamentally, it is linked to the object that has been lost and has left its traces in the unconscious (Lacan, 1998). It is impossible to make up for this loss, and *jouissance* is marked by this absence – the impossibility of fulfilment, beyond the pleasure principle. Desire arises only in relation to an Other that is, by definition, absent.

In the structural model of the mind, Freud went one step further in connecting sexuality, repetition and trauma through the discovery that there is something that he designates "beyond the pleasure principle". The activity of discharge is now linked to the Nirvana principle – the aim of reaching a state of "nought" tensions that he linked to the death drives. *Jouissance* now cannot be fully attained because it would lead to death.

Because of its links with death, the concept of *jouissance* cannot be translated as "pleasure". *Jouissance* arises from one's own body, especially the border zones – mouth, anus, genitals, eyes, ears, skin (Lacan, 1973). Anxiety about *jouissance* is one of being overwhelmed by one's own drives.

*Jouissance* thus designates an excess of pleasure, a satisfaction that is overwhelming, that brings suffering as a result of a prolonged state of internal excitation, in a mixture of the life and death drives. Freud gives several examples of this state that are beyond the pleasure principle: the *fort–da* game, the dreams of traumatic neurosis, the compulsion to repeat, the negative therapeutic reaction.

Laplanche has suggested that the death drive is *"itself* a deepening of sexuality in its most radical aspect" (1999, p. 188; see also Perelberg 2007). He understands the concept of the death drive in terms of sexuality:

> The patient … is obliged to repeat the repressed material as a contemporary experience instead of, as the physician would prefer to see, remembering it as something belonging to the past. These reproductions, which emerge with such wished for exactitude, always have as their subject some portion of infantile sexual life – of the Oedipus complex, that is.
>
> (Freud, 1920g, p. 18)

### e The role of the other in the constitution of the psyche[6]

A new paradigm present in contemporary French psychoanalysis highlights the crucial importance of the unconscious discourse of the adult in the constitution of the child's sexuality. The key point of reference for this shift can be found in Lacan's work and his notion that the individual is born into language. This language is present in the adult Other and pre-dates the individual's existence. For Lacan, this was expressed in terms of *le grand Autre* (the big Other), referring to the whole of the symbolic order itself. A whole generation of influential analysts – including André Green, Jean Laplanche, Pontalis, Aulagnier, and Rosolato – attended Lacan's seminars for many years, are implicitly, if not explicitly, engaged in a dialogue with him, and found their own ways of conceptualizing this.

Green suggests the concept of framing structure as being at the origins of representation. When holding her infant, the mother leaves the impression of her arms on the child, which constitutes the framing structure that, in her absence, contains the loss of the perception of the maternal object, as a negative hallucination of it. Green believes that it is against the background of negativity that future representations of the object are inscribed. The negative hallucination of the mother and of the mother's body creates the condition for the activity of thinking itself, as well as the capacity to symbolize. The negative hallucination of the mother is, therefore, a precondition for thought. Green's conceptualization of the mother as the "framing structure" is also the erotic mother, the mother that – as Freud argues in *Outline of Psycho-Analysis* (1940a) – is the first seductress of the infant through the care that she gives him and her general attitude to him. This framing structure, by its implicit reference to the father linked to the mother's absence, is also an indication of thirdness. It is at the heart of Green's formulation about the psychoanalytic setting itself (see also Perelberg, 2016).

Another crucial contributor to the current theoretical framework on the connections between "inside and outside" is Jean Laplanche, who has suggested that infantile sexuality develops under the influence of the parental and primarily maternal "enigmatic signifiers" (Laplanche, 1987, p. 125). These signifiers imprint the mother's unconscious on the child's erogenous zones, along with the erotic link she has with the father and with the father's own unconscious. Infantile sexuality is endogenous inasmuch as it follows a course of development and passes through different stages, and exogenous inasmuch as it invades the subject from the direction of the adult world (since the subject is obliged from the outset to find a place in the phantasy universe of the parents, and since they subject him to more or less veiled sexual incitement). Laplanche suggests an account of the origin of the psychic apparatus and the drives, starting from the adult–infant relation. This theory supposes that, in the sexual domain, such a relation is asymmetrical, the sexual message originating in the adult Other. It is the impact of the Other on the constitution of the psychic apparatus that is the conceptual reference here.

The maternal feminine at an oedipal level is present in the notion of the *censorship of the mother-as-lover* introduced by Fain. Braunschweig and Fain indicate the misrecognition of feminine sexual pleasure. This formulation emphasizes the role of the mother's own internal relationship to her sexuality and that of her lover in the constitution of the child's internal world. The concept of the *censorship of the mother-as-lover* reinforces the impossibility of direct access to the maternal without the intervention of the law of the father.

All these different authors emphasize the impact of the parental discourse in the structuring of the psychic bisexuality of an individual. This process is therefore not only endogenous, but also something that comes from the adult other. These ideas are implicitly, if not explicitly, present throughout the chapters in this volume.

31

### f Primary homosexuality

The term "primary homosexuality" was first formulated by Fenichel, who introduced it in connection with female homosexuality:

> The first object of every human being is the mother: all women, in contradistinction to men, have had a primary homosexual attachment, which may later be revived if normal heterosexuality is blocked.
>
> (1946, p. 338)

Kestemberg (1984) proposed the concept of a primary homosexuality that is common to both sexes.

One returns to Freud, in "A Case of Paranoia Running Counter to the Psycho-Analytic Theory of Disease" (1915f), where he offers a theoretical understanding of the patient's homosexuality that relates to the primal relationship to the mother: the "powerful emotional attachment to her mother", the "homosexual dependence on her mother" is transposed to the "elderly superior", and it is this bond that is at the root of the patient's difficulties.

Freud further states that:

> The manifestation of the neurotic reaction will always be determined, however, not by their present-day relation to her actual mother but by her infantile relations to the earliest image of her mother.
>
> (1915f, p. 268)

This formulation relates implicitly to the relationship between the girl and her mother. Paul Denis (1982) extends the concept to include the relationship between the boy and his mother. "Anatomical sex is therefore not adequate to define relational modalities" (p. 642).

His point of departure is Freud himself, in his statement in *The Ego and the Id*:

> before a child has arrived at a definite knowledge of the difference between the sexes, the lack of a penis, it does not distinguish in value between its father and its mother.
>
> (Freud, 1923b, p. 31)

This is a key Freudian formulation that is prevalent in French psychoanalysis: the lack of awareness of sexual differentiation in young life. It is castration that inaugurates, retrospectively, an awareness of sexual differences (Mitchell, 1982, 1999). Denis suggests that it is the progressive recognition of sexual difference that puts an end to primary homosexuality (1982, p. 645).

Freud suggests that tenderness is born of a gradual process of desexualization of the relationship between the child and the caregivers. French psychoanalysis has emphasized the centrality of the distinction between day mother and night mother. The mother of the night turns her erotic relationship to her husband/partner, who is not the baby (Braunschweig & Fain, 1975). I have suggested that an interpretation of Freud's "The 'Uncanny'" (1919h) is the distinction between the day father (who is the benign father, the counterpart of the mother who exercises the maternal function) and the night father (sexual father, who is "repulsive" and diabolical and who takes the mother as his lover) (Perelberg, 2015b, p. 228). Sexuality is thus traumatic for the child and poses an enigma that the individual tries to make sense of throughout his life.

## Sex and gender

A conceptual differentiation between *sex, gender* and *sexuality* seems crucial to elucidate some of the questions and themes that permeate the chapters in this volume.

All societies are faced with the task of differentiating between the identical and the different (Perelberg, 1990a, 1990b, 1997b, 2015c). Sex refers to a biological differentiation at the base of the cultural attribution of gender roles. Sexuality, in contrast, at the base of psychoanalytic theory, refers to unconscious phantasies present in the life of each individual. Sexuality is to do with desire and is always in conflict with prohibition and the Law against incest.

The division of gender roles according to sex is universal; it is present in all human societies. Making sense of it is a task, perhaps a lifelong one, for each individual.

According to Héritier, the differences between male and female bodies and between their roles in reproduction are at the base of all systems of representation, and especially beliefs about difference, such as hot/cold, dry/humid, high/low, inferior/superior, light/dark, and so forth (2002, 2012, p. 20). Binary systems, she adds, are at the base of universal categorizations. Héritier addresses the universals surrounding the notions of masculine and feminine in a variety of kinship systems, as well as the cultural images that are present in these differentiations. These are constructs of the culture, not biological givens. Héritier suggests that differentiation between masculine and feminine should not be regarded merely as an addition to the three pillars of culture suggested by Lévi-Strauss (1969 [1967]) – the incest taboo, the sexual division of labour and a recognized form of sexual union – but as actually lying at the origins of the other three.

The recognition of the differences between the sexes and the generations, as an outcome of the incest taboo, universally marks the passage from nature to culture (Lévi-Strauss, 1969 [1967]). Each known society, however, attempts to find its own solutions and responses to the fundamental enigma of these differences through the structures of kinship systems and rituals. An example is that of the ritual *Naven*, among the Iatmul people of New Guinea, in which men dress as women and women dress as men. These ceremonies are performed to celebrate certain acts and achievements of the *laua* (sister's son) by the *wau* (mother's brother) (Perelberg, 2016).

There is an inherent contradiction in Iatmul society between the nature of an individual's relationship with his mother's clan and the behaviour that is expected from the men – that is, the masculine ethos. Two main dichotomies organize social life: the opposition between men and women, and that between the individual matrilineal and patrilineal ties. It is through these contradictions that Bateson analyses the Naven, particularly the transvestism and pantomime that it involves (Bateson, in Perelberg, 2015b).

In what concerns the distinction between the sexes, Bateson (1958 [1936]) indicates that men put an "emphasis and value set upon pride, self-assertion, harshness and spectacular display" (p. 198). They are occupied with violent activities. There is a tendency to histrionic behaviour that transforms harshness into irony, which can turn into buffoonery. The women have a less consistent ethos as, according to Bateson, their lives are more geared towards getting food, rearing children and "reality". "The normal life of Iatmul women is quiet and unostentatious, while that of men is noisy and ostentatious" (p. 201). In the ceremonial house men display their skills in oratory and in the spectacular; the tone of the debates is, according to Bateson, noisy, angry and ironical.

Bateson suggests that the difference between the sexes should be understood as acquired through learning and imitation. In the Naven ceremony, the exaggerated elements of the *wau*'s behaviour reflect patterns of behaviour accepted among ordinary Iatmul men.

In a different context, in the annual Brazilian Carnival rituals, men dance and parade in the *Escolas de Samba* dressed as women in ways that at times indicate a parody or a caricature of women. These are just a couple of examples of the way in which the enigma of the difference between the sexes permeates different times, spaces and cultures. If sexual difference "means no more than one sex is not another" (Mitchell, 2015, p. 84), might one see the infinite variation of expressions and heterogeneity of gender identifications in contemporary societies also as attempted answers given to the mystery of this basic difference?

If the responses to the question of difference between the sexes vary from culture to culture, what is constant and universal, according to Héritier, is inequality between the sexes across cultures. She quotes from the 1995 report of the United Nations, which states that full equality between men and women is not to be found in any society. Feminist writers, activists, academics and clinicians have amply addressed this issue in extremely important ways.[7]

Reading Héritier's texts reminds me of what I wrote in 1990, in *Gender and Power in Families*:

> Gender differences are culturally selected from among biological characteristics and are turned into "natural differences" between the sexes (La Fontaine, 1985). What westerners regard as the natural characteristics of men and women are neither universal nor natural. The literature abounds with examples which illustrate the variation in these "natural" characteristics. There are parts of New Guinea, for instance, in which men are prudish and flirtatious, preoccupied with cosmetics and their appearance, while women take the initiative in courtship (Mead, 1935; Rosaldo & Lamphere, 1974).
>
> (Perelberg, 1990a, pp. 42–43)

The terms "man" and "woman" are therefore social constructs that legitimize patterns of behaviour (La Fontaine, 1981). However, most societies – whatever their kinship organization or mode of subsistence – tend to give authority and value to the role and activities of men. The diversity in the relationship between the genders is tempered by a common factor of subordination. In a later work, I suggested that the universal subordination of women across cultures may be understood as ways that societies have tried to control the unconscious fears of the all-powerful primitive maternal imago (Perelberg, 2008, p. 22).

In terms of the framework that is outlined in this Introduction, one must also consider Freud's notion of the universality of the (unconscious) repudiation of femininity as the universal signifier of a lack and incompleteness.

The term "gender" was introduced into the psychotherapies by the sexologist John Money (Money, Hampson, & Hampson, 1955) and was then taken up by Robert J. Stoller (1968), who coined the term "core gender identity" (Laplanche, 2007). Stoller was one of the first clinicians to listen to transsexuals. He puts forward a definition of gender that is linked to a biological conception, and he linked sexuality to procreation (Stoller, 1968, p. 4). He suggests, nevertheless, a distinction between sex – as determined by biology – and gender, a term that is psychological or cultural (p. 9). He also integrated the importance of the mother's desire for the establishment of gender into his conceptual framework. When the mother feminizes a boy, he will later wish to become a girl.

In recent decades the issue of gender has become prominent in the spheres of health and human rights. It was in 1994 that the gene DSS, which is responsible for sexual abnormalities, was discovered. These discoveries have introduced a change in contemporary views on gender. The debate has perhaps become confusing because of a lack of differentiation between sex, gender and sexuality.[8]

## Sexuality, bisexuality

The object of psychoanalysis, however, is not gender but psycho-sexuality, which establishes a link between sexuality and the unconscious. The latter is permanently challenging our apparent unity as subjects (Rose, 1982, p. 30). This unity, as we have seen when discussing Lacan's notion of the mirror stage, is a specular construction that enables the individual to enter into the realm of symbolic exchanges.

In discussion with Butler, both Mitchell and Rose (Butler, 2015; Mitchell, 2015) emphasize the fundamental principle of sexual difference within the law within culture that prohibits incest and murder. This is an irreducible principle in psychoanalysis and is to be distinguished from the variations of sexual desire.

Freud pointed out the fluidity that is the hallmark of identificatory processes. This fluidity contrasts with the individual quest for a *coherent* identity, a sense of cohesiveness that is denied him by the very nature of the psychic apparatus.

Laplanche has coined the term *"le sexuel"* – by definition, multiple and polymorphous – which refers to infantile, perverse sexuality. He stresses that the *"sexuel"* is the psychoanalytic object (2007):

> The infantile sexuel, the "sexual," is the very object of psychoanalysis. A matter of drives and not instinct, functioning according to a specific economic system that is the seeking of tension and not the seeking of tension reduction, having at its origin the fantasmatic object, at its origin and not at its outcome, hence reversing the "object relation," it comes to take up all the room by trying to organize itself in a way that is always precarious, until the upheaval of puberty when the instinctive genital will have to come to terms with it.
>
> (p. 218)

Laplanche argues that the introduction of the term "gender" into psychoanalysis colludes with those who want to diminish the impact of the Freudian discovery.

Lacan has coined the term *sexuation*, as distinct from biological sexuality, to designate the way in which the subject is inscribed in the difference between the sexes, specifically in terms of the unconscious and castration, that is, as "inhabiting language" (1998, p. 80). The process of sexuation passes through what comes from the discourse of the other. For him, there is a fundamental, specular, imaginary aspect to this.

Three moments of sexuation are identified (Morel, 2011). They include anatomy, in the first instance, a sexual discourse in the second, and in the third moment, the unconscious choice of sex by the subject. These would have some correspondence with my distinctions between sex, gender and sexuality.

In 1931, Fairbairn published one of the earliest analyses of a patient concerned about her "real" sex. She had been in analysis for nine years. I will focus for a moment on this patient as it is derived from an analysis, and there is some material about the individual's unconscious phantasies. The patient had been depressed, which had led her to stop teaching, but she also had doubts about her "real" sex. At puberty, she was found to have a genital abnormality: she did not menstruate, and her growth was abnormal. When she was 20 years old, it was revealed that she had external genital organs but a very minuscule vagina, and that she had no uterus. Although she had been a tomboy in her childhood, she had always been attracted to boys and had never had any doubts about her femininity. When she started to work, she became too harsh with the children she taught. She alternated between periods of mania and depression.

Her mother had been an energetic person, and her father insignificant and passive. The authority in the family resided in her maternal grandfather, who had died a year before the patient started her analysis.

Initially the patient responded well to the analysis with Fairbairn and had an awakening of her sexuality. A period of excitement surrounding this sexual wakening was followed by increased anxiety in relation to men. Fairbairn understood this as her penis envy, oral-sadistic in quality, which provoked enormous unconscious guilt in the patient. The analyst focused his interpretations on the patient's sadism. Morel (2011) indicates that "penis envy was not theorized as a symbolic lack, but rather as the very concrete envy of, and desire for, an object, like a chocolate she had wanted to steal from the fridge" (p. 170). She emphasizes that Fairbairn's technique "consisted in making his patient feel guilty about her immoral desires". Lacan wondered whether the analyst's technique could have led to a "paranoidization of hysteria" (1991, p. 272).

Morel goes through the details of the case and identifies how, as a child, the patient had a masculine identification:

> In her imagination she was a man, and the depression she experienced at the time of her "adventures" can be explained by the fact that, when confronted by a man, her narcissistic image, her masculine ego was snatched away. ... The analysis should have enabled her to elaborate her castration complex and helped her to assume her privation (the real lack of the symbolic object, the phallus). ... Fairbairn, by interpreting the desire for a penis as if it was the desire for a real object, could not allow her to go beyond Penisneid.
>
> (2011, p. 172)

Moreover, by concentrating the analysis on the mother–daughter relationship and forgetting about the father, he was eliminated in analysis. Hysteria, however, as we have also discussed in relation to the case of Dora, "is dedicated to exposing the father's impotence" (Freud, 1905e, p. 47).

Morel (2011) concludes that the unconscious choice may remain unrecognized without an analysis (p. 177). The biological abnormalities in this classical psychoanalytic case did not determine the choice of the process of sexuation. In some cases of transsexualism, she suggests, the wish to eliminate the sexual organ is "not requested so that the subject can experience the sexual jouissance of the other sex, but rather for reasons of 'being' (appearances, social identity, change of status, etc.)" (p. 187; see also Lemma, 2013). Lemma also emphasizes the visual aspect: some transsexuals wish to have an operation to remove their penis in terms of how they look, rather than it being a question of desire. In the case of her patient, Ms A, she observed that "her body felt shut down, turned away from anything alive, like a ghost dressed up with nowhere to go" (p. 281).

In a recent paper, Lemma has suggested in the analysis of her patient Celine, who declared herself as "trans" at the beginning of their work together, that she was rather lost, confused and unable to sustain intimate relationships. This is also the case for several of the clinical cases presented in this book. The individual feels alienated, "neither dead nor alive" (Rolland, 2007), "caught up in an obsessional doubt, neither yes, nor no" (Green, 1986c [1977]; see also Campbell, Chapter 11, and Green, Chapter 12, in this volume), or unable to be neither one *or* the other, or one *and* the other (Chabert, Chapter 2, in this volume). At times these patients attempt to deal with these alienating identifications by establishing a sense of identity, saying "I am this, and not that and not that" (see Chabert, Chapter 2, Zilkha, Chapter 7, and Campbell, Chapter 11, in this volume). One is thus not addressing the choice of the object of desire but, rather, the individual's disturbed relationship to their body and their unconscious identifications. To my way of thinking, the pitfall is, once again, for a conscious discourse to be taken literally.[9]

Following a Lacanian formulation, Morel suggests that this demand for an actual change in the body may be understood as the outcome of the foreclosure of the signifier of the phallus.[10] It is an attempt to make a correction in anatomy, whereas the real issue lies at the juncture of the real and the symbolic (2011, p. 186). In some of the cases of women wanting to have a penis, something that belongs to the symbolic level (castration) is taken as a concrete reality. In reality, however, there was no castration!

Gozlan suggests that transsexuality can be viewed as a "particular embodiment of sexual difference that captures a universal enigma at the heart of subjectivity" (2015, p. 12). He believes that when gender is conceived as naturally given or, at the other extreme, as "a matter of choice" (Gherovici, 2010) "what gets foreclosed is the incommensurability between the symbolic articulation of gender and the real of sexual difference" (Gozlan, 2015, p. 13). The relationship between the sexed body and gender identity is fragile "at best". Psychoanalytic theories move between what he considers is the "compulsion" to uphold the normative binary gender system and the acknowledgement of the radical heterogeneity of the drive.

In his account of Aron, a female-to-male patient, Gozlan (2015) understands transsexuality as a way of avoiding the experience of engulfment by the parents. Gozlan openly shares with the reader the way in which, for quite some time, he had become stuck in his countertransference by the patient's conscious doubts about whether or not to be a man or a woman. I think that one can read this case in the light of Green's chapter in this volume, as an attempt to be neither a man nor a woman but the phantasy of the neuter gender, neither masculine nor feminine.

Gozlan suggests that the question of transsexual surgery should be understood in terms of "transitioning" and not reassignment and that this opens a new discourse of agency (p. 92). Transsexuality can thus be conceptualized as a signifier for a liminal space that challenges the finitude of gender and calls for a recounting of history, one that is ruptured, opaque and incomplete.

I believe that there is at times a confusion between the patient's conscious discourse and the analyst's interpretations. Rather than attesting to the incompleteness and fragmented, perverse nature of sexuality, the transsexual individual paradoxically appears to insist on a clear categorization. Within a psychoanalytic framework, as Mitchell well emphasizes in her Foreword, and as discussed by all the authors in the present volume, we are all bisexual and there is no definition of an individual's sexuality and desire outside this framework.[11] I wonder if a distinction between sex, gender and sexuality might enable one to firmly remain within an understanding of masculinity and femininity as psychic positions.[12]

In psychoanalysis, taking into account the fluidity of identifications discussed in this Introduction and throughout the chapters of this volume, it is clear that absolute certainty about one's identifications expresses a confusion of registers – addressing as real something that belongs to the symbolic sphere.

## Structure of the book

Chapter 1, by Christian David, offers a formulation on psychic bisexuality that constitutes an important marker in this volume, permeating several chapters. David identifies two discernible lines of thinking on the question of bisexuality in Freud's work:

a   successful repression of the initial bisexuality – the more sexual difference is asserted, the more bisexuality becomes involuted and virtualized;
b   the differential integration of sexuality goes hand-in-hand with an authentic bisexual fulfilment.

Freud assigns the psychoanalytic treatment of homosexuality the goal of the "re-establishment of a complete bisexual function" while emphasizing the difficulties of such a result, an ideal outcome for which we can only strive.

David introduces the concept of a bisexualization process in order to describe the integration of masculine and feminine dimensions in the psychosexuality of both men and women. The bisexualization process corresponds, in both sexes, to the possibility of acquiring "the mental capacity to fantasise, understand and share the sexual and psychosexual experience of someone of the other sex"; this implies acceptance of the incompleteness of both sexes, experienced as castration, and not its denial, as we find in actual bisexual behaviour.

Following Freud, David goes further, to say that sexual intercourse exists, and relationships between the sexes exist, because bisexuality exists: "In all of us, throughout life, the libido normally oscillates between male and female object."

The analytic situation intrinsically consists of a testing of psychosexual characteristics and identity and simultaneously a stimulation of bisexuality. It is a process, not of the abolition nor the exacerbation of sexual difference, but its relativization: it requires the

41

resumption of the unconscious bisexualization process in the service of establishing "full bisexual function" (Freud, 1920g).

There is an inherent incompleteness of sexual differences, as no human being is able to completely give up father or mother.

In Chapter 2, Catherine Chabert reminds us, in her analysis of the Rat Man (1909d), that the great references to masculine and feminine are not to be confused with man and woman. They not only embody father and mother, but they emphasize an intertwining: "their swings and hesitations allow us to follow and theorize the traces of an ever-active bisexuality. The more sexuation comes to impose its differences, the more it empowers bisexuality, as if sexual identity went with its necessary maintenance."

The Rat Man could be regarded as the key example of the tortures inflicted by object choice and the vicissitudes of psychic bisexuality. Freud centres his understanding of the case on the father, but Chabert indicates that many of the fragments of the narrative may be understood as referring to the mother, who is present in several of the scenes and memories. They have, however, been repressed from the published case on obsessional neurosis, in favour of the father. She understands this as evidence of the oedipal repetition, but Freud does not say that the "venerated lady" has replaced the mother as "sexual object". Yet bisexuality, integrated into the difference between the sexes, might be the very condition of the double choice, the double identification and its major underlying conflicts. Chabert suggests that the Rat Man's inability to move from one point to another might be a representation of the wish and at the same time the immense difficulty he experiences in attempting to move from one parent to the other.

Chabert concludes that the "bisexuality of all human beings" exposed by Freud (1950 [1892–1899], Letter 52) indicates the impossibility of considering either the masculine or the feminine without its link to the other sex: they are defined by their difference. "Bisexuality … definitely does not mean a confusion of sexes but maintains the existence of both, masculine and feminine, with their usual or extraordinary articulations."

In her patient Hippolyte, who struggled in his identifications with wanting to be on the side of one *or* the other, Chabert understands the profound separation of the primal couple. The patient was unable to grasp his parents' sexual identity – his father as a man and his mother as a woman. Without these representations, this incapacity made his own sexual identity very complicated: he could be neither, neither one *or* the other, neither one *and* the other: "the impossibility to stand the primal scene obliges one to overinvest in bisexuality in its narcissistic form, erasing any difference in order to avoid any desire and to ensure protection against horror and exclusion." In this process castration anxiety is avoided, but it leaves the individual unable to find his *jouissance*.

In Chapter 3, Monique Cournut-Janin indicates how the concept of bisexuality emerged in Freud's work through his idealized relationship with a man. Bisexuality and transference are discovered together. This theme is developed further in Chapter 13, by Gregorio Kohon.

In any analysis there is an oscillation between the archaic and the oedipal – the narcissistic pull, on the one hand, and the relationship to the object, on the other. Our patients' narratives contain their unconscious infantile sexual theories: the universality of the penis, the delivery through the anus, the sadistic primal scene between the parents, and the lack of knowledge of the vagina. The loss of the breast, the separation from the object, leave profound traces in the mental life of individuals. Birth is a disturbing event shared by mother and child. For the child, it is the loss of a protective world; the mother, in turn, is confronted with the real baby, not the baby of her phantasy (see also Davies, Chapter 9, and Green, Chapter 12).

For both patient and analyst, bisexual identifications are intrinsic to the analytic process, with the participation of the parental imagos where the interplay of the masculine and feminine are delineated – perhaps not too clearly.

Cournut-Janin offers us clinical vignettes of the analyses of Louise and Violette. Louise had repressed a memory that she had offered the analyst in the first period of her analysis. As a child, she used to play with one of her grandfather's fingers, deformed by shrapnel during the First World War; she moved this glinting, metallic fragment under the amused and tender gaze of this grandfather. When she comes back for a second period of analysis, this memory has been forgotten, making the analyst doubt her own memory.

Violette does not accept that she is a woman, as this would mean not being able to be both a boy and a girl. She hates her analyst for having offered her an analysis and for not saying that she was unanalysable. The analyst experiences herself at times as enclosed in

43

a carcass, dead. Cournut-Janin argues that anality was at the centre of the treatment. It enabled her to avoid her mother, the analyst, her sex and sexuality. The challenge for the analyst is to find a third that enables her to escape from this enclosed universe. A dream or a word may facilitate this for the analyst.

In Chapter 4, Rosine Jozef Perelberg suggests that in the analysis of women by women a melancholic core may be encountered at the centre of the transference–countertransference situation that is an expression of the loss of the primary maternal object that has never been mourned. The attachment to the primary lost object may be preserved in a melancholy, invisible way, and the longing to which it is connected might reach representation only in the *après-coup* of the analytic process. The links between this primary love, melancholia and the unrepresentable in the analysis of women are explored.

This discovery of a fundamental passion for the mother, a later discovery in Freud's formulation, permeates many of the chapters in this volume. As Hirsch says in his Chapter 8, quoting from Romain Gary: *Avec l'amour maternel, la vie vous fait à l'aube une promesse qu'elle ne tient jamais* [The *Promise at Dawn* (Gary, 1962) is the original unconscious promise made by every mother to her child, *which is then always contradicted by life.*]

The chapter links these as expressions of the pre-oedipal domain, or Oedipus 1, as described by Kristeva, that can only be constructed in the context of an analysis and indicates the contact with women's fundamental psychic bisexuality. These analyses powerfully evoke the relationship to the somatic. The internalization of the body of the mother, which is a requirement in the development of a woman in order for her to take on her feminine sexuality, can take on frightening, fragmented, part-object qualities. The chapter describes a period in Emma's analysis when there was a breakdown into the somatic. The analyst understood this period, *après coup*, as a regression into a *primary homosexuality in the transference*, before a *secondary femininity* could be constructed in the vicissitudes of the transference and countertransference. The analytic process required the analyst to be able to be receptive to the patient's somatic suffering and to respond with an attitude of containment and (symbolic) maternal care. This was predominant for a period of time, before a more potent interpretative function could be established – an expression of a paternal function that was then reached. This analysis illustrates that the movement from the maternal to the paternal can be reached in the analyses of women patients by women analysts. Perelberg also raises the question of whether the analysis of women by women analysts makes this archaic transference more easily accessible. The relevance of the gender of the analyst in the process of transference is also raised by Jacqueline Godfrind (Chapter 5), Denis Hirsch (Chapter 8) and Nathalie Zilkha (Chapter 7). The concepts of *primary homosexuality* and *secondary femininity* are also discussed by Jacqueline Godfrind (Chapter 5) and Denis Hirsch (Chapter 8).

In Chapter 5, Jacqueline Godfrind, a Belgian analyst who has made important contributions to the understanding of femininity, hypothesizes a *primary core of the organization of bisexuality in women*:

> Behind the sometimes deadly hate that exists between daughter and mother, suddenly there appears a bewildered love for the mother, a fascination that rivets the daughter to the mother, appealing to an encounter "de trou à trou" – "hole to hole" – the daughter being totally attached to the mother, bewitched, a link I call "primary homosexuality".

When there are psychotic aspects in the mother's functioning, this exacerbates the difficulties linked with the conflictualization of the primary homosexual relation. Her patient Jane expressed her distress in her sessions, during which the deadly alliance between daughter and mother came to the fore and to the transference. How is it possible to escape the deadly ascendancy of a mother, who is so fragile, when this separation raises the risk of destroying her?

In these configurations, the father is idealized. The penis loses its quality as a partial object, a signifier of male attributes, and becomes a phallic antidote with respect to the "narcissistic hole" hollowed out by her existential dependency on the mother:

> This idealized image of the father functions as a guarantee of the daughter's integrity and femininity. Enclosed in a crypt carefully preserved from any questioning, a phallic identification with father is hidden, a solidarity that has been indispensable to building the primary femininity.

The power attributed to the father is an antidote to the terrifying fascination aroused by the mother and the threat represented by the temptation of giving herself to her.

Godfrind suggests that lengthy analytic work is necessary before femininity and masculinity can reach what she has called "the peace of the sexes".

In Chapter 6, Marilia Aisenstein and Harvey Rich are particularly interested in masculine identifications in women and feminine identifications in men. They present two clinical cases: that of "Byron", a young patient followed by Harvey Rich, and a more succinct vignette relating to a session of a female patient, "Antigone", in analysis with a woman analyst (Aisenstein).

Byron's analysis illustrates how much the bisexual listening of the male psychoanalyst (Rich) can help the patient to build a bisexuality that had been undermined by his family history. Byron's openly declared bisexuality was aimed, the analyst thought, at hiding the failure of psychic bisexuality and his fear of relationships with women. When he asked for an analysis, Byron spoke of himself as either homosexual or bisexual; he complained of difficulties in forming relations with others rather than of difficulties of identity. During his analysis, Byron was able to explore the homosexual passive position in relation to the father with a male analyst who was capable of accepting and working through the homosexual transference. This contributed to reinforcing Byron's predominant heterosexual position.

The authors understand the material present in the patient they call "Antigone" as a lack of equilibrium – the bisexual investment in her by the father was not in tune with the investment of the mother, who loved her for her success at school but had never been able to invest in the daughter's femininity. Analysis with a woman was able to invest in the patient all the registers of their respective bisexualities. The chapter includes the vignette of a session, which reveals a moment when the analyst comes to understand the mother's rejection of the patient's body from the patient's reaction to the analyst's body in the session. Antigone was seen not as a failure in the construction of bisexuality (as was Byron) but "a lack of equilibrium" due to a lack of investment in her femininity by both parents.

In Chapter 7, Nathalie Zilkha reflects on the process whereby the feminine is constructed and organized with the support of the experience of a gendered body. It takes shape through the feminine aspect of the mother and through the feminine aspect of the father. She considers that is the work of adolescence, however, that gives meaning and fabric to the feminine. "Throughout this process and beyond (since it is ongoing), multiple occasions for stumbling blocks, obstacles, singularities and impasses occur – as well as for creative solutions" (Zilkha, p. 155, Chapter 7, in this volume).

Zilkha understands her patient Ms A's psychic bisexuality in the initial stages of their work to operate in clusters (*en îlots*), in a split or "fragmented" (*éclatée*) manner, against the backdrop of a femininity *in abeyance*. Her female body was experienced alternatively as walled-in, as empty or as dangerously permeable, causing her to suffer. The maternal object was omnipresent in her bodily experiences, and this blocked her freedom of being and capacity for pleasure. At the same time there was a question as to whether Ms A's mother had tried to "impose" a "masculine" ideal on her. The father was portrayed as a pale figure.

In the course of the analysis, the patient begins to progressively take an interest in external signs of femininity (make-up, jewellery, etc.). At the same time, she begins to "act like a boy" in order to conceal from the maternal object that the analyst represents the woman that she is. In this context, she tells the analyst that, after seeing a television programme about menstruation, she thought: "And me, I don't have them … so there!" "Both girl and boy? Neither girl nor boy?" The analyst replied, choosing to portray both issues at stake, hysteria and that of the negative. "Both girl and boy", Ms A replied.

Progressively, Ms A was able to weave a more personal, more satisfying and, above all, less restrictive fabric of the feminine, paving the way for a certain play between feminine and masculine identifications.

In considering the repudiation of the feminine in women and penis envy, Zilkha suggests that it may be thought of a resistance of the superego to a maternal imago of an incorporative nature. Like the other authors in this book, Zilkha emphasizes that it is the work of the transference and countertransference that will offer opportunities for reorganizing identifications.

In her reflections on Winnicott's text (Winnicott, 1966), Zilkha suggests that when bisexuality cannot be played out intrapsychically, it may be dramatized on the stage of the transference and countertransference. Winnicott shares

> his receptivity to a fundamental alterity or otherness by which he
> can let himself be permeated and carried, and to which he gives

freedom of expression through his interpretations. He can let himself be affected by this radical alterity that is the madness of the maternal object and let it speak in him.

Zilkha concludes that Winnicott's patient's resistance, which had taken the form of penis envy, "expressed a need to have a part of himself recognised and, more fundamentally, to a lack of being".

Denis Hirsch opens Chapter 8 with some reflections on *La promesse de l'aube*, a novel by Romain Gary. It is an account of Gary's childhood with his mother, who loved her son unconditionally. This is a narrative of a struggle against adversity so that the son is able to fulfil his mother's dreams. Hirsch suggests that this story expresses the unconscious promise that every mother makes to her child. In spite of the inequality of the relationship between mother and child, it is a reciprocal promise, a narcissistic contract that will have an impact on the construction of the individual's sexuality and on psychic bisexuality. In his formulations, Hirsch is following a tradition in French psychoanalysis that considers the impact of the parental unconscious life on the constitution of the child's sexuality (see Perelberg, 2013b, and Chapter 4, in this volume).

Hirsch points out that some alienating pacts in the relationship between mother and child act as an impediment in the structuralization of the child's sexuality. He considers the "heroic pact" between Romain Gary and his mother and then an example of "black pact" between mother and daughter in an analytic process. Romain Gary's pact with his mother requires him to sustain a phallic identification and a pseudo-masculinity. He remains an object of narcissistic satisfaction for his mother and is required to deny the desire for the father. The father as lover of the mother (Braunschweig & Fain, 1975) is obliterated. This is a theme that one can also identify in Donald Campbell's Chapter 11, in this book.

In the analysis of his patient named Justine, Hirsch considers the effects of bisexuality in the countertransference in an analysis of a woman by a male analyst. The account is of a *primary homosexuality* that was expressed in the relationship with the father that the mother could not sustain. The death of her father when Justine was still a young adolescent constituted a trauma and was experienced as a punishment against incestuous phantasies in relation to the father. There is an overcompensation in her looking after the mother. It is interesting to contrast this chapter with those by Perelberg (Chapter 4) and Godfrind (Chapter 5), as some of the themes re-emerge. Whereas Perelberg and Godfrind address the theme of a primary homosexuality in the analysis of women by women analysts, in this chapter, Hirsch analyses the way in which this can also be expressed in the analysis of a female patient by a male analyst, and the challenges that this poses for his own countertransference.

The beginnings of the analysis reveal in the transference an inconsolable mourning for the father. The "black pact" between mother and daughter takes the shape of a denial of the masculine in a love–hate relationship between mother and daughter. There is a demand on the male analyst towards his feminine and maternal identifications. Hirsch follows the vicissitudes of this analysis and the various configurations that are presented and analysed. He suggests that independently of his/her gender, the analyst must be able to work with his own psychic bisexuality. The author defines many terms that are part of the vocabulary of contemporary French psychoanalysis. Some of these terms are also defined in the Glossary at the end of the book.

In Chapter 9, Rosemary Davies explores the links between transvestism and hysteria in connection with bisexuality. She describes Mervin Glasser's patient, Mr Webster, a man who was compelled to dress like a woman and wanted to be freed of his transvestism, about which he felt deeply ashamed (Glasser, 1979a). He would dress up carefully, paying attention to all the details, and would then masturbate, looking at himself in the mirror. He often fantasized about making love to himself as a woman to a woman. Glasser sees the concept of the *core complex* as central to the understanding of the transvestite patient: the dressing up is highly important, but it is the undressing that is crucial, as it becomes the enactment of getting rid of the mother's engulfment. Rosemary Davies examines the parallels between Mr Webster and the Wolf Man (Freud, 1918b) in several details of the story, and ultimately it is the identification with the mother in the primal scene as well as the longing for the father who would provide a source of masculine identifications. The core complex is enacted in the treatment in that the patient avoids any recognition of feelings as a defence against the intense desire to merge with the analyst.

In the transference, her own patient Jack enacts the struggle to move from the maternal to the paternal order. He is ruminative and is unable to make decisions, like several other patients described in this book. In one session Jack told the analyst that he was demolishing a concrete ramp that his mother had needed to access her garden. "I have to be careful when I am breaking it up not to damage the manhole cover or the drain." The analyst reflects:

> When Jack described breaking up a concrete ramp that his mother needed to enter the garden, I wondered whether he was communicating to me the challenge of breaking the deadly tie to his mother that had done such damage to the whole man (the manhole), denying him a sexual identification with his father and preventing him using the garden of his own adult sexuality – very much the hysteric's predicament.

Davies suggests that hysterics attempt to avoid the disruption of sexuality and find an "apparent resolution" through remaining both one thing and the other, saving themselves "from the trauma of adult sexuality and the mourning entailed". The account of the clinical material indicates movingly her patient's tentative movements towards entering the "challenging, risky world of male sexuality".

In Chapter 10, Rachel Chaplin explores the theoretical conundrum offered by Freud: bisexuality is universal in human beings, and yet both sexes repudiate femininity, "the alpha and omega of Freud's thinking about psychic sexuality still have live currency in our clinical thinking".

She offers an interpretation to her female patient, Christa: "You want to be one of the racing boys and men." The patient responds that she felt "stabbed" by it. In reflecting on her patient's reaction, Chaplin indicates that she had thought that her observation of her patient's masculine identification had been available at a preconscious level. However, she now thinks that her interpretation expressed her own failure to fully register her patient's otherness: at this point in the analysis, the sexual action had not yet been metaphorized, and Christa could only experience her analyst's comment as intrusive sexual action. Chaplin wonders whether, with her comment, she is introducing the fact of sexual difference:

> To say to Christa that she wants to be one of the racing men is implicitly to point to her bodily femininity, and to tell her that

she is castrated. I have spoken from a position in which sexual difference is known and the fact of castration is accepted, but my introduction of sexual difference seems to be premature and traumatic.

The patient's response, as her analyst understands it, is to assert her "supremacist bisexuality": "I am both, both more male and more female." Chaplin understood that her patient remained "stateless" in terms of her internal identifications and therefore in her bisexual functions.

Chaplin goes on to suggest that "the pairing of analyst and patient in the sexual action of the analytic session activates the analyst's bisexualization process as much as the patient's, prompting the analyst to move intrapsychically between experiential passivity and representing activity". This is also suggested by Hirsch (Chapter 8).

In Chapter 11, Donald Campbell discusses his work with Mr Jones, who felt unable to choose between a male and a female sexual object. He declared he was gay and sought analysis because of what he called his ambivalence, never being able to decide on something (one's thoughts go in the direction of the Rat Man case above and Sodré's views on obsessionality). Mr Jones had homosexual and heterosexual fantasies, but he could not enact them in intercourse with another person. He retreated to the safety of masturbation, as his own masculine body became the sexual object of choice. He expressed no affect and no real emotional contact with the analyst. Campbell indicates that the patient felt empty because he did not know who he was.

Campbell progressively understood aspects of Mr Jones' homosexuality as protecting him from heterosexual phantasies, as this would include the threat of being enveloped by an all-engulfing mother. The father, in turn, was critical, either attacking the patient or being rather passive in relation to the mother. Mr Jones inhabited a "no-man's-land" between heterosexuality and homosexuality.

This was enacted in a session that the author offers us in detail: the patient entered the consulting room in a disoriented state – as if it were a much bigger room than it was – moved past the couch and proceeded as if he was going to sit next to the analyst. A succession of dreams enabled the analyst to understand that the transference to the mother aroused psychotic anxieties in the patient about loss of body boundaries. In this dissociated state, Mr Jones moved towards the masculine object, expressing his wish for the analyst to help him claim his masculinity. Campbell suggests that if sexuality is characterized by inherent incompleteness, our thinking about sexual identity is likely to lack resolution.

In Chapter 12, André Green states: "Although, for psycho-analysis, *difference* is sexual, the question of bisexuality is related to psychoanalytic theory as a whole." The "counterpart and comple-ment" of psychical bisexuality, which is a fantasy of the "neuter gender, neither masculine nor feminine, and dominated by absolute primary narcissism".

His patient opened the consultation with him by saying: "*My mother hated me before I was born.*" While he was a prisoner of the Germans, they had carried out feminizing experiments on him; now he was preparing to undergo an operation. She[13] produced a photo-copy of a document from the French Ministry of Employment cer-tifying that she presented feminine and masculine attributes with a feminine dominance. She was taking steps to have her identity changed.

She had an artificial cycle every twenty-eight days "*through rectal porosity*" and described how irritable she was prior to her periods. Following her material, Green said to her: "In fact, you don't want to be either a man or a woman", to which she replied: "*I think you're the first person to get to the heart of the matter; I don't want to give up any of the advantages of the two sexes.*"

As a child, she had been brought up and dressed as a girl, until she started school. The transvestite practices began at around the age of 16 or 17.

He lived together with an older woman, and they engaged in sadomasochistic practices. Thus, on Sundays, she sometimes wanted to go out but was not allowed to do so by this friend who chained her to a stove to make her finish her housework first. The patient accepted this treatment. The anality of this configuration was also expressed in the dirtiness of their flat. She longed to be in a passive position. She said at the same time: "*It is as if my body were divided into two; as if below the belt I didn't exist, or was another person.*"

Green discussed the options with the patient, with transvestism and transsexualism as two possible solutions. The patient replied that she neither wanted to be emasculated nor did she want to live as a man. Green thought that she wanted to live as a masculine woman.

In a complex account by the patient of actions that involved burglary and submitting naked to a bullying, castrating man, Green identifies a primal scene whereby a man would repeatedly castrate the woman with the penis. The fantasy of the neuter gender may be a sign both of "obedience to the mother's desire as well as vengeance on her, through the violent rejection of her". The phantasy has as its final goal "the extinction of all excitation, of all desire, whether it is agreeable or disagreeable".

Green emphasizes the importance of the parental impregnation on their children's sexuality, given that the parent is himself (or herself) caught in a conflict with respect to psychic bisexuality. He suggests that "the counterpart and complement of psychic bisexuality, whether manifest or latent, thus seems to be the fantasy of the *neuter gender*, neither masculine nor feminine and dominated by *absolute primary narcissism*". This goal is never fully achieved, unless perhaps through suicidal behaviour.

Bisexuality is thus closely linked to the difference between the sexes. Where there is bisexuality, there is also difference. Where there is difference, there is a cut, a caesura, a castration of the potentialities for *jouissance* of the complementary sex: inverse and symmetrical.

Green makes a distinction similar to David's, in Chapter 1, between psychic bisexuality and a declaration of being bisexual. "*Claiming real bisexuality means refusing sexual difference insofar as the latter implies the lack of the other sex.*" If, by definition, each sex lacks the other, then putting both sexes, so to speak, on the same level denies that lack. Green believes that both Freud and Klein expressed their limitations in that domain. Freud struggled with the maternal transference to himself, whereas Melanie Klein failed to identify the paternal transference.

Sexual reality refers to the sex, which is determined and fixed before the third year; psychic reality concerns the phantasies that converge with or diverge from sexual reality. In an analysis, the psychic bisexuality of the patient unfolds through the transference in its conflictual form. The challenge for the analyst is "to tolerate, to allow to develop, to interpret with precision, the transference concerning the imago of the sex that is not his own".

In Chapter 13, Gregorio Kohon offers a conceptual framework to examine the confusion existing between gender and sexuality in the contemporary psychoanalytic literature. In this chapter, in the words of a reviewer of this book, "theory itself is used to question its own value".

Kohon starts by tracing the fundamental differences between Freud's and Fliess's notions of bisexuality. He suggests that loyalty to Fliess hindered Freud from fully developing his own views. He also examines the influence of Groddeck and Jung, whose, "notion of bisexuality was also, like Fliess's and Groddeck's, imbued with a sense of harmony, offering an illusion of totality, a unified Self" (p. 265).

Butler's ideas on sexuality as "performative" and her notion that the sexed body is culturally constructed by regulative discourse had enormous influence in the 1990s and became central to queer theory. In its commitment to deconstruction, queer theory, in turn, "makes it nearly impossible to speak of lesbian or gay individuals: it cannot, by definition, offer a framework for examining their selves, their subjectivities, and/or their sexuality".

Kohon argues for the "division and precariousness of human subjectivity itself" (Rose, 1982, p. 27). However, as he reminds us: Rose spoke of "division" not "multiplicity" – a truly crucial distinction between human subjectivity as divided (as in psychoanalysis), rather than multiple (as in queer theory).

Kohon suggests that queer theory has desexualized identity. The concept of sexual difference, a concept specific to psychoanalytic theory, "was expelled from theoretical discourse and reduced to a biological distinction". He argues for the recognition of humans' finitude and acceptance that desires can never be fulfilled. "In sexual difference, there is always something missing." He quotes Mitchell: "because human subjectivity cannot ultimately exist outside a division into one of the two sexes, then it is castration that finally comes to symbolize this split..." (Kohon, 1986a, p. 393). Castration conveys, above all, something about the uniqueness of each sex.

All the chapters in this volume contribute to a profound psychoanalytic understanding of sexuality. Psychoanalysis's object is psychosexuality, which is, in the final analysis, determined not by having a male or a female body, but by the unconscious phantasies that are reached *après coup* through tracing the nuanced interplay of identifications as they are projected, enacted and experienced in the transference and the countertransference in the analytic encounter. I would wish to make it very clear that analytic treatment does not imply the possibility of a curative treatment for sexuality; it aims to offer an understanding of the underlying unconscious phantasies. In the words of Rose: "However clear you are in your own mind about being a man or a woman, the unconscious knows better" (2016, p. 12).

The paradigmatic example is that of Winnicott, as discussed by Zilkha. Winnicott says to his patient: "You are a man, but I am listening to a girl, and I am talking to a girl. I am telling this girl: You are talking about penis envy." "If I was to tell someone about this girl," the patient replies, "I would be called mad" (Winnicott, 1971a).

Sexual difference is the basis of a psychoanalytic understanding of sexuality and should not be confused with *sexual differences* (Mitchell, 1999, 2015). The former is to do with an organizing principle that indicates that completeness is not possible, that one cannot possess one's mother or kill one's father. It is at the order of the law (Perelberg, 2009, 2015b). The oedipal configuration confronts the child with the fact that they cannot have both sexes and cannot possess either of their parents. The latter – sexual differences – refers to a variety of ways in which individuals decide to practise their sexualities. Sexual difference is inaugurated by the law that prohibits incest and murder, the constitution of the superego and repression. These are the key concepts of a psychoanalytic understanding of sexuality and bisexuality. Bisexuality is a psychoanalytic concept (Mitchell, 2015, p. 80).

These are some of the ideas that permeate the chapters of this volume. The authors are all clinicians, and most of the ideas are illustrated with detailed clinical material. Vignettes of fifteen analyses are presented: six men, eight women, and one man in doubt about whether to have an operation, but who wishes to be neither a man or a woman. Their fictional names are given by the imagination and associations of their analysts: Romain, Hippolyte, Byron, Mr Webster, Jack, Mr Jones; Louise, Violette, Antigone, Emma, Jane, Ms A, Christa and Justine. There is also Romain Gary's portrait of himself, as understood by Denis Hirsch. They all come alive in their struggle with their sexual identification and with bisexuality, as vividly expressed in the transference–countertransference in their analyses. The challenge for the analyst is to be receptive to the movements in their sexual identifications and forms of *jouissance* through the derivatives that are enacted and expressed in their sessions. In the process, the analyst's capacity to be receptive and to elaborate their own psychic bisexuality is also mobilized.

## Notes

* This section was originally published in Perelberg, 1999b.
1 Leclaire has suggested that the question of the hysteric is "Am I a man or a woman?" (Leclaire, 1975; see also Kohon, 1986a; Lacan, 1981). It is a question of shifting identifications in an attempt to retain one identification, which is phallic. This is also present in some violent patients (Perelberg, 1999a, 1999b).
2 Michel Fain has suggested that sexuality is a constant oscillation between hysteria and orgasm (in Schaeffer, 1986, p. 944).
3 Chasseguet-Smirgel has suggested that femininity stands for receptivity (1964b, 1976). M. Eglé Laufer, in numerous published and unpublished papers (e.g. Laufer, 1993), has addressed the active and passive identification and the relationship to the body in adolescence.
4 Some of these concepts are discussed in "The structuring function of the Oedipus complex", in Perelberg, 2016, pp. 125–160.
5 I am grateful to Susanne Calice who introduced me to the work of Geneviève Morel.
6 This section first appeared in Perelberg, 2013b.
7 The legislation about the relationship between men and women in the political and economic sphere attests to the fact that equality between the sexes has not been achieved. Nowadays this has become more complex when considering the slow progress towards achieving full LGBT rights. In 2011, the United Nations Human Rights Council passed its first resolution recognizing LGBT rights, which was followed up with a report from the UN Human Rights Commission documenting violations of the rights of LGBT people, including hate crime, criminalization of homosexuality and discrimination. The UN Human Rights Commission urged all countries that had not yet done so to enact laws protecting basic LGBT rights. There is a huge variation in the recognition of these rights around the world.
8 In 2016, national legislation was proposed to make self-declaration the qualifying pivotal factor of gender identity (House of Commons, 2016).
9 Morel has suggested that Stoller's concept of "gender identity" is based on his theory on the conscious discourse of transsexualism (Morel, 2011, p. 59): Certainly he is faithful to the clinic of transsexualism, but at the same time his theory of gender identity remains too close to what is said by the subjects he listens to, which is taken almost literally. What they say should rather be elaborated and interpreted in a coherent theory of sexuation. (p. 60).
10 Similar views are expressed by Ambrosio (2009), Chiland (2005), Gherovici (2010), Millot (1990) and Wolf-Bernstein (2011).
11 Gherovici (2010) and Verhaege (2009) have developed the view that transsexual surgery may be understood as a way of claiming one's

desire. As discussed in this introduction, however, I believe that at times there may be a disjunction between the wish for an appearance, a gender identity on the one hand, and desire, on the other. It is also perhaps impossible to disengage the demand for surgery from the family and cultural context in which it takes place.

Preciado coined the term Pharmacopornographic era to describe the way the pharmaceutical and pornography industries, and late capitalism, are integrated in their responsibility for the regulation of the cycles of reproductive and social control of the human body (2013). Preciado states that the political and technological management of the body and sexuality is a major twenty-first-century industry. Contemporary society is inhabited by toxicopornographic subjectivities: "There is nothing to discover in sex or in sexual identity; there is no inside" (p. 35). Sex becomes "sex design"; pharmachopornographic industry invents the subject (p. 36) and makes it impossible to think about the demand for a fabricated body outside the context of the current technological framework of contemporary post-imperialist society. The penetration of the body is the outcome of an entire industry (Preciado, 2013, p. 32).

This has become a larger topic than it is possible to discuss in the framework of this Introduction. I am offering a few points of reference in the discussions only.

12  Gozlan suggests that Anish Kapoor and Louise Bourgeois are both preoccupied with the enigma of embodiment and reveal in their work "the precariousness of our signifying categories in the face of the body's inexhaustible inscrutability" (2015, p. 19). He takes Kapoor's abstract sculpture *Memory* as expressing the inherent tension when approaching an enigmatic object. Bourgeois' work captures incoherence, "the borderline zone between being and not-being, separation and joining" (p. 19). However, even if he states that transsexuality is a signifier "that takes different meanings at different times" (p. 23), he paradoxically risks reifying the transsexual. In contrast, Juliet Mitchell in her Foreword to this volume refers to Bourgeois as "subjective bisexuality's most profound portraitist". Kohon has argued for the commonality of experience between aesthetics and psychoanalysis, and suggests that both art and psychoanalysis must be considered in their own terms (Kohon, 2016).

13  This note by Green explains that he alternated the use of masculine and feminine to refer to the subject to reflect how he, as "the misled spectator of this hybridisation, was alternately caught between illusion and reality". Nowadays in many contexts there is a requirement to call these patients "they".

# THE BEAUTIFUL DIFFERENCES[1]

## Christian David

The unconscious is said to have no knowledge of time. However, there are many signs that some fairly striking characteristics of our own are the progressive attenuation of conventional manifestations of sexual difference, even a trend towards the complete reversal of masculinity and femininity, hand in hand with a strange bisexual claim. The more of a stake this claims, the more it seems that sexually specific characteristics – which are undoubtedly among these "beautiful differences of nature" that Freud deplored Groddeck for seeking to disparage "in favour of tempting unity" (Letter of 5 June 1917, in E. L. Freud, 1960, p. 324) – tend to diminish, even disappear.

Does the half made-up, grotesque and disturbing countenance of the hero of Stanley Kubrick's sinister 1971 film *A Clockwork Orange* bring together in one hard-hitting, symbolic opening shot these recent psychosexual vicissitudes in our society? Does the strange expression that emanates from these ill-matched eyes, one with long mascara-coated lashes and fully adorned with make-up, and the other completely undecorated, contain something more than an ambiguous provocation – namely, the hidden meaning of a defusion of the drives? Does the conjunction of homosexual and heterosexual attitudes and behaviours, readily considered a feat and an achievement by certain naïve witnesses, in fact involve an insidious negation of sexuality, like a challenge to Eros, in the guise of an unleashing of erotism?

On the other hand, leaving the uncanny register of disturbing strangeness for what I would call wonderful strangeness, I will gladly make an opposite symbol of a countertenor voice heard the other evening. This presented to the listener not only through its unique inflections and timbre, but through all it conveyed of the artist's inner nature, an indescribable mixture of masculinity and femininity. Now Alfred Deller,[2] through his stature, his face and his words, appears an eminently "virile" character, and the quality of his voice, however close to the castrati of bygone days, is the fruit – if we are to believe some recent impromptu comments by the singer himself on television – of patient and exciting work intended to "bring out" and develop to its point of perfection the "head voice" that every man capable of singing has available potentially but without knowing it, without daring to use it or without thinking of doing so.

These are landmark images, key moments, of the kind also encountered in analysis, in which a world of affects and meanings is obscurely condensed, and I would like to convey its resonance so that at least on a preliminary basis this slightly over-abstract approach to the disturbing problematic presented here does not resemble an impossible detachment.

# I

Whether this is a question of sexual difference or bisexuality, an incontestable ambiguity – probably in connection with the constitutive duality of every drive – characterises the elaboration of these facts in Freud's work. Based on the anatomy and embryology of his day, Freud draws out the "psychological implications" of some elements that are inherently alien to psychology. Thus he regards bisexuality as a biological concept, which he extrapolates into a postulate of psychoanalytic treatment; however, in parallel, albeit from an entirely different perspective, he writes to Fliess – his well-known source of inspiration in this case – that he is getting used to "regarding every sexual act as a process in which four individuals are involved" (Letter of 1 August 1899, in Masson, 1985, p. 364). As for this "bisexual constitution" that everyone is said to possess, how is it manifested psychically? Through the masculinity and femininity of attitudes ... Moreover, although sexual difference assumes the status of "destiny", there is still no strict concordance between sex, psychosexual characteristics and the type of object choice. What is more: "We speak, too, of 'masculine' and 'feminine' mental attributes and impulses, although, strictly speaking, the differences between the sexes can lay claim to no special psychical characterization" (Freud, 1913j, p. 182). In fact, all that can ultimately be claimed is that activity and passivity are involved; now apart from the fact that these are inadequate connotations, they do not concern the drives themselves but the nature of their goals, and their "regular association ... in mental life reflects the bisexuality of individuals" (p. 182).

Has this argument not become somewhat circular? Freud never allowed himself to be impressed by obstacles of that kind: he always treated them with a sovereign disregard and a cool audacity. "But psycho-analysis cannot elucidate the intrinsic nature of what in conventional or in biological phraseology is termed 'masculine' and 'feminine'. If only! ... 'it simply takes over the two concepts and makes them the foundation of its work.'" (1920a, p. 171).

Admittedly, this was an inspired move, but also because these "works" simultaneously found other and better foundations, and above all perhaps because between the foot and the summit a real metamorphosis has occurred, from which it seems that we have only recently departed, having explained the full importance and theoretical implications. I am thinking in particular here of the definition of the drive in relation to instinct, and even more of the determination of the many effects of the extension of the notion of sexuality – this brilliant speculative master-stroke. We cannot in fact address the sexual psychoanalytically in clinical or theoretical terms without having made this extension *our own*. Certainly we must avoid being dragged here on to the path of a spiritualism that would not dare speak its name, neglecting the somatic basis and "scandalous" aspects of sexuality, but we must also remember that its conceptual extension is – like a difficult realisation fleetingly effected during the treatment – an acquisition that is permanently under threat. This can easily be seen with the creator of psychoanalysis himself, when its temporary overshadowing sometimes gives rise to a certain wavering in thought. Laplanche seeks to explain these eclipses as the inevitable confusion caused by

> a scientific revolution which suddenly enlarges the meaning of a concept [and] sweeps away, we might say, its very ground. Such is the case for Freud himself: at which point we see him taking refuge in the hopes for a biological, chemical, or hormonal

definition of sexuality ... or we see him simply repeating, as though he could progress no further, the reasons which force him to assimilate the domain he discovered to sex in the popular, 'genital' sense of the word.

(Laplanche, 1976, p. 28)

We must also be wary of overemphasising this similarity, as well as subjugating ourselves too narrowly to scientific advances, *on pain of losing the benefit of an epistemological leap through which the unconscious can be indicated as sexual and sexuality as psychic.*

The sexual certainly originates from far beyond the psychic, but analysis proposes to address the way in which it is represented. This is the case with anatomical sexual difference, which, as the object of conscious and unconscious representations, is introduced into analysis as a difference between psychosexualities. Then what about bisexuality? Certainly, we may think that Freud would have hesitated to introduce it into his theory if he had not believed he could give it a biological foundation, based primarily on the embryology of his era. But there again, bisexuality is linked in psychoanalysis not to the vestigial presence in an individual of a particular sex of certain characteristics of the other sex, but to psychic organisations that depend on many other factors. It is even certain that, as something psychic, it has only the most tenuous connection with these vestiges: one proof of this is that the advances made since Freud in the field of embryology (notably, imposing the concept of an embryonic differentiation that occurs not from a bisexual preliminary stage as previously thought but is absolutely phenotypically female) only seem to have to involve *ipso facto* abandoning the concept of bisexuality in psychoanalysis if the psychoanalytic dimension is seriously underestimated.[3] Although it may also be highly instructive as an analyst to study the psychic repercussions of a particular anatomico–physiological bisexual characteristic (true hermaphroditism, pseudo-hermaphroditism, transsexualism and so on), it is nonetheless true that psychic bisexuality is absolutely independent of the existence of such aberrations or other equivalents (endocrine malfunctioning). Bisexuality, as a coexistence of opposite psychosexual dispositions, some conscious and others unconscious, in each of us, proceeds – whatever its biological connections – from psychic processes. How otherwise, moreover, can we explain the universality of its role and how can we recognise that fundamentally

61

"we can only see that both in male and female individuals masculine as well as feminine instinctual impulses are found, and that each can equally well undergo repression and so become unconscious" (1919e, p. 202). Also, when in 1914 Freud reverses the determining priority in relation to repression that he had previously attributed like Fliess to bisexuality, and in respect of which he tried, as early as the Wolf Man case, to demonstrate how it is the ego that instigates the repression to the advantage of one of the sexual orientations, can it be said that he is finally giving bisexuality its specific psychoanalytic status? Is it not, in fact, highly revealing that it should be on this point alone that his position should have changed throughout all his works?

This subordination of sexuality to conflict is decisive, and this is probably what best elucidates the connection between sexual difference and bisexuality. Their relationship emerges as essentially dialectical. This is what I should like to emphasise in the course of the pages that follow.

To be born a girl or born a boy is – even more broadly and more decisively than being summoned to live the castration complex in one way or another – to be promised, as Green (1972) persuasively demonstrates, to a certain sexual destiny, according to an inescapable sexual reality: a man will never give birth and a woman will never impregnate, which are truths that are more comprehensive than the anatomical facts but equally restrictive. However, to be a man with certain female tendencies, or a woman with some male tendencies, *is to possess a potential sexual otherness and consequently to bear some indeterminacy.* If, therefore, on the one hand anatomy is destiny, then on the other sexual reality, or sexual destiny, we might say, *bisexuality is – or may be – anti-destiny.* The formula may be less surprising if we recall that the extended concept of bisexuality stems from that of sexuality. As with pregenital sexuality, there are grounds for conceiving of a pregenital bisexuality. The early relations with the mother entail a close relationship between the emergence of desire, the genesis of phantasy and the internal object, and the emergence of a psychosexual bipotentiality (e.g. receiving or giving pleasure in one mode or another), although admittedly this will be specified only later and in stages of bisexuality in the current analytic sense of this term. Furthermore, is it not part of the logic of sexuality, which is difference and division, that it promotes itself from one bipartition to the next, from one opposition to the next?

Bisexuality testifies to the internalisation of the active–passive polarity and the progressive introjection of sexual polarity. It is through these internalisations of difference that some *play* can intervene from the outset in the evolution of sexuality: in parallel with the maturational activity that prepares the integration of sexual identity, what I will call *an unconscious bisexualisation process* seems to be quietly at work, a process that clinical observation suggests does not necessarily involute when the specific psychosexuality is fully established.

Being closely connected with the configuration of identifications and their vicissitudes, the Oedipus complex provides the theory of bisexuality (and the problem of its connection with sexual difference) with its only means of achieving coherence and adequate clarity. Rather strangely, Freud does not seem to have resolved to make full use of this resource to elucidate the concept of bisexuality and to determine its integration in drive theory. I would again readily point to his biologism here. … However, on the nature and development of bisexuality, there are really two discernible lines of thinking in his work, which are difficult to reconcile. Often, Freud sees bisexuality as a primal and universal disposition, clearly morbid when it is very pronounced,[4] which has the natural (i.e. biological) destiny – depending on the consecutive demands at the primacy of genitality – of a gradual diminution in the course of libidinal development. Ultimately, it "normally" no longer consists in anything but subtle individual traits, aim-inhibited desires or capacities for socialisation and sublimation. Even if the orientation of the object choice is subject to discrepancies in relation to anatomical destiny, psychosexual identity – in the vast majority of cases – is finally integrated in accordance with the person's own sex: this presupposes the successful repression of the initial bisexuality. In other words, the more sexual difference is asserted, the more bisexuality becomes involuted and virtualised. Nevertheless, however dominant this genetic and dynamic correlation may be in Freud's conception of bisexuality, it has another non-biologistic aspect that may generally be understated. According to this, the differential integration of sexuality, far from excluding an active psychic bisexuality, and far from necessarily requiring its entirely successful repression in accordance with prevailing norms, can (in some cases even should) go hand in hand with an authentic bisexual fulfilment – if not in relation to the erotic choice of object and fulfilment, at least as concerns personal psychic characteristics and functioning. This viewpoint is eloquently illustrated in "The Psychogenesis of a Case of Homosexuality in a Woman" (1920a), where Freud clearly indicates that: "in normal sexuality also there is a limitation in the choice of object" (he does not refer to more hidden restrictions but to even more important ones that concern "psychical sexual characteristics" in general). He assigns the psychoanalytic treatment of homosexuality the goal of "re-establishing a complete bisexual function" while emphasising the difficulties of such a result, an ideal outcome for which we can only strive. He clearly states on several occasions that, especially in men, psychic hermaphroditism is independent of physical hermaphroditism of whatever nature and degree, as well as that these two sequences are independent of the type of object choice. The three characteristics vary independently of each other and occur in combination in the most diverse fashion in different individuals. It would be making a concession to the layperson and adopting his frequent conformism to favour the modalities of object choice and also to fail to recognise that "In all of us, throughout life, the libido normally oscillates between the male and the female object" (p. 158); it would also be attaching little importance to unconscious sexuality and losing sight "of the general bisexuality of mankind" (p. 143).

This second aspect of the Freudian conception seems to me to be the only one to do justice both to the meaning shift in the concepts of bisexuality and sexuality in psychoanalysis and to the reformulation of the psychosexual problematic in accordance with the oedipal structural model (the "complete" Oedipus complex with all its implications and resonances). It is also the only one to account for the compatibility of sexual difference with bisexuality and to point towards any possible resolution – at least in part – of the divergence of their respective dynamisms. Finally, it is the only model that enables us to imagine their functional association, according to an ideal goal, beyond their many conflictual potentialities.

## II

The sexual is not the sole object of analysis, but is its constant object. The transference in the analytic situation could be said to correspond to the principle of libidinal co-excitation postulated by Freud as a consequence of the possible extension of erogeneity to the entire human body. There is in fact nothing in the field this defines that cannot and must not be considered an effect – proximate or remote, pure or combined – of the transference, whether in the strict or broad sense of the word. There is nothing, then, that cannot be considered a sign of the drives and consequently, given the actual conjunction represented by every psychic phenomenon, a sign of sexuality. What is expressed and lived and, in the process, disguised and neglected in the analysand is impelled by a sexual dynamic (even if it is never the only thing in play), pursues the satisfaction of desire and is perpetuated in accordance with an ever-recurrent dissatisfaction. Just as the essence of sexuality could be said to reside in the very impulse that separates the sexual drive from the vital function on which it is based, it is equally legitimate to regard the inherent restrictive conditions in the analytic treatment as a form of experimental reproduction and, consequently, *an enforced intensification of this fundamental separation.* It is not from the vital function that the sexual dynamic tends to extricate itself here, but from the discharge function. And just as the genesis of sexuality involves its perversion (human sexuality always bears at least some traces of this origin), so the channelling of the drive expression solely according to the possibilities of the analytic transference brings an artificial increase in these first conditions, leading innate perverse sexuality ultimately to become an "affective perversion".[5]

These general observations are connected with the more specific aspects of our problem. In fact, this capacity for separation revealed by the libido, a sign of its plasticity, applies not only to that from which it separates but also in regard to itself. "It is my belief that, however strange it may sound, we must reckon with the possibility that something in the nature of the sexual instinct itself is unfavourable to the realization of complete satisfaction" (1912d, pp. 188–189), writes Freud. This contains the bold but suggestive and productive hypothesis of an intra-libidinal negativity. Thus, irrespective of the fact that the libido follows a particular specific developmental destiny according to whether it animates an anatomically male or female being, there pre-exists in it a potential internal division, the beginning of a splitting that could be seen as both the mark and the origin of a primitive *"sexion"*[6] (Lewinter, 1969).

It is clear where this is leading: the very close affinity in the sexual between the positivity of desire and the negativity of inhibition altogether represents a prefiguring of bisexuality and the herald of sexual difference. In other words, the duality, a contrasting dynamic duality, emerges as their common principle, but when this intrinsic antagonism is externalised into a trans-individual sexual dichotomy, then it promotes itself less visibly by establishing an intra-individual psychosexual polarity. This gives rise to two major lines of conflict in sexual life, which are, of course, inseparably intermingled, one relational and the other intrasubjective. Introjection and projection enmesh them from the outset on a canvas on to which the destructive drives are also placed, to which I am deliberately only referring to the extent that they reinforce intra-libidinal negativity.

Within a psychoanalysis, such a reinforcement, as I have emphasised, intensifies solely under the impact of the transference and the elective appeal of "psychical participation" (Freud, 1905d).

This enforced internalisation is never a smooth process; however, we can consider that *the analytic situation intrinsically consists in a testing of psychosexual characteristics and identity and simultaneously a stimulation of psychic bisexuality*, in which regression always generates some psychosexual de-differentiation. Everything occurs as if this dual incitement must temporarily find its response if a redistribution of the drive economy is to be achieved; as if a quasi-experimental amplification of the potential for psychosexual indeterminacy had to occur for new choices and a better functioning to become possible at a secondary stage. But this manifestly implies that the activation of bisexuality generated by the treatment can have a destructuring effect. Against this, various defence reactions are instigated that can form resistances that are difficult to lift or alternatively barriers that are too fragile to allow time for a re-elaboration of psychosexuality to mature for the benefit of the complete development of the analytic process.

"When I come in here, there's always a smell of perfume or eau de Cologne, never the smell of tobacco, or smoke! ... Ah! If only you smoked a pipe. You're colourless, odourless and tasteless. ... No! It's not true what I said just then. ... It's when I think about what you have and what I would like to have that I get sad. Sometimes I even feel a desire to tear you to pieces." – *"To emasculate me."* – "Oh! I see things in a less clear, less localised and more general way. It is more about power. It is that I can't simply desire a man I like; I immediately have to imagine appropriating for myself the thing by which he would seduce me if I followed my first impulse, if I could let myself be charmed..."

It was in this context that at the end of the session, of which I have just approximately transcribed the initial phase, this young person, whose female status has constantly represented a painful problem ever since she attained self-awareness, directly raised the question of sexuality in the analytic situation:

"Altogether, it's as if neither you nor I had a sex here, don't you think? Yes, really, what difference can it make that I'm a woman and you're a man?" – "*You regret this though*" – "That, I've no idea. ... Oh! I'm thinking back to the interview I had with an analyst, to ask her advice and possibly for a referral to a therapist. I made it very clear at the start that if a psychoanalysis was recommended for me, I would only consider doing it with a man. She reacted in what I felt was rather an impulsive way, replying curtly that once the analysis started it made no difference at all whether it was conducted by a man or a woman. I argued that in my view with my current state of mind, it wasn't the same thing at all and that it was very important to me to undertake my analysis, if I decided to do this, with a man. With a woman, the whole thing seemed impossible, intolerable. That was a while ago, and now I realise that this analyst was right! In reality, in fact, what difference can it make that you're a man?"

Beyond the obvious defensive impact of this negation of the role of sex and sexuality in the analytic situation, this patient is both right and wrong at the same time. She is wrong because in spite of the strong predominance of projections over perceptions in her relationship with me, her transference experience incorporates an aspect that belongs not to the revival of past affects but to current turmoil in which my sexual identity, my voice and my character as she perceives them during the sessions play a distinct role. She is also wrong in the sense that sporadically she reacts to my presence with an erotic excitation or tender emotions that she wishes to forget, but, above all, in the sense that within the fabric of her discourse (including, of course, the sequence reported here and even – as we see – when the sexual and sexual difference are being revoked) everything that she says – and does not say – is inscribed in the psychosexual dimension (in which genitality only represents a privileged component); only she has an acute resistance to recognising that inscription. She is right, on the other hand, to the large degree to which the analytic situation and the incomparable relational modes it establishes hardly depend on the analyst's sex, even often play with sexual difference, while actively appealing to each protagonist's bisexuality. The fundamental rule has the dual and contradictory quality of a barrier raised before incest *and* of an almost provocative systematic seduction of the sexual fantasmatic. "Here again is the present–absent, accessible–elusive, lost–found object of your desire", the analyst implicitly states in every session. Such is the "liberty" that he proposes for the associative process: we imagine that he must be responding to this with evenly suspended attention, in-difference, some suspension of the drives and a maximum of bisexual availability. It is in particular through this availability, as Cathérine Parat pointed out (during some work that clearly demonstrated the primacy of psychosexuality and phantasy over external reality and the sexual in the "popular" sense) that analysts find themselves undergoing, by assuming some of their patients' fantasies, affective experiences that they would never have been able to have in any other situation because of their sex (Luquet-Parat, 1962).

Closer examination of the sequences just reported initially reveals an active and passive castration phantasy. Now, this phantasy is explicitly related to a bisexual conflict, emerging in all its acuity. Let us note here the dual ambiguity of the standpoint from which the question of the role of sexuality in the analytic situation is formulated: both a negation of my masculinity *and* an acknowledgement that she feels me to be male (the paternal transference is currently fairly intense); accordingly, a masochistic assertion of her female position in terms of the phallic illusion (fully in play in her at this point in the treatment) of the assimilation of femininity to a castration that has been effected *and* a rejection of this position by the admission of her current incapacity to adopt a passive attitude that is nevertheless desired (forcing her to attempt a narcissistic retreat). Given the excessive ambiguity of the situation at the point that the question with which we are concerned arises, it is hardly surprising that this question itself should be posed in a fundamental uncertainty, in a great indeterminacy: that today it is no longer at all important in her view – she says – that we should be of different sexes, even that we should have a sex at all, although she used to imagine that it took place altogether differently. Admittedly neither the unconscious nor the analyst take account of this opposition between present and past, particularly given that a latent homo-sexual desire is implicitly outlined that intensifies the disappointment and pique created by the analytic frustration. *Another impulse to negate sexual difference can be seen to instigate the awakening of bisexuality here.*

This is evidenced by the dream that she presented fairly soon afterwards:

> A young man is visiting a blonde, curly-haired woman who is clearly older than him. She is an enchantress. In the large, rather dark room in which she is standing, the windows are open. On a nearby table is a bottle of perfume, opened. Affected by the aroma of this perfume, the young man loses his head, feels an upsurge of anxiety, until it becomes intolerable. No longer able to stand it, he suddenly throws himself out of the window.

The associations – the reader will not have failed to notice in passing certain parallels between the dream text and the above session report – reveal very clearly that this young man represents her, while I am the enchantress. The reversal of our respective genders, as a product of the dream work, can easily be related to the conscious and vigilant expression of her desire to appropriate for herself, "the thing by which a man would seduce her if she allowed herself to be charmed", and therefore also to her emphasis on my lack of certain specifically masculine signs (smoking a pipe, for instance). It can be noticed that the simultaneous negation of the erotic atmosphere of the session and the role of the analyst's sex is accompanied here by a perception of me as effeminate or, in the dream, overtly feminised. In parallel, she often states that she is feeling uneasy in her women's clothes. She therefore projects on to me her own feeling of castration by condemning us both to a sort of amorphous undifferentiated destiny that excludes any sexual attraction. For this to be exerted she considers it necessary for sexual difference to be strongly in evidence, but because of her unresolved conflicts she rejects her female "destiny" while also contesting my masculinity, and she inadvertently instigates all the resources of her unconscious homosexuality in order to rid her relationship with me of any eroticism; at least, this is how things are proceeding at this stage of her analysis. She exhibits a sexuality that she feels is weak: she is not the boy her parents wanted and that she would have liked to be; neither is she "a real woman". Moreover, she is exasperated by women who are regarded as highly feminine. As for me, rather than being the masculine man for whom she hoped, I am someone fragile and ambiguous.

Here we see again the effects of the unconscious androgynous phantasy: elimination of sexual difference and diminution of the sexual drive. Psychic bisexuality is then in functional opposition with psychosexual specificity. It is from difference that the drive seems to draw its energy, whereas the emphasis on analogies and reciprocal exchanges only weakens it. From this perspective – but it is not, as I have already indicated, in any sense the only one – in which bisexuality "works" to diminish sexual differences and *seems to be directed at the mythical realisation of a form of unisexuality*, it constitutes a factor of erotic impoverishment, a source of degeneration of male and female, a kernel of de-eroticisation, de-differentiation – in short, of lethal desexualisation. While it is true that a man's desire to be a woman responds to a woman's desire to be a man, this commonality of the desire to be the other is a very long way from founding an entire, less still an exclusive, similarity...

Also, in contrast to the picture I have just presented, clinical experience often provides the opportunity to observe how, through the realisation and integration of latent homosexuality, and non-apparent and more or less effectively repressed femininity or masculinity, as well as through the reconciliation of conflicting identifications, the re-establishment of the bisexual function instead tends to liberate energy, an irreplaceable innovatory factor in relational modalities that also enriches the functioning of the psychic apparatus. Now, such a re-establishment is antinomical to the defensive implementation of a hermaphrodite phantasy, of realised ambisexuality: it certainly presupposes its transcendence and dissolution. At the conclusion of these felicitous analyses, both the repudiation of femininity and the overvaluation of phallicity will have been recognised as reactions linked to misunderstanding and illusion, whereas the progressive perception and acceptance of neglected psychosexual potentialities, of unknown desires and pleasures, will have entailed a more accurate and deeper appreciation of masculinity and femininity. The process that led to such a result does not tend towards de-differentiation – which was nevertheless required in the early phases of the analysis – but this time in a resumption of the introjection (in the Ferenczian sense of the term) of differences. Admittedly, its completion is never achieved, but this is not necessary for the subject's specific sexuality to be harmonised with his psychic bisexuality, or for him to find and develop his own sexual formula, which is moreover oscillating because alive. Such a successful outcome does not involve the unconditional and massive disengagement of the thwarted psychosexual pole, but only its qualified reintegration in the various directions. Furthermore, it assumes *neither the abolition nor the exacerbation of sexual difference but its relativisation,* and it requires the resumption of what I have called the unconscious bisexualisation process (totally incompatible with unisexualising goals) in the service of establishing what Freud terms the "full bisexual function" (1920a, p. 151).

## III

Although because of its length and its teeming abundance, the story of Kamar-ez-Zemán and Princess Budoor, one of the most delightful in the *Thousand and One Nights,*[7] contains too much "material" to be used satisfactorily in the context of an article, I cannot resist the pleasure of referring to it here – which will at least introduce a note of colour into the grey tones of the picture. Both its content (manifest and latent) – which in my view gives an opportune illustration of the dialectic of sexual difference and bisexuality – and above all the trajectory taken by the many twists and turns of a story that always starts again seem to me *to demonstrate the possibility of a precedence of libidinal plasticity over anatomical destiny and the key role of bisexuality in this precedence.* To demonstrate this, I will first summarise this never-ending tale, strangely enlivened by what I am inclined to call the *sexual romance.*

King Sháh-Zemán, at an advanced age, belatedly has a son, Kamar-ez-Zemán, who is so perfectly beautiful that he is known as "the Moon of the Age". He loves him so much that he cannot part from him for a moment, even at night. However, worried about his lack of descendants, he then decides to arrange a marriage for this son. Fiercely misogynistic, the son categorically refuses to do this. At his failure, the father – with a heavy heart – finally imprisons him in a tower – with very little idea of what will happen there – in the hope that the isolation will make him reflect. In this prison, haunted by jinns – male and female – of the air and the earth, Meymooneh, illustrious among all the daughters of the jinns, surprises

Kamar-ez-Zemán in his sleep. She is captivated by his beauty and therefore immediately decides to take the young man under her protection to defend him against any male jinn who, attracted by his charms, might wish to exploit them. Then she meets Dahnash, an evil jinn, who tells her how in the great El-Ghayoor's kingdom in China, he happened to discover Budoor, the monarch's adored daughter, in identical circumstances: indescribably beautiful, she too is rejecting every marriage proposal her father conveys to her: "O my father, I have no wish at all to marry; for I am a princess, and a queen, ruling over men, and I desire not a man to rule over me" (p. 82). She threatens to kill herself if her father tries to force her to take a husband. So El-Ghayoor also has her imprisoned in a tower.

The two jinns then make a bet that the object of their respective discoveries is unsurpassably beautiful. Meymooneh immediately leads Dahnash to Kamar-ez-Zemán's bedside. He concedes he has never in fact seen so many perfections in an adolescent's body but adds that the mould that made him only broke after producing a female version, Princess Budoor. He sets off to send for her so that Meymooneh can compare them. She first observes that the resemblance between the two young people is so perfect that they would be taken for twins if they did not differ in their environment and origins. The same moon-like face, the same delicate waist, the same rounded behind ... and on Budoor the breasts advantageously replace the embellishing penis that she lacks. However, Meymooneh tells Dahnash that anyone would have to be blind or mad not to agree that the male surpasses the female. They then appeal to the arbitration of a third person (from the brotherhood). Having acknowledged that the young people are equal in beauty and only different in sex, he suggests a way of determining who should win the bet: it is enough to awaken and then put back to sleep first one then the other young person, having brought them together: "the one who shall be most inflamed with love for the other shall be confessed to be the inferior in beauty and loveliness" (p. 87) because he will have recognised the superior attractions of his companion. Initially conquered by the beautiful Budoor, Kamar-ez-Zemán soon finds he cannot resist the desire to penetrate her, when suddenly it occurs to him that this may be a ruse of his father's to force him into marriage. He therefore resolves to defer his satisfaction and only puts a ring on the young girl's finger. As for her, once she has been awoken, after a moment of fright and confusion, she behaves as if under a spell. With increasing emotion, soon, no longer worrying about anything, she becomes bolder, discovers Kamar-ez-Zemán's penis and immediately understands its specific purpose because, we are told, just as desire in women is much more intense than in men, so their intelligence is infinitely quicker to grasp the relations between the organs of pleasure. Meymooneh therefore wins the bet.

Having returned to their prisons, the two protagonists utter loud cries for their partner of the night. They are both thought to be mad. Kamar-ez-Zemán, however, provides some tangible evidence of his story so that his father, convinced, then leaves with him for an island to lament "their" misfortune there. But Budoor meanwhile does not manage to persuade her father. Believing her to have gone mad, he imprisons her and promises her hand in marriage to anyone who can cure her of her madness. Budoor then gets her foster brother, Marzawán, to leave in search of the mysterious lover from the tower. Through a combination of circumstances, he arrives at King Sháh-Zemán's court because fate has decreed that he should cure Kamar-ez-Zemán of his melancholy. Marzawán, who is also astounded by his foster-sister's resemblance to the prince, reveals to him his mission, which is enough to bring him immediately back to life. Using a ploy to leave his father, who would not spontaneously allow him to leave, he leaves the country with Marzawán to rejoin his beloved in El-Ghayoor. Having arrived, he disguises himself as a wizard and easily manages to get a letter transmitted to Budoor into which he has inserted her ring (for she also put one on his finger). The princess comes back to life in turn. Kamar-ez-Zemán reveals his identity to everyone and tells their story to general astonishment. The marriage is celebrated with no further ado. After a honeymoon, one night Kamar-ez-Zemán has a dream in which his father is in tears. He convinces Budoor to accompany him to her father-in-law's court. On their journey, the prince – contemplating his young wife asleep one evening – discovers an extraordinary cornaline jewel hidden in her pubic hair. When he has made it glitter between his fingers, a bird swoops down from the sky, snatches it from him with his beak and takes it away. Kamar-ez-Zemán rushes after it, in vain ... for ten days, he dares not return to Budoor without her jewel. This quest finally leads him to an island where he is greeted by an old gardener, who takes him to help, becomes attached to him as to a son, and showers him with gold when he dies not long afterwards.

Meanwhile the princess, in despair at having lost the object of her desire again, disguises herself as a man to make her journey. When she arrives several days later at King Armánoos's court, she pretends to him that she is Kamar-ez-Zemán. Armánoos, with an only daughter Hayát-en-Nufoos, is overcome by the exceptional beauty of this young Adonis, not guessing his cross-dressing, and he immediately asks him to accept both his succession and Hayát-en-Nufoos's hand. Budoor realises that there is no question of refusing if she wants to stay alive. The marriage is celebrated. The night after the wedding night, Armánoos and his wife, furious that the marriage has not been consummated, make some alarming threats with regard to the false Kamar-ez-Zemán. Budoor therefore tells her young companion about the situation and with her tender agreement, they simulate the defloration with a chicken's blood. The royal couple having been comforted, Budoor continues to share Hayát-en-Nufoos's bed but, we are told, less innocently than before.

In the meantime, Kamar-ez-Zemán miraculously finds the lost cornaline and hides it at the bottom of an earthenware jar. This jewel, which he had planned to take away with him when he could leave his island, ends up without him at Armánoos's court because of a missed departure. Having asked for the cargo of the boat that transported the jar, Budoor finds the cornaline in it and faints. The captain is then asked about its owner and he reveals that it belonged to a gardener's assistant who fled in fear of being punished for having cruelly sodomised one of his chef's assistants. On royal orders, the alleged cook is then seized: Kamar-ez-Zemán clearly has no idea what is happening to him when he feels a hand placed on his shoulder. Once he is facing Budoor in men's clothing, he does not recognise her and believes that the young sovereign is a great lover of handsome boys. ... Despite the extreme reticence that he shows towards her, Budoor becomes more and more insistent, and finally entreats him to spend the night with "him". To persuade him better, she says she wants him to play the active role. Kamar-ez-Zemán, believing he must play along with this if he wants to save his skin, only asks his tyrant to at least do him the honour of agreeing that the act should take place once only, in hope of showing him that he would do much better to embrace heterosexuality. When the moment arrives, Kamar-ez-Zemán discovers – to his great surprise! – that his seducer is a woman and that this is none other than Budoor. The joyous reunion follows. The reunited couple reveal the whole truth to Armánoos who, in a generous impulse, offers his daughter again – still a virgin – in marriage, this time to the real Kamar-ez-Zemán: she will be, if he likes, his second wife. This suggestion is accepted happily by everyone, including Budoor and Hayát-en-Nufoos themselves. The two women continue to live in harmony, giving their nights to their husbands but granting themselves the daytime hours together. And they lived happily ever after.

Quite apart from all the general reasons against it, there could be no question here of subjecting this dry summary of a luxuriant narrative[8] to an actual interpretation. I merely offer it to the reader's associations (I hope, inspiring him to read or return to the text) and will only present some of mine in the form of a few observations.

Anatomical in manifest content, and more complex undoubtedly in the latent content and symbolic import of this story, sexual difference plays a decisive role here since it constitutes – constantly we might say – the impetus of the story. However, from the outset, bisexuality is an equally strong theme in the strong indication of the father's latent homosexuality towards the son and that of the son towards the father, as well as in the way that Kamar-ez-Zemán's misogyny, just like Budoor's androphobia, become associated, in both of them, with an intense and touchy narcissism in which fantasmatic bisexuality plays a part. Auto-erotic retreat and father fixation are only transcended by the impact of a dual trauma inflicted on narcissism by the exhortation that is successively external and internal towards heterosexual union. It should also be noted that the connection is made here in favour of the extreme resemblance and equal beauty of the two protagonists, who resemble twins. Can we not perceive there an echo of the myth of Plato's *Symposium*[9] in the idea of the mould that made Kamar-ez-Zemán only having broken after producing a female version, Princess Budoor? This "split" represents the origin of sexual differentiation, but this has been experienced in the bisexual mode of oedipal identifications and narcissistic fantasies long before the irruption of desire and the breakthrough of the feeling of incompleteness instigate the quest for the lost complementary object.

According to the same phallocentric tendency that leads Meymooneh to state that with equal beauty it would be mad not to recognise the male's superiority to the female, the particular intensity of Budoor's desire, in her initial contact with Kamar-ez-Zemán, is presented by the arbiter jinn as proof of the princess's inferiority. Does this not raise doubts as to the unconscious motivations for this highly Platonic criteriology: what male envy in regard to female desire and pleasure, what denial of the unknown,[10] what precarious repression of femininity do they not conceal? Whatever the answer, there are grounds from this perspective for recalling that the day after the crucial night when the two heroes are brought together, the young man's father immediately shares his melancholy, and his impetus towards a narcissistic and homosexual retreat, whereas El-Ghayoor will hear none of his daughter's "madness" and temporarily banishes her. It will certainly be said that the oscillations between male and female continue to occur incessantly at every level throughout this extravaganza, as in everyday life. If the young people were able to spend their auto-erotic isolation in the deliberate pursuit of the object, no sooner found than lost, it is indeed through the brilliance of the other's desire, but it is also because this otherness is the object of a recognition, a reminiscence – a term as dear to Freud as to Plato – because the other's mute, hidden internal and internalised presence is re-externalised and largely re-projected. *The possibilities of psychic bisexuality combine here to accomplish the "sexual destiny"*.

Reading – in Mardrus's text – the story of Kamar-ez-Zemán and Budoor, it is soon obvious that everything happens as if the circulation of libidinal and loving cathexes were always occurring through the presence of small mediating objects, which have a symbolic as well as a quasi-transitional quality that is gradually imposed on the mind. This particularly involves rings and jewels that are gradually discovered, transmitted, lost and found, each event accentuating the long erotic apprenticeship of the hero and heroine. Thus Budoor "recognises" her lover without seeing him when, in a message he transmits to her, she finds the ring she had given him; the same thing happens later when, after many trials and tribulations, she identifies her lost cornaline, which Kamar-ez-Zemán placed at the bottom of a precious jar. However obvious the sexual symbolism of these objects may appear, there is nevertheless a sense that they cannot always be assigned a fixed and unequivocal meaning.

Every time the loving encounter finally occurs, the witnesses marvel and the story of the adventures and wonders that have taken place give the signal of the festival – the festival of the reunion of the separated halves – but the satisfaction and joy born of the long-anticipated union are only said to endure at the end of the story (perhaps because an end has to be put to it after all). Otherwise, once the honeymoon is over, a gnawing dissatisfaction is seen to re-emerge. On two occasions, this is the act of Kamar-ez-Zemán: scruples about his father and regret for his absence, or curiosity about Budoor and the acute blame directed at the consequences of this curiosity. Thus the primacy of genital heterosexuality, under the dual sign of pleasure and fertility, does not long stifle the aspirations and desires linked to each character's bisexuality. It is because Kamar-ez-Zemán does not find in Budoor the complete fulfilment of his wishes – he would vainly seek there his father, with whom he has always shared a very close bond – that he risks losing for a second time the long-concealed object of his desire. As for Budoor, she pines for her young spouse at Armánoos's court, but this does not prevent her benefiting from the opportunities presented to her by her cross-dressing to involve Hayát-en-Nufoos in some homosexual games that do not long remain "innocent". Rather, having rediscovered the object of her strongest love, she does not baulk at sharing him with a rival whose erotic partner she will also happily continue to be. Far from weakening them, the satisfaction of the heterosexual drives thus intensifies the homosexual drives. Admittedly this is merely an oscillation, more or less rapid and intense, in the object cathexis, but do the latent resonances of our tale not invite a duplication of what occurs in this order with analogous oscillations in others: in both protagonists' relationship to themselves following the fluctuations of their narcissistic cathexes and their psychosexual characteristics, as relatively independent of the type of object choice and even the modalities of their object relationships?

In any case, it is obvious that the trajectory followed by the unfolding of the entire story (even if proven to be the result of successive additions over time, that would not change anything from our point of view) is jointly and constantly determined by the inherent incompleteness of sexual difference and by a complex and variable combination of homosexuality and heterosexuality, a combination that can only be conceived with the help and in terms of psychic bisexuality. Is it not also remarkable that through so many trials and tribulations of all kinds, a progression or, better, an expansion is emphasised and confirmed, from the initial phobogenic fixations to the supple complexity of the ultimate polygamous situation? There would probably be a great deal to say in passing on the role of cross-dressing and make-believe in this development. A particular character's disguise in fact regularly contributes to the resolution of conflicts and the mobility of situations. It simultaneously provides, under the cover of usurped external fulfilments, authentic affective and sexual accomplishments.

By taking into account some recompense for homosexuality – especially female – and polygamy, here the expression of a tradition, while also reserving its place to a constant freeing of the latent from the manifest, is it not finally rather tempting to see this ambiguous extravaganza as an illustration – both naïve and esoteric – of the "full accomplishment of the bisexual function"? Is it not significant from this perspective that in the closing scene in which Kamar-ez-Zemán is supposed to have to submit to his tyrant's homosexual demands, his intense surprise on noticing in "his" partner the absence of the anticipated penis (an absence presented, let us recall, at the beginning of history as equivalent to a real lack of being) then becomes the marvelling rediscovery – of a wonder that this time is just as great as Budoor's in the episode of the tower – of the entire female body and especially the vagina, described as a "paradise regained"?

The economy of each person's sexuality (to give the word the full wealth of meaning that psychoanalysis confers on it) is based on an ever-fragile relationship between the assertion of bisexuality and the assertion of sexual specificity. Reckoning with the oscillation between femininity and masculinity – a constant in our psychic life – with the highly composite nature of the concept of sexual difference and with the fact that the individual psychosexual position – I mean each person's position on the infinitely varied spectrum of concrete sexualities – is the result of a long and hazardous drive-related and personal evolution, it becomes evident that the "psychic participation" has transformed human sexuality into an extremely plastic and polymorphous reality. Admittedly, sexual reality indisputably limits this plasticity, this polymorphism, but is it not counterbalanced, at its very core, by another reality that is potentially antagonistic: the sexual fantasmatic, with its powerful modulating effects?

When psychosexuality, in a subject or a group, submits to a costly and contrived effort with a view to compartmentalising sexual choices and attitudes and is pledged to a highly contrasting simplification of the inherent vocations and characteristics of each of the sexes, libidinal tension will probably be increased and perhaps the species – at least its reproduction – will benefit; but the living communication between people, genuine exchanges between men and women, are compromised: an end is made to potential similarities and affinities, as well as opportunities for agreement and unity.

However, if the opposite transpires (might this be the case today in some of our societies?), if "bisexualisation" stimulates an opening up of the male and female universes and an attenuation of sexual difference as the source of insurmountable conflicts, in short if the commonality between men and women increases, libidinal tension probably loses by it, and there is even a risk of a certain involution of sexuality occurring, but communication becomes livelier and more complete...

Unless, of course, the economic equilibrium is broken by an excessively strong bisexualisation, for, from then, the vulnerability of Eros to the destructive drives becomes more pronounced, the drive defusion is facilitated, and soon what it seemed could only extend or create communication breaks it down, and the happy introjection of the other sexuality turns into a narcissistic androgynous phantasy that is toxic in nature: then an end is made to those effective and beautiful differences!

## Notes

1 Originally published in 1975 in French. Translated by Sophie Leighton for Birksted-Breen, D., Flanders, S., & Gibeault, A. (2010). Reading French Psychoanalysis London: Routledge. Pp. 649–667.
2 Alfred Deller (1912–79), an English singer and a musicologist, was one of the main figures in popularising the use of the countertenor voice in Renaissance and Baroque music, a voice that had been forgotten since the castrati of the sixteenth and seventeenth centuries. [*Eds.*, 2010].
3 As was the case, for instance, with S. Rado as early as 1940, E. Bergler (1956) and, more recently, M. J. Sherfey (Rado, 1940; Sherfey, 1972).
4 Accordingly, Freud (1908a) regards the bisexual nature of many hysterical symptoms as "an interesting confirmation of my view that the postulated existence of an innate bisexual disposition in man is especially clearly visible in the analysis of psychoneurotics" (pp. 165–166).
5 This notion was presented in 1977 in a lecture I gave at the British Psychoanalytical Society; it could briefly be defined as the psycho-affective fetishism of an internal object or as a kind of intimate and repetitive fantasy scenario.

6 This term for the establishment of gender also implies a cut, through a play on the French word *section*. [Translator's note].

7 The summary of this story is based on the French translation by Dr J. C. Mardrus (1990, vol. 5). Quotations are from Lane (1883).

8 In particular, the story contains various poems that I have not taken into account.

9 The myth of the origin of love and sexuality, according to which the human being was originally a male and female creature that was split by the gods into two halves, each of which has ever since been in search of its counterparts.

10 During one of the princess's initial descriptions (in the Mardrus version), it is mentioned that the sleeves of her blouse were embroidered with the lines: "Three things prevent her from granting men a look that says 'yes': the fear of the unknown, the horror of the known and her beauty."

# 2

# TELL ME WHOM YOU LIKE BEST[1]

## *Catherine Chabert*

One day, he finally met the woman of his life. He was going on 40 and had always been a bachelor. He fell madly in love with Laura. Quite soon they decided to marry – a traditional, classic marriage – and they had a child, a little girl. He had never imagined such bliss. Right after the baby was born, the young mother, Laura, became seriously ill, and she died within a few weeks.

There are no words to describe Romain's distress: his falling apart, his whole self going to pieces, losing all he cared for – all except one exclusive care, the love for his baby girl. He gives her all his time. She cries quite a lot like inconsolable babies do, but the cause of her distress is obvious. One day, as he is in despair of calming her wailing, he comes upon a forgotten piece of underwear that belonged to his wife: he wraps the bottle in it, the baby sucks and falls asleep.

From there on things go very fast: Romain is tempted to wrap himself in Laura's clothes, then to wear them, he has them tailored to his size, buys a wig, blond as she was, and from then on dresses thus to look after the child.

The procedure seems natural to him: since then, not only does the baby seem consoled, but he also is coming out of the deep despair that had been over him – as though with this ruse death and absence could be cancelled. "A child absolutely needs its mother!" says he, "but it also needs its father…" "Well, I can be both!"

He remembers that at the death of his mother he had kept her fur coat and sometimes wore it at home, examining himself in a mirror: he could smell her feminine perfume, he walked as she did, she was there! Then, one day, he stopped, even though the coat was still there, at hand, hanging amid men's clothes.

The core of this story cannot simply be summed up as a particular modality of grief: what is at stake with troubling intensity goes beyond the curiosity that the other sex excites: it reveals how Romain holds an unwavering belief that the only way to bridge the gap of the difference, which for him means a terrifying absence, is to feed his passion for femininity, which gives him a feeling of existing totally. All visible expressions of femininity fascinate him: he humbly and patiently tries to learn the paths that will allow him to conquer it. When asked: "What does being a woman mean to you?" he replies with amazing candour: "I can do everything I am not permitted to do as a man!"

Romain could peremptorily answer the questions raised by the notions of psychic bisexuality and difference between sexes! No, there is no problem of object choice; it would be absurd to wonder, "Whom do I like best, my father or my mother? Whom do I love most, her or him?" No, there is no point being on one side *or* the other, and there is no risk losing the love of either one. Yes, absolute bisexuality makes all possible: it allows father *and* mother to be united into a single being, indivisible and inseparable. And yes, the pain one might feel when confronted with their life in common, their relationship, their desires – all that makes no sense. Since one *is* the other, any way you look at it, choosing one or the other amounts to choosing the only omnipresent one always in coexistence with the other without ever having to renounce either. The reversibility acquired through unfailing bisexuality allows the passage from masculinity to femininity in a triumph that ignores castration and its woes. A single person but two sexes offer themselves as figures of identification and object choice: "I can be the father *and* the mother" could be the motto of pure bisexuality, having undone all ties with castration.

One thing is certain: even though Romain is devoured by his will to *be* a woman, his powerful sexual drives are always directed towards women: he passionately desired his wife and now aches for her best friend, who has become his own. He is not attracted to men and was not particularly pleased by his single homosexual experience, which took place at the end of his adolescence. What is at stake for him is to be able to be both: man and woman, father and mother. His identity entitlement is conditioned by his double sexual belonging: looking like a woman when he wants to and having no doubt as to the existence of his penis. What fascinates him most are the manoeuvres of transformation that allow a perceptible visual passage from masculine to feminine; in his very particular way he is experimenting with the question raised by Freud: "How does one become a woman?"

But Romain is not Romain – or, rather, he is Romain Duris, but in the role of David, the hero of François Ozon's film, *A New Girlfriend*. A disturbing film – doubly disturbing – because of the active developments of bisexuality it presents and dramatizes through the massive affects attached to the images on the one hand, and because of the deep conviction at work that brings us face to face with infantile beliefs and their surprising brutality, on the other.

However, the happy end – the final image, gathering a happy trio: David in transvestite gear, his new friend whom he has made pregnant, and the little girl – is not convincing. One cannot help wanting the return of two badly missing awols: the father of the hero, and the conflict! It is as though erasing the father had taken away the slightest signs of affects and contradictory representations. David might be an illustration of the most idyllic descriptions of manic love: no separation, no renouncement, no anger, no hate; he is all love – a fool's love – with unending generosity; but at the same time his candour and wonder concerning femininity could make him into a simpleton who would die if he were to give up this stubborn audible and visible bisexuality.

The involvement of castration with death has long been a given fact: but it is the way(s) this tied game is played that should capture our attention. The narrative and the fantasies are developed in François Ozon's film with obvious implications for affects and sexuality, but they may not be suspected by him, even though he associates them in the film. Bisexuality might contain a manic element, which, beyond the narcissistic base, would ensure the triumph of the ego over the lost object, and even the triumph over castration as well. The economic advantage of bisexuality could be obtained by the megalomaniac excitation that is associated with the conviction of belonging to both sexes, and to the setting aside of any pain due to the loss of a loved object.

Thus the ambivalence of feelings, which is an essential and motivating experience of life, has come to be rubbed away, to a point where worry and terror loom: what anxieties, what destructivity, what melancholia can be hiding behind the idealization of a dead woman who is ever-present in all the compulsive incarnations aimed at denying her disappearance?

It is this ambivalence, and the conflicts it generates, that Freud evokes concerning the treatment of Ernst Lanzer: beyond his symptom and the repulsive name that made him famous, Freud's young patient, the Rat Man (Freud, 1909d), could be considered the very example of the tortures inflicted by object choice and the vicissitudes of psychic bisexuality.

The beginning of Ernst's illness goes back to a romantic situation that was both complicated and quite ordinary: he had long loved a young girl, but he met another, whom he resolved to marry. His illness let him avoid deciding: he could not choose one rather than the other, and this brought on a symptomatic turmoil that became increasingly invalidating; contaminating oscillations, constant and repetitive, left him torn between what Freud calls the unconscious "conflicting choice between the father and the sexual object". At first glance, this construction seems puzzling: why and how does Freud replace the impossible choice between two women, the old and the new, by the agony of choosing between father and sexual object?

The father is clearly Freud's choice: several fragments of the cure concern the mother, who is present in many scenes and memories related in the analysis of the Rat Man, but they have been practically eradicated, repressed from the published opus on obsessional neurosis (Freud, 1909d), in favour of the father, who is set up as the central figure. For us, this appears as an evidence of the oedipal repetition, but this construction is not explicitly formulated by Freud: he does not say that the "venerated lady" has replaced the mother as "sexual object"; he insists on a crystallization of guilt and castration around the father. At the same time, one can wonder whether this ambiguous passage from one couple to the other is not precisely what contains all the complications of bisexuality, at all its narcissistic, identificatory and objectal levels. How far is bisexuality, integrated into the difference between sexes, the very condition of this dual choice, this dual identification and its major underlying conflicts?

I wonder about the overinvestment of displacement in Ernst's cure; this process interests me all the more since it is the very root of the transference: his obsessive ideas are initially concerned with the total impossibility of going and getting the small object he has lost. This inability to go from one point to another, from one place to another, could be a representation of the wish and at the same time immense difficulty he experiences in attempting to go from one parent to the other. Certainly the father is there, extraordinarily present despite – or because of – his death: he is present to the point of hallucination, and Ernst is paralysed. Does this mean that he cannot go back to his mother now that the murder of the father has been accomplished, which has the effect on his life that he cannot go towards any woman – that is, to allow himself to desire, have pleasure and be a man? Another interpretation could be that this impotence is also linked to his love for his mother, to his guilt and fear of loving "another", as happened at the start of his illness, when he was tempted to marry a new woman.

If bisexuality imposes both object choice and identifications; one can easily imagine the alternative relations that can help one to understand the difficult object choices of the Rat Man. The coexistence of the two forms of Oedipus complex, the positive and the negative, determines a dialectic of identifications that lead him to love or hate one or the other, then one and the other.

It is the Oedipus complex that orchestrates ambivalence *in fine*. It implies a distribution of drives that breaks up and delegates quantities of excitation that are more mobile, attach them to one, to the other, link them together, unlink. ... But it does happen, as Freud notes, that love may not manage to attenuate hate, that hate remains and grows on very actively in the unconscious. How else are we to understand the major place of death within obsessional neurosis? And how else are we to grasp the meaning of this constant threat?

The problem is not so much that one or the other sexual object can specifically mobilize different drives – more libidinal or more aggressive: it is well known that masculine and father are not necessarily the bearers of regular activity of power, strength and domination. The same way, feminine and mother do not necessarily engage passivity and submission – far from it! What happens, rather, is that the dynamics of phantasies take hold of opposite couples – activity– passivity, masculine–feminine, sadism–masochism, and mostly love– hate – and assign them to the father or to the mother: these are the original figures and objects of love, and their trace remains in the ordinary representations of masculine and feminine.

85

Both these great references of masculine and feminine (which are not to be confused with man and woman) concern us not only in terms of the figures that embody them, father and mother, but also in terms of their intertwining: their swings and hesitations allow us to follow and theorize the traces of an ever active bisexuality. The more sexuation comes to impose its differences, the more it empowers bisexuality, as if sexual identity went with its necessary maintenance. Every time a difference imposes itself, an overinvestment of the contrary also imposes itself because of the narcissistic attack this implies.

In fact, bisexuality is anchored to the narcissistic origins of psychosexuality and can be maintained throughout life by dependence on the alienating and unmovable omnipotence of a same object. But bisexuality also inherits from the Oedipus complex and the vast movement of differentiation it determines, establishing a firm super-ego, sexual identifications and object choices.

The "bisexuality of all human beings" that Freud exposed (1950 [1892–99], Letter 50) means that it is impossible to get near the masculine, or the feminine, without considering its link to the other sex: both are associated intrinsically, linked, paradoxically, by their difference. The logic of this difference supports the existence and recognition of internal objects belonging to the net of the sexual matter, which is partly detached from its narcissistic mechanisms and moves away from an identification with the same until death, while the logic of the different operates within the projection of love and hate, considering the object with immoderate excess, taking it or leaving it radically.

As for the Oedipus complex, it is not simply a structuring configuration: the difference of sexes and generations is not admitted without hesitation. Yet, the infantile is not exclusively maintained within the opaque zones of non-differentiation; it inevitably comes upon differences, and must deal with them, more or less. Bisexuality, which is a formidable construction proposed by Freud, remains incredibly vivid and leans to one side only by a "much more" of one than the other; it definitely does not mean a confusion of sexes but maintains the existence of both, masculine and feminine, with their usual or extraordinary articulations.

I turn now to another issue – that is, another obstacle that is determined by the question, "Tell me whom you like best, your father or mother?"

Hippolyte was going on 40 when he decided to have children. His companion wished the same thing, and they joined their projects in a marriage. However, this engagement had a radical effect: Hippolyte ceased to desire his wife, definitively. He became obsessed with this symptom, which he did not experience as sexual impotence in the ordinary way but as the result of it being impossible for him to become a father. His whole life was turned upside down, and he was submerged by anxiety.

His parents had divorced when Hippolyte was 10: he remembered the parental couple only through images of violent scenes, and his childhood through images of moments spent with his father. Obviously his mother had existed, she never abandoned him, but she did not appear in his memories of everyday life: no signs of her left in the house, no clues to the presence of a woman anywhere. With her departure, all feminine marks had manifestly and perceptively disappeared from his domestic life. However, girls, and then women, always had a great place in Hippolyte's life: he could not live without them, had regularly been dividing himself between two loves, feeling remorse and guilt but always needing both women and being incapable of bringing himself to choose without terrible pain. His decision to marry had been a great victory – one that did not last long. He mentioned the obligatory and repetitive behaviours of his love life with some embarrassment, since, whoever the woman may be, he regularly got angry with her, verbally at first then more violently, until they came to fight physically. During these scenes, he no longer knew who he was, he himself or she, a man or a woman, a boy or a girl. He remembered that when he was an adolescent he had stopped eating in order to stop growing and preserve the tender ambiguity of the fragile little boy his parents loved so much: was it a way of fixing in his unchanged body the image of an only child, loved by a loving couple? Later on, he had methodically exercised to transform his child's body into that of an athlete. During his analysis, he complained of the way his father had wanted him to perform domestic chores while they lived together. Years later he was suddenly revolted and furious about this and re-experienced with me some of this intolerable submission. He did not want to be the eternal child depending on the will of his father whose valet he had been, no, his manservant, no, even worse, his maid, his wife ... But he was able to say all that only after he had recovered during his analysis his place of preferred son of his mother, her treasure, her passion-child. The reintegration of his mother in his psychic life had allowed him to finally discover a conflictual position with his father, recognizing his submission and his rebellion.

However, what did remain cut off and could not be considered or even thought of was the desire existing between his parents: one could hear his insistences on their quarrels and fights as representations of sexual primal scenes. However, Hippolyte could simply not admit an ordinary memory or recognition of their spent love: something more fundamental stood in the way, his incapacity to grasp their sexual identity – his father as a man and his mother as a woman. Without these representations, this incapacity made his own sexual identity very complicated: he could be neither, neither one *or* the other, neither one *and* the other.

He was completely on the side of one *or* the other: on the side of him, who speaks, who separates, who enunciates, who forbids, who seduces, on the side of his father? Or, on the side of her, who touches, excites, contains, confuses, on the side of his mother? As though this separation, this alternative, remained indispensable in order to install one *and* the other in different places, to set up each in his kingdom and make the thought of their meetings, desires and pleasures quite impossible: what Winnicott calls the "splitting" of masculine and feminine elements.

One thing is obvious: by being on the side of one *or* the other, he separated them and did not see them together, could not represent one beside the other, precisely at times when he was alone, waiting, filled with distress. In such situations, the impossibility of being able to stand the primal scene obliges one to overinvest bisexuality in its narcissistic form, erasing any difference in order to avoid any desire and to ensure protection against horror and exclusion; to be outside the parents' desire, in exile from maternal or paternal soil, to be banished from their bodies and amorous relations.

Here are two dreams Hippolyte reported: in the first *he was piloting a small plane, a two-seater, and his mother was beside him sitting in the passenger seat. A bump while they fly shoves them one against the other, and they find themselves lying on the floor, he over her.* The dream really disturbed him: it happened towards the beginning of the cure, at a time when he was convinced he did not love his mother and that she had no importance for him. Had he, could he still, desire her?

In the second dream, which occurred much later, *his father intro-duces his new wife to him.* Hippolyte says this woman looks like me, maybe his father's wife in the dream is really me! And he remembers with some terror what she says to him: *"I can no longer be your analyst. I am your father's wife. You must find another!"*

He rebels and complains: "Another woman, another analyst, what else? Are they all for him? Everything for him! No, I'll leave him his wife, but the analyst I keep."

Let us briefly consider Freud's conception towards the end of his life, concerning the articulation of psyche and the difference between sexes: his thesis is that of an anatomical or biological difference that has psychic consequences that develop with the perception of these differences, and then essentially with the Oedipus complex and the delayed arrangements of these perceptions. The biological basis on which the psychic differences are anchored marks the gap between both sexes in terms of "having or having not", and this dissymmetry is displaced and transferred to a psychical dissymmetry that determines the vicissitudes of psychosexuality.

Here is a commentary made by J.-B. Pontalis:

Why is man so afraid of being a woman? ... Why does woman have so much trouble renouncing – and perhaps never does renounce – her desire to have, to obtain a penis? That is the rock. Freud tells us there is an obvious correspondence between the two themes, that of man's refusal and that of woman's envy; "something, which is common to both sexes, has, because of the difference between the sexes, been modelled into different forms of expression".

(1974, p. 19; translated for this edition)

Pontalis calls this something that is common, the "ungraspable in-between".

### Note

1 Translated by Laurence Apfelbaum.

89

# 3

# THE ORIGIN OF PSYCHOANALYSIS BETWEEN BISEXUALITY AND TRANSFERENCE[1]

*Monique Cournut-Janin*

The history of the human could be related in terms of being first one, a single encompassing/encompassed unit, then two, the child and his mother, but two is three, and then at least four, then one in the midst of a multitude from whom he must differentiate himself as best he can; or, alternatively, it could be seen as an undifferentiated sphere, though one that is already marked by differences, with a perceiving, enjoying and suffering body; or again as an inextricable mixture of everything and nothing.

In France, we readily call the small child "*ma puce*"; a "flea" is tiny, but it stings and is irritating. Is the human child irritating from the beginning and terribly disappointing in comparison with what we had imagined? He is at once the bearer of expected perfection and of inevitable disappointment, and this will continue to gnaw at him throughout his life.

To complicate matters, he has a body that it will take him his whole life to learn to inhabit; this body is sexual and the two primordial differences will have to be taken into account. There are grown-ups (adults) and children. And one day he (or she) will have to recognize and accept that he is on one side of the difference of the sexes, a boy or a girl, even if he would like to be both or neither. And, however interesting they may be, "gender studies" can also serve as a screen to avoid speaking about sex and the difference between the sexes, an avoidance that Freud fought against from the beginning of his career. It has to be said that after his studies on eels, whose sex was so difficult to determine, his arrival in the world of mental illness left him no respite – with Charcot in Paris, with hysterics, women mainly, then with his patients, almost all of whom were women, and then with the women at home.

Freud felt the need to have social or human interactions to take him out of his solitude as a researcher. It was around the age of 40 that he wanted to communicate with a man, a scientist like him, and of the same generation. He wrote to Wilhelm Fliess who had given a paper that he had appreciated. They established a relationship, at first by correspondence, then through meetings to which he looked forward feverishly, in which personal problems and scientific questions could be evaluated critically to the mutual enrichment of both men.

It was in the context of this relationship that the term "bisexuality" first emerged, introduced by Fliess, a reputed otorhinolaryngologist for whom the nose was an organ just as important and erectile as the sexual organs. Freud was immediately seduced by Fliess's theories. Female periods of 28 days had their male equivalent of 26 days, and both of them were investigating the effects of such periods on themselves, the masculine representing for them activity, above all intellectual and creative,[2] and the feminine passivity, associated with an experience of painful inhibition.

It was thus in Fliess, a chosen and idealized double, that Freud confided his most hidden lines of questioning, but also the very first outlines of what was later on to become the metapsychology, a theory that made it possible to think about mental illness, and then human functioning in general.

During the first three months of the year 1893, Freud was faced in his personal life with the problems that he was studying as a doctor and researcher in his patients of both sexes. At that time, methods of contraception were very haphazard. Freud, who had waited a long time for marital life with his fiancée Martha, was faced with the dilemma of enjoying a satisfying sexual life with births at close intervals, or of having recourse to diverse means of contraception that were more or less frustrating for both partners. Such are the subjects of the first letters and manuscripts of this fruitful period, during which his great work began to take shape through Drafts A and B. Freud gradually became aware of those aspects of the notion of bisexuality that were his own and those that were based on the intuitions of Fliess. Moreover, it was around the question of the paternity of this notion that their relationship gradually began to deteriorate and become embittered, before finally breaking down.

Freud understood later on that he had "transferred" onto this man everything that was troubling him during a period marked by the treatment of patients, by his own marital problems and by his relationship with his father. "My old father (age eighty-one)", he wrote to Fliess at the end of June 1896, "is in Baden in a most shaky state, with heart failure, paralysis of the bladder, and so forth" (letter dated 30 June 1896, in Masson, 1985, p. 193). Freud found it difficult to accept his father's physical decline, which made him question, through identification, his own image of himself and exacerbated his doubts about who he was. "No one can replace for me the relationship with a friend which a special – possibly feminine – side in me demands" (Letter dated 7 May 1900, in Masson, 1985, p. 412).

Death, and the guilt of those left behind, would be recurrent themes in his self-analysis.

Bisexuality and the transference were thus at the origin of psychoanalysis.

Reading the Freud–Fliess correspondence makes us reflect, in turn, on the difficulty of thinking, theorizing and working with our patients when we are ourselves concerned and involved in the transference that they make onto us and in that which we cannot avoid, unconsciously, making onto them. The series of papers Freud wrote on the transference a few years later (*Papers on Technique*, 1912b, 1913c, 1914g, 1915a) are not, in spite of the title under which these writings are subsumed, technical texts in the usual sense of the term, but, rather, a reminder to every analyst that the transference is the very basis of analytic practice, but also its greatest risk. Through his own self-analysis, Freud discovered that it was the analyst's own infantile sexuality that is awakened through the narrative that he/she listens to on the couch.

In this twenty-first century, the time of the unconscious refers to the same depths of violence, hate, inhumanity and struggle (which the subject wants to know nothing about) as at the beginning of the last century, when Freud was beginning to theorize it.

In September 2014,[3] writing about bisexuality as it is expressed in the session might, at first sight, seem derisory in the light of the onslaught of terrifying news items: decapitations of human beings,

Ebola epidemic, sabre-rattling in large parts of the world, and climate change. Or we can tell ourselves, in the manner of Freud writing *Moses and Monotheism* (1939a) during the Nazi years, that attempting to think about what is enacted on a couch may help us avoid being engulfed by the immediateness of things, without in any way denying the existence of what surrounds us, whether at home or abroad.

Freud explored mental functioning, sexuality first, and then destructiveness, whether or not we call it the death drive. The presence of murder and incest in human history makes it possible, admittedly, to recognize the full organizing significance of oedipal symbolism. But the oedipal configuration (*l'Oedipe*) does not suffice to tackle the fundamental question, whether or not we wish to call it psychotic, which is a constant source of problems for every "civilized" individual.

Racism, in all its forms, has not diminished in importance. Is it worse than at the time of the Black Death, the Inquisition or the wars of the past? Maybe not. Perhaps we are always tempted by denial, just as we would like to continue to believe in the innocence, the purity of the young child.

Psychoanalysis is no longer in fashion – and perhaps it never was. Believing in better days, while idealizing the past, is a universal tool that is used as much by the individual as by society.

There are two ways of approaching Freud's work: one consists in fitting into its mould as if it were an unalterable protective house, avoiding confrontation with the outside; the other is to follow the path of the author, his hesitations, his steps forward and his steps back, constantly re-examining the questions raised by the psyche throughout his life.

These questions echo those of childhood: Who am I? Who am I for whom? What is the sex of this other? Is it the same as mine or not? In any case there are at least two "others", one of the same sex, the other of a different sex. The first deception is not to be all. Being gendered (*sexué*) is another, as it excludes being all. Belief in a higher being who lacks nothing and is omnipotent can take over and serve as consolation for the evidence of one's own incompleteness. This is reminiscent of Freud's reflections in *The Future of an Illusion* (1927c).

Writing requires one to take one's time, to refine one's sentences and the words one uses because they are not adequate for expressing what one is trying to think about. And in so doing, writing obliges us to be more precise, not in order to find the right word but, rather, the one that is most suited to giving form to what remains, ultimately, necessarily inadequate for expressing the unknown. Our time is waiting feverishly for answers, when, in fact, it is questions that can help us to think.

Between the lack of control over reality, which offends our sense of omnipotence, and the frantic quest for active ways to modify it, the role of psychoanalysis might be to introduce an element of uncertainty. Not without baggage, the practice of psychoanalysis offers some possibilities: the belief in the unconscious and in the irreducible inadequacy of words to represent things, and in particular the traces that subsist in us of our infantile sexuality.

The analysis of Louise, with pauses and resumptions, took place during various key moments in her life: first, on becoming an adult, then during a pregnancy, and finally when the child she gave birth to took us back into the turbulent waters of a past that had already been explored in the analysis, but which returned in quite another form.

I could still recall memories that had come back to her during the first period of analysis. She herself could not remember them and complained, on the contrary, of having no recollections of her childhood; the repression had been so deep and effective that I even doubted my own memory. One memory, above all, was absent, which had nonetheless had an important place in the earlier period of analysis. It concerned a finger of her grandfather which had been deformed by a piece of shrapnel during the First World War, and of her mixed pleasure in moving this little fragment with metallic glints under the amused and tender gaze of this grandfather.

What I want to relate (narrate?) here took place two years later when Louise's little girl was just a few months old. She was playing with the hands of her daddy, Louise's husband, and Louise was upset not to have any memories of the hands of her own father. My intervention, "And with your grandfather?" simply provoked an irritated reaction from her concerning the approaching holidays which, she complained, I was taking at a time that did not suit her (even though it was planned and usual). The following week brought nothing further on this subject ... and I went away on holiday, almost doubting my memory.

94

Two weeks went by, during which Louise and I lived our own lives, and I, in any case, thought about this matter with some perplexity. On my return, Louise said she had spent a pleasant holiday with her husband and daughter and told me this dream: "*I was looking upwards and there was a bird – in fact, a bit like the one in the painting above the couch – it was getting bigger and at a certain moment it fell to the ground and was broken into a thousand bits, like a crashed plane.*"

Her associations to the dream led to the idea that her mother could have been in the plane that had crashed, of which she had seen pictures the night before. If I heard a death-wish addressed both to her mother and to me in the transference, I refrained from interpreting it ... (my English colleagues, however, might feel it would have been pertinent to do so). I waited. ... Louise brought another dream at the next session: "*I was at the seaside and there was a huge creature in the sea which I was following in the water; I don't know whether it ate me or whether I ate it.*" And she added, "*What's strange is that it was actually quite a pleasant dream.*"

What are we to think about this sequence? The presence, in her eyes, of the tender physical proximity between daughter and father had evidently put her in touch with clearly oedipal death wishes, with her in the position of an excluded third party. It also seemed to me that the relationship with me, the "basic transference" as Catherine Parat[4] (1995) would have said, had protected both of us from a flight from analysis, or worse, a psychic or somatic disorganization in Louise.

The second dream had to do with a deep physical relationship, that of a baby for whom eating and being eaten can be terrifying ideas, but also to the very happy buried memory of physical contact, of shared touching. ... It was only a few weeks later that Louise came to her session with the recollection of handling her grandfather's finger, one she felt she had had for the first time. The return of this memory plunged Louise for quite some time into the need to separate herself, to leave behind something of her childhood. She described that in this way: "I cannot love them, though, in the same way at the same time." Not in the same way, it's true.

These moments from Louise's analysis raise the issue for the analyst of choosing whether to interpret or not, and at what level, reflecting the complexity in each analysis of what circulates between the patient's unconscious and that of the analyst. They also evoke the deep changes that occur during each stage of life, leading to a reorganization of psychic life. The lack of contact during sessions between the bodies of the two protagonists, who are nonetheless physically stimulated, confers on the transference a force which it is the analyst's task to understand and control. Freud, and also Ferenczi in his research, came up against this fire of the transference which it is important not to deny, which one cannot, without negative effects, help hearing, and which the analyst will have to interpret as being related to his function as an analyst and not to his person, in spite of what the patient claims. Dreams, but also the facts of everyday life, allow this work to take place, which goes hand in hand with the need to get out of the dual relationship and to triangulate.

Bisexual identifications will play a part in this process, harking back, of course, to the two parental imagos, but not only, and without the notions of feminine and masculine, of passive and active, being clearly discernible. Identifications can be parallel, but also shifting; a father who has long been seen as purely phallic may reveal a maternal imago that one might have thought was reserved for the mother. The role of siblings, in what Freud called the "nursery", may also, at many other moments in life, allow for identificatory processes and the elaboration of jealousies or idealizations, alleviating to some extent the burden of parental images. It is only necessary to listen, later on, to the problems teachers have with the flaring passions of their pupils or alternatively the violent rejection by these pupils of this or that teacher, to see the importance of the stepping-stones that socialization offers the psychic life of the infant who is so handicapped at the beginning by his dependence on the care of another person.

To return now to what appears, in what is reconstructed from this retrospectively, as the time of the first identifications. Every infant initially finds himself immerged in the maternal feminine. Poets write about it; patients with their innumerable dreams of the sea, talk about it in analysis. It was in the sea that Louise located the huge creature, mother and analyst. Every child will have to separate from this maternal feminine that was so present, even though the subject was not yet a subject, in order to experience himself as different and not as an integral part of this first object.

For the mother, this child was at first imaginary, caught in her own relationship with the child's father, but also, more deeply, in the phantasy activity that places him within a paternal and maternal line of descent. Unconsciously, this pregnancy awakens her own oedipal conflicts, the incestuous child made with her own father or her own mother. The birth is an upheaval shared by the infant and his mother: he is separated from a protected world; she loses an inner dream child and discovers a real baby.

We come up against this problematic issue in analysis, and on both sides. The patient (whether man or woman) expresses disappointment and idealization; the analyst must be perfect, just as the first object should have been, which was so disappointing that it was idealized in an attempt to repair it. Thanks to the transference that is established by the analytic situation, the patient brings to the sessions his/her rage and the anxiety that this destructive rage will trigger the fear of being destroyed in turn, according to the ancient law of retaliation.

In order not to let him/herself be caught up in this dual situation, it is in the analyst's own capacity to integrate the third element that he or she will find the capacity to think. "In advance, or ahead of, an analysis", as André Green used to say, he or she will hear, in an apparently closed discourse, like an offshoot of the unconscious emerging from the couch, something that will inject new life into the process. A word, an image, a dream, an unusual way of behaving, however minimal it might be, will help him to free himself from the encompassing force of the transference to which he is subjected.

There seems no point in denying that repetition, which is always identical, and sometimes boredom, plague the analyst. Linking them up with the unconscious wish to send the analyst to sleep, but also with the compulsion to relive – albeit retroactively, and even if apparently unrecognizable – an early traumatic experience that is embedded in the infantile, which is still alive, helps to give meaning again to the process.

As Freud taught us, the infantile is certainly in the order of the sexual, but an *infantile* sexual order (*sexuel infantile*). Through the body, the sense-organs, the infant absorbs the external world, animate or inanimate objects.

Knowing how to hear and feel via his/her transference onto the analyst, the excited presence of an erogenous zone, the buried trace of a wound or ecstatic pleasure (*jouissance*), reanimates a psychic functioning (deferred and subject to revisions retroactively) that had seemed at a standstill, bogged down.

Perhaps the greatest difficulty for the analyst is to feel, in each session, and sometimes even in the different phases of each session, the switch from archaic conflicts to oedipal conflicts, and to recognize the value of defence at each moment. The conflict between narcissism and object-cathexis underlies what is played out throughout an analytic treatment.

The infantile is bound up with tenderness, but not only. Freud, through his self-analysis, his dreams and those of his patients, and thanks to the research that he engaged in with his collaborators in the Vienna Group, appreciated the degree of conflict that every child experiences between his wish to be loved, to conform to his parents' wishes, and that of giving free expression to his impulses. The analysis of Little Hans (Freud, 1909b), which he followed closely, confirmed and enriched the ideas he had about the infantile sexuality of a little boy. Hans and his analysis show how much the bisexuality of the child is created within the shifting richness of the identifications with everything that surrounds him, cows or horses, but also his pants or excrement. And all this in blissful ignorance of what, according to "adult" rules, "should" be feminine or masculine. At a playful age, moreover, when these two terms do not have a fixed meaning. In his text "On the Sexual Theories of Children" (1908c), Freud describes the gap between the answers of parents to the questions of children and the theories that the latter elaborate. "The nuclear complex of a neurosis", he writes, "is in this way brought into being" (1908c, p. 214). For Freud, this first cleavage, after repression has subsequently covered over this first flaring-up of murderous and loving impulses, will persist in the unconscious.

Let us think again, in our own times, about these infantile theories: one penis for all, birth taking place via the anus, the sadistic primal scene between the parents, and the ignorance of the vagina. There is no real difference between the sexes at this stage. When one listens to patients of both sexes, these theories seem neither outmoded nor exclusive. The child's imagination creates and builds, resisting any adult attempts to inculcate a so-called truth. The adult world and the infantile world cannot communicate without restrictions. These restrictions are a source of richness for the child's capacities to think. It is the basis, after repression, on which the complexity of the different paths of the bisexual drive solutions are organized, even if repression or other defences have intervened to ignore them or disguise them.

Violette cannot accept not being everything; she prefers to be nothing, for to be a woman would be to give up being both a boy and a girl. She hates me for not having told her that she was unanalysable; she makes fun of me, of my incompetence. I am bourgeois, feminine and frivolous, everything that she loathes about bourgeois women, or alternatively I am bad and despise her. Thus, using all the means at her disposal, Violette tries to limit her destructivity towards me by establishing a "difference" between her and me, because she is so afraid that I will "throw her out". Those are her words. At certain moments I feel confined within a "carcass", something metallic, inanimate, or perhaps a dead animal. ... The analysis continued and I told her what I was feeling; this made her agitated and she had associations to a decaying carcass. In the following sessions this image led to the sexual images that children look at, taken aback, which excite and shock them. I only emerged from the state of drowsiness into which I was slipping at the price of risking greater closeness by telling her what she was making me feel. It was after a long period of analysis and I had already tried to lessen the distance at which she was keeping me. This time, it worked. Later, after a few very long months, in a poetic reference, she recalled the decaying carcass. Here we touched on a sexual theme and an image of death but after they had undergone a process of elaboration, and even sublimation.

Violette and the controlling attitude she subjected me to provide me with the opportunity of revisiting this aspect of the drive envisaged by Freud at different moments in his work. Every relationship with the other, and especially with the first other, is characterized by a mixture of investments involving mastery. The infant takes hold of the mother's breast, sucks it or drinks from his bottle, and he lets go of his mastery with a degree of ecstatic pleasure (*jouissance*) which, for the observer, is evocative of an orgasmic peak.

Paul Denis (1997) has put forward a conception of the drive which has the potential to resolve, in part, the latent conflict between the Anglo-Saxons who give prominence above all to the object-relationship, and the French who are traditionally more attached to the quest for pleasure, even if it is masochistic. By considering that "the drive is formed from the combination of two currents of investment, 'in the mode of mastery' and 'in the mode of satisfaction'", he has opened up a path that may be fruitful.

What remains, in the adult, of this memory of the body, of the need to take hold of and not to let go of the object? Separation, with which the human being is constantly confronted, puts psychic life in permanent danger of disequilibrium. The loss of the breast, of faeces, separation from the object, mother and father, leave deep traces. The flexibility of bisexual identifications can open up new paths.

*Something is missing. The complaint is addressed to the analyst, and he or she is asked to make up for this lack.*

Castration and its complex are certainly one answer. We know it is insufficient, which does not exclude the possibility that it is also pertinent. The worst form of castration is to be nothing for want of not being everything.

Through the asymmetry that it establishes, the analytic situation puts the patient in a position of submission. Depending on his/her mode of functioning, but also on the moment in the analysis for a given patient, the situation will evoke infantile experiences of dependence, along with various affects ranging from rage to shame, or pleasure.

In "Analysis, Terminable and Interminable" (1937c), Freud concludes his text by speaking of the bedrock of the feminine to which he attributes, in both sexes, the most insurmountable resistance to analysis.

The feminine might be considered as that in the mother which, in the unconscious, is so difficult to get rid of, a feminine that signifies, if we follow Freud, being beaten, subjected to sexual intercourse, and giving birth in pain. ... In short, more than passivity, it implies a "passivation" excluding all pleasure other than that which is masochistic. This masculine theory of sexuality is a phallic theory which Freud was reluctant to review.

Nevertheless he himself gave us the keys to imagine another theory, by insisting, at the end of his work, on the multiplicity of bisexual identifications in both sexes. The phallic, from this perspective, is no longer the monopoly of men, any more than the feminine is of women.

And, irrespective of its sexual affiliation, pleasure might be not only a phallic, but also a feminine pleasure.

On the couch, adult sexuality is not spoken about much, especially when the relationship is a happy one. We hear about it through the material of dreams or other unconscious outcomes. Not infrequently the adult on the couch keeps well hidden the sexual pleasure which, as a child, he concealed. It is as if only painful affects may be given expression. As for shame, it is fruitful to rediscover its sources in the erogenous zones, and first and foremost, the anal zone. In his text "On Transformations of Instinct as Exemplified in Anal Erotism" (1917c), Freud shows that activity has a double purpose, that of retaining and expelling. Passivity is felt at the same time as activity. Mucous membrane and musculature procure pleasure and an experience of mastery over the internal object, faecal first, then imaginary. They offer a representation of container/contained, capable of permitting fruitful journeys back and forth, because they are sometimes regressive and sometimes progressive. Within oneself, what penetrates and what receives represent a royal path towards bisexuality, for both boys and girls.

When I was speaking about Violette earlier on, what I had experienced was the sensation of being captured within an anal interior. In *Anal and Sexual*, Lou Andréas Salomé (1916) has shown this proximity between the anal and the genital, often a motive for shame. Money is the heir of the faeces – it is said that money is dirty – and, in French at least, the expression *dirty money (argent sale)* is used to describe the illegal use of money. Overcoming shame, in analysis, will often involve returning to this richness of a "product" that was given with pride, before the notion of "dirty" had the effect of blocking the pleasure of exchange.

Michel Fain (1982), fine clinician that he was, used to explore his countertransference by asking himself which erogenous zone was excited in him through contact with the patient's discourse. In the dream of my first patient, the themes of eating and being eaten certainly reflected anxieties, but also oral pleasures, which would be contained by the words heard and proffered.

With Violette, anality was at the centre of the treatment. It allowed her to avoid confronting both her mother and me. Her gender and her sexual identity were vigorously excluded.

She was only able to talk about her father and her affects in relation to him (oral activity), once we had got beyond the trap of anal shame.

As Freud had rightly intuited, we cannot sublimate everything. The violence that Violette did to herself and to me was probably an experience she needed to go through. Subsequently, the idea of wanting a child from the father, rather than a worthless intestinal product, nourished her fantasies. It was then possible to work on guilt, which is better than shame. We were then in a world of desire, where three persons are imagined. The primal scene remained an obstacle. It is unbearable not to be involved in a moment of ecstatic pleasure in which one is both present and absent, but this has to be worked on, probably throughout the whole of one's life … as one patient said to me at the end of a long analysis, as he was leaving.

The primal scene remains unthinkable. This does not mean, though, it cannot be elaborated. Traces are always present in the unconscious fantasies re-enacting the erogenous zones, oral and anal. Projections of sadistic images onto the genital organs of the parental imagos may, depending on the uncertainties of life, trigger regressive moments in which a phallic imago attacks a weaker imago. The violence of destroying one or the other of these imagos, or both, or oneself through a reversal, is encountered in every analysis, whether of a man or a woman. Neither the feminine nor the masculine, let me repeat, is the monopoly of one sex. It is for the analyst in the session (who is not spared either from the effort of continually doing this work) to hear these reminders of an undatable past and to know how to link them up with what, in the present, reanimates these figures of the past.

## Notes

1  Translated by Andrew Weller.
2  As contraception did not exist at that time, the successive pregnancies of Martha, his wife, led him to give up the hope of enjoying a satisfying sexual life. He understood, in the course of his self-analysis, how much this had affected his image of himself.
3  Writing initiated in 2014.
4  She distinguishes "two relational elements, the transference and the relationship", which she also calls the basic transference. If the analysis of the transference constitutes the very substance of the analytic technique, for her, "the relationship corresponds to the cathexis by the patient of the analyst's person, coloured by trust". She refers to Freud's statement in "On Narcissism: An Introduction" (1914c): "what possesses [by implication the physician] the excellence which the ego lacks for making it an ideal, is loved" (p. 101).

# 4

# LOVE AND MELANCHOLIA IN THE ANALYSIS OF WOMEN BY WOMEN

*Rosine Jozef Perelberg*

## Introduction

In the analysis of women by women analysts, one may be confronted by a melancholic core in the relationship to an internal maternal imago. The attachment to this primary love object may be preserved in a melancholic, invisible way and reach representation only in the *après-coup* of the analytic process. It is my suggestion that attacks on the body that take place in the course of such an analysis are expressions of the attacks on this primary object at the same time as this object is preserved in oneself.

These analyses bring to the fore intense somatic experiences that tend to be expressed in fragmented, part-object terms, so that what emerges in the analysis are bodily parts, such as the breasts, the uterus, ovaries and anus (see Cournut-Janin, 1998a, 1998b). The process of bodily fragmentation that takes place makes it difficult at times to recognize whether one is dealing with a hysterical presentation or with melancholia. The differentiation will be brought out in the analyst's countertransference, as this chapter demonstrates, so that the issue at stake is experienced by the analyst not in terms of a battle between love and hate but, more accurately, in terms of life and death. The experience is that the very life of the patient may be under threat.

The pre-oedipal relationship to the mother was a later discovery in Freud's work. He referred to the archaic relationship of the little girl to her mother as a "dark continent", difficult to access in analysis because it belongs to the pre-verbal, sensorial domain,[1] he hoped that women analysts would be more able to shed light on these processes. Freud nevertheless identified the little girl's sexual longings towards the mother and the wish to give her a baby.

Julia Kristeva has suggested a psychosomatic fatigue present in the woman that expresses her inability "to choose the sex of her object of desire, because she has failed to work through her bisexuality" (2012, p. 115). Women are in the impossible positions of wanting their mothers *and* their fathers in one and the same love object. This constitutes an inherent bisexuality in women in that the love for the mother is never given up.

I believe that melancholia for the mother may be encountered in the analysis of women and that it is potentially intensified in the analysis of women by women analysts.

Melancholia, in contrast to mourning, is characterized by the experience of the individual not consciously knowing what has been lost; it is related, in some way, to an object-loss that is withdrawn from consciousness. It is my suggestion that *it is only in the analytic process that the lost, primary erotic object will be found and constituted in the vicissitudes of the transference and countertransference.*

Freud also states that "in mourning it is the world which has become poor and empty; in melancholia it is the ego itself" (1917e, p. 246); the patient represents his ego to us as worthless. This, Freud explains, is due to ambivalence. The analysis of a melancholic patient may thus lead to potential impasses that could give rise to a sadomasochistic relationship in the analysis.

There are interconnected ideas in this thinking:

1   The attachment to the lost primary object is preserved in a melancholic, invisible way, and the longing to which it is connected might only reach representation in the *après coup* of the analytic process. The links between this primary love, melancholia and the irrepresentable in analyses of women, as well as their representation reached through the vicissitudes of the transference and countertransference, are explored further here.

2   There is an attempt in many of these analyses to organize such inchoate, at times frightening bodily experiences into a sadomasochistic relationship with the female analyst. The sadomasochism and the suffering that it entails are, however, secondary to the melancholy that such experiences mask. This perspective

raises profound questions of technique in that interpretations that focus on the destructive function of the sadistic attacks (on the self and other) may miss the underlying longings that these attacks conceal. Green identified a crucial point of technique: "to interpret hatred in structures which take on depressive characteristics amounts to never approaching the primary core of this constellation" (1986a, p. 146). This echoes something that Riviere had stated: "Nothing will lead more surely to a negative therapeutic reaction in the patient than failure to recognize anything but the aggression in his material" (1936, p. 310).

3    The somatic in psychoanalysis must include unconscious phantasies about the body. This perspective evokes what Freud referred to as the mysterious leap from the psychic into the somatic that was the foundation of psychoanalysis in the studies of hysteria. In psychoanalysis, the somatic is intrinsically linked to the sexual and includes infantile phantasy life.

4    The somatic is indissolubly linked to the primary relationship to the maternal object.

## Hypothesis: the core conflict and bodily symptoms

It is perhaps not surprising that so many women's struggle to turn away and separate from their mothers involves a bodily symptom. Most of the analyses described in *Female Experience: Four Generations of Women Analysts on Work with Women* (Raphael-Leff & Perelberg, 1997) involved a bodily symptom. Thus, Enid Balint suggested that a woman needs to feel that she was satisfied by her mother's body as an infant in order to feel that her own body satisfied her mother (Balint, 1997). She described the way in which her two women patients' sexuality was an expression of their relationship to their mothers (Balint, 1997). Burgner (1997) discussed the analysis of a 17-year-old bulimic girl who had attempted suicide. For her patient, Cara, bingeing and vomiting were her only possession and her way of separating from her mother, whom she experienced as intrusive and invasive. Mother and daughter were bound to each other through a crazy and addictive sexuality. The transference–countertransference was an important source of information about the patient's affective states and one that allowed the patient's preverbal states of mind to be understood in the process. Birksted-Breen discussed the case of an anorexic patient in terms of "her wish for, and fear of, fusion with her mother" (1989, p. 30). She suggested that in the anorexic patient there is a disturbance in the area of symbolization that does not allow a space to be developed between mother and daughter. Whereas in the boy this conflict might lead to a perversion, in the case of her patient it leads to anorexia as an attempt to have a body that is different from her mother's (Birksted-Breen, 1989). She quotes from Boris, who discusses fusion in terms of a "not me" and "not you" space (Boris, 1984, p. 319), and suggests that the anorexic girl fails to maintain a transitional space in the relationship to her mother.

My patient Maria presented a series of bodily symptoms in the course of her analysis. I understood the convulsive twitching that she showed throughout many months on the couch as "the concrete experience of her contact with me, where she felt both excited and attacked by me". They expressed her experience of a maternal intrusion that felt murderous in the transference, as well as her bodily discharge of her murderous and erotic feelings towards me (Perelberg, 1997c, p. 67; see also Perelberg, 1996, 2016).

In my introduction to *Female Experience* (1997a) I suggested that many of the bodily experiences of some women seen in clinical practice represent attempts to have a body and a sense of self that are separate from the mother. At the same time, these symptoms seem to represent an aspect of the relationship with the mother that has not been properly internalized: this is the mother as protector against the child's own sexual and destructive phantasies.

What is also a source of struggle is the primary erotic and ambivalent relationship to the mother. Symptoms may have a paradoxical function, thus expressing the conflict between longing for and fear of fusion with the mother. The girl, says Irigaray, "has the mother, in some sense, in her skin, in the humidity of the mucous membranes, in the intimacy of her most intimate parts, in the mystery of her relation to gestation, birth and to her sexual identity" (1989, p. 133). This is the conflict at the core of perversions that Glasser has discussed (1979b), but it may have a wider relevance, as being found at the core of each individual's relationship with their mother. It is my suggestion that this pre-oedipal pull is more prevalent in the analysis of women by women analysts. Although some of the cases discussed in that book may seem extreme, I would suggest that they highlight some of the archaic forms of the little girl's relationship with her mother. In my experience, it is not uncommon that the analyses of women by women involve bodily symptoms. Is it that in her conflict between identification with and differentiation from her mother's body, the woman will locate her conflict in her own body? Is this in contrast with boys, for whom the conflict is externalized? I have previously contrasted Breuer's patient Anna O's hysteria with the violence of the patient whom I named Karl. I then asked:

> Is it that Anna O's attacks in her own body the body of her mother, whereas Karl has to find in the other, the (m)other?
>
> (Perelberg, 1999b, p. 186)

Freud was the first to point out, in 1920, the relevance of the analyst's gender, when treating a female homosexual who developed a negative transference to him (1920a). Later, in 1931, he also emphasized the importance of the ability of women analysts to gain more access to the pre-oedipal transference in female patients (1931b). It has been women analysts who have mostly written about the analysis of women in a way that takes into account their gender and sexuality in the transference (Perelberg, 1997a). Why should that be? Might it be that a bodily identification is more easily available in the analysis of women by women analysts as their bodies resemble each other? This raises interesting questions about the way in which the body of the analyst might be internalized at the perceptive level and reach representation as a framing structure in the course of an analysis (Perelberg, 2016, forthcoming).

Many analysts have suggested that the sequence of material presented in the transference may reflect the sex of the therapist, early pre-oedipal material being more frequently identified in analyses with female analysts. Balint (1973), Blum (1971), Glover (1955), and Pines (1993) also point out in their work with female patients that there are specific issues that arise in the transference to female analysts. Pines believes that "a woman analyst's physical capacity to be a mother appears to facilitate the transference of primitive feelings arising from partial maternal deprivation" (1993, p. 24). This is in contrast with the transference to male analysts, which often tends to be reported as presenting itself in an erotized pseudo-heterosexual way.

In all this, one must not lose sight of the eminently oedipal configuration of the analytic situation. Chasseguet-Smirgel (1986) has pointed out that in analysis the analysand is offered a womb, a potential for regression, but in the setting itself, with its framework and rules, the limits are also indicated, in the same way as the father separates the mother and the child. She discusses the issue in terms of how the femininity of analysts – whether male or female – affects their professional practice. I have come to think, nevertheless, that there is a powerful pull in the analysis of women patients by women analysts for the pre-oedipal domain to express itself more vividly.

The following clinical case illustrates a five-times-a-week analysis that enabled me to deepen these ideas.

## Emma

Emma came to analysis in her early twenties because of her constant intense anxiety that had a paralysing effect on her life. She came from a Latin American country, and the analysis was carried out in her mother tongue. Emma had an exacerbated preoccupation with her body and experienced different kinds of transient ailments that tended to abate when anxiety subsided. She was also extremely anxious at the first consultation and could not decide whether she wanted to come to see me again. Looking at the books in my consulting room, she was concerned that I would not have a space for her in my mind – a transferential expression of her relationship to her father, a famous novelist who, she felt, had not had a space in his mind for her, especially after her mother had died. Emma had experienced her father as more focused on his older son, who had followed in his footsteps and was also a well-known writer.

Emma came for several consultations before she was able to decide to come for analysis, and she was reluctant to lie on the couch. After a few months of sitting in a chair facing me, she eventually did lie on the couch and started a five-times-a-week analytic process. In the very first dream she brought after lying on the couch, *I had joined her and we were locked in an erotic embrace*. That first dream, after she had been reluctant to lie on the couch, alerted me to the pull of the erotic pre-oedipal domain that she felt she had to protect herself from.

The first years of Emma's analysis were dominated by accounts of the traumatic events of her life. As a young child she had had a very close relationship with her mother and remembered wanting to follow her everywhere. Her mother seemed to have been very dedicated and loving to both her children. She had been a pianist until before her children were born, but she had retired after their birth and only performed occasionally. The family lived in a major city in Latin America. They constituted a small family, as neither parent had siblings. They spent their weekends at a farm two hours away that had been in the mother's family for many generations. It was at this farm that her mother had a horse-riding accident when Emma was very young, broke her spine, and died a few weeks later. This took place during a week of holidays, when Emma and her mother were alone on the farm. Her brother was away, spending time with their paternal grandfather. Emma had tried frantically to reach someone to help her, but she felt it had taken a long time before she was eventually able to reach an adult. Her experience was that they were very distant from the dramatic situation she was immersed in. I then felt able to understand the experience that was so pervasive in the consulting room for quite some time: a frantic, ever-present anxiety, a sense of a catastrophe that was always in the process of happening. I put this forward to her in the following interpretation:

> The experience is of a catastrophe that has already happened but is, nevertheless, always happening.

This (open) interpretation (Perelberg, 2003, p. 590) linked her constant state of anxiety to the experience that preceded her mother's death and her experience of being left with no help. Our subsequent work centred on this event and led to a long period of calm and development in Emma's life. She married, had two babies, and undertook a post-graduate academic course. I often had the thought that she had not had a mother to witness her development as a teenager and young woman, and I felt very moved by her achievements.

A few years later, as I raised the theme of ending of the treatment, Emma developed a series of bodily sensations – palpitations that evoked fears of a heart attack, as well as various other worrying and undefined symptoms. A dramatic weight loss in the space of a few weeks raised the fear of cancer, which led to tests, the results of which were all negative. She described them as *feelings with no thought*. She undertook a series of medical investigations by endocrinologists, neurologists and gynaecologists, all of whom consistently told her that there was nothing physically wrong with her. Eventually, after a few months, the sensations concentrated on her vagina. These were described at great length throughout her sessions. For many months, I experienced a sense of helplessness as I listened to detailed accounts of Emma's experiences and trips to see doctors – mainly men – and of her bodily sensations. I experienced myself as very supportive during this period and made just a few attempts to interpret these symptoms as part of a symbolic chain.

It seemed to me that my suggestion that we should end the analysis had evoked the fear of trauma and death, and a powerful repetition of her inner state of anxiety and fear after her mother's accident and during the period of some weeks that preceded her death. Throughout the ensuing months of her analysis, I was deeply concerned about her state of health. Progressively, as the various medical doctors could not find anything wrong with her, I became more certain that this had been a reaction to my suggestion that we should begin to think about a date to end the analysis. It was more possible to offer tentative interpretations that addressed psychic meaning.

I will give an example of a session which took place towards the end of this period:

*Thursday*
Emma comes in on time, and lies on the couch. She tells me at the beginning of the session about a letter from the neurologist, which he had sent to her GP earlier in the month.

PATIENT: I am going to see him tomorrow. He also said that if the situation deteriorates, he will undertake further investigations. I don't want any more tests; I don't want any more doctors. I am afraid of going to sleep, as I don't know what will happen during the night...

I had this dream last night: I can see the visual image of it extremely clearly. *I went to the hairdresser. There was a most horrible scene. There were all these women, lying on their backs – like in a beauty salon, or also a dental chair. They were all naked, quite old, with no skin; you could see their muscles, their flesh. It reminded me of a kind of art exhibit last year, where they were showing dead bodies. There were, then, these eight women lying in a morgue, having their relaxed treatment. On one woman one could see all her veins – it is a shame I can't have a snapshot of it for you to see.* [I had a vivid image of what she was describing that felt horrific.] *There was some kind of emphasis on the pelvic area. They were all so old.* At my hairdresser's, I meet quite a lot of old women.

When I went to do one of my tests a few weeks ago, I saw a woman like the one in the dream. This was a disturbing dream. It was a shock to look at these bodies. They were very taut. One image I have in mind is of the torso. There was no bleeding. They were intact bodies without skin. I had a funny incident – not funny, really. When I went home, I put a key in my door and could not open the door. I assumed someone must have left and had locked it from the inside. I was feeling cold and tired. I thought that it would be less expensive if I broke a pane on the back door. I was going to do that, but I decided to try the lock once more and was able to open the door.

[Silence.]

I feel this dream is occupying my head...

ANALYST: It was such a horrific dream. ... Perhaps this is what you are afraid will happen in the night if you go to sleep; you will have such a horrific dream.
PATIENT: Exactly! I feel despairing.
ANALYST: I wonder if the dream expresses the experience of coming here for all these eight years: the confusion between the dental chair, the hairdressing salon, the tests and the morgue. It is a horrific experience at the moment; you feel exposed, fragile, without a skin, and frightened that we will not have the key to open that door...

[I was also thinking about the presence of the body of her dead mother in the background, throughout all these years.]

PATIENT: I am terrified of having to do a lumbar puncture or a spinal test. ... I agree about the dream; it is so shocking, this whole idea. All we talk about now is my body, and my vagina and my veins.
ANALYST: Yet you *were* able to open the door and go in...
PATIENT: All I do is to talk about my sick body. I have no doubt that there is a disturbance of sensation in that area [the vagina]. It makes me want to cry...

111

ANALYST: Perhaps it feels safer to talk in the language of symptoms, even if it is, at the same time, so upsetting...

[Silence.]

PATIENT: ...But I am so worried about it all. I am totally convinced that there is something wrong with my body. I cannot believe that my psyche would have the power to provoke all this.

One could see the beginnings of Emma's capacity to open the door to a way of thinking about her bodily experiences. The depicting of the dead bodies in the dream was horrific; it conveyed, via very distressing images, what had felt impossible to put into words ... the way she felt dead inside, in identification with the dead mother. It also conveyed the struggle, over the last few months, to keep myself as a live analyst who would be able to offer a dialogue that would facilitate the emergence of a lively woman. Yet there was also a door that was starting to be opened. The end of the session indicates how tentative all this was – opening the door felt like something almost impossible, and Emma went back to her despair about her bodily symptoms.

A few weeks later, Emma described the events surrounding the death of a neighbour who, she was told, had lived in the house next door to her all her life and only left there to be buried. She described the coffin being taken away in great detail.

When thinking about this neighbour who just left his house, dead, I found myself saying to her:

This makes me think about the experience of the last few months; we have both lived inside your vagina; we cannot escape from this experience, or give any meaning to it. We just have to be there, until one of us dies.

She stopped for a while, surprised, and then became immersed in her thoughts, quiet, until the end of the session. I was myself surprised at this interpretation, which conveyed so much my experience of being with her over the last few months.

While up to now she had kept telling me that there were no thoughts connected to her various bodily sensations, progressively she was able to relate more about conscious fantasies. These included

112

scenes between women. Four of these scenes were especially disturbing to her, and she told me about them in detail, hesitantly and with a very real sense of shame/excitement.

Emma sounded despairing: as these were recent fantasies, was she becoming a homosexual after all this analysis?

I thought that all the stages of libidinal investment in the relationship with her mother/analyst were present in these scenes – from the surface of the skin to the oral, anal and phallic dimensions. I said to her that *these scenes expressed the various ways of penetrating/ being penetrated by a woman through all possible orifices and surfaces of the body. These were also ways of preserving that woman.* Emma felt immensely relieved.

The sequence of the sexual scenes between women that she described seemed to constitute a somatic/erotic memory/phantasy of her relationship to her mother/analyst, evoking Emma's infantile memories of the different ways of incorporating her mother and her body.

There followed a period when she told me about memories of bodily contact with her mother that expressed the nature of her passionate attachment to her mother as a child: burying her face in her big breasts, hugging her, sitting on her lap, smelling her buttocks when showering together when she was little and her head only reached that height. These different memories had now become eroticized, leaving her feeling bewildered and frightened, at the mercy of a tidal wave that seemed to destroy all the existing barriers and protectors erected by repression. Emma was seeking to understand the here-and-now her own sexuality as a woman through the memories of her exploration of the mystery of her mother's body and sexuality.

This phase of Emma's analysis was lived by both of us as a real trauma being repeated over and over. Each memory/phantasy felt like a "*coup*" (blows, trauma), potentially developing into symptoms that were felt in each part of her body, and one could not be sure whether the analysis would eventually lead to working through in a process of *après coup*, or whether it would continue to be just a repetition of the trauma. In the many symptoms that Emma experienced during this period of the analysis I was not sure whether she was, indeed, seriously ill, or whether we would eventually be able to understand her symptoms as part of a symbolic chain. Paradoxically, this thought enabled me to feel myself freer of her symptoms.

After many months of agony, confusion and symptoms, the analysis progressively moved into a different phase – one of dreams, associations and working through. Emma's symptoms progressively disappeared. Eventually, two years later, Emma was able to take on an academic position, and she started to write. A process of identification with her father and the analytic function came to the fore. This analytic function enabled her to emerge from an enmeshed identification with her mother, and a real work of mourning started to take place. The image of her mother itself became a livelier presence in her mind.

## The encounter with the melancholic feminine in the analysis of women

Freud states that in melancholia there is an *identification* of the ego with the abandoned object:

> Thus, the shadow of the object fell upon the ego, and the latter could henceforth be judged by a special agency, as though it were an object, the forsaken object. In this way, an object-loss was transformed into an ego-loss and the conflict between the ego and the loved person into a cleavage between the critical activity of the ego and the ego as altered by identification.
>
> (Freud, 1917e, p. 249)

The loss of the object leads to its incorporation within the ego, and this, in turn, becomes a way of taking possession of the object. Incorporation has bodily emphases – in contrast to identification, which requires the relinquishment of the object. Torok has suggested that the term "incorporation" applies to a loss that occurred "before the desires concerning the object might have been freed" (1994, p. 112). This loss acts as a prohibition, and "the prohibited object is settled in the ego in order to compensate for the lost pleasure and the failed introjection" (p. 113). Torok suggests that incorporation may occur by means of representations, affects or *bodily states*. While introjection ends dependency on the object, *incorporation reinforces the imaginary ties to the object* (p. 114).

Judith Kestenberg proposed a distinction between "inner" and "outer" anatomical configurations and the associated phantasies (1968). The little girl's representation of her genitals as an inner

114

space has an impact on her experience of her femininity. Kestenberg's views have been very influential among French analysts, who have indicated the relevance of the *construction* of inner space in the sequence of women's development, from being in the womb and then being held in the mother's arms to the construction of the potential inner space from the mouth to the anus and, finally, to the vagina, leading eventually to the actual inner space of the woman's womb in pregnancy and its externalization during childbirth (Cournut-Janin, 1998a, 1998b; Kristeva, 1995; see also Brierley, 1932). The three orifices (mouth, anus, vagina), as well as the sensory surface of the skin, working as a boundary, comprise the main ways that women progressively experience inner space (see also Chasseguet-Smirgel, 1976). It was as if, through the breakdown of Emma's experiences into sensorial, bodily experiences, she was structuring her feminine body in her analysis. The encounter with the feminine in an analysis may be a voyage into that which characterizes the unconscious itself: disruption, discontinuity and incoherence (e.g. Abraham & Torok, 1994).

The middle phase of Emma's analysis plunged the analytic couple into a somatic universe made up of bodily parts: breasts, uterus, ovaries, anus and vagina. We were living in a domain of somatic confusion, fragmentation and suffering, plunged into a massive regressive movement, in a process of rupture with anything that it was possible to think about: the emphases were on bodily sensations that were overwhelming and experienced as lethal.

Monique and Jean Cournut (Cournut-Janin & Cournut, 1993) have referred to a type of transference in the analysis of women as an archaic memory of a maternal imago that gives the impression that the analytic work meets "dead bodies" – the residue of mortal combat. Their description is very evocative of my experience with Emma in this middle phase: that of being involved in a deadly battle, where one does not know whether the patient or the analysis will survive – a confusion between life and death. This is also the description of the pre-oedipal domain to which one can have access only within the framework of an analysis.

I am aware that Emma had suffered a particular trauma in her life, losing her mother so early. It is my experience, nevertheless, that what we had access to in her analysis are the pre-oedipal elements that are present in the analysis of many women by women analysts.

Kristeva describes the pre-oedipal as a play of bodily rhythms and pre-linguistic exchanges between infant and mother: it is the domain of the semiotic. She refers to what Plato, in *Timaeus*, called the *chora* as the site of the undifferentiated bodily space that mother and child share. With the Oedipus complex, the symbolic − the domain of unified texts, cultural representations and knowledge − is dominant. This distinction between the semiotic and the symbolic is, however, *retrospective*, as it is only through the symbolic that one has access to the semiotic. For Kristeva, subjectivity is founded on a constitutive repression of the maternal, the *chora*, the semiotic, the abject (liminal states, like pregnancy). Perhaps one could say that in this analysis we had access to the experience of the abject, a potential disintegration of the body into bodily parts, before a process of reintegration could take place.

Kristeva suggests a two-sided Oedipus phase for the girl: "Oedipus 1" relates to both boys and girls, where the desire for the mother is dominant, before there is a change of the object for the girl towards the father:

> Masturbation, incestuous desire for the mother: here is the first aspect of the Oedipus complex (I will call it Oedipus 1) that structurally defines the girl, as well as the boy, before she arrives at Oedipus 2, which causes her to change objects (the father instead of the mother). Yet, starting with this structuring (Oedipus 1), there are differences between the girl's phallicism and the boy's.
>
> (Kristeva, 2000, p. 99)

Kristeva emphasizes women's inherent bisexuality in that the passion for the mother is never given up. They are destined to continue to desire their mother, and this characterizes their fundamental *étrangeté*. Women are in the impossible position of desiring both their mothers *and* their fathers in one and the same love object. Kristeva suggests that the cause of women's extravagance is their inherent bisexuality (Oliver, 2012). "The female subject (is subjected) to an eternal psychosexual incompletion: tiring, exhausting hesitation between unstable, undecidable objects of desire (as 'marked psychic bisexuality requires')" (Kristeva, 2012, p. 120). In this formulation Kristeva follows Freud, for whom "bisexuality … comes to the fore more clearly in women than men" (1931b, p. 227).

Kristeva believes that in psychoanalytic treatment a woman can move through the borderline state that is her inherent bisexuality towards "serenity". This serenity actually explodes the illusion of oneness and wholeness in order to love passionately and yet let go of that love to embrace life. Like childbirth, analysis – and writing, art and mysticism – can bring "a time of new beginnings and rebirths and a certain serenity" (Kristeva, 2012, p. 120).

## Melancholia and eroticization

From the above, one can identify a crucial dimension that is present in the analyses of these female patients: *a struggle with a melancholic core that cannot be elaborated.* (For the way in which this melancholia may also be found eroticized in the analysis of a man, see Perelberg, 2011.) The core of melancholia is the murder of the primordial object that is lost for ever, yet in a way is never entirely lost, because the subject will always be attempting to find it again. It is this object that was never possessed that these female patients try to recover through apparent sadism and cruelty towards their objects and, in their analysis, towards their own bodies and towards the analyst:

> If the love for the object – a love which cannot be given up though the object itself is given up – takes refuge in narcissistic identification, then the hate comes into operation on this substitutive object, abusing it, debasing it, making it suffer and deriving sadistic satisfaction from its suffering.
>
> (Freud, 1917e, p. 250)

This quotation establishes a link between melancholia, sadism, masochism and the negative therapeutic reaction in which the patient "refuses" to get better. This would mean letting the maternal object go. It was, indeed, when I referred to the possible ending of the analysis that this period that I have been describing was precipitated. The experience in the countertransference during this phase of the analysis is that of inutility, an expression of the power of the forces of narcissism. The analyst is required to re-live in the process the same fate as the lost/destroyed object. I cannot overemphasize the despair I felt about whether Emma would survive and emerge in a more "serene" way from her

117

analysis. I struggled with whether it was ethical to continue, as Emma seemed to be getting worse rather than better. Throughout this whole period, however, she never missed a session and always lay on the couch. This left me, at the same time, with a profound sense of a working alliance between us that underlined the whole experience.

Towards the end of the second phase of her analysis, Emma brought another dream: *She was in a bathtub, and there were lots of tubes coming out of her, including her mouth. She was being fed in this way, somewhere between life and death.* The memory was that of her mother on her deathbed. But the tubes also reminded her of recent examinations of her genitals, where the injection of a contrasting liquid left her with burning sensations.

The equation is present between the mouth and the genitals, the feeding situation and excitation, life and death. My comment to her was as follows:

On the couch, there is a confusion between life-giving nourishment, sexual excitation and death.

### *Après-coup*

Emma's analysis illustrates the issue of repetition linked with the sexual and the traumatic, the fractality present in the *après-coup* (Chervet, 2009; Perelberg, 2006, 2015a). A fractal is a complex geometric structure, the properties of which repeat themselves: an image contains a smaller copy of itself, the sequence appearing to recur infinitely; the repetitions reflect the structure, exactly the way mirrors reflect each other to infinity.

At one point in the analysis, Emma had the following dream:

*A man had come to install a special kind of mouthwash in the bathroom – it looked like some kind of hotel bathroom, with a huge dispenser, with lots of loops. It had a mirror. I also wondered why there were so many mirrors, what did it say about me? Above the sink, on the other wall, there were also many mirrors. It made me wonder how persecuted I feel, as if I have lost my sense of reality.*

There were many associations in that session, including to a friend of her mother's who had had breast cancer and a mastectomy.

Emma remembered the name of an autoimmune disease that implies cell death.

At that session, Emma's intense anxiety was again palpable in the room. I said:

> Perhaps the many mirrors present in the dream refer to the question of how many mirrors one actually needs in order to see what has been happening, that *can lead to cell death…*?

I also had in mind at that moment the many times Emma had looked at her vagina in the mirror, trying to identify what was happening to it. The looking in the mirror at her hidden, feminine sex seemed to be a way of working out the castration of her sex. How many mirrors does she have to look at to come to terms with that fact? These were my thoughts, which linked Emma's experience of being ill to her femininity, but I did not say so to her at that moment.

One is reminded of Freud looking at Irma's throat. Jacques Lacan described Freud's action of looking inside the throat of Irma in the following way:

> There's a horrendous discovery here, that of the flesh one never sees, the foundation of things, the other side of the head, of the face, the secretory glands *par excellence*, the flesh from which everything exudes, at the very heart of the mystery, the flesh in as much as it is suffering, is formless, in as much as its form in itself is something which provokes anxiety.
>
> (Lacan, 1978, p. 154)

The various phases of Emma's analysis were like these mirrors that reflected each other, like a fractal. In Phase 1, Emma repeated her anxiety in the face of the mother who had died, and her attempts to reach someone to help her. In Phase 2, chronologically later in the analysis but referring to earlier experiences and phantasies in her life, there was a breakdown into the somatic. We were facing incomprehensible, despairing attempts to reach an Other who is not there, indifferent, cruel even – a mirror image of Phase 1, but in the language of a regressive pull: there was no narrative, but acts and sensations being repeated over and over. This second phase can be described as one of pure trauma, with no content, expressed as a fear of a breakdown that has already occurred. At the beginning of the third phase, the conscious fantasies came to the fore. They now had a more explicit sexual content and an explicit sexual longing for the analyst. It reminded me of what Godfrind has called good *secondary feminine homosexuality* (2001), which is essential in the structuring of femininity. The erotic rapprochement with the mother/analyst and the identification it enables open the way to the blossoming of a feminine sexuality.

On reflecting on the terms *Nachträglichkeit* and *après-coup*, Chervet has pointed to the masochism present in the word *tragen*, which suggests "to bear" and "to carry" (2009). *Coup* thus refers to sadomasochism, but equally to the traumatic. *Après-coup* points to the essentially traumatic dimension of a psychoanalytic treatment as well as to what enables that to be worked through. Its economic function is to transform repetition compulsion into the pleasure principle.

## Conclusion

Analytic experience shows that there is a melancholic core to be found in the analysis of women that is an expression of the loss of the maternal object that can never be completely mourned (Chabert, 2003). This melancholic core emerges in the narrative of the analysis and becomes a construction in the *après-coup* of the analysis. This melancholia can take refuge, however, in anxiety that floods into the room, or it can lead to a somatic breakdown, as in Emma's analysis. We were thrown into a universe of bizarre bodily experiences that express both the longing towards that primary maternal object and attempts to separate from it: love and the hate towards the primary object come to the fore in a potentially lethal battle.

One can identify the different scenes in Emma's analysis. The first register was directed towards external events in her life. The second register involved a collapse into bodily and sensorial registrations, dominated by unacceptable affects that, until then, had not been thought about. It was experienced as a breakdown into the somatic, before symbolization could take place in the third phase, in a process of the *après-coup*.

Many women's struggle to turn away and separate from their mothers involves a bodily symptom. I have often understood the bodily experiences of the women seen in clinical practice as representing attempts to have a body and a sense of self that are separate from the mother. At the same time these symptoms seem to represent an aspect of the relationship with the mother that has not been properly internalized. This chapter proposes that a breakdown into the somatic points to the following: a melancholic core in the relationship with the mother; an internal, potentially lethal battle in the relationship between desire and renunciation that has not been elaborated. This analysis illustrates that this somatic breakdown can reach such profound depths, and it is my experience that the presence of transient symptoms is not uncommon in the analyses of women by women analysts. In such analyses the presence of somatic sensations and disturbances expresses primitive experiences of fusion with the ambivalently loved mother's body.

For Emma, the father did not offer an alternative to the relationship to the mother. As in the configuration present in the analyses of the famous hysterics, the father appeared, at best, as absent, leaving Emma at the mercy of the frightening maternal imago.

As a final comment, one cannot overemphasize the demands that such analyses place on both patient and analyst – the pain, despair and collapse of symbolic representation, raising the analyst's anxiety about the patient's capacity to literally survive the process and transform it all into language. The process I have described is that of a massive regression to the somatic, which expresses a refusal to separate from the body of the mother and the analyst. This process may take a long time to be worked through. One is referring to something that had never before been put into words. Pontalis (1977) has evoked the experience of another space: words come from that space, it is not language that makes language.

From that space comes a narrative of death, sexuality and love.

## Note

1  "We know less about the sexual life of little girls than about that of boys. But we need not feel ashamed of this distinction; after all, the sexual life of adult women is a 'dark continent' for psychology" (Freud, 1926e, p. 212). If in the *Three Essays* Freud had postulated an analogous development in the sexual life of both boys and girls, progressively he was to discover the prolonged attachment of little girls to their mothers.

# 5

# FROM BISEXUALITY TO THE FEMININE

*Jacqueline Godfrind*

The concept of bisexuality, introduced by Freud from the very beginning of his work (Freud, 1950 [1892–99], p. 238), is not without some ambiguity. This is why it is necessary to clarify the use one makes of the concept. Mainly, bisexuality is considered with reference to identifications to both sexes – identifications that are the result of what is called "the decline of the Oedipus complex". In this sense, bisexuality is linked with neurotic functioning. It implies the free use of attributes associated with genital identifications, masculine and feminine. On this level, analysis is concerned with the conflictualization of that use, as it refers to the oedipal organization. Even if this level of analysis remains essential, it is not sufficient to resolve the troubles that prevent the unfolding of a harmonious bisexuality. My clinical experience has led me to question the substructure of the neurotic organization on which the genital organization of bisexuality has been built.

It is the bisexuality of women that I have been particularly interested in. Clinical experience has led me to discover a *primary core of the organization of bisexuality in women*. My hypotheses are based on particular cases, connected with particular situations, and after a very long analysis. But I think that these hypotheses, even their exaggerated character, can contribute to understanding the complexities of bisexuality in women in general.

I am referring to women whose mothers present a psychotic structure that is more or less compensated. These mothers show character features that are deeply insecure for their little girls.

Unstable, unreliable in daily life and unpredictable, they tend to create an anxious atmosphere. Sometimes tender and appealing, they suddenly become stand-offish and contemptuous, capable of a disrespectful intrusion into the girl's psyche – even into her body. Their psychic absences evoke the syndrome Green has called the "the dead mother complex" (1983). Their presence expresses a demand for an exclusive adhesive love as well as for transparency. In spite of such maternal pathology, these women have an apparently solid psychic organization. All of them have adequate accomplishments in their lives: they have been able to reach a successful professional situation; they are married; they have children. All of them have already undertaken an analysis with a man. I qualify them as "modestly phallic" or "discreetly phallic", in reference to a masculinity I shall come back to later on. As "superwomen", their hyperactivity is the expression of a strong need for reparation. The possibilities of their being successful in their social life prove the existence of an authentic neurotic sector of functioning of an oedipal quality. Nevertheless, the distress they express in the consulting room reveals the existence of a problem that has been fiercely hidden until now. They are seeking help for affective difficulties: instability in their love affairs, anxieties, lack of confidence, and so forth.

## Jane

Jane is an illustration of such cases. When she came to consult with me, she was 35 years old. She is divorced and has two children. She is working as matron in intensive care in a health service and brilliantly assists the chief physician, a man. Her childhood was marked by her mother's psychotic state. She was an only child and was idealized and adored by her parents. Her father suffered from multiple sclerosis. He struggled against the progression of his illness by way of a phallic–narcissistic attitude that disguised his suffering and created a bewildered admiration for him in his daughter. The parental couple was experienced as close-knit, each partner taking care of the psychic and somatic wounds of the other. A first analysis with a man opened her to psychic reality and weakened the narcissistic defences that protected her from anxiety. She appreciates the benefits of that first analytic work. She carries the memory of a warm and sustaining analyst.

However, the improvement she experienced did not last long, and Jane is in analysis now in a state of intense distress. This time she wants to be analysed by a woman.

## Analysis of femininity

A first period of the analysis allowed us to analyse the *neurotic organization*. We were confronted with an oedipal problematic marked by the maternal pathology. Jane evoked the rivalry with her mother, associated with the hate expression of which was particularly difficult because of her mother's fragility. We spent much time in the analysis elaborating, as far as possible, the genital part of the relation with her mother, an analysis that was supposed to lead to a feminine identification integral to the bisexuality we are interested in. But still obstacles remained, which hindered the harmonious resolution of the oedipal problematic.

Finally, her associations gave us access to the *deepest level of the psyche*, allowing analysis of the drama of the primary relation with the mother in reference to what I have called "primary homosexuality" (Godfrind, 1997, 2001). I shall briefly elaborate this concept. If the analysis of the relationship with the mother is conducted with enough depth, it leads to the development of splitting, which, in turn, reveals what I have called a *crypt*. The crypt contains the part of the relation with the mother that I have described in terms of a "black pact". Behind the sometimes deadly hate that exists between daughter and mother, suddenly there appears a bewildered love for the mother, a fascination that rivets the daughter to the mother, appealing to an encounter *"de trou à trou"* ("hole to hole"), the daughter being totally attached to the mother, bewitched, a link I call *"primary homosexuality"*.

The psychotic components of the mother's functioning exacerbate the difficulties linked with the conflictualization of the primary homosexual relation. So it was for Jane. When these problematics came to light, we shared distressing sessions during which the deadly alliance between daughter and mother was expressed in dramatic words. I quote:

Her eyes have a haunting attraction, they fix me, I would like to disappear into their gaze – the call of a mirror that suddenly smashes to bits. Then her eyes vacillate, invaded by madness. I am caught in a mad whirl, I am re-joining her, she and I both mad. ... Sometimes her eyes abandon me ... gripping her, I don't see anything other than the void of her absence. ... Death inhabits her, and I am trying, desperately, to revive her ... but we are only two children drifting away to an emptiness that is calling them.

How to separate from such a mother? How to abandon to her destiny such a mad and deprived mother in order to become autonomous? Jane's repairing love for her mother prevents her from breaking away from that vampire mother. Hate, which we know is necessary in order to become separate – "the object is born out of hate" – has not been able to operate against such a bewildered mother. "The drama of the gifted child" (Miller, 1984) – is actualizing itself, with all its toxicity. We discover a child attached by the tentacles of and for mother's love, clinging to her to secure her survival through control and mastery, an attitude that also protects her from aspiration to fascinating nothingness. But such a position tragically hinders the development of feminine qualities. The risk of experiencing feminine receptivity exposes one to dissolution in the abyss of the "hole to hole". How is it possible to get free of that mother, her deadly ascendancy hindering the development of a feminine identity?

Fortunately, the mother is not alone in contributing to the construction of the girl's identity. Totally excluded during the moments of closeness with the archaic mother I have just evoked, analysis progressively resituates the presence of the father, his place in carrying the masculine identification necessary to building bisexuality. Inside the daughter's desperate struggle to separate herself from her mother, signs of the father's presence are progressively appearing in the material in the form of metaphors of the "saving penis". A phallic form represented in characteristic dreams or fantasies is filtering into the gash between mother and daughter, into the caesura operated by the analytic work. One day, Jane recounts a dream that opens new horizons:

I am on a raft with a woman. The sea is slack, infinite, distressing. I have a wound on my breast. The woman is bending, she is going to kiss my wound ... but crawling maggots are escaping from it ... they are disgusting, but I feel hugely relieved and released...

125

## Analysis of masculinity

Before considering the particularities of the relationship with the father appearing when the deepest levels had been reached, I return to some aspects of the analysis of the relationship with the father in the neurotic organization previously analysed. This part of the analysis gives a first general idea of the impact of the father on the destiny of femininity with respect to its bisexual component.

The relation with the father is sustained by the intense love every girl feels towards her father, oedipal longings the expression of which is subject to heavy interdictions and conflictualizations. Analysis always makes it possible to find traces of the love of an oedipal little girl for her father, who, in her fantasies, feels the same love. The conflictualization of the love for father is at first due to the oedipal prohibition by mother. In Jane's case, I have mentioned that any rivalry with mother is made particularly difficult by mother's fragility, which raises the risk of destroying her. But the daughter also fears destroying the mother by depriving her of the support the father represents for her. For these reasons, the love for father can be disguised, it can be turned off in many ways. It can be masked by violence, hate or disgust. Often, the disorders of adolescence settle the defences against the closeness with the father, either through fear of sexual proximity due to puberty reworkings or through the oedipal movements of the father. This can be hidden, but also expressed, by the eroticization of a sadomasochistic relation. And we know, anxieties due to the sadistic fantasies are associated with the relation with the father. Such anxiety is particularly strong when it is the transposition of an abusive penetration previously experienced with the mother and associated with the risk of alienation.

But analysis of the "neurotic part" of the relation with father cannot, of course, avoid consideration of "*penis envy*" (Freud, 1937c). Its manifestations particularly concern my subject, since they contribute to the conflictualization of the use of male attributes. Of course, "penis envy" is the feminine problem that mainly feeds polemics, the one most criticized by feminists, the most disturbing for men. Freud himself considered it to be the *centre of gravity* of femininity, linked with his "mono-sex" theory in his early writings. What can still be said that has not been said before? I add my personal thoughts from the point of view of my subject here.

Let us briefly summarize the main features of the question of "penis envy". Every woman is supposed to come in touch with it during her analysis. On the genital level, the penis, specifically characteristic of the man's body, is symbolically representative of qualities and privileges usually attributed to men – attributes that depend on the period, the cultural environment, even the family. We know that inequalities still weigh on a woman's destiny, in relation to professional success, sexual freedom, and so forth … and it is for this reason that girls feel interest, curiosity but also envy for the symbolic penis. This envy is associated with a woman's intense fantasies of stealing the prerogatives of men in order to assert her femininity, actualizing a rivalry with the penis at stake. The violence associated with the theft of the penis is responsible in a woman for the inhibition of the use, by identification, of the paternal attributes experienced as a guilty appropriation.

Janine Chasseguet-Smirgel (1964b) has described an interesting compromise to resolving this problem. She imputes, as a counterinvestment to the sadism associated with the desire to steal the penis, the existence, for the girl, of an attitude of being the *"bras droit"* – the "right hand" – of the father. It is true that penis envy expresses itself differently according to the violence, the aggressiveness and even, of course, the sadism linked with it, and such a compromise can be useful. Nevertheless, a long period of analysis will be necessary to reach an appeasement of penis envy, liberating the woman from hindrances that prevent her from using the resources owed to paternal identifications experienced until now as usurped from father, forbidden to women. In this way, such an appeasement contributes largely to the unfolding of a harmonious femininity taking part in a well-balanced bisexuality.

Let us come back to Jane. At a genital level, she was a good illustration of Chasseguet-Smirgel's hypothesis. The analysis has revealed a paternal identification, which sustains her professional accomplishments, but at the price of her subordination to the "chief" – a man she admires and with whom she works as his "right hand", corresponding to the "modestly phallic" I discussed above. Nevertheless, even if an apparently satisfactory evolution of the relation with masculinity at a neurotic level was evident, I was struck by the permanence of hindrances that still interfere with her use of masculine attributes. I was particularly sensitive to the idealization of the father that still remained. Behind the disgust, criticism, violence that still could be expressed, the analysis showed more and more her fidelity and attachment to the image of an idealized father, an image fiercely defended and preserved in continuity with the image developed by the oedipal little girl. It seemed that something remained in suspense, an unsatisfied interest, sometimes violent, towards something male, which intrigued me, as well as a "phallic demand", claimed with accents full of revenge, which were still masking the expression of a calm femininity. I felt an uneasiness without being able to understand its origin. What was it, around the question of masculinity, that still preoccupied Jane, preventing her from profiting from a harmonious development of her femininity, enriched by an integrated "male part"?

### Primary masculinity

To answer that question, I have to come back to the deepest level of the primary homosexual relation with the mother. We left Jane confronted with the appearance of male symbols that put a mark on the tear in her attachment to her mother. And, in spite of the intensity of her confusion, I hear Jane crying out her demands for a feminine identity – demands that she has never uttered with such firmness but also such pain. She is a woman. She wants to assert herself as a woman, but that assertion means a cruel separation from mother. The tearing apart she wants is experienced in violent pain and necessitates considerable energy.

Also, linked with the analysis of the separation from the primary mother, Jane cries out in a desperate appeal to the father as a support to the separation. Theoretically, we know the function of "the third" as a foundation of psychic life, the presence of the father providing the birth of symbolization. But it is one thing to theorize, and another to discover clinically how such a problematic appears. In the material, the recourse to father's love, to a male love able to sustain the daughter's attempt to escape from mother's ascendancy, is pathetic; the deadly power of attraction of such a mother needs an antidote strong enough to allow her to resist the siren song. And that antidote is one that the daughter hopes to find in the image of an omnipotent, powerful father.

We are reaching analytic moments that awaken an archaic functioning specific to the solicitation of problematics of splitting. Parallel to the crypt that contains the primary characteristics of the relation with the mother, another crypt is revealed through the recourse to the father. Disclosure of that core reveals its archaism by the radicalism of its mechanisms. Envy of the omnipotence of the father expresses itself with violence. I think we are coming into contact with the substructure of penis envy. Its principal quality here is, paradoxically, as a saving penis, a protector against the mother. So the penis loses its quality as a partial object, a signifier of male attributes, and becomes a phallic antidote with respect to the "narcissistic hole" hollowed out by her existential dependency on the mother. But to succeed in that mission, the penis has to be omnipotent. This implies the imperious necessity of transforming the father into an idealized object who could become an efficient object of identification. This explains the power of the idealization of the father.

This idealized image of the father functions as a guarantor of the daughter's integrity and femininity. Enclosed in a crypt carefully preserved from any question, it hides a phallic identification with father, a solidarity that has been indispensable to building the primary femininity. The daughter's efforts to maintain an idealized image of the father are pathetic, frantic. The girl has developed her identity thanks to her identification with the paternal qualities able to sustain her efforts to avoid the alienating identification with mother. One can think that these particularities – control, mastery, phallic assertion – are those the father has used to differentiate himself from his own mother. We know the specific difficulties a boy meets in his development. Like the girl, the boy encounters the mother as his first object of identification – a primary feminine identification – so that the boy then has to summon up considerable energy in order to develop a male identity. Hence the qualities just pointed out – narcissistic defences erected to protect oneself from the primary mother – could be considered as specifically male, the male qualities included in the primary individuation process. I will go even further in my hypothesis: might it not be the existence of this basic core to which we can attribute women's unconscious bias in support of these male qualities, participating in that way in the cultural phallocentric prejudices we know so well...?

Exceptional qualities, magnified by the daughter, are attributed to the father. The choice of these qualities is not innocent: the power attributed to the father is intended to counter the terrifying fascination aroused by the mother and the threat represented by the temptation of giving herself to the mother – "mad, she and I". So, it is not surprising that the essential qualities the daughter attributes to the father and that she wants to be identified with are those that permit her to protect herself against being swallowed up by the mother: mastery, control, assertion: these are the very qualities that are considered to be "male" – even "phallic" – by our culture.

Nevertheless, these early identification processes establish the substructure of the "male part" of primary bisexuality, a component of feminine identity. The excess of "phallic attitudes" of certain women I have described is the manifestation of these primary identifications with the idealized father, which are necessary to protect oneself from the mother. "Penis envy" is finding here its basic roots – a "narcissistic penis". This phallic identification sheds a new light on the problematic of the "right hand of the father" that I mentioned earlier. Such an attitude now appears also as a way of contributing to maintaining paternal omnipotence, responsible at the same time for an undamaged image of the father but also for the protection it ensures for the mother.

## When the crypt is cracking

At the same time that analysis of the relationship with the primary mother is going on, the analytic work is also aimed at de-idealizing the image of the father. This process is a very difficult one. To abandon the image of a sustaining, strong, reliable father, loved and admired, and to acknowledge the reality of a human father, fallible, fragile, and sometimes also weak and contemptible, is a very painful moment. And that is what the material shows: the daughter's illusions are breaking down, and she is no longer the dupe of her father's semblance of power expressed by phallic–narcissistic characteristics, nor of his efforts to maintain a control, the obsessive rigidity of which is now appearing. Disappointed love, hurt love, has to be integrated by the daughter into the new reality she has to face. But it is also a narcissistic wound with which she is confronted. She has to alter her narcissistic organization, in which the identification with father constitutes a central element. Behind the images of idealized identification, images of a castrated, damaged, diminished masculinity are appearing. Feelings of impotence, inferiority, grief, even shame also arise during this painful period of the analysis. And it is amazing to discover the mechanisms of disavowal that have contributed to the construction of the father's idealized image. It is with perplexity, sometimes bewilderment, even incomprehension, that the daughter is questioning herself about her blindness. In Jane's words:

> How has it been possible to deny to such a degree what he was, to shut my eyes to reality? However, I think I knew, I had a presentiment, but no, it is not possible. ... I didn't know more ... however, I knew. ... Today, I can only cry because of his mediocrity, his coldness, our endless distance ... and experience my hatred for what he never has been, for what he didn't give to me ...

She is simultaneously both questioning the qualities of her father's love for his daughter and acknowledging her femininity.

The softening of her narcissistic defences associated with this stage in the analytic work allows us access to violent fantasies of the primal scene hidden up to now behind the idealized image of a narcissistically fused couple. Now that this image is changing, archaic images of masculinity and femininity are emerging. Femininity is associated with the "feminine hollow", threatening, by the fascination it awakens, to being mortally swallowed up. Masculinity, on the other hand, is associated with the erect, piercing, penetrating, violating penis. These ancestral images are coming from the deepest times. They contribute to a phantasmagoria of the encounter of the sexes expressed in body images, a primary bisexuality that haunts any realization based on the exercise of a genital bisexuality. Very lengthy analytic work is necessary before femininity and masculinity can reach what I have called "the peace of the sexes" – time that is necessary for the woman to introject a peaceful image of a harmonious encounter of the sexes, time for the de-idealization of the father, which then allows the introjection of modestly human male attributes, time for reconciliation with the image of a "good-enough" masculinity that fecundates her femininity, allowing the development of a genital bisexual feminine identity liberated from the alienating chains.

In conclusion: I have used clinical material to show access to a harmonious bisexuality that can be considered a positive result of analysis. It means the free use of the attributes of both sexes articulated on sexual identity – feminine identity for women. I have come to the conclusion that the conflictualization of bisexuality comes not only from an oedipal problematic but also from troubles linked with the primary relationship with mother and father: primary bisexuality. I have stressed the painful struggle to separate from the alienation of the mother, and then the need to build an idealized image of the father. As I have said, the analysands to whom I am referring belong to a familial constellation that has contributed to emphasizing the clinical difficulties in the construction of bisexuality. But is it not the destiny of every woman to follow that difficult path? Even when it is not so extreme, does every woman not have to separate painfully from the primary mother in order to achieve her full feminine identity? And is it not necessary to lean on an idealized image of the father to achieve autonomy? Perhaps is it possible to attribute to that problematic the tendency of many women in love to idealize the loved one, in their search for the father whom the repetition compulsion still preserves in the deepest unconscious.

But that is another story.

# 6

# ON BISEXUALITY

## Being born with two eyes[1]

*Marilia Aisenstein and Harvey Rich*

Bisexuality is a concept that was introduced by Wilhelm Fliess back in 1896 (in Masson, 1985, p. 212). It became a central notion in the work of Freud, who, in 1899, had planned to write an article with the title, "On Human Bisexuality", but it never saw the light of day. In his book, *Woodrow Wilson: A Psychological Study*, he states nonetheless "to be born bisexual is as normal as to be born with two eyes; a male or a female without the element of bisexuality would be as inhuman as a cyclops" (Freud & Bullitt, 1967, p. 64). If Freud speaks of being "born bisexual", he nonetheless rejects the biological basis that Fliess wanted to ascribe to this notion. Fliess sees it as the equivalent of bilaterality in the human being. For Freud, bisexuality is psychic and a corollary of his conception of repression. Its proportion, on the other hand, is constitutional. Thus, in "Dostoevsky and Parricide" (1928b), he puts forward the idea that "a strong innate bisexual disposition becomes one of the preconditions or reinforcements of the neurosis" (p. 184). That is why we think it is interesting to go back to the bisexual cathexis of the child by the parents and thus to the question of identifications. One of us has been particularly interested in masculine identifications in women (Aisenstein, 2012), while the other has focused more on feminine identifications in men (Harvey Rich).

The first identification prior to object-choice is, for both boys and girls, identification with the father of personal prehistory:

Identification is known as the earliest expression of an emotional tie with another person. It plays a part in the early history of the Oedipus complex. A little boy will exhibit a special interest in his father; he would like to grow like him and be like him, and take his place everywhere. This behaviour has nothing to do with a passive attitude towards his father; it is on the contrary typically masculine. It fits in very well with the Oedipus complex, for which it helps to prepare the way.

(Freud, 1921c, p. 105)

Though it is well known and clear in boys, this identification also exists in women and is at the origin of the ego-ideal tied to the superego, itself essentially constituted by identifications with the early parental objects.

The formation of the female superego is made more complex by the double position of the father as at once the original seducer but also guarantor of the law. Later, the girl may give up her oedipal attraction for the father by laying hold of him through identification.

We now want to present two clinical cases: that of "Byron", a young patient followed by Harvey Rich, then a more succinct vignette relating a session of a female patient, "Antigone", in analysis with a woman analyst, Marilia Aisenstein.

Byron is a young man followed in analysis by a man, and it seemed to us that this material illustrates how much the bisexual listening of the psychoanalyst can help the patient to build a bisexuality that had been undermined by his or her family history.

## Byron's history

I will call him Byron because he was the image of a Byronic hero. He was tall, pale and quite thin, with a loving and pleading visage. He was also quite sexy, for some reason that was not apparent at first glance. Byron was referred to me by a colleague in California who offered him some short-term therapy before Byron left for Paris, where he was to take up a post at an international research institute. When my colleague made the referral, the only thing he said to me was that, "Despite having earned a doctorate in his field, he was 'a bit spacey'." I did not get that impression at all, but I was to later find out why he presented himself to my colleague that way.

134

Byron, who was 37 years old at the time of his consultation, complained that he felt "out of sync" here in Paris. He said that he had received a very indifferent reception from his colleagues at the institution where he worked. In fact, he corrected himself, "Some of them were downright rude and hostile." He worked in English, so the fact that he could not speak very much French was not a problem there. But he couldn't help feeling that others were talking about him within his earshot. He could not get down to the business of his research because he felt so out of sorts.

Byron sought refuge by cutting short his work day. He put in the 40 hours a week, but no more. When he was really involved in his research, he could spend 80 hours in the laboratory. He also sought refuge with his French–American girlfriend. They lived in separate apartments but spent most evenings and nights together. He said that he was not yet sure if she would be the first woman with whom he felt a real liaison and safety. Safety would prove to be a very important affect state for Byron. He could not say what was the phantasy or fact from which he sought safety in a relationship, except to say that demands and expectations of him were the key to his getting upset and seeking an out, either through a sexual relationship outside the relationship or simply by moving away from the particular woman who was the cause of his disquiet.

Byron was born to a dysfunctional marriage, which ended in divorce when he was less than 2 years old. He was raised in South Dakota – the real Wild West of the United States. His mother was a strict Christian (Protestant), and Byron was forced to attend church services three times a week. His life was completely controlled by his mother, who would not let him become the "drunk" that his father had become. Such "control" included multiple "groundings" (forced to stay either in his room or in the house) when she perceived any aberrant behaviour on Byron's part. Those misbehaviours could include various adolescent adventures (rather innocent) with his male friends or dating a girl and staying out too late. He recalled that once he was kissing his girlfriend in the car parked outside his home, and his mother started throwing snowballs at the car and grounded him for a week. He related this part of his history without affect – if anything, with a bit of ironic smile.

Byron's father was largely out of the picture for many years. He remarried and moved to the East Coast. He had a second family.

He also got sober and seemed to have a good deal of money. However, as Byron's mother refused him contact with Byron, he refused to pay child support. As a result, Byron was very poor during his childhood, living on what his mother could earn as a waitress in a local diner.

Byron sought out his father when he was 16 years old. He found a man who was much less terrible than the picture his mother had painted. He was able to tell his father how angry he was that his father had abandoned him, though he did so with no show of angry emotion. His father spoke of his regret. They began to build a cordial relationship, but Byron remained very hesitant to ask his father for any support for his further education for fear of being disappointed. It turned out to be a correct fear.

Academically, Byron excelled. He came under the tutelage of a few excellent scientists and thrived in that atmosphere. He began his doctorate studies at a major university but had a great problem with his supervising professor, who was singularly critical and not helpful, without apparent reason. He became so depressed that he eventually switched to another university (also excellent) and thrived under kinder supervision. During this difficult time, he treated his depression with extreme exercise and "entering mind voyages", where he would go into a meditative state and "travel" to exotic places. He also sought relief with sex, but not fidelity.

As I mentioned before, Byron had met a woman in Paris who was half-French, half-American. For a first time, he very tentatively fell in love. He spoke of it only when asked and then quite hesitantly. "Why so hesitant?" I asked. "Because it is a new feeling and one I'm not certain of. I think this feels quite different. She does not make me feel cornered by demands and expectations. I met her parents – nice people. They, too, did not seem to have expectations" (laughs), "at least not in front of us." As he spoke of her, I really had no sense of who she was from what he said: I could not even picture her in my mind. I had to ask specific questions to understand the nature of the relationship: how often they saw each other, did they live together? what she did for a living, how did they relate? This was all absent from his commentary. It was as if he protected this relationship from me.

This stood in marked contrast to how Byron related to me. From the start, he took to the analytic process seemingly easily and with curiosity. He presented a dream early on:

*It was a giant conch shell floating in space. It had a clock imbedded into its side. The hands of the clock were going in the opposite direction. Then the shell tipped forward and matter started pouring out. I awoke.*

His spontaneous analysis of the dream was about his starting the analytic process and going back to his beginnings. "Why the shell itself?" I asked. "Oh, that is clearly me. I live in a shell of self-protection. This process is the antithesis of that."

I noted the contrast between Byron's approach to women and his ease with me, but I did not comment upon it. Instead, as I listened over the following months, Byron spoke of several intimate (non-sexual) relationships with men that had endured the test of time and distance. There were two in particular – a childhood friend who had become a minister and never married, and an older gay man who retired to his South Dakota region to rehabilitate an old hotel. Both these relationships were placed deep at the core of his sense of personal safety.

I think it timely for me to speak of my own countertransference to Byron at this time. I had become comfortable with my own bisexuality over many years. I have often pointed out that, except for my own analyst, all my mentors since elementary school happened to have been women. I think this a fortunate occurrence. I like being a man and I like men as friends and colleagues, and, thanks to that very female background and probably my own medical vocation, I have enjoyed being a medical doctor, and I like to nurse and take care of my patients. Men can be maternal, and I am one of those. I hold my patients as a woman would. Before becoming an analyst, I was a medical doctor with the real sublimation to cure and heal. It so happens that I see more very tough men than women. I cannot say whether this is by chance: we know very well that Freud did not believe in coincidences. I should also say that this is probably linked to the physical location of my practice. Eventually, by word of mouth, some men came reluctantly to seek consultation with me – but they generally did continue their treatment. I found that I could be equally firm with them, but in a loving and containing way. They responded well to this – perhaps they felt understood within a good holding. I would dare to say that they probably experienced a bisexual cathexis.

Byron appealed to me. I mean that on many levels. He was physically appealing, even sexy, despite the lack of effort he put into that. He was appealing to me as a man who sought to be loved safely. I guess one can say that my heart went out to him. He wanted to be loved but feared surrendering to that desire lest he be disappointed or even worse – betrayed.

As the second year progressed, Byron was filled with anger at his colleagues at work. They were petty and at times even tried to hamper his progress. One woman was spoken of as "the bitch", and one man "betrayed" him by creating allegiances behind his back and to his detriment after they had seemingly befriended each other. This hurt him more than he would say or show. However, when I told him that he was denying how hurt he felt, he laboured to agree, fending off tears, and spoke of his how his father had betrayed him all his life.

His work excelled: a fact that became evident to all his colleagues. He was unable to see their jealousy and envy, despite their obvious manifestations. When I pointed this out, he was amazed that he had not seen it. He was also blind to the fact that people were attracted to him physically as well. A woman secretary actually harassed him to the point that he had to speak to his superior to avoid any untoward future consequences. Byron was completely oblivious to his physical qualities and to how others might react to them. He made no attempt to enhance his own appearance, wearing rather shoddy clothes and being poorly groomed. Despite that, the aura of his sexuality was also apparent but never commented upon. I did comment upon it: "You shrink like a hurt puppy when you feel betrayed rather than rejoice in the fact that they feel it necessary to do those things to you out of jealousy or envy." Again, Byron was both surprised at his own denial and somewhat pleased to think about it.

Moving further into his analysis, Byron described the painful details of a mother who literally beat him with a leather belt, producing welts on his skin, and visits to his father, who unpredictably railed at him for reasons that were not clear. He had no visible affective response to these descriptions. His mother's intrusiveness was far beyond reasonable limits. She often entered his room when he was not there, rifled through his belongings, and even took and wore intimate items, such as a ring that a girl had given him. She was not respectful of his privacy and occasionally entered at very inappropriate and inopportune moments.

Byron was beginning to connect his inexplicable behaviour, such as sudden abandonment of girlfriends who placed "demands and expectations" upon him, to his history and the absent emotional reactions both then and now.

One Sunday morning, as was my habit, I was shopping at a large outdoor street market and inspecting the vegetables. Byron suddenly approached me. He noticed that I was buying kale, a vegetable only recently introduced to the French market. He spoke about cooking with kale and seemed to enjoy the out–of–context contact. It was a cordial encounter, which lasted only a few minutes. At the session following the encounter at the market, Byron presented me with an envelope containing kale seeds from his own window garden. He thought I might want to plant them in my own window boxes.

I asked Byron to speak about his offering and say what came to mind beyond it being a generous gift, and what more it might mean. He laughed and said: "I guess I want to plant my seeds in you as you have been doing with me." We spoke of intimacy between men. He spoke of a deep wish to have profound intimacy with the two men mentioned before. "Not necessarily sexual," he insisted, "though I wouldn't mind that either." He spoke of one incomplete homosexual encounter with a roommate in Spain during a year abroad. He withdrew from it, causing the eventual breakup of the apartment arrangement. Had he possibly sent out sexually inviting signals, I enquired? He laughed and said, "Probably – he was very attractive."

I felt it necessary to accept the seeds he proffered; not to do so would be a repetition of the myriad rejections of his father. Though it was a bit awkward to do so, the following discussion awoke a part of his psyche that would flourish later.

Nearing his third year of analysis, Byron announced that his girlfriend wanted to move in with him, both as a practical matter of economy and because "it was time". He was nervous about this. The issue was once again his exposing himself to demands and encouraging expectations. However, he felt that he had made enough progress to let it happen. He even liked the idea, despite his fear of such close proximity. Byron and his girlfriend decided to take a vacation. They chose a "hippy retreat" in Spain. The question of nudity arose. It was the optional style of this retreat. He was not inclined to do that. "I don't mind being naked with my girlfriend, but in front of all those hunky Spaniards, I'm not so sure." "What do you fear?" I asked.

139

Byron went on to say that he tended to wear tighter clothes than most men (something I could not particularly notice) because he hated all the loose and baggy clothes his mother had forced him to wear in his childhood, "and, I guess, I feel sexier in them". "And who is your audience", I asked. "Oh both men and women", he said proudly. He then spontaneously went on to speak of a significant girl-friend who had thought he was gay. As a matter of fact, many people thought that, because of "those imperceptible signals one sends out". She pointed out that he showed more "excitement" over his relations with men than with her and with other women.

"I guess she was right", he said. "It is easier with men. Men are safer and more responsive to being charmed and charming me in return. Particularly my gay friends, but really all men in general are easier. When you try to be charming to a woman, they immediately start feeling they have a right to make demands and have expectations. This is not the case with men."

"So what, then, is the difference between showing your sexiness clothed and not clothed?" I asked.

"Ah, then I am open to judgement. They will see all of me, and the whole package, and judge me."

"Well, yes, they probably would, but you feel judgement means negative judgement, whereas there could also be positive judgement", I said.

"That's true," Byron responded thoughtfully, "I always felt judged negatively by all around me. Do you think it is possible to feel that as a newborn baby in your mother's arms? I think I did feel that, even then. I was always just seen as wanting."

"I have found much more comfort in the arms of my men friends. Some wanted to have sex with me. I wouldn't have minded, but I just couldn't get into it. Well, once I did. A very close friend was comforting me during the worst of times in grad school. We were hugging, and we kissed. I felt so comforted" – silence – "and even a little excited, but we did not go further."

He began to take a daily interest in my person and my office. He noticed and commented upon my clothing and any changes in the office décor, such as flower arrangements. I pointed this out to him with some trepidation, fearing it would be taken as a rebuke. However, he laughed and said that he loved to look forward to seeing me and observing my person and my space. He said that his family could never appreciate those aesthetic aspects of a relationship. He went on to say that he now thought that my presence in his life was much as that of his two friends. "I think that I could never permit S. (his girlfriend) to move in, if I didn't have you to back me up."

Relationships with women, he went on to explain, were based on trust. He laughed and said, "More like mistrust." He had the image of two men on a trapeze, muscular and wearing tights. One man let go of the trapeze and flew through the air, confident that the other man was there to catch him. That confidence he had with men, but it was not there with women. "You are there to catch me."

In a moment of terrible coincidence, both of the men from his past of whom Byron spoke with love and devotion died, a week apart. The younger man died of causes unknown; the older died of a stroke that killed him instantly. Byron was visibly saddened and even dazed. He cried as he told me about this. He set about to contact family and friends of the deceased and took it upon himself to arrange memorial services for both to be held during the summer ahead. He spoke of his love for both men and his regret that he had not been there for them in their last days. His persistent inquiry regarding the death of his younger friend led to no response. He assumed finally that his friend was gay and closeted, though they had never spoken of it, despite their closeness. In fact, the older friend – who was gay – had thought that to be true many years earlier. He sadly admitted that being a closeted gay Baptist minister in South Dakota would have been a challenge at best, and unsupportable over time. "He must have killed himself. But why didn't he call me? If he told me he was gay and suffering, I would have comforted him" – sobbing – "I truly loved him."

In the following days and weeks, Byron worked to gather the friends and family of his two deceased friends and arrange memorial services for both. He would travel to South Dakota in the summer to accomplish two goals. He wanted to introduce his girlfriend to his family and friends – a first ever – and eulogize his two deceased friends. He felt he could do this well and commenced to work on the eulogies to honour his friends.

Byron brought a dream to a session during this grieving process:

*I was with R [the older gay man] and K [his Baptist minister friend] and enjoying a moment of complete comfort and ease – no fears. There was also the presence of another person off in the back of the room.*

*We were discussing intimate things, like sex. K had no real experience. R said that he should really try it and not be afraid. K looked at me, and his desire was clearly in his eyes. I was concerned about where this was going, but I wanted to comfort him. I thought that if having sex with him would help, why not? Actually, when I looked over at R, he understood and nodded his agreement and approval. With R looking on, I approached K, who looked frightened but excited also. I told him to relax. I stroked his hair and leaned in to a kiss. I was aroused, and so was K. He had been sitting on a couch, so he lay down, and I was on top of him. It became quite sensual. I awoke.*

I was not upset by the dream, but very sad. I would have done anything to bring him peace – even have sex. I would do anything to have him alive now. R always thought that K wanted me, but he never said that it was mutual. I would laugh it off. In the dream I was quite excited, even though I had not had that kind of attraction to K during the many years of our friendship. However, he and R were the only people who understood my mother and how bizarre she was. K would call and say, "Are you grounded today?" We would laugh.

He sobbed again. "I am really looking forward to bringing S. [his girlfriend] to meet my friends and family, and be beside me during the services."

"And the presence in the back of the room?" I asked. He chuckled, "Oh really, do you really need to know? You are always there, for better or worse – mostly worse." He laughed.

Byron was feeling that he needed to move on from the institute where he was currently working. "They are too much like my family – not helpful and well-wishing for me. I know I can find a more welcoming environment."

Byron had a habit of coming anywhere between two to five minutes late – a pattern that I commented upon but did not insist on analysing. He was always winded and dishevelled upon entering. He always had a big smile on his face, with a slight ironic apology to give. On those occasions when he would be on time (or, rarely, a bit early), he would expect a grand celebration from me. When finally, I asked him to associate to this pattern of relating to me, he was thoughtful and began to speak about demands and expectations.

This led to a dark place. I think it fair to say that the mood of the sessions took on a darker tone. He spoke of the continuous and endless series of broken promises by this father: how his father with-held money that had been promised for his tuition for college, and even up to recently he was withholding Byron's own money from the sale of a car that had been completed after Byron had left for France.

He felt helpless. When he gathered the courage to speak to his father about this, he was greeted either with an explosion of invectives or outright denial that any promises had ever been made. After such encounters he felt "empty inside". He said that recently when his girlfriend did something even remotely like that, saying she did not remember an agreement that they had made regarding where to spend their meagre monetary resources, he became very angry (out of proportion to the moment) and awoke the following morning feeling that he had no personal value as a human being, and all his work had amounted to nothing. I interpreted that what his father had done – and his mother too, in different ways – was to deny his humanity and thus drain him of his own sense of the same. His helplessness was the remaining feeling state, which protected both him from his own rage and his parents from having that same rage aimed at them. "Yes", he said, "I fear that all of what little love there was would be lost forever."

The recent experience with his girlfriend was different. He was now able to speak of his feelings and not just leave her, as he done so often in the past with previous girlfriends. Most surprisingly, she was able to appreciate his distress and resolve the dispute.

I offered that my wanting to see him on time for our appoint-ments was seen by him as a demand, and that he was asserting his own humanity by coming at *his* time and not *mine*. "I don't know exactly what has changed in me, but I now feel that some of the hole in me is filling up. I think it is my trust in you and confidence that love will not be lost, no matter what in here." He then laughed and said, "You see what comes from planting seeds in each other?"

Byron was missing the essential bisexual bond with his father and any surrogate father figures. It is this bond that in normal develop-ment protects boys from their instinctual fear of others.

It seems to us that Byron is one those patients – men or women – who present flaws in the construction of their bisexuality. Our hypothesis is that this had its origin in infantile suffering, where, setting aside mournings and losses, there may have been a lack of bisexual investment by the two parents.

The fact that he was invested in by the father as a boy but also as a little girl whose grace and elegance the father admired, and by the mother as the future man and also as the little girl whom this mother liked to cuddle, permitted the construction of psychic bisexuality suited to opening up a wide range of possible identifications and, consequently, of rich and varied human relationships.

The vicissitudes of a lack of bisexuality are very diverse and can range from active homosexuality that aims to avoid psychic bisexuality to homophobia, or to conditions such as "social phobias", which conceal a terror of linking.

In Byron, a heterosexual young man, an openly declared bisexuality aimed to hide the failure of psychic bisexuality and his fear of relationships with women.

When he asked for an analysis, Byron did speak of himself as either homosexual or bisexual; he complained of difficulties in forming relations with others rather than of difficulties of identity. He had never known his parents as a couple. His mother had prevented him from investing in his father in any way and even deprived him of the material support that this father wanted to give him. How, then, did this mother, whom we imagine to be a "phallic narcissistic" personality, invest in him?

We would say that she probably wanted him to replace his father without resembling him. Consequently, she prevented him from having any access to his own passivity. During his analysis, Byron was able to explore the homosexual passive position in relation to the father with a male analyst who was capable of accepting and working through the homosexual transference. This certainly contributed to reinforcing his predominant heterosexual position.

## In women

The female Oedipus complex is more complicated than the male's. It presupposes a prehistory that Freud called the Minoan–Mycenean period, due to its tie with the mother. If prior to any object-choice the first identification is with the father, then, because of her pre-oedipal attachment, the young girl will identify with her mother. This is a tender pre-oedipal phase of attachment that is critical for the establishment of all later identifications. The girl's primary identification with her mother is closely related to primary homosexuality. In *Totem and Taboo* (1912–13), Freud mentions in this regard a verse from the Bible: "This one is bone of my bone and flesh of my flesh." In the course of her oedipal development, the girl will turn away from her mother, who becomes a rival. The post-oedipal identifications with the father represent a pathway towards resolving the complex: she takes hold of the object through identification so as to renounce it erotically.


## Antigone

Our second vignette concerns a woman who is still quite young (47 years old), and who is in analysis with a woman.

Antigone is a doctor who works in a prestigious department of internal medicine. Her career gives her much satisfaction, and she hopes to be appointed to the post of professor because, she says, the department head invests a lot of interest and hope in her. She had consulted someone three years earlier on account of "serious weekend depression". Her weeks go well: she is more than busy, and she likes that. Each weekend, she declines invitations, dinners, and shows so that she can "rest quietly at home", which is what she longs for. Once she is at home, she is unable to profit either from books that she has bought or from her music. She suddenly sinks into a depressive state that she is familiar with, drinks a bottle of vodka, sleeps like a log, and does the same thing the next day. Antigone feels ashamed and doesn't understand what is happening with her.

Her childhood had been quite happy, with parents who were simple but loving. She is appreciated and has many friends and a variety of interests.

However, despite of being pretty and wooed, Antigone's love life has always been complicated. She gets attached repeatedly to married men or to men who are so busy that they are always absent. She has not had a child or even got pregnant – nor has she ever wanted to.

She fiercely denies the "nonsense of psychoanalysts": for example, she has never been in love with her father, who is adorable but small and fat, nor jealous of a mother who is neither intelligent nor beautiful and whom, "fortunately, she does not resemble".

The following session, during the fourth year, took place face to face. Following a discal hernia, Antigone was wearing a corset, which, for the last month, had prevented her from lying down on the couch. I noticed that, as a result of this change in the setting, she felt very uneasy looking at me.

PATIENT: I saw you from a distance at the opera yesterday; you were with a man. It seemed to me that it wasn't your husband. He was too good-looking, too elegant. ... I don't know why I thought that...
ANALYST: You allow me to have a husband on condition that he is not handsome – perhaps small and fat?
PATIENT: (surprised) I don't know, I don't know anything, and in any case, you look tired this morning. And, anyway, I couldn't care less about what you do outside the sessions.

She then gave a long description of her consultation that day. It was a difficult diagnosis: she had been brilliant. Her boss had told her that she was the best[2] in the department.

ANALYST: The best? His favourite son?

A short silence followed. Antigone told me that her father, who ran a café, used to be so proud of her marks that he would display her school reports behind the counter. He used to say to his clients: "My daughter is not only beautiful but more intelligent than three boys."

I thought at that moment that her father was able to love and invest interest in her, both as a daughter and as a son. What happened with the mother?

Antigone described her mother as dull, poorly dressed, soft, helpful, always busy in the kitchen. What drama was this woman hiding behind her silence and her relentless housework? I am mentioning the history of this mother because I know that she lost her twin brother in a tractor accident and was then married to a man in another village who was a good man but whom she hardly knew.

I am thinking of Green's article "The Dead Mother" (1983) and imagining a young mother in mourning making her little girl experience moments of a sudden withdrawal of investment. Antigone got by thanks to the precocious development of her intellectual and fantasmatic capacities (Green, 1983, p. 180) but would find her "dead mother" again at the weekends, identifying massively with her. I said to myself that during the week she was protected by her

146

identifications with an active, efficient, hard-working father, but at the weekends, as soon as she yearned for some peace, a maternal identification reappeared.

After a short silence, Antigone said to me:

PATIENT: I am bothered by your body, your posture, you look "cool".

ANALYST: On the couch, how do you imagine my body?

PATIENT: I think I imagine you sitting up very straight, tense, like my mother who would never lean back fully in armchairs.

ANALYST: Straight, rigid, or sunk into a deep sleep without dreams, like when you have drunk a litre of vodka?

PATIENT: I would never have made the connection but, yes, my mother was very active all day and then would collapse like a dead person.

ANALYST A: A rhythm that you reproduce, but you it's "*week/ weekends*".

PATIENT: I had never thought that I resembled her; I have done everything to be different.

ANALYST A: Consciously, yes.

PATIENT: I think I understand now finally that I must have loved her too. ... In any event, she loved me, she admired me for my studies, my success, and so on.

ANALYST: You have never told me, have you, whether she complimented you on your physique?

PATIENT: Never, never, never, and that hurt me when I was a young woman; it was as if my body shouldn't exist.

ANALYST: This explains why you were so comfortable on the couch and so uneasy at seeing my body in the armchair.

The session ended in a silence that felt to me to be rich and peaceful.

I had chosen the name of Antigone without thinking; it was only later on that I remembered the devastating grief of Antigone after the death of her brother Polynices. I then realized that the death of a much-loved brother was part of the history of my patient's mother, not the patient herself. This "moment of vacillation in my countertransference" in which I was confusing the generations seemed to me to confirm the hypothesis of an unconscious identification between Antigone and her "dead mother", in the sense that André Green gives to these words.

147

Towards the end of the session I became interested in this mother who, it seemed to me, had loved her daughter but had not been able to approach her female body or show interest in her femininity. Antigone had had a love life; during the analysis she got back together with a friend/lover from the past and is living with him now. She has not wanted to have a child; I would avoid making a symptom out of this lack of desire for a child (Aisenstein, 2005) but cannot help making a connection between it and Antigone's infantile or transgressional history.

During our discussions, Antigone seemed to us to be different from Byron. We would not speak in her case in terms of a failure of the construction of bisexuality but, rather, of a lack of equilibrium – as if the bisexual investment in her by the father was not in tune with the investment of the mother, who loved her for her success at school but had never been able to invest in the daughter's femininity. An analysis with a woman who was able to be attentive to this difference and to invest in the patient all the registers of their respective bisexualities enabled Antigone to say, at the end of her analysis four years later: "If I had done this analysis ten years earlier, I might have thought about having a child."

Affirming the unavoidable dimension of psychic bisexuality, Freud writes, in a letter to Fliess, dated 1 August 1899 (in Masson, 1985), that each sexual act should be considered a process that involves four people. This also applies to the analytic couple in the process of a session. The listening of the psychoanalyst necessarily oscillates in all the registers of his/her bisexual functioning. In short, every session is also a process involving four people.

At the conclusion of this article we linked the aphorism "being born bisexual..." with another affirmation by Freud, this time in "The Dissolution of the Oedipus Complex" (1924d): "anatomy is Destiny" (p. 178). It is trite to say that the actual gender of the analyst is of little importance. This assertion is based, precisely, on the assumption of bisexuality. Is there not good reason to suppose, however, that the destiny of certain analyses is played out precisely between the psychic bisexuality and very real anatomy of the two protagonists? In his book, *La bisexualité psychique*, Christian David (1992) sees bisexuality as an organizer of psychosexuality: "It obeys a dialectic that goes beyond the sexual while including it" (p. 9). He points out that the phoneme "bi" does not indicate a difference but, rather, a synthesis of separated

148

elements. The Freudian psychic apparatus is organized around the notion of conflict. In Freud's work, sexuality is subordinated to conflict. The fact of being born a girl or a boy – the anatomical destiny – translates into living the complex of castration in one way or the other. In this sense it can be said that sexual destiny is played out according to an ineluctable sexual reality. Irrespective of the means of medically assisted procreation that exist today, a man will never be able to give birth, and a woman will never be able to fecundate. She can, within a homosexual marriage, give her partner an egg (or oocyte) but not sperm.

## Conclusion

Bisexuality is psychic, and, as such, it is what completes and enriches the anatomical destiny by making it possible to internalize the difference between the sexes and the integration of the poles of activity/passivity.

Clinical practice shows how much so-called bisexual behaviours, whether openly heterosexual and homosexual or practised simultaneously, often mask or make up for difficulties related to this integration.

In a very interesting volume of the *Nouvelle Revue de Psychanalyse* from 1973, entitled *Bisexualité et différence des sexes*, the article by André Green (1973) is called, "The Neuter Gender". This remarkable text raises the question in these terms:

Although for the psychoanalyst *difference* is sexual, the question of bisexuality concerns psychoanalytic theory as a whole. What is the position as far as abolishing or as far as the phantasy of abolishing this difference is concerned? So two stages are involved: first we must establish the theoretical framework for our project, and then, within this framework, we will attempt to elucidate the nature of this object of our study which is called the *neuter gender*.
(Green, 1973/2001, p. 158)

Green illustrates brilliantly how the psychic sex of the individual depends on how it is perceived and lived by his father and mother, on their convergent or divergent desires towards him, and on his desires towards them. This culminates in the phantasy of the primal scene, which organizes contradictory identifications.

When conflict and phantasy do not contribute to the organization of the psyche, "the counterpart and complement of psychic bisexuality", Green writes, "will be the phantasy of the neuter gender, neither masculine nor feminine, and dominated by absolute primordial narcissism" (p. 161).

Well anchored in a clinical narrative and over four decades old now, this article seems to us to be visionary because it links up with and predicts a current phenomenon that has often come up in our exchanges and which we call "the vogue of the neuter gender".

On 1 November 2013, Germany was the first European country to allow parents to register "indeterminate sex" on birth certificates. This decision was taken in Berlin on the recommendation of the Supreme Court. The *Nouvel Observateur* reported that, in Sweden, crèches and nurseries for children whom parents wish to be "neuter" propose indeterminate games and require non-distinctive clothing.

We need to take into account today a certain tendency, arising from extremist feminist movements, to want to erase the differences between girls and boys. Thus many mothers and associations demand "neutral" clothing, neutral toys, and so on.

This social phenomenon is all the more formidable in that, under the pretext of aiming to achieve greater equality between the sexes, it attacks the very roots of psychosexual identity and, at the same time, risks impeding the constitution of psychic bisexuality. It thus rests on a real misunderstanding, for instead of favouring the integration of differences, it seeks to erase them. As Green writes, more than the "counterpart of psychic bisexuality", the phantasy of the neuter gender is its antithesis.

What is this obscure fear of that which is different, which inevitably reminds us of xenophobia, racism, and anti-Semitism and is leading some today to fight against the difference of the sexes?

### Notes

1  Translated by Andrew Weller.
2  In the original French, the boss had said: "*le* ... docteur" – i.e. the best (male) doctor.

# 7

# STUMBLING BLOCKS OF THE FEMININE, STUMBLING BLOCKS OF PSYCHIC BISEXUALITY[1]

*Nathalie Zilkha*

Analytic work invites us to consider, in all its complexity, the psychic bisexuality that unfolds during the treatment. It assumes various modalities, and a session may be marked by different forms and nuances. Our listening and our countertransference work allow us to appreciate this complexity and to put it to work without reducing it.

I would like to approach this theme by linking it with the question of the stumbling blocks of the feminine in both sexes, given that these hitches can weigh heavily in the organization of psychic bisexuality and in the potential for play that is related to it. A *fragmented, split or inoperative bisexuality* then seems to dominate the clinical picture more than a *silently structuring and organizing psychic bisexuality* or than a background of supple bisexuality, with its share of tension and conflicts, but also with the space of psychic play that it sustains. Unless, that is, the individual has yielded to the sirens of the "phantasy of the *neuter gender*", as Green conceptualizes it: "neither masculine nor feminine, and dominated by absolute primary narcissism" (1973, p. 161; see also Green, Chapter 12, in this volume).

I shall begin with some general thoughts on the stumbling blocks of the feminine and of psychic bisexuality inspired by clinical material, before moving on to some theoretical considerations. This will lead us finally to compare Freud's hypothesis concerning the repudiation of the feminine in both sexes with the opening that emerges from Winnicott's (1966) text, "The Split-off Male and Female Elements to Be Found Clinically in Men and Women". Indeed, the latter opens up new perspectives for us precisely where Freud's hope seemed to falter.

## Some thoughts inspired by clinical material

Why is the feminine so important? Why can its stumbling blocks be so devastating? These questions may seem strange. Our answer will vary depending on whether we are referring to the feminine of man or that of woman. It will also depend on whether we choose to give priority to the feminine on the side of being and identity or to the feminine that emerges with the genital organization of the drive in complementarity, and to some extent woven with the masculine, of course, but also with femininity (Cournut-Janin, 1998a, 1998b). I agree with Cournut-Janin concerning the valuable distinction she makes between "the feminine hidden inside" and "femininity shown on the outside" (1998b/2010, p. 624): "femininity is what the woman displays – attractive in her finery, make-up, everything that makes her beautiful ... and deflects the gaze from the genital organs ... Femininity can therefore be understood as the unconscious organisation of a lure" (p. 624).

Far removed from analysis, *Wild Tales* (*Relatos Salvajes*, 2014), a film by Damián Szifrón, explores the theme of instinctual savagery and offers us a striking cinematographic illustration of the stumbling blocks of the feminine which involve psychic bisexuality. In one of the sequences of the film, the director takes us along a long deserted road. An elegant man in a beautiful car tries to overtake a less flamboyant vehicle which is travelling in the passing lane and is driven by a rougher-looking man. The latter refuses to move over; the apparently elegant driver tries to overtake in the other lane, but the other driver moves over in turn. I will pass over the details of the sequence. As far as I recall, the apparently elegant man finally achieves his ends, but accompanies his laborious victory with a triumphant one-finger salute and the remark, "You're jealous." Further on, the elegant man has a breakdown. His anxiety is palpable. The other driver arrives, goes past him, but then returns, threatening him and urinating and defecating on his windscreen. The tension rises further, and the violence increases exponentially;

neither of them can back down. The two protagonists are found dead, carbonized, their two skeletons interlaced. The emergency services that the first driver had succeeded in contacting comment: "They must have loved each other a lot, those two."

However grotesque it may be, this scene evokes for me a lack of organization of masculine–feminine complementarity. When the latter cannot function in a sufficiently stable and organizing way, the phallic–castrated and activity–passivity logics quickly gain the upper hand and regression can be massive. In the situation of the film as I understand it, without a mechanism to put a check on the instinctual regression and narcissistic haemorrhage, death is in the air.

Clinical work leads us fortunately to think in a much more subtle way about psychic bisexuality and the stumbling blocks of the feminine in both sexes. Our psychosexual organization is not smooth or made of one piece, and analysis offers the setting and the time for some of the stumbling blocks in its organization to reveal and deploy themselves, especially as the feminine has a very particular affinity with analysis. It is particularly brought into play through the necessary investment of receptivity to our psychic reality. Correlatively, the analytic process quite naturally elicits the stumbling blocks or hitches of its organization.[2]

Moreover, although it is deeply familiar to us, the feminine, like the masculine with which it is articulated, is very difficult to circumscribe and define. The analyst recognizes it, does he not, as much through its stumbling blocks – as many sticking-points for him – as through its essence? The stumbling blocks of the feminine, whether they reveal themselves through fantasies, identifications, transference actualizations or the countertransference, are all ports of entry into its complexity.

The feminine, like the masculine and psychic bisexuality, is built on the experience of a gendered body (*corps sexué*). From this point of view, the gender of the analyst is not a matter of indifference. But some patients challenge us more acutely than others around these questions. If it is frequently the case that an analysand questions the pertinence of his/her choice of a man or woman as analyst, it is less common for it to become a major issue in the process, and, more precisely, one of the prominent points that serves as a basis for the deployment of the patient's psychic reality.

An analysand of mature age, who is well into the analytic process, tells me repeatedly that because I am a woman I am fundamentally incapable of understanding and helping him. This crucial thought, which takes the form of a resistance and has the force of a conviction, has developed in the course of the analytic work. I am sensitive to my patient's attempt to explore in this way the difference of the sexes and the limits of psychic bisexuality. ... By proxy, I feel like adding, as if this reality concerned and affected me primarily and did not concern him so fundamentally. Initially I was surprised, moreover, to find myself feeling deeply touched and tempted to "defend" my capacity to understand him sufficiently none the less.

These inner movements led me to wonder about the element of illusion that underpins our utilization of the concept of psychic bisexuality. Without speaking of individual differences, the feminine of a man is not the feminine of a woman, and vice versa. The same is true for the masculine or for the experience of psychic bisexuality. It is an obvious fact, one of those that can unsettle our ideal of an analyst or therapist. To return to my patient; behind his complaints − transference complaints in short − I can hear as much an appeal to a paternal object (the masculine element of a man) as his fear of my feminine self. But what feminine are we speaking about? About the feminine self of his mother? Or that of his father? Or again his own feminine self projected on to the woman analyst that I am?

Another cinematographic sequence comes to mind associatively, in relation to the issues at stake in this treatment, taken from *Rebel Without a Cause*. In this film, directed by Nicolas Ray, in 1955, James Dean plays the role of a young teenager, Jim Stark, who often gets into fights because he is called a "chicken". When he tries to meet his father man to man, he finds him on his knees, wearing a kitchen apron and picking up what has fallen off a meal tray that he wanted to bring to his wife, the mother of Jim, whom he is afraid of. Jim tries to help him up but his father doesn't understand. With a few touches, the director manages to make us feel that the feminine side of his father fills Jim with shame and rage and that it prevents him from being able to introject the feminine himself. As a result, he finds himself in situations where he has to put his life at stake to defend his honour − that is, to prove to himself, as much as to others, that he is a man.

The character of "Jim Stark" and the patient that I referred to above invite us to consider that the stumbling blocks of the psychic bisexuality of an individual − this is particularly striking when, as in the film, it concerns an adolescent – may reflect those of his parents, of each of his parents. They also invite us to think about how they try to deal with them. I am not thinking, obviously, in terms of a simple linearity or causality, especially as the creativity of the adolescent is mixed up in it at least as much as his defences. If the adolescent is functioning well enough, with a bit of luck, he/she will find the means to go beyond what seemed like an impasse, by investing interest in his/her peers, for example.

I pointed out earlier that the feminine is constructed and organized with the support of the experience of a gendered body. I would add that it discovers itself, too. In fact, it takes shape through the feminine aspect of the mother and, beyond primary identification and primary homosexuality (Kestemberg, 1984), through the feminine aspect of the father. The psychic work arising from the recognition of the difference of the sexes, the phallic–castrated logic, and the Oedipus complex give density to the feminine and throw light, retrospectively, in a different way, on the logic (activity–passivity) of the anal organization of the drive. It is the work of adolescence, however, that really gives meaning and fabric to the feminine. Throughout this process and beyond (since it is ongoing), multiple occasions for stumbling blocks, obstacles, singularities and impasses occur – as well as for creative solutions.

## When the feminine aspect of the woman is in abeyance

What are the particularities of psychic bisexuality when the feminine is *in abeyance* and the oedipal situation is not fundamentally the organizer of bisexuality? To put it differently, how is it played out and how does it fail to be played out when what predominates is a certain agonizing identificatory struggle (masculine–feminine, maternal–paternal) rather than a silent tuning of the identifications of the superego, or a situation of conflictuality against the backcloth of a certain – or, according to Freud, a "full" – bisexual function (Freud, 1920a, p. 151), and especially primary homosexuality? Concerning these situations, I would readily speak of a *bisexuality in clusters* (*en îlots*) or of a *fragmented* (*éclatée*) *bisexuality*, against the backcloth of a feminine *in abeyance*.

Certain women analysands in particular have helped me to approach the complexity of the different dimensions of the feminine (precocious, infantile, adolescent and adult) which are interwoven. I am thinking, for example, of women who, in spite of having sometimes a very rich emotional and professional life, feel that a fundamental dimension of their feminine self remains inaccessible to them. They attest to this by speaking in particular about the lack of deep pleasure in their life, or alternatively through the representation of their body and its functioning. I am thinking, for example, of anorexia, aboulia, constipation and amenorrhoea.

I agree with Perelberg in thinking that, in these women, bodily symptoms are essentially linked to difficulties of differentiation from the maternal object, and that they are indicative as much of the attempt at differentiation as of its limits. She writes:

> It is perhaps not surprising that so many women's struggles to turn away and separate from their mothers involve a bodily symptom. I have come to understand many of the bodily experiences of some of the women I have seen in my clinical practice as representing attempts to have a body and a sense of self that is separate from the mother. At the same time these symptoms seem to represent an aspect of the relationship which has not been properly internalized.
>
> (Perelberg, 1997a, p. 24)

In this passage, Perelberg emphasizes that this lack of internalization principally concerns an aspect of the maternal object that protects the child against its own destructive fantasies. Other dimensions of the maternal object and exchanges are also present, particularly the internalization of shared pleasure, a perspective that is similar to Perelberg's ideas.

The women analysands who are the source of inspiration for my remarks – particularly those who suffer from amenorrhoea – often speak about the impression they have of still being preadolescents; but they may add almost immediately that they feel they have the same age as their mother. Their body itself seems to escape any temporal inscription, even if only at the level of rhythmicity, a dimension that is particularly interesting to consider for the feminine. Do they see themselves as "too young" to have their periods or "too old" to still be having them? Are they subject to an agonizing temporal struggle? Freed from time? Or are they excluded from human, and feminine temporality in particular?

With these analysands, the idea of closed or condemned orifices often coexists with that of extreme permeability. Together these ideas reflect as much a ruthless defence against their own drive functioning, and against the sway of the maternal object, as its relative failure. They also constitute a way of dealing with what has not been inscribed as shared pleasure with the primary object.

The transference actualization also reveals the turning around of the mastery of the maternal object into self-mastery and into mastery of everything that the mother (and the analyst) says or does not say, does or does not do. ... They find themselves hanging painfully on her piercing gaze and on all its inflections and paradoxes concerning their femininity. Fascinated by their mother's body, these women can observe it in a detailed way in the desperate quest to make up for the flaws of primary homosexuality. The questionings of the little girl and of the adolescent that they were around the enigma of their mother's feminine self also find expression in this way. A major issue at stake in analysis will be to permit these women analysands to weave a more personal, less constrictive fabric of femininity, a femininity open to life, to different objects, and to transformations.

I am thinking of a young analysand, Ms A., in whom psychic bisexuality seemed, in the initial stages of our work, to operate in clusters, in a split or "fragmented" manner. Furthermore, it was entwined with the paradoxes of the maternal object, as Ms A. had internalized them. Her female body, which she experienced alternatively as walled-in, empty, or as dangerously permeable, caused her to suffer without her really being able to feel this suffering or make it her own. It belonged to her, of course, primarily on account of her symptoms, among which was amenorrhoea; but, even then, not completely: the maternal object was omnipresent in her bodily experiences and in the ideas she has/d about them, and this blocked her freedom of being and capacity for pleasure.

When the maternal transference reactualized her mother's grip on her weight and her food intake, one remark, among all the memories that emerged, stood out with insistence: *"Tu as forci!"*[3] The expression her mother used took her aback. Indeed, the effect of the mother's remark was all the more exciting in that the word *"forci"* expresses an ambiguity. Ms A. asked herself: "In the maternal ideal, must a woman be strong like a man?" Had her mother tried to "impose" on her this "masculine" ideal, an ideal that she had tried to comply with, while communicating to her a depreciated image of the woman that she is? My analysand is caught in this double and split characterization.

What's more, in the early stages of our work together the paternal object cut a pale figure, even if great expectations and profound disappointments converged in him. This configuration continued until the analytic work allowed (and above all until I could hear it) a highly invested paternal incorporated object, hidden from the intrusive and desubjectivizing gaze of the maternal object that I embodied in the transference, to emerge. It took the form of the sensation of having a foreign body in her body. At first, what she described made me think of a faecal stick that could serve her as a spinal column, an axis and pillar. With time something gradually changed both in my listening and in the patient's psychic functioning. I then became sensitive to another dimension of her experience: the phantasy of possessing the paternal object and of keeping it preciously, all to herself, away from the control of the maternal object.

A new interiority had woven itself in Ms A. which is related to a different investment of anality and underpinned by a certain transformation of the maternal object. As Perelberg points out:

> This sense of bodily space and mental space is linked to a mother who is able to tolerate life in her children and also able to let them be alone in her presence, who is neither too intrusive nor too abandoning of her children.
>
> (1997b, p. 222)

In this movement, it is difficult to know what was related more directly to the development of the patient and what was contributed by my work of countertransference. At any rate, I then had the feeling that my analysand was less threatened by the analytic adventure.

Psychic bisexuality now manifested itself in a new way and was marked by new conflicts. Ms A. expressed, for example, the feeling that she was not sufficiently intelligent for analytic work, which we linked up with the idea conveyed by her father that women should not lay claim to a man's job. She began, moreover, freely and with pleasure, to take interest in the external signs of femininity (make-up, jewellery, etc.). At the same time she began to "act like a boy" in order to conceal herself better, and to conceal from the maternal object that I represented, the woman that she is. At another level, her investment of the external signs of femininity also functioned as an anti-cathexis against her jealous rage to do with the fact that boys have received other "family jewels" that she would never have. It was in this context that she told me, with a certain pleasure and a note of defiance, that, after seeing a television programme about menstruation, she thought: "And me, I don't have them ... so there!" "Both girl and boy? Neither girl nor boy?" I said to her, choosing to portray both issues at stake, hysteria and that of the negative. "Both girl and boy," she replied. A certain renunciation would come later. For the time being, the tonality of pleasure and defiance revealed her underlying feelings of pain and frustration.

In the course of the analysis, Ms A. was able to weave a more personal, more satisfying and, above all, less restrictive fabric of the feminine. Moreover, the reorganization of her identifications opened the way for a certain play between feminine and masculine identifications and, correlatively, as much for conflicts as a certain tuning between them. In configurations like that of Ms A., the work of remembering does not suffice to permit a reorganization of identifications. The various transference actualizations offer opportunities for reorganizing identifications and a new tuning between them, provided that the analyst's work of countertransference helps to give them shape and meaning. I have tried to give an account of this with my patient. We will come back to it later with Winnicott.

## A few theoretical considerations

The concept of psychic bisexuality, with its implications for clinical work, runs through Freud's work, from the beginnings of psychoanalysis in Freud's correspondence with Fliess up to the *Outline* (1940a) – that is, over a period of forty years. In a certain way, the developments on the feminine and the masculine have taken place against this background, and vice versa. I can only give a quick overview of it here, one that is very schematic and determined by my argument, but it will enable me to explore a fundamental contribution of Winnicott on this subject.

In the course of his clinical experience and theoretical developments, Freud had time to deepen and give greater complexity to these concepts which also benefited from the more general development of his theorization. Different dimensions of the feminine and of bisexuality are thus entwined, albeit without one replacing the other. Since Freud, other significant theoretical advances have left their mark on these concepts. I am thinking in particular of adolescence and of everything that touches on what is "primary". What is important is to be able to bring this greater complexity into play and to gain greater freedom and depth of listening.

My reading of Freud on this theme is oriented by my interest in the contrast between two conceptualizations that structure his work temporally: on the one hand, that of an unconscious fantasmatic bisexuality which finds expression and compromise in the hysterical symptom, that is, a bisexuality that is apparently flexible but always mobile; and, on the other, the so-called "biological bedrock" (1937c, p. 252), that is, the repudiation of the feminine in both sexes, an essential form of resistance in analysis and the potential cause of its interminable character. Between these two figures, Freud articulated bisexuality with the Oedipus complex and the post-oedipal superego wonderfully, in what constitutes the high point of his conceptualization of psychic bisexuality.[4]

Let us look at Freud's text, "Hysterical Phantasies and Their Relation to Bisexuality" (1908a). At that time, Freud was attracted by the freedom that phantasies offered. Bisexuality was to benefit from this climate. Freud had already understood that a symptom generally refers to several unconscious phantasies of which one, in any case, is of a sexual nature. But the bisexual roots of certain symptoms surprised him: "Hysterical symptoms are the expression on the one hand of a masculine unconscious sexual phantasy, and on the other hand of a feminine one" (p. 165). Freud discovered above all how hysterical bisexuality serves resistance in psychoanalytic treatment:

> In the treatment of such cases, moreover, one may observe how the patient avails himself, during the analysis, of the one sexual meaning of the convenient possibility of constantly switching his associations, as though onto an adjoining track, into the field of the contrary meaning.
>
> (p. 166)

The clinical implications of the image of adjoining tracks seems particularly interesting.

In following the Freudian point of view, the slogan of the hysteric could be: *"Catch me if you can!"*[5] Or alternatively: I am "both girl and boy" and I play with that, "I show the girl in order to hide the boy better and vice versa ... in any case, I will never give up...". Phantasmatic bisexuality is noisy and demonstrative here. From this configuration, under the aegis of the pleasure/unpleasure principle, there emerges an *impression* of symmetry between the feminine and the masculine, and more precisely in the interplay between feminine and masculine identifications. Even though they do not have an equivalent value for the subject, their introjective nature allows for a sufficient – albeit interminable – interplay between them.

At another level, it is worth pointing out that, in the best of cases, the ordinary articulation between the feminine and femininity, as it emerges from the ideas developed by Cournut-Janin (1998a, 1998b), has its roots in the hysterical dimension of psychic functioning.

With time, the sexual dimension extends to the Oedipus complex, both direct and inverted (Freud, 1923b, 1925j). Correlatively, bisexuality finds itself at the heart of the post-oedipal superego and becomes an organizer of it. The Oedipus complex and the post-oedipal superego form the peak of bisexual organization. I would readily speak of a bisexuality that is organizing for the Oedipus complex and silently structuring for the post-oedipal superego. But the difficulties that Freud encountered in his clinical practice (the treatment of the Wolf Man, the young female homosexual patient), and in his research into the psychosexual development of the girl, shook up the theoretical edifice of bisexuality and put an end to its apparent symmetry.

In "Analysis Terminable and Interminable", Freud (1937c) thus postulates a repudiation of the feminine in both sexes. The play of bisexuality is inoperative here. Officially, this repudiation takes a different form depending on the sex: penis envy in the girl and fear of homosexuality passivity in the boy. Following the perspective envisaged by Freud, I would add that this repudiation also unfolds in two phases (the two phases of the Oedipus complex): the phase of infantile sexuality with penis envy, and the phase of the sexual adolescent with the rebellion against passivity. Especially as the archaic is summoned again in adolescence – think of the terror of *passivation* that can be projected on to the feminine.

In this text, Freud highlighted particularly serious forms of resistance. Without minimizing their gravity or the discomfort in which they can put us, we are today more familiar and more at ease with their dimension of transference actualization. This leads us, drawing on our countertransference work, to try to deploy it in order to promote its transformation and clarification. I would like now to illustrate this with two examples.

Let us consider, first of all, penis envy in the woman, a subject that Freud returns to insistently in his theorization to the point of seeing it as a major point of resistance in the treatment. It is generally agreed today that it can have a defensive function. As Torok writes:

> The fulfilment of desires is not a matter of objective realities; it depends on our capacity to satisfy ourselves and on our right to satisfaction, that is, on our freedom to accomplish the relational acts of our bodies. The objective realities, invoked as so many – usually inaccessible – objects of lack and of envy are traps in therapy; they are meant to mask (and therefore sustain) the inhibitions linked to relational acts. These traps – all too often – imprison desire for life.
>
> (1964, p. 43)

Expanding on the ideas developed by Torok, it is my view that what seems to be penis envy may be the reflection of a stumbling block in the process of superegoization, more often than not linked to a maternal incorporated object. I am thinking of the quite unusual and paradoxical form that early inhibitions and their subsequent effects can take (Zilkha, 2013). The issues at stake in the process of superegoization can, in effect, weigh heavily in the elaboration of penis envy, even to the point of nourishing it. I also agree with Torok in thinking of penis envy as an "ad hoc invention to mask desire" (Torok, 1964, p. 44). The envied and idealized penis is elected to represent freedom, thereby masking a girl's desire to derive pleasure from her own body. Torok adds that this privation, or this renunciation of the self and of the *jouissance* of a girl's own body, is carried out for the benefit of the mother. I would add that in these constellations, the repudiation of the feminine, as it appears in the form of resistance in analysis, could be thought of as a resistance of the superego related to a maternal imago of an incorporative nature.

162

I would like to emphasize further that, in such configurations, the work of remembering does not suffice to bring about a reorganization of identifications. The various transference actualizations offer opportunities for reorganizing identifications and for a new tuning between them on the condition that the analyst's countertransference work helps to give them shape and meaning.

## A reading of Winnicott

To conclude, I would like to offer a personal reading of "The Split-off Male and Female Elements to be Found Clinically in Men and Women", a paper read by Winnicott to the British Psychoanalytical Society in 1966. This text echoes the Freudian perspective of the "repudiation of the feminine in both sexes". It constitutes a sort of response or counterpoint to it because it invites us to go beyond the stumbling block towards an opening and a transformation. The constellation is different, but penis envy is again associated with the idea of resistance and interminability, this time in a man.

Winnicott seeks to account for a precise moment in the analysis of a man of mature age. This movement concerning psychic bisexuality was the fruit of a long journey and proved to have significant repercussions for the patient. Winnicott points out that he was not his patient's first analyst and that while the patient could not envisage terminating his analysis, he understood that his patient would lose something essential if he stopped there. Moreover, even if this treatment seems to be subject to a schema that could be evocative of a negative therapeutic reaction (the good work done leads, repeatedly, to movements of destruction and disillusionment), Winnicott understands the profound coherence of his patient's reaction, because something fundamental remains unchanged.

The opening, the solution to the impasse, came from a tangible difference in the analyst's listening which allowed him to hear in a new way the "non-masculine element" (Winnicott, 1966, p. 73) in his patient's personality. More precisely, Winnicott was particularly sensitive to their (i.e. these split-off elements) transference dimension and to their incongruity in the transference address. (This last point is not explicit in the text but emerges quite clearly from it.) In fact, the feminine element of the analyst supports the work of transformation through the interpretations that would prove mutative.

Let us turn now to the first part of this text. After a preamble on psychic sexuality and on the time it inevitably takes to arrive at such significant moments in a treatment, owing, precisely, to resistances, Winnicott describes a Friday session in which the patient's tone and remarks are no different from usual. However, Winnicott hears them in a new way. His male patient speaks, paradoxically, of penis envy, which he interprets to him as follows:

> I am listening to a girl. I know perfectly well that you are a man but I am listening to a girl, and I am talking to a girl. I am telling this girl: "You are talking about penis envy."
>
> (p. 73)

Winnicott continues by describing the successive reactions of his patient to his interpretation:

> On this occasion there was an immediate effect in the form of intellectual acceptance and relief, and there were more remote effects. After a pause the patient said: "If I were to tell someone about this girl I would be called mad."
>
> (p. 73)

The interpretation that comes to Winnicott's mind surprises him. He takes the madness upon himself and transforms it into an environmental madness, a maternal madness: "It was not that *you* told this to anyone; it is *I* who see the girl and hear a girl talking, when actually there is a man on my couch. The mad person is *myself*" (pp. 73–74, italics in original). Winnicott adds that the interpretation "went home". Saved from the dilemma of knowing whether it was his madness or that of the environment, the patient then said that he felt healthy in a mad environment. And he added: "I myself could never say (knowing myself to be a man) 'I am a girl'. I am not mad that way. But you said it, and you have spoken to *both parts of me*" (p. 74, my italics). Winnicott says that the fact that he was able to take the madness upon himself permitted his patient to see himself as a girl from the analyst's position.

We know that Winnicott and his patient had already formed the hypothesis that the mother had seen him as a girl before seeing him as a boy and that he had had to adapt to this. But in this sequence, Winnicott, affected by the transference actualization, finds that he is receptive to the madness of the maternal object in a different way. In other words, he is able to let himself be permeated by this radical otherness and allow it to express itself through interpretations that astonish him. An offshoot linked to the mother's psychic reality and associated with primary homosexuality is actualized in the transference: it unfolds against the backcloth and with the support of the analyst's countertransference. Through his interpretations, the analyst supports the deployment of the "delusional" dimension of the transference (Winnicott speaks of a delusional transference). It is this dimension that is effective and that enables the patient to recognize emotionally his feminine part which had complied with the mother's gaze, and to begin to articulate it with his masculine part through the analyst's gaze, which can see both parts. This short sequence comprises an interesting interplay of mirror images. It is because the analyst can see him that the patient can see himself. Through the sensation, the perception and the representation that the analyst offers him of himself, the patient can genuinely begin to recognize the two parts of himself and at last feel whole.

This situation is obviously very different from one of conflictual bisexuality governed by repression. Winnicott makes it clear that here the masculine and the feminine are dissociated, which is evident from the way they develop differently. As I understand it, a female element had been attributed to this man before being repudiated. Correlatively, something had remained fixed in the eyes of the maternal object with which he himself had identified (he had identified with the girl looked at by the mother and with the mother looking at the girl).

Winnicott refers to this treatment in two other texts, including "Nothing at the Centre" (1959), where he elucidates the interventions that he made and the effects that they had:

> I had a very great deal of material available which enabled me to make the following interpretations. He was telling me in physical terms how his mother conveyed to him when he was a tiny infant that he was from her point of view a girl and not a boy. ... I was able to say that the mother did up his napkin in a way that would be appropriate for a girl baby, perhaps like a sanitary towel.
>
> (p. 51)

The effect of the interpretation was that the patient was able to picture himself as a boy urinating freely. And Winnicott concludes: "This is the first time that he can remember that his penis has felt to be his own" (p. 52). In the logic of interlocking problems, we could ask ourselves if we are not dealing with a stumbling block relating to the female part of the mother. What was the issue with the female part of the mother such that she needed to project it onto her son? With what dimension(s) of the feminine did she have particular difficulties? We are sufficiently familiar with the stumbling blocks of the feminine, linked to early infantile experience, but is not Winnicott's interpretation linking napkins and sanitary towels also evocative of the feminine in adolescence?

To return now to the clinical material in "The Split-off Male and Female Elements" (1966). Winnicott's case illustrates how bisexuality which cannot be played out intrapsychically opens up and is dramatized on the stage of the transference and countertransference. Winnicott shares with us here his receptivity to a fundamental alterity or otherness by which he can let himself be permeated and carried, and to which he gives freedom of expression through his interpretations which surprise him. In other words, he can let himself be affected by this radical alterity that is the madness of the maternal object and let it speak in him.

Winnicott notes that his first interpretation is close to playing, both in its form and content. The form of his second interpretation ("It is I who am mad") leads me to think that he was sensitive to the risk of accentuating the incorporation of the maternal object and her madness. In fact, he supports the projection with the aim of re-establishing the topography where the subject and object were merged, which helped his patient de-identify himself in relation to the maternal gaze that he had incorporated.

To continue with the text. The patient returns on the Monday and says he is feeling ill. Strangely, Winnicott chooses to tell him that he has flu and that his wife would suffer from it the next day. I wonder what led Winnicott to intervene by referring to external reality, disengaging himself thereby from the psychic reality of his patient and from everything that had been brought into play between them in the last session, and to tell us about it. Winnicott's change of register evokes for me the "historic" change in the way the mother looked at her son. In the co-construction of Winnicott and his patient, the mother saw the latter as a girl before seeing him as the boy that he was. In my view, like the maternal object, Winnicott found himself introducing external reality "in a forced manner". From this perspective, his intervention could be seen as the expression of a maternal countertransference position.

But the patient resists. He clearly wants Winnicott to interpret the illness and his thinking becomes clearer: he should have felt better because he had had a sexual relationship: Winnicott interprets: "I was able to leave aside the physical disorder and talk about the incongruity of his feeling ill after the intercourse that he felt ought to have been a healing experience" (1966, p. 75). It is worth noting in passing that the maternal madness has now given way to a sense of incongruity. Winnicott goes on:

> You feel as if you ought to be pleased that here was an interpretation of mine that had released masculine behaviour. The girl that I was talking to, however, does not want the man released, and indeed she is not interested in him. What she wants is full acknowledgement of herself and of her own rights over your body. Her penis envy especially includes envy of you as a male.

He concludes:

> The feeling ill is a protest from the female self. this girl, because she has always hoped that the analysis would in fact find out that this man, yourself, is, and always has been a girl (and "being ill" is a pregenital pregnancy). The only end to the analysis that this girl can look for is the discovery that in fact you are a girl.
>
> (p. 75)

A new conflictual situation emerges on the terrain of what was previously dissociated. According to Winnicott, the defence by means of dissociation gives way to an acceptance of bisexuality as a quality of the whole self. He also notes that following this session something had fundamentally changed with regard to the interminable character of the analysis.

With this patient, resistance, which had taken – or found – the form of penis envy, was linked to a need to have a part of himself recognized, and more fundamentally, to a lack of being. Moreover he began to feel alive again as soon as the dissociated and recognized female part found a "unity" with the analyst, which led

Winnicott to elaborate his concept of the "pure feminine", linked to being. But the resistance did not disappear for all that. It found another form – it invested Winnicott's interpretation itself: "It is I who am mad…" – in an attempt to turn it into a mere stylistic device and thereby to minimize its weight of psychic truth.

The ideas developed by Winnicott in this text are far removed from the Freudian perspective of penis envy in "Analysis Terminable and Interminable" (1937c), to which Freud returned in 1938, adding to it identification with the clitoris: "As a substitute for penis envy, identification with the clitoris: neatest expression of inferiority, source of all inhibitions" (1941f [1938], p. 299). It should be noted, however, that it is in this same famous note that Freud adds on the subject of "Having and being in the child", and taking the breast as a model, "The breast is a part of me, I am the breast. Only later: 'I have it' – that is, 'I am not it'" (p. 299). The so-called "envy of the penis" seems, does it not, perfectly designated here to represent the weight of the vicissitudes of "being" over "having"?

The path I have followed through different stumbling blocks of the feminine and psychic bisexuality has allowed me to identify different fantasmatic figures of psychic bisexuality: they are noisy and demonstrative in their hysterical dimension; organizing in the oedipal dimension; silently structuring where the post-oedipal superego is concerned; fragmented or in clusters when the male and female identifications are of a different nature and quality; and rejected or traumatic in the so-called "repudiation of the feminine in both sexes". In the situation illustrated by Winnicott – which I have tried to dialectalize with Freud's "concluding" position in "Analysis Terminable and Interminable" – bisexuality is marked by splitting as well as by an assignation by an object (in this case, maternal) with which the subject has identified himself incorporatively.

When it is a matter of deploying the so-called bedrock of the repudiation of femininity and other constellations of psychic bisexuality which overwhelm the capacities for tolerating conflict or which "are organized" at a more fundamental level than them, the female part of the analyst is particularly challenged. This is never completely self-evident, and resistance in analysis can obviously also prove to be a resistance of the analyst. Perhaps we never stress enough, moreover, our own resistance concerning the need to be receptive to radical alterity.

# Notes

1 Translated by Andrew Weller.
2 The specific effects of the stumbling blocks in the organization of the masculine on psychic bisexuality, and their deployment in analysis, would also be worth exploring in more depth.
3 Normally, one would have expected her to say, "*Tu as grossi!*" (You have put on weight"). But *forci* has the same root as *fort* = strong, which lends ambiguity to the neologism. [Translator's note].
4 Kamel (1997) emphasizes in particular the contribution of *Leonardo da Vinci and a Memory of His Childhood* (Freud, 1910c), the case of President Schreber (1911c), and "The Psychogenesis of a Case of Homosexuality in a Woman" (1920a).
5 To reprise the title of a very fine film by Spielberg in 2002 (but without reference to its content).

# 8

# UNCONSCIOUS PACTS AND THE BISEXUALITY OF THE COUNTERTRANSFERENCE IN THE TREATMENT[1]

*Denis Hirsch*

## I Unconscious alliances and the transmission of psychic bisexuality

The *Promise at Dawn* (Gary, 1962) is the original unconscious promise made by every mother to her child, *which is then always contradicted by life*. It is, however, a mutual promise, despite the ontological asymmetry between the baby and the primary objects. In exchange for parental love, the child is then "required" to fulfil the parents' *dreams of unfulfilled desires* (Freud, 1914c).

This narcissistic contract (Aulagnier, 2001) also goes on to have a critical bearing on the construction of the subject's gender identity and his psychic bisexuality. In fact, the construction of the baby's internal world and psychic topographies is based on the primary object's drive motions and primal fantasies but also the mother's psychic response to his drive demands.

But how are the two psyches of the mother and the child established from the outset? Many authors (Green, 1999; Kaës, 2009; Laplanche, 1989) have shown that the erotic and narcissistic bond between mother and child requires a work of the negative so that some of the mother's representations and drive motions can still be repressed. These concern in particular primary representations of bisexuality, primal fantasies and filiation, and the mother's infantile sexual theories.

These "unconscious alliances" (Kaës, 2002) between the mother and her baby have the purpose and effect – in each of the subjects concerned by this alliance – of keeping a desire, a defence, an agency, a phantasy and/or an ideal actively repressed, denied or foreclosed.

Accordingly, the unconscious alliances structure a "shared psychic space" between the mother and her baby. They form as soon as two or more subjects become part of an established and vital bond – in which I include the analytic bond that is one of its paradigms, as soon as these unconscious alliances *account for the part of the subject's unconscious that forms because of the other's unconscious* (Kaës, 2002).

## a. *Structuring alliances*

Some of these unconscious alliances that form the basis of psychic bisexuality and gender identifications are called "structuring alliances". Accordingly, a negative alliance underlies, for example, the "primary repression of the vagina" and the "censorship of the mother-as-lover" (Braunschweig & Fain, 1975; Schaeffer, 1994). These unconscious "censorships" are unconscious alliances induced by the mother in the daughter that organise their unconscious bond.

These shared repressions are therefore essential to the negative hallucination of the mother and the internalisation of the baby's framing structure (Green, 1999), and to the onset of fantasmatisation. A background of primal repression and "enigmatic signifiers" is thus constituted in the baby (Laplanche, 1989). This organises the transmission between mother and baby of what must remain outside consciousness to protect the latter from an excess of drive excitations that threaten his primary narcissism.

The infant's earliest gender identifications and part of the dynamic gendered unconscious are thus "hollowed out", like a "primary feminine" induced in the infant based on sexual and gender representations repressed and split off by the mother (André, 1995).

Another form of unconscious alliance that structures bisexuality concerns hysterical identifications that interconnect the subject, the rival and the rival's object of desire through an unconscious identification *in shared unconscious sexual desire* (Freud, 1900a, Vol. 5). Accordingly, these unconscious alliances shape the hysterical identifications and co-repressions shared by several subjects. They are

171

constitutive of each subject's psychic bisexuality, as well as his secondary feminine and masculine identifications, in connection with the resolution of the Oedipus complex.

## b. Alienating alliances

Other alliances are clearly more defensive, even restrictive, in relation to the integration of psychic bisexuality. In fact, the unconscious alliance between mother and baby can also become alienating when it is underlain by networks of narcissistic identifications and a "shared disavowal", particularly when this concerns the other's object of desire (Braunschweig & Fain, 1975). These alienating and defensive alliances – which Kaës (2009) then calls unconscious "pacts" rather than alliances – often impede the transmission of the feminine and the masculine. They assume a different form depending on the child's sex, as we will see later on.

These bonds of co-repression or shared disavowal, even foreclosure, are maintained by each of the subjects in the "negative pact"[2] – each being assured that the others of the bonds adhere to them as well, reinforcing the symbiotic ties, with no further possibility of psychic separation or individuation between the subject and his primary objects. Like Siren songs of the archaic and the primal, these alienating pacts are formidably tempting for the mother–infant dyad. They have a major impact on future gender identifications and the internalisation of psychic bisexuality and form part of the constitution of psychic bisexuality from the origin of life.

I would like to illustrate these "alienating pacts" that influence psychic bisexuality and to reveal the "untying" of these knots of identity and gender identification that form the heart of every analytic treatment. Starting from the "heroic pact" between Romain Gary and his mother, then a "black pact" between mother and daughter in a treatment (see Godfrind, Chapter 5, in this volume), I will explore the specific nature, according to the subject's sex, of the unconscious forms of maternal and paternal transmission of the feminine and the masculine.

On the analyst's part, the countertransference issues involved in the transference of these unconscious pacts in the treatment will be addressed in terms of the "bisexuality of the countertransference". Freud had emphasised that a so-called "individual" treatment involves four characters, according to both sides of the

Oedipus complex and the psychic bisexuality of patient and analyst respectively.[3]

However, the blind spots and unconscious collusions associated with the gender identifications of each subject in the analytic couple also vary according to whether the analyst is a man or woman. Here I will address some specific countertransference issues for a male analyst in the treatment with a female analysand.

## II A heroic narcissistic pact between mother and son

Here I will quote from Romain Gary's biography and his literary works to illustrate an "alienating heroic narcissistic pact" between a mother and her son and its effects on the constitution of the author's psychic bisexuality.

Gary (1962) gave this unconscious pact an evocative name – *the promise of dawn* – a wonderful and striking expression that emphasises its universal dimension – although here it constitutes a "unique" pact.

In *Promise at Dawn* (1962), which is more fictional than autobiographical, the author writes this famous passage that is so redolent of the essence of the founding bond of every human being:

> In your mother's love, life makes you a promise that it will never keep. You have known something that you will never know again. You will go hungry to the end of your days. Leftovers, cold titbits, that's what you will find in front of you at each new feast. After that first encounter so early in the dawn, each time a woman takes you in her arms and presses you to her heart and murmurs sweet words into your ear, you will always do your best to forget and to believe, but you will always know better. You will always crawl back to your mother's grave and howl like a lost dog. Never again, never again, never again. Lovely arms embrace your neck, gentle lips whisper sweetly into your ear, and in those eyes you will catch glimpses of beauty now and then, but it's too late, too little, you know where all the beauty lies, and from this first and final knowledge not even the sweetest breast can bribe you away. You have long since found the spring and you have drunk it dry. You will walk through the desert from mirage to mirage, and your thirst will remain such that you will become a drunkard, but each sweet gulp will only rekindle

173

your longing for the one and only source. Wherever you go, you carry within you the poison [burden][4] of comparisons, and you spend your days waiting for something you have already had and will never have again. I am not saying that mothers should be prevented from loving their young. I am only saying that they should have had someone else to love as well. If my mother had had a husband or a lover I would not have spent my days dying of thirst beside so many fountains.

(pp. 24–25)

This well-known passage, full of rage, black humour, passion and narcissistic suffering, is reminiscent of a quotation from Freud about the mother, the first caregiver, and already seductive, as "the first and strongest love–object and as the prototype of all later love-relations" (1940a, p. 188). It contains the interweaving of anaclitic and erotic seductive ties, those of the drives and the object relationship.

Here Gary condemns his revered and hated mother's original promise, the illusion of an absolute maternal love that is always – fortunately – contradicted by life, at the cost of disillusionment and narcissistic injury.

For Gary's mother's phallic, imperative and grandiose narcissistic aspirations for her son to become a great writer, a heroic diplomat and a man adored by women – her maternal demands – do not constitute a structuring contract but an imperious narcissistic pact in which the threat of losing the mother's love assumes the status of a threat of psychic death.

In exchange for his mother's recognition of his identity as a man and the guarantee of her absolute love, Gary then devotes himself to the phallic–narcissistic and oedipal realisation of the mother's plans. In this, Gary finds an identificatory support to the masculine, supported by his mother's ego ideal.

A son is erotically cathected here as a man, provided that he agrees to submit to the mother's poorly repressed phallic–narcissistic erotic fantasmatic and to submit to a relative disavowal of the father. The promise of an absolute maternal love – generally a source of opening to the paternal third and introductory identifications – serves here to maintain a shared idealisation of the masculine and a disavowal of the feminine. This entails an alienating narcissistic pact and a shared denial that seals a "pseudo"-masculine.

Furthermore, however, this alienating narcissistic pact is pad-locked by a drives issue and another shared denial: it involves blend-ing into an ideal ego, remaining the object of narcissistic satisfaction for the maternal power and denying the desire for the father. The censorship of the mother-as-lover is blocked, the mother's father-as-lover is eliminated by common agreement, and each is the guar-antee of this shared rejection. Gary's ego ideal is infiltrated from then on by the ideal ego, an "agency" that is not really one, which maintains the lack of distinction between mother and son in a gran-diose shared delusion.

All that counts from then is a mother–son couple in which each gives birth to the other. Thus, Gary goes on to write: "I had my mother very late; she was 36 years old when I was born" (1974, *Pseudo*, translated quotation). This is a man's identification with a mother who gives birth to her own mother in a self-procreative and retro-procreative phantasy that erases generational difference and psychic temporality. The gender identification is captured by the subject–object agglutination, leaving in the child a deficit in narcis-sism and identity: "I have always been an other to myself", writes Gary, alias Émile Ajar in his last book, Vie et mort d'Émile Ajar (1981, p. 30, translated quotation).

The narcissistic and erotic alienation imposed by the mother – this game of reciprocal inclusion, this "*double-voiced I*" (Bauduin, 2007) – marks the very essence of the unconscious narcissistic pact in which the two subjects are held by their mutual complicity. Gary attempts to realise the maternal plan while also escaping from it in order to exist as a subject.

Accordingly, Gary – great seducer and "procreator" of unique works – realises the plan brilliantly, demonstrating its structuring effects on narcissism and bisexuality. Nevertheless, the impossible promise of an absolute love gradually turns out to be an abyss and a deception. Gary later commits suicide despite a final masterpiece written under a pseudonym that grants him a recognition that is exceptional but off-limits by deceiving his readers and society with a disguised identity.

These pretences then leave Gary more exposed than ever in an abyss of identity and a fundamental need for love:

Seagulls land ... in a moment or two, they will settle on my shoulders, in my arms, press their feathers against my neck and

175

against my face, cover me completely. ... At the age of forty-four, I still catch myself dreaming of some universal and total tenderness.

(Gary, 1962, p. 5)

### III A "black pact" between daughter and mother

What happens with the unconscious alliances that structure the filiation of the feminine and the masculine between mother and daughter? I will now refer in detail to a "black pact" between mother and daughter that relates to a joint rejection of the feminine and a shared melancholic female destiny (Godfrind, 1994).

This feminine version is not reserved to women, any more than the "heroic pact" described in Gary is the prerogative of men. The unconscious pacts assume a paradigmatic but therefore necessarily reductive value here as they concern a preferential incidence in either sex. Nonetheless, the issues are clearly differentiated, as are the identifications with the father and the mother, with the feminine and the masculine, of both parents. I will emphasise in particular how these unconscious pacts are replayed in the dynamics of the transference and countertransference in a female analysand's treatment with a male analyst.

Justine, who was 35 years old when she first came to see me, seems to have had to pay a high price for her life with an expiatory masochism and a constant, fruitless reparation of her objects, particularly with self-destructive men whom she wants to save at all costs. Justine asks for an analytic treatment because she is afraid that her life as a woman will pass her by. Her major professional successes do not compensate Justine for a sense of emptiness, inhibition and depression.

Justine's mother is described as "hysterical", "extravagant", "seductive" and "narcissistic". But since her earliest childhood, Justine has sensed how much her mother hates her own femininity and her status as a woman. This does not prevent a compulsive need to seduce men, especially from her daughter's circle or generation.

Justine goes on to tell me that her mother had post-partum depression shortly after the birth of her only daughter. She would have preferred to have a boy and does not hide the fact. But she hated her pregnancy and does not want any more children. The father, however, is described as an unassuming, silent, almost enigmatic but reliable and gentle man.

Justine was a clever baby, weaned early, subjected to her mother's phallic narcissistic demands. The parents travelled a lot together, leaving Justine with nannies, in an experience of solitude and exclusion. In a screen memory, she sees herself shouting at the top of the stairs in the house when her mother was leaving, all excited, to go to her lovers while the father was away on one of his frequent trips.

But her father at least wrote her many beautiful letters, very tender, almost too tender, as if she were becoming his confidante. They would exchange their shared love of books, which Justine read at an early age, anticipating the enjoyment of discussing them with her father in his study. The enjoyment was all the greater because the mother felt excluded and made this known. But this oedipal triumph did not truly fill the gap of a secret pain connected with the lack of a tender maternal cathexis.

The father's oedipal cathexis enables Justine to free herself a little from the mother's melancholic shadow, her narcissistic demands and anal control over her body and her psyche. She can build herself a foundational female identity by identifying hysterically with a father who cathects her libidinally as a little girl but at the risk of an incestuous overheating. Justine also seems to find a tender maternal substitute and a primary homosexuality in her father that the mother does not seem to be able to maintain (Hirsch, 2009).

Justine's father suddenly leaves his wife and daughter when she is 15 years old. He gives few further signs of life, sends no more letters and now only cathects his new family. Justine's process of adolescence is petrified and frozen by this abrupt paternal decathexis, possibly in connection with his daughter's excessively demanding puberty. Justine is also confronted with a further breakdown in her deceived mother, who relives a melancholic time, as at Justine's birth.

After the father's departure, the mother and daughter are united in shared mourning for this idealised man. Justine repairs her mother just as she repairs herself narcissistically through her academic successes. She will become a scientist, far away from

emotions and anything unpredictable. Justine tries to relieve her own unconscious guilt masochistically with an unlimited devotion to her mother whose disavowed femininity she finds very difficult to tolerate, while warding off the threat of a depressive breakdown in both herself and her mother. But she thereby becomes, finally, her mother's special partner.

The father's betrayal seems to be experienced as a punishment for Justine's oedipal love for this idealised father. Her phallic identifications become essential to preserve living traces of the paternal internal object but at the cost of a conscious and unconscious guilt. Yet her loving cathexes towards boys and then men never consist of anything more than anaclitic, disappointing bonds. In the end, like the father they always leave her. Justine thinks with dread that she will never be able to become a mother and will always remain the gifted nurse sacrificed to the other's narcissistic needs: her mother, her current lover, and soon her analyst.

### a. First transference movements: the melancholic shadow of the paternal object and the hole-to-hole of the feminine

In the treatment, an initial stage of positive oedipal transference impetus – more manic than introjective in quality – is followed by a very painful elaboration of the loss and the betrayal of the oedipal father who abandoned her.

But the dual mastery of an alienating pact between mother and daughter is then replayed, this time in a maternal transference on to the analyst-man. This transference probably reproduces Justine's early infantile history with her father. But it brings to light the "black pact"[5] (Godfrind, 1994) that was previously split in Justine. Its identification includes the elaboration of the analyst's countertransference, in essentially dual and identity-related registers.

Justine dreams that she is walking hand-in-hand with her mother, when a lorry threatens to run them over and chases them. They run away to try to escape from it; mother and daughter hide and lie down on the ground, in each other's arms, clinging to each other like a closed shell. The lorry falls into a ravine and bursts into flames. They look at the lorry's charred remains, the driver is dead or else he has disappeared.

The narrative of the dream and Justine's associations evoke the inconsolable mourning for an oedipal love towards the father and the melancholic shadow of this father who disappeared: what remains is the exciting, incestuous body-to-body of a homosexual scene with a manic quality that protects against the threat of a shared, fatal, melancholic solution.

The alienating but vital pact between mother and daughter takes the form of a pact of disavowal of the masculine, sealed and compensated by an incestuous adhesion between mother and daughter. This is what Godfrind terms a "hole-to-hole" adhesion (1994, pp. 86–88), which serves to foreclose and disavow the hollow of the feminine,[6] in a mutual bond of love and hatred between mother and daughter.

From this point, the male analyst's female and maternal identifications are increasingly called on, as he grapples with the analysand's "melancholic feminine" (Chabert, 2003).

## b. Perverted oedipal triangulation and bisexuality of the transference

A perverse pact then emerges in the realm of the transference, through various forms of acting out and dreams that include an apparently oedipal triangle consisting of Justine, her mother and a male character: a paternal figure, a lover, then ultimately the analyst.

> Justine has a dream about a disused factory with a tall imposing chimney. She is there with a male friend and a female colleague in the middle of a crowd. The noise is such that none of the three characters can hear what the other two are saying.
>
> Justine wants to speak in confidence to her friend (an older colleague who is harassing her), who is keeping silent (which reminds her of her father and the analyst), in the woman's hiding-place. Justine talks to her in a low voice so that her colleague cannot hear. The crowd in the factory is making more and more noise. The colleague no longer seems to be paying attention to the couple. Justine then talks with her friend about some very private things.
>
> But in fact Justine knows that her colleague understands everything they are saying and moreover that the colleague knows that Justine knows it. Justine also wonders whether the man also knows that her colleague could hear everything.

At first sight, the dream features the oedipal erotic issues projected by Justine on to each of the other two characters in the dream, which can be analysed in both the maternal and the paternal transference on to the analyst.

The dream features a perverted and perverting alliance that unites a mother, her daughter and the father–analyst in the transference: each finds an unconscious advantage in not condemning the other's pretence; each of the subjects represented is complicit – including the analyst – so that the unconscious alliance that holds them around a shared unconscious phantasy can continue to be denied.

Here the three characters know that the colleague (the mother) can hear everything, when the girl approaches the friend (the father, the analyst). So the daughter has access to an oedipal primal scene with a man as long as the mother is not excluded from it. But the interchangeability and the displacement that operate on the dream work allow the dreamer to be identified with each character in this inseparable trio. This ambiguous game in fact simultaneously enables Justine not to leave the body-to-body with the mother, to satisfy her homosexuality (primary and oedipal) there, to control the parental primal scene, to possess both the father and the mother without renunciation or exclusion and finally to avoid the primary hatred and rivalry towards the mother.

Nevertheless, this "ideal" solution – as I have suggested with Romain Gary – impedes a mourning for the primary object and a structuring introjection of the maternal and erotic feminine that takes on the configuration of thirdness with the father.

Justine's dream, which recurs, then alerts the analyst to his own countertransference collusion and his unconscious complicity in maintaining the alienating pact that threatens the analytic process. This requires that the three subjects are interchangeable provided that the bonds are maintained in a shared denial that can be formulated by stating the Freudian formula of splitting and denial in fetishism (Freud, 1927e). Here, this would be: *"I can't hear anything, but all the same."*

For it is certainly the dreamer who controls the noise level and the interference as an auditory deception. The analyst's countertransference work has enabled a paternal complicity (the analyst's in the transference) to be realised in this primal scene with three characters. The manifest dream text expresses it very well: *Justine wonders if the man himself also knows that her colleague could hear all their confidences.*

The father's betrayal has from then assumed other fantasmatic and libidinal forms in what is clearly a less idealised register.

The transference here is therefore not only a transference of imagos – paternal then maternal. It is also about the acted-out transference of an alienating unconscious pact that imprisons Justine's masculine and feminine identifications in the toils of a collusion with the analyst, identified simultaneously with her mother and her father, if not with a combined object (Bleger, 1985).

This perverted oedipal triangulation is sealed by a shared disavowal of generational and gender difference and the denial of exclusion from the primal scene.

The three subjects are held immobilised by this unconscious pact – each being able to take another's place, as long as the three subjects of the bond are kept associated, placed on the same level, in an incestuous primal scene that is undifferentiated, eternal and interchangeable, with no excluded third.

Through her phoric function as a *dream-bearer* (Kaës, 2010),[7] Justine indicates where and how she assigns the analyst in the transference as a capturing maternal figure. In the same movement, she condemns this inescapable mother–daughter pact with which the father is complicit. Ambivalently, she hopes for a paternal third who will snatch her away from the maternal captation and who assumes – as in Justine's childhood history – an oedipal father's role in separating and differentiating the agglomerated mother–daughter couple. That is, unless Justine instead identifies with her capturing mother and castrates the father, who is then reduced to a part-object that she offers to her mother in a mother–daughter collusion.

The dream also allows the dimension of mutual voyeurism to be realised in a perverse triangle in which the analyst participated, in all unconscious non-recognition … probably like Justine's father in the past. The analyst had to rid himself of the unconscious fascination of this scene which, ultimately, offered the omnipotent illusion that both the analysand and the analyst could simultaneously be man and woman, father and mother, the mother's daughter and the mother's mother.

At the cost of this very painful renunciation, Justine stopped needing to tell her mother her private dreams.

## c. *Incorporation of the melancholic feminine*
## *"into" the male analyst*

Another unconscious pact was revealed in the emergence of a "transgenerational phantasy of identification" with an infanticidal maternal imago (Ciccone, 2012). This phantasy was transmitted from mother to daughter like a "statement of certainty" (Aulagnier, 2001),[8] intended to assume the force of family law from mother into daughter over several generations. The incorporated phantasy related to the catastrophe for a mother of giving birth to a girl rather than a boy, and fundamentally to mothers' murderous wishes towards their baby daughters.

This is a fundamental violence transmitted between mother and daughter, which condemns to death the girls who are guilty of the crime of not following the same destiny as the mother. Well beyond the oedipal rivalry, this was the crime of having left the mother's womb, of being impelled by an active pressure to be born and to cathect the world and its objects with her drives.

In the session, this phantasy is presented in the hysterised form of a telescoping of generations (Faimberg, 1995). A "wild maternal" imago (Abensour, 2010) and a denied infanticidal phantasy have set the tradition of women over several generations. From mother into daughter, this is about not separating in order to counter a threat of post-partum melancholic depression in connection with this infanticidal mother phantasy. The detachment from this infanticidal maternal imago could only be worked through at the cost of Justine's melancholic and hateful transference onto the analyst as a maternal transference imago. Here in a primary maternal identification the male analyst had to incorporate and "carry" in his "psychic womb" the melancholic enclaves incorporated by Justine, and beyond that, by the entire line of mothers into daughters.

In a kind of identity of perception with Justine, the analyst is inhabited in the session by the stubborn sensation that a tide of black, dirty, sticky lime is indelibly staining his study, driving him urgently and literally to want to wash the study blinds! This could be seen as the symbolic equating of the murderous melancholia of the feminine and the maternal that arose in a double transference movement.

The bisexuality of the male analyst's identifications probably assumes the value here of the internal third confronted with the dangerous and fascinating double dive of the transference into the abyssal depths of the analysand's melancholic feminine.

### d. Bisexuality and bivalency of the countertransference

This sequence then makes it easier to address Justine's primary and secondary homosexuality[9] towards the male analyst as a maternal object.

The "bisexuality of the analysand's transference" onto the analyst calls on the analyst's maternal and paternal, masculine and feminine, identifications. It involves countertransference work by the analyst that specifically relates to his psychic bisexuality and therefore also the bisexuality and rhythmicity of his bisexual analytic functions of evenly suspended listening and active interpretation (Houzel, 2003).

This stage proves to be essential for the emergence of a true imagoic transference, the transfer on to the male analyst of a maternal imago that is from then on more clearly ambivalent. The hatred in the transference that emerges in such configurations entails the analyst tolerating his unavoidable hateful countertransference movements, manifested as a lengthy silent retreat.

The bivalency of the analyst's hateful countertransference involves some functional splitting: on the one hand, a retreat by reprisals in complementary identification with a hateful and melancholic maternal object (Racker, 1953); on the other hand, a self-preservative retreat in order to try to establish a third with his own thoughts and theories and so to be able to remain in empathy with the analysand. This "bivalency of the countertransference" has different effects according to whether the analyst is a man or a woman.

Primary homosexuality – misused by the violence of the passionate and hateful bond to the mother – can be brought back into play by the unconscious bond in the treatment between Justine's feminine part and the male analyst's feminine and maternal identifications in their function of containing and receiving the analysand's projections.

The transference of primary homosexuality mobilises in the male analyst very primitive phallic–narcissistic identifications and incorporates[10] those which have served him specifically as a boy for support and anchoring in order to differentiate himself from the incestuous and alienating attraction to his own original mother and his primary female identifications.

This raises the question of the analysand's choice of a male analyst and the impact of the analyst's real sex on the dynamics of the treatment. What is promoted and what is impeded by the fact that the analyst is a man in the unfolding of such a regressive dynamic, which summons up murderous and melancholic maternal imagos? This line of questioning leads us to another form of unconscious alliance that structures the feminine and the masculine in the treatment.

### e. *"Being the analyst-father's right arm"* *(Chasseguet-Smirgel, 1964a)*

How are hatred of the feminine and the potential of an infanticidal maternal imago interwoven in the treatment of Justine, with her undeniable infantile hysterical neurosis?

If the analyst must take into account the alienating internal objects and the traumatic vagaries of the psychic filiation of the feminine, the turns and about-turns of the unconscious seeking to fulfil secret desires are unlimited.

For it is important not to underestimate how far the analysand remains the author of a reconstruction that transforms, however incorporated and archaic, the transmitted destinies of the feminine, to the benefit of her own infantile neurosis and her life narcissism.

For all that, given the *"attractive force"* (Pontalis, 1999) of archaic fixations, what supports does this archaic register provide to Justine's infantile psychosexuality and hysterical core?

Godfrind (1994) has emphasised two distinct issues of "idealised penis envy" in some women in a treatment: on the one hand, "offensive": the envy of a paternal penis cathected with the capacity to satisfy the mother sexually. On the other hand, more "defensive": the envy of the paternal penis idealised as an omnipotent attribute to protect the daughter against the threat and temptation of fatal fusion with the mother.

This idealised masculine identification becomes a phallic antidote confronted with the mother's fascinating and vampirical narcissistic hole. It seals a relational pact with an idealised father.

Accordingly, Justine then attacks the analyst's thinking, considering it "too feminine", too "receptive", whereas she would like an analyst whose "masculine thought" would impel her to cease turning towards the past and seeking realms of suffering.

This movement of the treatment emphasises the essential role of masculine and paternal identifications in the destiny of the feminine and the maternal in the girl. These contribute to the constitution of a *"female narcissism"* that is adequately differentiated from the internal mother – a foundation necessary to the onset of female psychosexuality.

Here we rediscover Romain Gary's phallic heroic pact with his mother, in a father–daughter variation.

### f. A hysteria shared between father and daughter

Finally, the treatment evolves towards another mode of unconscious alliance between analysand and analyst. This time, entirely in collusion with the analyst, Justine settles into a more authentically positive oedipal paternal transference, where the erotic play is no longer a deception but an erotised (and interpreted) game of hide-and-seek.

Similarly, this time a mother's condemnation of a daughter to death becomes the mark of an erotic masochism connected with the guilt of daring to abandon the maternal imago and throw herself fully into the transference love with the analyst's masculine component. This is at the cost of an anxiety that he might not survive the violence of her erotic drives, like the real father who ran away when his daughter was turning into a woman.

The integration of psychic bisexuality into the secondary identifications is consolidated by the elaboration of the mourning for the primary objects and the resolution of the depressive position and the Oedipus complex, key elements of every analytic treatment.

From then on, it becomes possible for the analysand's childhood and adolescent history, and that of her future as a woman and mother, in connection with her psychic bisexuality, to be written in a subjective version and in deferred action (Hirsch, 2014).

Accordingly, it transpires that the analyst's "fixation", from now on defensive, in the maternal and archaic zones, confirmed to Justine the dangerousness of her feminine erotic drives and reinforced her unconscious construction of her guilt in relation to her father's sudden abandonment in her mid-adolescence.

Conversely, it can finally be hypothesised that "the force", vitality and drive qualities of the cathexis of the analyst helped to "revive" Justine's masculine identifications, hitherto shaken by the mourning and disappointment with regard to the idealised father.

The economic dimension of the mutual cathexis in the treatment thus plays a part in the reorganisation of the gender identifications and the primal scene, henceforth less split or perverted.

The phantasy of the murder of daughters by mothers is transformed into a masochistic phantasy: *"a girl is being killed/desired/beaten"*, henceforth testifying to an oedipal guilt and a life-preserving masochistic pleasure (Rosenberg, 1988; see also Perelberg, 2011, and Chapter 4, in this volume).

## IV Conclusions

This extensive account of Justine's treatment shows how a deficit in narcissism and identity in our analysands' psychic bisexuality is defensively sealed by unconscious pacts. As in all treatments, these are brought into play in bi-gendered transferences and by the mobilisation of the male analyst's feminine as well as masculine components. In the analytic journey, the compass of the bisexuality of the analyst's countertransference is from then on essential.

Through two illustrations – one literary, the other clinical – I have emphasised the benefit of thinking about the elaboration of psychic bisexuality in the session in terms of the transference of unconscious pacts. In fact, the unconscious intersubjective alliances that are woven from the start between mother and baby are necessary for the psychic transmission of the feminine and the masculine and of the bi-gendered identifications from one generation to the other.

I have sought to identify various clinical forms of these unconscious alliances as they are woven from the origin of the treatment between analyst and analysand. These transferences of configurations of psychic bonds replicate the primary unconscious pacts between mother and baby, and specifically those that have sealed the identities and gender identifications of the analysand's psychic bisexuality from the origin of psychic life.

These "unconscious pact transferences" are specifically governed by shared repressions, denials, foreclosures and disavowals between primary objects and baby. They account for the work of the negative that is necessary for the onset of psychic bisexuality. They are forged from the origin of the treatment and structure the transference–countertransference field of the treatment. They particularly mobilise the analyst's "blind tasks" as regards his or her own unconscious gender identifications.

Every analytic treatment therefore sets in motion a countertransference work of bisexuality that echoes the bisexuality of the analysand's transference. Whatever the analyst's sex, the psychic response requires drawing support from a work of integration of psychic bisexuality, which can be conceived – ideally – as the link between a feminine which is articulated in a configuration of thirdness by the masculine and a masculine which is inhabited by the feminine.

## Notes

1   Translated by Sophie Leighton.
2   Negative pact: The negative pact accounts for the transmission between the subjects of a group or the transgenerational transmission inside a family; it is also a "meta-defence" because it creates, on the whole and in each one, areas of silence which keep the subject as a foreigner to its own history. These imply shared mechanisms of repression, denial or foreclosure shared by each individual, so that some representations remain unconscious in each of the related subjects.
3   In a letter to Fliess, dated 1 August 1899 (in Masson, 1985), Freud suggested that each sexual act should be considered a process that involves four people (editor's note).
4   The original French word here is not "*poison*" but "*poids*", meaning "weight" or "burden". [Translator's note].
5   The "black pact" described by Godfrind is one of the unconscious pacts that is transmitted between mother and daughter. This pact relates to the transmission of a non-subjectivised part of the maternal unconscious that alienates the girl's unconscious. Its unconscious content relates to a shared hatred of the feminine. But this masks a boundless, incestuous and fusional love between mother and daughter, sealing a shared denial of otherness and the third.
6   The "*female hollow*" is the site of female castration, in which the vagina and uterus together are indissociably linked. It represents the symbolic support of female attributes and is situated at the source of female creativity. This hollow also evokes the function of receptivity and passive–active dynamics that characterise the female organising fantasy.
7   According to Kaës, "the phoric function" is a function borne unconsciously by a subject, for himself but also for a set of other subjects with whom he is connected within a couple, family, group or institution. Several phoric functions can be identified: the spokesperson, the scapegoat, the symptom-bearer, the ideal-bearer, the dream-bearer. The *dream-bearer* can elaborate thanks to its oneiric function an

internal conflict that belongs to it but which, by identification, is connected with a similar psychic conflict and shared by all the subjects in the group. So these are linked by an unconscious alliance. Accordingly, in the treatment, a patient's dream can be dreamt not only for himself, in his transference onto the analyst, but also be dreamt for his analyst who is confronted with a blind task that is similar or complementary to the patient's task.

8 Aulagnier has theorised the *narcissistic contract* that links the child and the social group to which he belongs. The narcissistic contract defines the place of a subject to be born in the generations, his unconscious missions, in exchange for the care given and the parental and collective narcissistic cathexis. The *"statements of certainty"* are the words that convey to the child the meanings, cultural bearings and taboos shared by the group that establish the bond of mutual recognition and collective collaboration. These statements also help to define the alien, the stranger and the enemy to be excluded from the group.

9 Primary homosexuality relates back to the original experience of satisfaction and pleasure shared between the mother and her baby, boy or girl. It concerns the primordial relationship, mainly undifferentiated, at the heart of which the baby encounters the mother as "similar to him". The mother agrees to merge into her baby's emotional states and to respond in a specular way to his needs. She establishes the foundations of primary narcissism. Secondary homosexuality relates back to the oedipal genital attraction to the parent of the same sex. It concerns the homosexual identifications of the inverted Oedipus complex. It contributes to the constitution of psychic bisexuality.

10 By the oral incorporation of the maternal object, a bodily model of introjection, the earliest experiences of satisfaction and pleasure shared between mother and child are constituted and, at the same time, the creation of the unconscious within the psyche. By extension, an "incorporate" refers to a set of bodily sensations, fantasmatic representations and affects that build up in the psyche.

# 9

# "NO SEX PLEASE, WE'RE BRITISH"

## Some reflections on bisexuality in contemporary clinical theory[1]

*Rosemary Davies*

---

After many years struggling with a dilemma around whether she felt herself able to manage a relationship and a baby, Caroline became pregnant. She and her partner were delighted, and her experience of pregnancy was calm and relatively uncomplicated. She decided to take a break from treatment and wondered, indeed, whether she would want to return after the baby was born. A few days after the expected date of arrival I got a telephone call from Caroline, she wanted to see if I had some time to talk: Josh had been born a few days previously, the delivery was straightforward. Mother and baby were well. But Caroline had suddenly felt swamped by powerful depressive feelings three days after the birth and was frightened that she was going to sink into a post-puerperal depression, not unknown in her family history. Anecdotal experience and research evidence told me that here was a case of the "three-day blues": hormones shifting, the milk "coming in". After some conversations with her, Caroline let me know that all was going well, and she had recovered her equilibrium and her and her partner's pleasure in the new baby. A not uncommon tale, but one that led me to consider the phenomenology of the famous "three-day blues". When a mother is delivered of a baby, she is, at the same time, *not* delivered of the other fantasized baby. Phenomenologically, this is particularly represented in the recognition of the reality of the gender of the baby. Whether or not she has known throughout the pregnancy what the gender is of the baby she is expecting, I think it remains the case that by the third day she knows she has in her arms a boy, not the girl she might have had; or a girl, not the boy she might have had. The psychic impact of this is powerful for some women and resonates with the mother's own story of her acquisition of identity, her relationship to her own bisexuality. Freud (1937c) noted in one of his last papers "every human being is bisexual" (p. 244).

The very experience of pregnancy and early motherhood might in David's (1973) terms represent his telling of bisexuality. David describes the activity of desire and the negativity of inhibition as representing forever a bisexual conundrum (p. 656). The mother's desire is met, she is active in conceiving and bearing her baby, but in nursing the child she has also, to a certain extent, to inhibit her own desires as a sexual woman, however passionately she engages with feeding. French psychoanalysts have never lost sight of the "sexual breast" in their writing and practice. They also explore the mother's erotic desire in the elaboration of Laplanche's (1992) notion of "enigmatic signifiers": the erotic and libidinal desires she herself brings to her relationship with her infant. By contrast, British psychoanalysts, with their characteristically pragmatic stance, follow the detail of clinical reports, focus on the pre-oedipal, hone in on separation, privilege loss, and are preoccupied with the mother/infant nursing dyad: the breast as feeding, not the sexual breast. In his characteristically iconoclastic way, André Green illustrated the view that British psychoanalysts, in particular, had abandoned the central place of sexuality. Green riposted to a British colleague at the 1973 IPA panel on hysteria "to consider sexuality as a defence looks more like a denial than a theoretical advance" (in Laplanche, 1973).

This pithy comment encapsulates something that has been central in contemporary debate on clinical theory and practice in British psychoanalysis: the relative neglect of sexuality. As I have argued elsewhere (Davies, 2012), more recently there has been an appeal against the hegemony of the pre-oedipal nursing couple, denuded of the paternal presence and the sexual breast. There has been an argument for a reinstatement of centrality of sexuality: the theory of the Unconscious, which places sexuality, desire and transgression at the centre of the puzzle, leading to repression that remains the cornerstone of psychoanalysis to this day. Kohon vividly depicts this:

The Oedipal drama has been transformed into a totally banal sequence of events and anecdotes: everybody can talk – and even joke – about it. But the joke is on us: what makes sexuality in humans specifically human is repression, that is to say, sexuality owes its existence to our unconscious incestuous fantasies. Desire in human sexuality is always transgression; and being something that is never completely fulfilled, its object cannot ever offer full satisfaction.

(1986b, p. 371)

I would argue that there are two examples of how sexuality has continued to have a central focus in British psychoanalysis, and in both cases bisexuality is to the fore. First, in a quiet corner of British psychoanalysis, there has been a thread of theory and practice where the centrality of sexuality in the structuring of the Unconscious has never lost its hold: the clinicians at the Portman Clinic[2] in London, in particular the work of Mervin Glasser.[3] Below I consider how Glasser's work with a transvestite patient at the Portman vividly illustrates this. Second, an entente cordiale has developed and flourished in recent decades through, for example, annual Anglo–French Colloquia (co-chaired by Anne-Marie Sandler and Haydée Faimberg) and the British French Colloquia on Sexuality (co-chaired by Rosine Perelberg, Monique Cournut and Chantal Lechartier-Atlan), and a number of distinguished British psychoanalysts – for example, Bollas, Flanders and Breen, Kohon, Mitchell, Parsons, and Perelberg – have made vital links with French psychoanalysis and recovered[4] the Freudian privileging of sexuality, in particular, infantile sexuality and bisexuality. Drawing on some of these authors' contemporary conceptualization of hysteria, I consider here the role of bisexuality in the analysis of a patient of mine, who presented with hysterical symptomatology.

## Transvestism and bisexuality

In a clinical case of Glasser's (1979b), the continued focus on sexuality, and, in particular, bisexuality, was central. He describes a transvestite patient, Mr Webster, who was in analysis with him. Mr Webster displayed no feminine gestures or mannerisms and seemed, in fact, an "ordinary good-natured young man, though somewhat

tense and brooding". He said he wanted to be freed of his transvestism, about which he felt deeply ashamed. Glasser writes:

> His transvestite act consisted of dressing up as a woman, paying
> careful attention to the minutest details: the exact size and shape
> of the padding put into his brassiere and the precise degree of
> tightness in its straps; the smoothness of the texture of the panties
> and the feel of their tightness round his waist; the matching
> blouse and skirt, tights and shoes; the hairstyle of the wig; and so
> on – all to ensure that what he saw in the mirror was a neatly and
> attractively dressed woman. It was important that there was
> nothing in his appearance and bodily-feel to dispel this experi-
> ence of himself as a woman. For example, he could not wear his
> ordinary wrist-watch even if this was hidden by the sleeve of his
> blouse. He would then masturbate looking at himself in the
> mirror, arranging himself in such a way that his penis was not
> visible in the reflection. A frequent phantasy was to imagine
> himself as a woman being made love to by a woman.
>
> He could not resist carrying out this act from time to time
> despite his strong feelings against it – he said it made him feel
> abnormal and deeply ashamed and that he was "not a proper
> man". Apart from the sexual pleasure, it also gave him a feeling
> of relaxation and a sense of freedom, particularly when he was
> aware of the sensation of the smooth, soft undergarments.
>
> He carried this "playing the role of a woman" beyond the
> sexual situation: he enjoyed going about the house performing
> the domestic activities such as house-cleaning, bed-making and
> cooking; but he would always end such an episode by masturbat-
> ing. He never lost his awareness of being male and never doubted
> this fact.
>
> (1979b, pp. 163–164)

Mr Webster gave characteristically concrete expression to his longings for "envelopment" in imagining himself crawling up the birth
canal and snuggling up inside the womb. But this gradually became
supplanted by annihilatory fears expressed in terms of "getting stuck
inside", and he went on to think of various pot-holing incidents all
centring round the theme of being trapped underground. Glasser
describes how these feelings came into the transference very clearly
in Mr Webster's treatment and proved a constant problem. His

comparison between dressing up and getting into a warm, protective nest could be related to his envelopment wishes in the transference and how this led to his feeling stifled by the sessions and his feeling of wanting to break out. He told his analyst how he could well imagine what it must feel like to be a chicken in an egg, wanting to burst out of its confining, suffocating shell.

In the course of his treatment Mr Webster described witnessing blood pouring down his mother's legs after a brutal attack by his father, who had hurled the garden shears at her; he recalled the enema that had been administered when he was hospitalized as a child as the curative factor; he talked about, as a child, holding back stools by all sorts of manoeuvres and ending up with explosive soiling. Mr Webster identified with the stool in his anus as the penis, which protects him, fetishistically, from the recognition of mother's castrated state. He wished to feel like a woman being made love to, and he imagined crawling up the birth canal and snuggling up inside the womb. Mr Webster dreamt of *a pyramid of seven men who balance in a precarious way and tumble into terrifying darkness.* He spoke of longing for a father who would make him feel man enough to counteract his libidinal strivings for his mother.

An echo rings out – the parallel is striking. Serge Pankejeff, Freud's Wolf Man (1918b), identified with his bleeding mother as she spoke to him of her bleeding body. Through the functioning of the *après-coup,* Freud reconstructs the dream as revealing the little boy's sighting, at the age of 18 months, of the primal scene, as intercourse being a violent act, leaving mother bleeding. The Wolf Man recalls a story about a pyramid of wolves, which collapse in a terrified heap when one loses his tail. The Wolf Man wishes to be inside the mother's womb in order to replace her during intercourse, to take mother's place in the primal scene. He holds on to his stools but explosively soils his detested governess's bed. He longs to be anally penetrated by his father, to make a man of him, to protect him from his identification with his mother. Mr Webster leads his analyst to conclude that from childhood, the transvestite patient has a memory of primary identification with the mother, which, at the same time, terrifies him with fears of suffocation: the dressing up matters, but the undressing is equally crucial, since it aims to escape the suffocating terror. In the Wolf Man, Freud is keen to exemplify his proposition on the theory of infantile sexuality: the libidinal stages and the concept of bisexuality.

193

The transvestite brings into treatment the conflict of wishing to be "enveloped" by the object and needing to ensure his "freedom" from the object. This, as many authors have attested, is vividly depicted in treatment. The patient energetically and persistently avoids in the transference any recognition of feelings that reflect his intense desire to merge with the analyst, or his frustrated rage. The nearest he comes to acknowledging this is experiencing the analyst as he has experienced the mother and her successors – namely, as ungiving, uncaring and essentially self-interested, and the unjust suffering and deprivation he experienced because of this. Even then these feelings are generally expressed about "the analysis", "the treatment", and so on, rather than in relation to the person of the analyst himself.

The dressing up as a woman represents a primary identification with mother, alongside a fetishistic wish to deny her castrated state; the undressing may illustrate a repudiation of the wish to be like mother. The use of the fetish is an attempt to prove there is no castration (Freud, 1927e). And, as Spillius writes in an unpublished 1975 paper on the treatment of a transvestite patient:

> The transvestite patient moved to and fro between a precarious state of self-sufficiency and an even more precarious fantasised state of fusion with his object in which fear was transformed into excitement and the object was possessed and controlled.

Glasser's clinical work described here is characterized by an emphasis on the patient's struggle to contain and conceal his aggression and sadism:

> from the most primitive levels onwards he experiences the greatest difficulty in dealing with intense rage and destructive feelings, which threaten to overwhelm him and negate the object. The sexualisation of these forces affords him mastery.
>
> (1979a, p. 166)

Mr Webster illustrated what Glasser (1979b) described as the "core complex", which he regards as fundamental: a concept often cited in contemporary British psychoanalysis. One of the main ingredients of the core complex is the intense longing for a condition of satiety and security, which is, of course, a component of the most normal of loving desires, but in the disturbed patient it is achieved through fusion with the mother expressed as a longing for union or merging. But this concept of fusion carries with it the risk of complete possession by the object, particularly the mother, and the risk of total annihilation. In the transvestite, the manifestation of the core complex is particularly vivid, for it is exhibited in the bodily envelopment by the clothes:

> In the transvestite, this longing for complete union with the object takes a characteristic form, namely the wish to get inside the object's body, to be "enveloped" by the object. This wish for "envelopment" is, of course, expressed in the act of getting into the woman's clothes. ... Thus undressing at the end of the transvestite act is as crucial an element in the whole experience as any other.
>
> (1979a, p. 164)

Glasser's adumbration of the diagnostic specificity of transvestism through his case of Mr Webster is a reprise of bisexuality. Glasser describes the "dimorphism of the object", which results in a vicious circle:

> the object in which he desires to be enveloped is always felt as having the opposing attributes of offering fulfilment and protection on the one hand, but of being engulfing and obliterative, on the other.
>
> (p. 164)

McDougall (1980) describes how

> The transvestite ... plays at making his genital disappear as he glides into his mother's clothing in a simulated attempt to purloin her identity while still protecting his own sex.
>
> (p. 193)

The patient hides away his penis in the belief of its violence. At the same time he offers up his penis to his mother in the mirror with the fetishistic idea that it will deal with the terrifying notion of her castrated state, from which he has to escape in the act of undressing and the becoming again the heterosexual man. Glasser describes

195

how this is re-enacted repeatedly in the analysis. In a commentary on the analysis of a transvestite, McDougall sees how the transvestite solution aims

> [to] mend the tatters so brutally torn in the fabric of his identity ... the scenario serves as mask to disguise the sexual truth, the container for the rage and mortification.
>
> (1980, p. 188)

> sexuality becomes merely an instrument for repairing rifts in the feeling of identity.
>
> (p. 147)

A choice has to be made, and the transvestite, through the disguise of the sexual truth, declines in some ways to make this choice.

## Hysteria, bisexuality and loss

McDougall's "tatters" and "fabrics" bring to mind an enduring image in Freud's paper "Hysterical Phantasies and Bisexuality" (1908a) in which the patient imagined trying to tear her dress off with one hand, as a man, while holding on to her dress with the other hand, as a woman. Freud's conceptualization of hysteria and bisexuality was extensively outlined in this paper:

> Hysterical symptoms are the expression on the one hand of a masculine unconscious sexual phantasy. ... The bisexual nature of hysterical symptoms, which can in any event be demonstrated in numerous cases, is an interesting confirmation of my view that the postulated existence of an innate bisexual disposition in man is especially clearly visible in the analysis of psychoneurotics. An exactly analogous state of affairs occurs in the same field when a person who is masturbating tries in his conscious phantasies to have the feelings both of the man and of the woman in the situation which he is picturing. Further counterparts are to be found in certain hysterical attacks in which the patient simultaneously plays both parts in the underlying sexual phantasy. *In one case which I observed, for instance, the patient pressed her dress up against her body with one hand (as the woman), while she tried to tear it off with the other (as the man).*
>
> (Freud, 1908a, pp. 165–166, italics added)

In psycho-analytic treatment it is very important to be prepared for a symptom having a bisexual meaning. We need not then be surprised or misled if a symptom seems to persist undiminished although we have already resolved one of its sexual meanings; for it is still being maintained by the – perhaps unsuspected – one belonging to the opposite sex. In the treatment of such cases, moreover, one may observe how the patient avails himself, during the analysis of the one sexual meaning, of the convenient possibility of constantly switching his associations, as though on to an adjoining track, into the field of the contrary meaning.

(p. 166)

Serge Leclaire (1980) interrogates the hysteric's demand as to whether she is a man or a woman, contrasting it with the obsessional's existential cry, "do I exist?" Kohon (1999) drawing on Leclaire's work, writes in his seminal paper on Dora and hysteria:

the hysteric demands *Am I a man or a woman?* ... The hysteric wanders between one object and the other, unable to choose between them, frozen in a gesture of apparent resolution.

(p. 16)

Similarly, Nasio (1998), in his reading of Lacan on hysteria, describes how:

the hysterical subject is no longer a man, no longer a woman; he is now the pain of dissatisfaction ... unable to say whether he is a man or a woman, to say, simply, what sex he is.

(p. 10)

Using some clinical material from the analysis of a patient of mine I would like to illustrate how in hysteria, bisexuality and loss are crucially intertwined.

Just as the transvestite act circumvents, at times, an unbearable psychic challenge, so contemporary theory on hysteria,[5] representing in part, a return to Freud's ground-breaking work on hysteria, illustrates how hysterical symptomatology may be an "apparent resolution" defending against the pain of mourning. In the hysteric's divalent conundrum, "Am I a man or a woman?", s/he regards the choice impossible and thereby circumvents the grief that would be

197

entailed. Yarom (1997) links hysteria to what she calls "narcissistic bisexuality". And Mitchell (1984) describes

hysteria the most Oedipal neurosis, the one most utilizes bisexuality.
(pp. 388–389)

Cixous (1981) puts it vividly:

The hysteric is a divine spirit that is always at the edge, the turning point, of making. She is one who does not make herself ... but she does make the other. It is said that the hysteric "makes believe" the father, plays the father, "makes believe the master". Plays, makes up, makes-believe: she makes-believe she is a woman, unmakes-believe too ... plays at desire, plays the father ... turns herself into him, unmakes him at the same time. ... She's the *unorganisable* feminine construct, whose power of producing the other is a power that never returns to her. She is really a wellspring nourishing the other for eternity; yet not drawing back from the other ... not recognizing herself in the images the other may or may not give her. She is given images that don't belong to her, and she forces herself, as we've all done, to resemble them.
(p. 47)

She is the mother and the father, the boy and the girl, the one who strips the woman naked and the one who clings to the dress as described by Freud (1908a). S/he

knows and does not know a thing at the same time.
(Freud, 1895d, p. 117)

In my description above of Caroline's recognition of her baby as also marking what he is not, the centrality of mourning is ever present. Recognition of gender identity brings the trauma of loss with it. Sexualization and eroticization are, even in common parlance, seen as a defence against the painful affect of loss. Hysterical symptoms seem particularly to demonstrate this: the hysteric in her dizzying theatricality, her over-identification with the other, exhibits an incapacity to mourn. Freud famously described in his own self-analysis, the ending of his "*petite hystérie*" with the death of his father in 1896 and the beginnings of a capacity to mourn (Anzieu,

1986). The loss of his father inaugurated the possibility of internalizing the lost object, in contrast to the denial of the loss through hysterical identification, as Freud did in his somatic ailments, mirroring his elderly father's deteriorating health. Later authors have in their conceptualization of hysteria, seeing it as the most oedipal of neuroses inevitably marking loss inherent in the triangularity, alluded to the link between loss and hysteria. For example, Mitchell (2000) writes:

> one of the characteristics of hysteria is that the hysteric does not have access to the process of mourning. ... Mourning requires the acknowledgment that the dead person is gone forever and cannot return ... there can be an internal image or memory of the dead person, instead of a kind of incubus within. The hysteric still has the incubus or the revenant.
>
> (p. 32)

Furthermore, in recent decades retrieval of the life stories of Freud's hysterics has demonstrated the catastrophic losses many of them suffered (Appignanesi & Forrester, 2000). Perelberg (1999b), in a reprise of Anna O's history and treatment, attests to the link between loss and hysteria. She describes how, in the hysterical drama of Anna O's illness, loss is avoided, and she shows how the traumatic history confronts her physician, Breuer, with his own unworked-through losses. Perelberg goes on to link the hysteric's avoidance of mourning with bisexuality. She convincingly describes how, for example, Anna O's hysterical pregnancy reflects a denial of separation from her beloved physician, but it also confirms her omnipotent belief in being a woman who produces babies not through intercourse, but through magical parthenogenesis. Anna O is imitating the sexual act in the characteristic mimicry of the hysteric, rather than identifying with a parental couple (p. 185).

My patient, Jack, described relationships with women that were intensely tantalizing: he was an engaging, handsome young man, with a captivating intellectual and verbal fluency. There was something of the Don Juan about him. Mitchell (2000) persuasively argues that Don Juan is the classic example of the male hysteric. Jack had many relationships with women, but nothing felt truly connected and consummated – "always at the edge", as Cixous describes. He seemed to decline entry into the actual sexual universe, moving restlessly between identification with a depressed over-weening mother and faint memories of an absent and now dead father. His professional life seemed similar: he perseverated and bemoaned his incapacity to complete tasks, despite encouragement from mentors who knew him to be intellectually able. But there was, at the same time, a certain excitement in the non–fulfilment, a gratification in relationships with an endless string of amorous and intellectual mentors who were keen to help him complete things while he resolutely but unconsciously avoided such an outcome. There was a theatricality about his reporting of his restless move- ment between various women. As Bollas (2000) describes the hysteric's theatricality:

> When we think of hysteria we think of people who are troubled by their body's sexual demands and repress sexual ideas; who are indifferent to conversion; who are overidentified with the other; who express themselves in a theatrical manner; who daydream existence rather than engage in it; and who prefer the illusion of childlike innocence to the worldliness of the adult ... only the hysteric brings these together in a single dynamic form.
>
> (p. 1)

In one session, Jack described being unable to stand on his own two feet. He felt as though he was always being suckled, and he found that once he was unattached, he couldn't work on his own. He said he needed some kind of seepage from the women he was with to make him "viable". He had been watching a television programme involving women talking about breast-feeding. An ex-newscaster spoke of how she was still breast-feeding her child at the age of 3½. He thought, "I work because of what others give me, I don't work on my own, and in some ways I am reluctant to acknowledge that." He mentioned a long list of women and their children with whom he had been involved and how "they animated me, they made me feel creative". He described feeling "lost in the large-breasted woman":

> I feel I have only ever worked because I have been attached to the breast of someone else – physically attached to my mother, not my father, he was a conundrum. But this is no way of being, I've got to make things work without it.

Listening retrospectively to his acknowledgement of the suffocating danger of being dependent on another, I think he was also telling me something about the danger of moving away from the large-breasted feeding mother, towards the "conundrum" that was the father, the marker of the sexual not the feeding breast, the emblem of masculinity: the challenge of entering the sexual universe, mourning the loss of omnipotence of bisexuality: "I can be both." He had alluded to the "deathly" nature of the desired capacious female body: the risk of being drawn back, like the passive little boy who stayed at home, to the incestuous shared bed with mother, mirroring the risk of being trapped and suffocated in the maternal bed of the transference. Perhaps in the reference to the ex-newscaster still feeding an infant of 3½ years he was noting, in the third year of his analysis, the risk of being lured back to the maternal breast, obscuring the paternal presence – the "conundrum", as he put it – the hysterical decline of the trauma of the paternal representation of sexuality, the to and fro of the divalent refusal to choose.

At the centre of the psychoanalytic endeavour is the question of origins: the child asks repeatedly, "where did I come from?" and the first question that is answered in the delivery room – or nowadays in the sonographer's scan – is, "is s/he a boy or a girl?" Perelberg (2015b, p. 132) describes how that which is fundamentally not known and known is the fact of the division of the sexes: sexuality is created through division and discontinuity.[6] The hysteric tries to deny this division and discontinuity: "the fractured sexual subject" as Mitchell describes (1982, p. 26). The hysteric papers over the cracks by being both the seducer and the seduced, living always in the liminal space, excited by being on the edge, neither one thing nor the other. Like Jack, the hysteric abhors consummation, talking sex but preferring not to complete it. S/he never faces the loss of the object, for s/he has never had to separate the male and female dimension – both man and girl, as Freud so vividly describes.

Britton (1999), in what he called the erotic psychodrama of Breuer's treatment of Anna O, also writes of the centrality of the theatricality, the denial, the double consciousness and sexuality. He notes Freud's crucial development of the idea of "negative hallucination" in his description of hysterical symptomatology. Freud's first description of the negative hallucination is in the case of Anna O:

Some ten days after her [Anna O's] father's death a consultant was brought in, whom, like all strangers, she completely ignored

201

R. Davies

while I demonstrated all her peculiarities to him. "That's like an examination", she said, laughing, when I got her to read a French text aloud in English. The other physician intervened in the conversation and tried to attract her attention, but in vain. It was a genuine "negative hallucination" of the kind which has since so often been produced experimentally. In the end he succeeded in breaking through it by blowing smoke in her face. She suddenly saw a stranger before her, rushed to the door to take away the key and fell unconscious to the ground. There followed a short fit of anger and then a severe attack of anxiety which I had great difficulty in calming down.

(1895d, p. 27)

Perhaps, in contemporary consideration of hysteria, the negative hallucination can be characterized as a device for blowing away the reality of being male or female. Britton elaborates this when he describes how his hysterical patient inserts herself into the parental couple, taking in one moment the father's place and in another the mother's place. In this fluidity of identification the hysteric's bisexual phantasy protects her from the pain of mourning. In Britton's description it is the negative hallucination that allows her to cast away the bad parental couple who exclude her, and in her bisexual identification with both partners she resists knowledge in the sexual realm. Britton concludes:

in hysteria there is a further question: whose sex is it?

(1999, p. 12)

Bollas (2000), too, sees sexuality as the problem in the origins of hysterical psychopathology. He focuses on the pre-oedipal and oedipal shift for the child in relation to the mother. And his theory of the hysterogenic mother focuses on how there is a lack of an unconscious sense of maternal desire for the child's sexual body, although in other respects the child often experiences maternal investment and care.

The infant–mother relation is erotic right from the beginning, transformation of the mother as comforter into the mother as sex object breaks up the particular sense of her as a sensual provider.

(p. 14)

202

Bollas argues that for the hysteric the layering of memory and experience makes the sexual epiphany of the move from the maternal order to the paternal order traumatic. With the arrival on the scene of father, mother is no longer seen as "mum the provider" but "mum who desires". There is a failed maternal libidinization of the body: a maternal decathexis of the child's sexuality. Sexual engagement seems defiling, best left in the realms of the imaginary. He argues that hysterics decline psychic entry into the actual sexual universe, preferring instead to appropriate sexual discourse and use it in place of the real. Bollas goes on to comment:

The past is available for proper thinking in the later course of time.

(p. 90)

This is, again, reprised in the analysis of the Wolf Man. Through the workings of the *après-coup*, the little Russian boy realizes the impact of a previously non-comprehended event: the witnessing of the primal scene. But his comprehension, revealed through his associations to the dream of wolves, depends on knowledge and maturation. What he couldn't make sense of as an infant he can make sense of as an older child, through his experimental researches with Nanya and Gruscha and the sheep on the estate: the reality of sexual difference.

This trauma of the move from the maternal to the paternal order was illustrated in a later session in Jack's analysis. Jack told me he is demolishing a concrete ramp that his mother had needed to access her garden. "I have to be careful when I am breaking it up not to damage the manhole cover or the drain." He had been thinking yesterday about whether things are dispensable. He said he had felt good yesterday, but he had talked as if there was a problem. It was as though he was somehow unravelling something, picking endlessly at a thread, and he wondered whether both he and I had been thinking that yesterday. He spent some time ruminating in a very characteristic and circular way about what he should be doing and when he should be deciding to do it. He went on to talk about issues of recognizing dependence: he can see that he is dependent on coming to analysis but also that he feels lost in that state. He said that things might be pleasurable, but nothing is a fixture – no relationship can be. He said he didn't think of himself as stable enough to be that which is needed, not like other people whose feelings don't change. He talked about how he felt his feelings change for

203

all the different women he knows, but other people offer a sense of self that they believe is unchanging and fixed.

When Jack described breaking up the concrete ramp that his mother had needed to enter the garden, I wondered whether he was communicating to me the challenge of breaking the deadly tie to his mother that had done such damage to the whole man (the manhole), denying him a sexual identification with his father and preventing him using the garden of his own adult sexuality – very much the hysteric's predicament. The patient is prevented, by the mother's privileging of the delibidinized connection to the pre-oedipal relationship, from entering into the realm of erotic pleasure in becoming, for example, her father's little princess or the little prince's sexual identification with father. Jack's view of others as fixed, like Echo, was a crucial element in his experience of his objects. Dismantling the concreteness of thinking, the concrete ramp, ushered in possibilities of differing symbolic modes exemplified by his thought of us both thinking and "unravelling a thread": the thread of our connectedness between and within sessions.

The hysteric eschews the fragmentation, the discontinuity, the disruption of sexuality and finds an "apparent resolution" through avoidance of moving out from the shadows of the liminal space and remaining both one thing and the other, "the predisposition to bisexuality" illustrated by Dora (Freud, 1905e, p. 112). Faced in Bollas' conceptualization with the awareness of two mothers, two fathers, two selves, genital and pre-genital, the hysteric dances a dizzying tarantella where, like Ibsen's Nora, the dizziness renders her unable to see, to differentiate, to complete the journey and step into the realm of recognizing herself as a man or a woman.[7] In her vertiginous confusion she cannot decide whether she is a man or a woman – the "frozen gesture" Kohon describes. But at least in that confusion she saves herself from the trauma of adult sexuality and the mourning entailed. Perelberg (1999b) describes how the hysteric brings to mind the ruby, the jewel that absorbs and retains all other colours but rejects and expels red – as the hysteric who looks red, displays sexuality, but there is no real consummated depth to the encounter.

Later in his analysis, Jack movingly began to recall his father, "the conundrum", and his affection for him. Father seemed not to fit into his pathologically limited libidinal world. He described very hazy images: he could remember him in his darkroom in the basement developing photographs, but "I couldn't make him out", and he remembered him thoughtfully watching his fish in the fish tank, but "I couldn't see his face". Jack went on to report a dream in which *he was with his girlfriend's sister, and they had to be careful not to get their legs wet in a canal lock that was filling up with sewage. He could not open the lock gates.* The dream scene changed, and he went on to describe another dream, in which

> I'm sort of here in the consulting room, but not here. We are coming to the end of a session, and you give me something, but I cannot understand it. You come to stop me getting up from the couch and hold me down and cradle my head against your stomach. I put my arms around you. We should have finished the session. It's odd, and I go downstairs, and there are other people around, perhaps other analysts. I feel embarrassed and conspicuous.

In these moments of analysis I understand Jack to have begun to imagine moving away from the lure of the "mum as comforter" to the imaginings of the father as a source of identification, but difficult to discern in the "dark room". In the dream he illustrates his struggle. Jack is fighting to open the lock gates, perhaps sensing how momentous the task is to enter the challenging, risky world of male sexuality. The sewage is getting higher, and he has to avoid getting wet. Is he struggling to own his maleness as it slips into the manhole, into the sewage, the undifferentiated anal universe so vividly depicted by Chasseguet-Smirgel (1985), where exciting difference is denied and immersion in the waters of adult sexuality is avoided? In the latter part of the dream he is embarrassed and exposed by the woman/analyst who fails to heed the boundaries of the analysis and pins him down, "cradling" him. Getting away from the identification with the mother, the suffocating cradling, is endlessly repeated in the act of dismantling and then covering up. Completion and consummation of the sexual act are avoided in the circularity of the theatricality of the *mise-en-scène* of the hysterical state of mind. But there are "others" around, perhaps a trace of something "other" with which it might be safe to identify.

The centrality of identification in the cases of Mr Webster and Jack illustrates Mitchell's (2016) reprising of the Freudian conceptualization of bisexuality. She emphasizes that Freud considered bisexuality first and foremost as a subject position. Mr Webster, for example, in his transvestite acts, experienced himself as a woman in identification with his mother. As Glasser (1979a) described, Mr Webster "wanted to ensure what he saw in the mirror was a neatly and attractively dressed woman". This is a subjective disposition, not necessarily implying a bisexual object choice. And Jack, in his sense, as he put it, that "no relationship can be a fixture", seemed to imply that his relationship to his own masculinity remained fluid. In treatment I had no sense of a vacillation between male and female object choice, but Jack's anxiety about the protection of his masculinity, encapsulated in the image of the possible damage to the manhole cover in the garden, seemed to me to indicate primarily a subjective issue. Thus, in my view, the question, "Am I a man or a woman?" remains the central locus of the psychoanalytic reading of bisexuality.

## Notes

1 *No Sex Please, We're British* was a show that ran in London's West End for many years during the 1970s.
2 The Portman Clinic was established in the 1930s, offering psychotherapeutic help to patients with perverse and forensic problems.
3 I also discuss this case in D. Campbell (2018) *The Core Complex, Violence and Perverse Solutions: Mervin Glasser's Contributions to Psychoanalysis*.
4 In this context of recovery, Bollas (2000) writes, "Next time we think hysterics have disappeared, let's ensure someone asks after us and calls for help" (p. 79).
5 In contemporary clinical theory, a consensus is emerging that clinicians still do see hysterics in their consulting rooms, but the clinical presentation may differ from the late nineteenth-century hysterics and is seen, for example, in eating disorders and chronic fatigue syndrome (see, for example, Bollas, 2000; Brenman, 1985; Mitchell, 2000; Showalter, 1997).
6 This creation in discontinuity is not unlike, Philip Roth's description of love:

> The only obsession everyone wants: "love". People think that in falling in love they make themselves whole. The Platonic union of souls? I think otherwise. I think you're whole before you begin. And the love fractures you. You're whole, and then you're cracked open. She was a foreign body introduced into your wholeness.
>
> (2002, pp. 99–100)

7 At the end of her frenetic dance, Nora declaims, "it's a wonderful thing to be waiting for a miracle" – reminiscent of the hysteric's pleasure of being on the edge, the excitement of anticipation, not of completion.

# 10

# HOW TO BE BOTH, BY NOT BEING BOTH

## The articulation of psychic bisexuality within the analytic session[1]

*Rachel Chaplin*

At the exhilarating birth of psychoanalysis, Freud responds to a suggestion from Fliess: "I avail myself of the bisexuality of all human beings" (Freud, 1950 [1892–99], p. 211). In the closing pages of his gloomy, valedictory work of 1937, "Analysis Terminable and Interminable", Freud speculates that it is the "repudiation of femininity" in both sexes that causes analysis to stagnate. These two thoughts – bisexuality is a given of human subjectivity, the rejection of femininity is a given of human subjectivity – the alpha and omega of Freud's thinking about psychic sexuality, still have live currency in our clinical thinking.[2] So how are we to make sense of the apparent conflict between these two givens of psychic life?

### A dangerous lullaby: the analyst falls asleep

After I have recounted an early session from Christa's analysis to some colleagues, they seem uneasy. During the session I have spoken very few words, and those more to reassure myself that I still could than because I felt I had anything inside me that I needed to say. Christa, meanwhile, has been active: she has described, in compelling filmic detail, events from her adolescence. I have been transfixed by the eerily beautiful images Christa evoked in my mind, as teenagers roamed the night-time countryside, set fire to the grassland surrounding their male teacher's house, and then rained heavy stones down upon the roof under which he was sleeping. It is only after the session that I can think that someone was asleep and needed to be woken up, through a violent shock. My colleagues' unease suggests they feel the same about me: I was problematically asleep during the session and needed to wake up. I can hear and acknowledge their concern that I have been submerged in a deep passivity, seduced by the dreamy beauty of the images Christa brings, but I feel as if I am deep underwater, just able to hear words coming to me from the surface.

The impact of this session is not so unusual in this analysis, though the imagery here is particularly beguiling. It repeats a specific situation: an observer, immobilized, perhaps horrified, perhaps excited, watches a violent scene. In these sessions, Christa's words carry me from one alarming scene to another as she describes her memories and dreams: I see piles of crashed go-karts with bloody, broken-limbed children waiting to be rescued, vans carrying children and adults sliding down mountainsides, soldiers at war, teenage boys falling to their deaths and scenes of "*gladiatorial combat*" as she puts it. Most recurrent is the theme of dangerous racing, corresponding to Christa's speed in the session, moving me from image to image, her mind running ahead of mine. I feel like a child carted from exciting trauma to trauma by a deranged, excited and unthinking mother: my eyes take everything in, I can see it all, but I cannot think. My situation is also Christa's situation in many of these accounts: frozen and passive, she cannot tear her eyes away from what she sees.

In these sessions my working analytic openness seems to lay me open to utter helplessness as my mind is paralysed by an intrusive rush of exciting imagery against which I cannot shield myself. At the same time, I have no thoughts with which to penetrate the surface of Christa's images, which construct a protective screen, a compelling surface that arrests my mind, and behind which Christa can remain safely out of contact.

After some discussion of the first session, one of my colleagues suggests, "We have to trust the analyst." I had felt that the session was one of a pair, and when I go on to recount the second session, we are all relieved to find that my mind has, in fact, woken up, and I am able to think again. It is a cliché: trust the analyst. To do what?

To go through a process in time, moving from what appears to be a "passivity more passive still than any receptivity"[3] to an active capacity for representation and thought, derived, I suggest, from underlying psychic bisexuality.

## Freud's final bedrock: the repudiation of femininity

In "Analysis Terminable and Interminable", Freud asks why his patients refuse to take in and use the analysis he offers. His speculative answer succinctly binds the psychic sphere, the taking in of an analysis, with the sexual: the cause of the resistance is the repudiation of femininity, which he defines as the fear for a man of passive submission to a man, and for a woman as the unmoveable desire to possess a penis:

> the resistance prevents any change from taking place – ... everything stays as it was. We often have the impression that with the wish for a penis and the masculine protest we have penetrated through all the psychological strata and have reached bedrock, and that thus our activities are at an end. This is probably true, since for the psychical field, the biological field does in fact play the part of the underlying bedrock. The repudiation of femininity can be nothing else than a biological fact, a part of the great riddle of sex.
>
> (Freud, 1937c, p. 252)

In this extract Freud despairingly turns to "biological fact" to explain the resistance to analysis. Yet throughout the years he had struggled with how to conceptualize the sexual and masculine and feminine in psychic life without recourse to biology. For example, "pure masculinity and femininity remain theoretical constructions of uncertain content" (Freud, 1925j, p. 257) or

> Psychoanalysis cannot elucidate the intrinsic nature of what ... in biological phraseology is termed "masculine" and "feminine"; it simply takes over the two terms and makes them the foundation for its work. When we attempt to reduce them further, we find masculinity vanishing into activity and femininity into passivity, and that does not tell us enough.
>
> (Freud, 1920a, p. 147)

209

Despite these terminological difficulties, Freud retains the differentiation between the two terms as the "foundation" of psychoanalytic work, and with the abstract terms activity and passivity he reaches for a way to describe differentiated modes of reciprocal relating. Each mode of relating needs the other in order to express itself: active needs to meet passive and passive needs to meet active.

## The primary conceptual bedrock: psychic bisexuality

The repudiation of femininity as a "biological" bedrock emerging at the very end of his work, runs counter to Freud's longest-held conviction regarding human sexuality – psychic bisexuality. This insight, foundational to his thinking, finds its theoretical flowering in his account of the complete oedipal constellation that consists of identifications with both father and mother and an active and passive relation to each parent. The desirable outcome of the Oedipus complex is a "precipitate in the ego", a structure consisting of these crossed identifications with both parents, "in some way united with one another" – a way to "be both", psychically. But Freud quietly notes that in some cases one or other of the identifications can disappear "except for barely distinguishable traces" (Freud, 1923b, p. 32).

Previously, in "The Psychogenesis of a Case of Homosexuality in a Woman", Freud had cautioned against attempts to reverse homosexuality, proposing instead that the aim should be to restore "full bisexual functions" (Freud, 1920a, p. 171). So it is a duality of psychic functions that is at stake in his insistence on the *two* terms masculine and feminine/active and passive as "the foundations" of psychoanalytic work (p. 147). And it is in terms of psychic functions, entailing active and passive modes of relating (with implications for the capacity for symbolization), that I will be exploring bisexuality in the session, not as a sexual practice.

When Freud cries out in frustration in 1937 that his patients will not renounce their "masculine protest" – understood here as a refusal of castration – sufficiently to take in his interpretations, what has happened to bisexuality? It is as if, facing the limits of his psychoanalytic potency, Freud issues his own "masculine protest", insisting that his patients should hand themselves over to his interventions in a state of "feminine" passivity. Yet I suggest that it is only when representing activity is available, if only quiescently, within the mind that a capacity for passively taking in becomes

210

possible. The "feminine" in this sense is dependent on the quiet presence of the "masculine". So one might read the unmoveable "masculine protest" that Freud encounters in his patients actually as a determined holding on to the possibility of a necessary psychic bisexuality. For both patient and analyst, deep passivity can only be endured or even desired if a "barely distinguishable trace" of the other identification with activity remains potentially available.

## Return to Christa

In her preliminary meetings with me, Christa appeared to be thoughtfully weighing up the prospect of an analysis. But at the level of action something very different was occurring. Before coming in for her first meeting, she asked where she would padlock her bicycle in future. She came to the second meeting without a padlock, so would I mind if she brought her bicycle into the waiting room? After our third meeting, in which we finalized the arrangements for the analysis, she left the padlock in the waiting room over the weekend. Adhesive attachment, intrusion or penetration, loss and theft, wakeful vigilance and sleepy inattention were all in play, awaiting analytic metaphorization. My permeability and receptiveness were already under unconscious scrutiny.

After an early break in the analysis, Christa had a fleeting conscious thought that the couch was a bed on which she might be raped. Later, wondering why she was telling me yet again about sexual trauma, she said: "It's a relief ... there needs to be someone listening to what happened. It's the point [of an analysis], getting in under something, breaking barriers..." She insists that I must interpret: she needs "a shock and an awakening" from a sleepy state. Yet at other times she hates me for the way I have "opened her up" through the analysis, to the insides of herself, to her unconscious mind beneath the surface. While the sexual dimension of such thoughts is loudly audible to me, Christa doesn't seem to hear it, suggesting that the sexual remains unintegrated in her mind. Yet the analysis is unconsciously a sexual scene for her, in which sexual *action* is a present danger. My analytic care, which she hopes will help her to develop an ego shield against the violent eruption of sexuality (experienced as coming from outside the self), even my provision of a couch for her to lie on, may presage a dangerous seduction or rape.

211

## A "stabbing" remark: sexual difference as trauma

This clinical sequence, from the first year of our work, reveals a complex pattern of four overlapping, coterminous psychosexual positions as they emerge in the transference and countertransference action of the sessions. First, there is a complete immersion in the archaic maternal universe, a kind of undifferentiated and amalgamated fusion in which there is no difference to be represented psychically. Second, there is a form of primary homosexuality as described by Denis (1982). The mother is separate enough to be cathected as an object, but she is cathected as a narcissistic double, and her sexual identity is assumed to be the same as the infant's. Denis views this "primary homosexual" cathexis as having a transitional function, in that it opens a path towards the acceptance of otherness and the recognition of sexual difference. Third, there is a form of phallic bisexuality in which sexual difference and castration are known but refused. And, finally, there is a form of genital bisexuality in which difference predicated on castration is both known and used. We could characterize these four positions in relation to sexual difference as identical, similar, different but denied, and different and used.

On hearing Christa's account of racing to keep up with her brothers as they ran for a bus, I suggested "You want to be one of the racing boys and men." She reeled from my interpretation, saying she felt "stabbed" by "the worst thing that could be said". I, in turn, felt shocked and baffled to find that I had said something so violently wrong. Christa explained that she despises men, apart from those in her family. How could she want to be one of them, and how could I think that of her? She attended her next session, a morning session, in a full-length black dress, as striking and glamorous as eveningwear. She had just come from the swimming pool, where she had swum faster than both the women and the men. She spoke of women having children as if they do it alone – men are peripheral. She interpreted her dress as a response to my remark of the previous day.

Christa's upset response to my interpretation was sharply dislocating for me. I seemed to have misread my patient's sexual identification and to have unwittingly committed raping violence, a *stabbing* penetration. We were both being woken up with a shock. I had thought my observation of her masculine identification was safely available at a preconscious level. Significantly, I think, I had referred this interpretation to myself, thinking that "I wouldn't find wanting to race with the men disturbing." In my attempt to identify her feelings, I have taken Christa to be *similar* to me in her sexual identification. As her enacted riposte the next day indicates, the content of the interpretation seems to be on the right lines, so the narcissistic identification had its use.

But I would stress that the interpretation is shaped by and enacts within the transference and countertransference underlying phantasies regarding the primal scene, seduction and castration. First, my interpretation indicates a realm in which there is similarity but not difference, as evidenced by my failure at an unconscious level fully to register her otherness. I have taken Christa to be my double. And yet, though my interpretation seems to originate from similarity, at this point in the analysis, when the sexual action between us has not yet been metaphorized, Christa can only experience my comment as intrusive sexual action.

But if we view this clinical moment from another perspective, we find that in my comment I am, unwittingly, introducing the fact of sexual difference. In saying to Christa that she wants to be one of the racing men, I implicitly point to her bodily femininity, telling her that she is castrated. I have spoken from a position in which sexual difference is known, and the fact of castration is accepted, but my introduction of sexual difference seems to be premature and traumatic. Perhaps I moved too fast, because I too felt under unconscious pressure to repudiate the feminine/passive: remember my experience of deep passivity in the first session. If the sessions implicitly involve raping/castrating violence – "gladiatorial combat" – then I might feel pressurized to assert *my* phallic activity by opting too soon for interpretive action. Christa's dress, racy swimming, assertion of parthenogenesis, and even perhaps her activeness in the session when she interprets her dress for me, represent self-protective "masculine protests" against this. She asserts her supremacist bisexuality by asserting: "I am both, both more male and more female." This androgynous stance simultaneously restores and constructs the illusion of sexual completion. And complete, there is nothing for my interpretation to penetrate. Her castration does not figure. Instead, she presents me with her fetish dress, covering over the fact of castration. In the logic of phallic monism there is no reciprocal position: passivity equates to castration and rape. The feminine may be outwardly worn as a dazzling phallic lure, but it can only figure inwardly as "being raped".

Christa remains "stuck" for a few days after this. A "white mist" descends on her mind – opaque, smooth, and white – sealing her in to a virginal state of mind and blocking all contact from me. Insight is dangerous, threatening the trauma that the premature representation of sexuality can bring. She freezes the analytic action, and I am held at a distance as a paralysed and castrated father. And she remains paralysed in a blurry, undifferentiated dyad with her mother.

Then she begins a session by returning to my interpretation:

I was agitated last night, I am confused about why I have come up against a brick wall, or why it feels as if I have. It is frustrating. [Analyst coughs, and Christa's cough follows on immediately.] One sentence hits a spot and gets me so stirred up. I am thinking that the person who lies on the sofa is not me, a different me. It is me, obviously, but a different person. I am not sure what part of me lies here on the sofa. I think I was agitated because I felt confused about being here. ... I have confused myself. ... This is hard to say: I think that I must have put myself across as a person you must not like, even despise. But this is supposed to be a professional relationship, so that should not come into it. But it is an anxiety I have built into a reality because I have said that I hate men ... [she pulls her jacket across her chest]. What bothered me was hearing you say that I wanted to be a man. It is different to say you want to be one of the racing boys or men. A different thing. But I have been very stuck with it for some reason.

After a while, I suggest: "If I think the same as you, if I hate men too, then nothing else can be thought, that is all there is."

She replies: "There's a problem. I assume how others are thinking about me. I am finely tuned, listening so I can gauge what someone is thinking of me. It does not feel very adult, it feels stuck ... like an adolescent. I should have grown out of it. ... Thinking it was the worst possible thing you could say is that I want to be a man – no, the worst possible thing you could say is that I am just like my mother. But why would you say that? You don't know her." [As a teenager, Christa found it very frustrating that when she complained about her friends, her mother could only agree and could not offer an alternative point of view.]

Christa is ready to resume thought-activity and to struggle with what happened when I "hit the spot". Her need to lie dormant beneath the white mist before resuming representational action mirrors my reaction in the first session, when my mind went to sleep for a time before I could get thinking again. Through the reversibility of roles in the transference and countertransference, we learn the structure of Christa's primal scene.

Now she can tell me that the touch of my mind on hers when I "hit the spot" overwhelmed her ego and dissolved the boundaries of her identity, leaving her unsure as to "what's me". My interpretive action has been traumatic. While she is able to articulate this in words, Christa's symbolic capacity is partial, and she is simultaneously having to manage the contact between us through bodily strategies. Her cough, almost perfectly synchronized with mine, suggests that we are operating as an undifferentiated dyad at an archaic bodily level. So she coughs me out, but then she needs her jacket – both as a second skin in which to wrap herself, raw at the separation, and to reinforce our separateness. The risk of regressively succumbing to a merger with the maternal is live. We both hate men, we think the same, we are the same: identical is all we can be: her mother who could only agree and who could not offer an alternative point of view is in the session.

Significantly it is only after Christa has concretely separated us, through coughing and wrapping herself in her jacket, that she recovers a capacity to identify difference: she notices that she heard me say that she wanted to *be a man*, not that she wanted to be *one of the men*. In other words, she heard me say that there was only one position to occupy, not one among several. I suspect that it was this active differentiating thought of hers that fed my capacity to identify the danger inherent in our "thinking the same", the danger that nothing else can be thought, we reach an impasse and all "our activities are at an end", to echo Freud. This time, because I interpret from a sufficiently *similar* position – "if I think the same as you" – Christa can accept my perception that there is a danger in our being trapped in the realm of the *identical*, and she voices the need to move out of her dyadic listening for "*what someone is thinking of me*". I can now name the risk that, in being identical, the trace of the other identification might be lost. She would then be "just like her mother", I would be unable to perceive the problem

215

and would not come to help her find her way out of the identical with an identificatory alternative.

At this point we are working as a generative couple, each of us moving between actively offering thoughts, passively receiving them before actively processing them, in a reciprocal dynamic. But what emerges more clearly in the next session is the insecure articulation of these "two" differentiated identificatory positions, correlated to the maternal and paternal and to active and passive relating.

Christa's daughter, Anna, has been in a panic all night, as has Christa. Should she have comforted her by lying down next to her or told her to manage alone? Her husband was clear that Anna should be left, but was he right? I notice I am starting to panic too: should I reassure her she was right, or leave her to think? Tell her which parent was right, or not? Christa says she feels as if she is just floating around lost, and I suggest that her questions are an attempt to feel that she has a secure hold on me. She associates to going to comfort her daughter and then sees herself in a jungle, trapped by vines – if she gives in to her daughter's plea for comfort, her daughter will never let her go. So she must not go to her. I link this to the long childhood afternoons she spent, alone with her depressed mother, trying to comfort her. She then recalls having said that our relationship is supposed to be a "professional" from my analyst point of view and asks, "But where does that leave me in terms of being looked after or cared about? It feels as if 'professional' is cold." The session continues:

ANALYST: If I am "professional", I am like a father saying the right thing is to "leave her to get on with it", including next week when I will be away from you?

CHRISTA: (*pulls her jacket across her body*) I don't know. It is confusing. ... I don't know why I cannot see through it. That's Paul's suggestion: leave Anna to cry, it's the only way she will manage. And it was my Dad's suggestion with my Mum too when she was crying in the afternoons. ... For some reason, I am feeling irrationally panicked right now. Too much coffee? I have a skin infection on my eye. I am worried the infection will go into my eye. Now I feel panicky. ... If I don't deal with it, I will go blind. I have got cream for it from the pharmacist, but I am worried it is the wrong cream and will damage my eyes. I might need eye-drops from the doctor but...

ANALYST: When I link my being "professional" to your father, you get really frightened you have not got a mother in me, only a father. [*An early question in the analysis: "Are you a mother?"*]

CHRISTA: (*coughs a lot*) Only in my case it is the mother who does the damage. Then I think of my father and his belt. That is damage. If I think of you as professional, there is no nurturing, no reassurance. It is hard to blend: it is black or white, there is no grey. When I say it aloud, my mother is the wrong one who causes the damage. But if I think of my father, that is not true. It is not just my mother.

ANALYST: So you have to run from one to the other.

CHRISTA: I run away from both of my parents – there is no running to them for comfort. I want the opposite direction. If I think in my mind of my mother and father, it is hard not to see "let her cry it out" without seeing the belt. Scary, harsh authority. I cannot see it with any softness. But the soft side is being manipulated. I flip from the right or wrong side and want to run away. It is guilt or the belt: you take your choice. Neither feels like I am giving Anna anything nice. Only wrapping her up and holding her – that will make her feel secure … well, wrapping her up and holding her securely, without guilt.

Christa is caught in a panicked oscillation between two dangerous parents and can only make fleeting contact with each object in her mind before running off in "the opposite direction". This phobic oscillation is triggered by the danger of permeability, of absorbing something that will only damage her: coffee, the dangerous cream offered by the pharmacist, the doctor's eye-drops. There is no safe care. My "professionalism", which we might equate with a paternal function that could protect her from being trapped inside the maternal object, leaves her cold, unprotected and floating. Though later in the session the father reappears and makes contact with her through beating, this potential seed of an erotized masochistic relation to the father, which might lead her away from maternal fusion, is bad and remains on the surface of her skin. She flips back to mother and daughter. But when she thinks of a daughter being comforted, wrapped securely in her mother's love, she falters and qualifies her thought, stressing that the wrapping must happen "*without guilt*".[4] The two objects – the mother who invasively wraps and secretes, the father whose distance intrudes as beating – are not,

217

in Freud's phrase, "in some way united with one another". Without this mediation, her mind is flooded with panic: there is no safe way to relate to me, and she cannot think.

Contact with either parent threatens a dangerous seduction that would entail giving up on access to the other sex. So she must yield to neither parent, refusing passivation[5] by both. This interferes with the process of identification with the parental objects. In the fourth year of our work, Christa was to say, sadly: "Actually I am neither, neither a girl nor a boy." She remains "stateless" in terms of her internal identifications and therefore in her bisexual functions. It is this double incompleteness – neither girl nor boy – that she screens with her phallic androgynous phantasy that she is more complete, able to overtake both the men and the women in the swimming pool. In terms of the four positions I outlined in relation to sexual difference, we see that when genital bisexuality, predicated on the acceptance of castration, cannot function, then patient and analyst are trapped in the realms of archaic fusion, primary homosexuality and phallic bisexuality and cannot relate reciprocally.

## Snake, analysis, father

In the fourth year of her analysis, Christa brought three dreams in which her predicament was clearly revealed:

*In the first dream I was being swallowed by a snake – it might have been a boa constrictor. I was inside it, being pulled down. Two men were there talking to each other, but oblivious to me as I was calling out to them to help me. The snake's digestive juices were eating me. Eventually I pulled myself out by holding onto the snake's teeth. When I got out I was shocked when I saw that I was all red and bloody because my skin had begun to dissolve. One of the men said: "It's not a problem. You're just losing your skin."*

*The second dream was that I forgot to come to my session.*

Christa had two associations: her daughter's need for laminated revision cards to help with her examination anxiety, and the breakdowns and bereavements of the two men in the dream. She then half-remembered being wrapped in a white blanket by her mother. But was her mother lovingly settling her for the night or quasi-murderously swaddling her, hoping to be free of her demands?

I linked the dream to her current frustration that she cannot "go right through" any process, that she has to pull herself out of immersion in any task. This includes the process of the analysis with me because of the danger (demonstrated by this dream) that in going right through the snake, she will lose her own self and be dissolved. Christa thought of the difficulty she had in "going through" adolescence.

The snake, with its bisexual dimensions, represents elements of both the maternal and paternal in Christa's mind.

First, constricted inside the pre-oedipal mother, with no separating membrane or placental wall, Christa risks losing the boundaries of her own self, illustrated by the terrifying dissolution of her skin by the snake's digestive juices. This is analogous to being comfortingly wrapped up by a mother who is simultaneously secreting guilt into you for existing. I recognized in the dream my recurrent countertransference experience of finding that my mind is dissolved in the encounter with Christa's. Then I sink into a deep passivity, a seductive and terrifying surrender to a murderous amalgamation in which my analytic aliveness is placed in jeopardy as I renounce my difference and yield to the pull of being "identical". Seduction by the mother's care promises not intrauterine paradise, but intrauterine hell: traumatic multiplication of the risks associated with passivation (Green, 1986b, p. 247).

Second, this dream provides an *après-coup* representation of the disabling trauma for Christa's adolescent ego when the reality of sexual difference burst in as rape on her unprepared mind. She is vulnerable because the father, standing for sexual difference and the threat of castration, has not succeeded in getting a secure purchase on her. In this context we can understand that my "premature" interpretation of sexual difference when I observed that she was not one of the racing men, was a structurally determined repetition of this adolescent trauma. In Christa's dream, the men who might rescue her from immersion in the maternal are damaged and oblivious to her, and she cannot make a proper relation to them – just as I struggled to hear and engage with my colleagues' concern that I was lost in the patient after I had reported the first session. The other parent is reduced to a "barely distinguishable trace", the danger Freud had noted (1923b). So Christa must rescue herself from the maternal, fight her own way out – a phallic solution. In a complex double move, she identifies with the father-as-a-phallus,

219

which she is simultaneously trapped inside in the form of the mother-as-a-phallus.

So although superficially the snake dream suggests that bisexual identifications are in play, actually it represents with terrifying clarity an underlying problem: a failure to establish two clearly differentiated foundations: Freud's masculine and feminine "in some way united" (Freud, 1923b, p. 32). Here it is the repudiation of the masculine, the father, that impedes the development of a genital bisexuality based on the acceptance of castration. Furthermore, Christa's second dream – that she forgets to come to analysis – suggests that there is a risk she will opt to rest dreamily inside her mother, unable to hear her analyst's words.

Then Christa brought another dream:

> *I was travelling through Russia, but we weren't in any particular state. I don't know where we were but we were trying to get to a race. Paul was with me in a big van, so it was hard to negotiate the roads. I was annoyed – why does Paul have to be here? I can negotiate myself. But I was also anxious, which is why he was there. Then there was a weird bit. I was on the top of a mountain, and the van was now a bus, and my sisters were on board. My father was driving and crashed the bus and we fell off the path. How could we fall off the path and crash? I could see someone – my younger sister – dead in the snow. And I saw my father's body in the snow too, and I ran over. Then I saw him pulling himself up out of the snow, shaking it off. It was like he had been buried in the snow and was coming out again.*

Christa reported that she had woken from this dream crying out for her father, not knowing what "state" he was in. In this dream she works through the repudiation of the father and his message of castration. Initially puzzled by her husband's presence, she realizes that she needs him because she is anxious: there is something *"weird"* and unsafe about the father. He has allowed her to assume a position of phallic omnipotence, leaving her vulnerable to a crashing fall. As she reflected on the dream, Christa was puzzled that eventually there are only two bodies: that of the dead girl, which "doesn't really seem significant" and "feels like [it] only really exists in my head", and the body of her father, which does seem significant. The sleeping father (previously represented by the teacher violently woken up by the stones on his roof) is now desperately called for.

He must be disinterred from the sleepy white snow in which he has been buried, in order to bring his daughter to life.

His task is to establish differentiated "states".[6] Christa is in no "particular state" in the dream and does not know where she is. When she wakes up from the dream, she does not know what "state" her father is in. And she feels that she is "neither, neither a girl nor a boy". As she progresses through this sequence of dreams – snake/analysis/father – Christa is moving from immersion in an undifferentiated "stateless" bisexuality via analysis of her phallic bisexuality towards the establishment of a differentiated psychic bisexuality. Simultaneously, the effectiveness of her symbolic functioning increases: at the start of the analysis a dream of being unable to get to her session was precisely enacted three weeks later, but now Christa does not forget to come to analysis. The father, standing for separation from the maternal, castration and access to symbolization, is waking up.

## Passivity is not inertia: passivity as medium

Freud proposes that the child's encounter with sexual difference is organized by the threat of castration, the father's prohibition of incest with the mother, and that it is in terms of this prohibition that the girl's lack of a penis is interpreted. His assertion was met by a well-documented chorus of protest.[7] Jones and Klein, for example, proposed a femininity predicated on presence, the bodily reality of the female sexual organs, which are more or less consciously known by the small girl and entail a primary heterosexuality. Klein (1928, p. 166) was first to use the terms "receptive" and "receptivity" in a psychoanalytic context when she refers to the "receptive aim of the vagina". An inheritance from this strand of thinking is our use of the term "receptivity" to designate feminine psychic functioning. It allows us to establish femininity as different from but equal to masculinity. Freud's "two foundational terms" – masculine/active and feminine/passive – can be re-phrased as feminine receptivity in relation to masculine activity. This sounds much more equitable.[8]

But we need to pay attention to the consequences of our conceptualization of receptivity. To opt for a receptivity premised on the fact of the biological presence of the vagina is to displace Freud's insistence on psychic sexuality: "we must keep psychoanalysis separate from biology" (Freud, 1935, p. 328). Freud's model allows us to acknowledge the complex vicissitudes of the construction of sexual identifications within the individual and hence of bisexual functions. There is no given heterosexuality.

In her summation of the evolution of thinking about the feminine, Birksted-Breen (2005, p. 148) persuasively argues for two feminines: a positive feminine derived from the female body ego, and a negative feminine organized by castration as a fundamental psychic structure prior to the self, represented by the father standing for the law. Here I wish to stay with the "negative feminine", because it allows us to see that the phobia of passivity, which prompts the repudiation of femininity, is tied to a fear of castration, when passivity is viewed from a phallic vantage point. Within the frame of negative femininity, the desire to receive the penis from the other is not biologically determined or primary but is the outcome of a process of working through phantasies of castration and seduction.[9] This receptiveness is initiated by the transition from phallic, supremacist bisexual functioning to "genital" bisexual functioning: finding a way to be both through not being both.

Perelberg (2003, p. 589) differentiates between passivity and receptivity. She writes that passivity is linked "(in terms of *après-coup*) to a 'phantasy' of a specific position in a scene of seduction in the primal scene." In contrast, receptivity "implies activity on the side of Eros". She contrasts this receptive mode with the lack of reciprocity, found when there is a rejection of the differences between the sexes and generations in a bid to retain a phallic position. The central issue is the desire to retain a phallic position: when there is only the phallus, there can be no reciprocal relating; to be passive is to be raped, and passivity is a phobic situation. Turning to the analyst for help with the construction of an ego shield that can insulate against the activity of the drive, the patient is threatened with a passivity that appears to repeat, or at least evoke, the primary traumatic flooding by the drive.

However, I would suggest that when genital bisexual functioning is operative, passivity can be desired and then function as the necessary medium through which two kinds of activity can meet and intersect. In a linked process, the activity of the drive is passively experienced and is then actively represented in the mind. For the patient, this is the experience of passivity in relation to the activity of the drive and in relation to the activeness of parental care. For the analyst, this is the experience of passivity in the face of the patient's expressive activity in the session, nudging her into a particular role in the countertransference (Sandler, 1976). The achievement of genital bisexuality ushers in, and is dependent on, a reworked primal scene in which there is a reciprocity of linked functions and passivity is a necessary and tolerable state. Passivity becomes a resource: "passivity–passibility" (Scarfone, 2010, p. 8).

## Bisexual functioning: an achievement for patient and analyst

Christa's snake dream with its suggestion that she had to stage her own emergency rescue from the constricting maternal supports her belief that she missed the adolescent process. Unable to take her time over the transition to genital sexuality, she encounters it unprepared by an early adolescent phase of fantasizing sexuality. An important element of this fantasizing is indicated by Cournut-Janin (1998b, p. 627), who suggests that at this stage rape fantasies can be used in the progressive integration of the desire to be penetrated, leading to the "full richness of bisexual identifications: penetrating, being penetrated". The snake dream graphically illustrates the absence of this integration and the need for the analytic process as an adolescent process, as time for phantasy.

Freud and Green focus on the patient's capacity to tolerate femininity/passivation. But isn't this also a work of the countertransference? For the analyst, seduced and castrated by the patient, passivity also brings its unconscious terrors, and the analyst may also long to repudiate femininity. Yet in order to learn, through experience, the shape of "masculine" and "feminine" in the patient's mind, the way that the primal scene has been configured by the patient, the analyst must be able to desire to be passive with the patient and to have the boundaries of her own sexual identifications broken open and dissolved. We may suspect that the degree and nature of the analyst's resistance to the prospect of passivity will be linked to the specific shape of the primal scene phantasy. The analyst may be most phobic about femininity/passivity when the primal scene is an undifferentiated crash in which two identificatory positions cannot be distinguished, let alone reciprocally connected. Or when it entails being seduced into an eternally passive fusion with the mother, as in the session I related to my colleagues. Or when it involves a phallic "gladiatorial battle" in the sexual action of the session – raping/phallic/active versus raped/castrated/passive – over who is to suffer femininity.

One of the "great riddles" of sexuality might be the apparent paradox that psychic bisexuality is a given in Freudian thought and yet psychic bisexuality is a desirable goal and achievement of the analytic session. We are born bisexual and yet we have to acquire bisexuality. The process of acquisition involves moving from fusion with the identical object to primary homosexuality in which the object is taken to be like the self in its sexuality; and then on through the renunciation of phallic bisexuality to genital bisexuality in which sexual difference is accepted and interiorized. This is the transition from bisexuality as defence to bisexuality as resource. Then the logic of "virtual complementarity" with respect to sexual difference pertains (David, 1975, p. 834): the masculine/penetrative/active necessarily requires the feminine/receptive/passive for its functioning, and vice versa. Now the functions represented by "the other to me" can be imagined and desired, claimed and deployed, in a fluidly dynamic interplay. According to David, the analytic treatment activates the bisexualization process, awakening or re-awakening the complementary shape of the potential "other sex" in the patient's mind, making possible the interiorization of sexual difference. This recalls Freud's insistence that both identifications need to be linked in some way through the Oedipus complex, and that we need to retain a trace of the other identification.

The pairing of analyst and patient in the sexual action of the analytic session activates the analyst's bisexualization process as much as the patient's, prompting the analyst to move intrapsychically between experiential passivity and representing activity. These linked functions of the primal scene, *being* both active and passive, lead to the construction of an ego shield for patient and analyst. It is the absence of this shield that Christa's snake dream illustrates: the absence of a permeable – neither "laminated" nor leaky – membrane securely placed between her mind and her drives and between herself and her primary object, protecting against traumatic anxiety. The analyst can only desire to be seduced and passivated by the patient if she can trust in her own bisexual functioning, that she can keep for herself a dormant capacity for representational activity, which will transform her passive experience of the patient. This dormant capacity for thought, buried like the father under snow, paralysed by the seductive or castrating action of the patient, is asleep but not dead.

We often preface our clinical accounts with a confident statement about the patient: she is a 20-year-old woman, he is a 16-year-old boy, and so on. But as Christa moved dreamily around in her mind one day, she thought of a photograph of a woman in a wedding dress, then one of a latency boy. Her brother? Her? Then she remembered being stuck in a stupid little white dress as a teenager. As sexuality plays itself out in the analytic setting, we have to hear the story of the patient's psychosexuality "more than one way at once" (Smith, 2014, p. 51), hear the "woman–manly" and "man–womanly" stories, the coterminous temporalities of psychic bisexuality. This demands of us that we allow the patient's phantasies of the primal scene, seduction and castration to *"get in and break down"* (as Christa put it) the stories we tell about our own sexual identifications in the session. Only in this way can the patient be enabled to access and link to the "barely distinguishable traces" of the other sexual identification in themselves, leading to the development of their own capacity for bisexual functioning.

## Notes

1 My title comes from Ali Smith's (2014) novel, *How to Be Both*, in which the reader has to mediate between two first-person narratives involving complex and fluid sexual identifications. As Smith writes, the task is to learn to "tell a story ... more than one way at once, and tell another underneath it up-rising through the skin of it ..." (p. 51).
2 For example, Birksted-Breen (2005, p. 148) writes: "The psychic possession of a good internal penis is necessary for both men and women as is psychic bisexuality for good mental functioning." And Green (1986b, p. 247) has reflected on how resistance to the analytic process lies in the repudiation of femininity.
3 Scarfone (2010, p. 2), quoting Levinas. Scarfone offers an evocative picture of the analyst's passivity when taken "hostage" by the patient, "besieged and persecuted". He argues that the analyst's task is to find activity within this extreme passivity. But, despite his linking this passivity to Laplanche's sexual "do not force your way in, do not rape me", Scarfone opts to desexualize the process. In doing so, he sacrifices the potential inherent in Freud's two-fold active and passive sexual identifications, the *"foundation"*, for Freud (1920a, p. 147), of analytic work.
4 In Laplanche's terminology, with the father we are in the neurotic world of implantation, messages placed on the surface of the skin. The father's contact struggles to compete with the world of the mother in which messages are passed through the skin as intromission: the maternal object secretes guilt into her. (Laplanche, 1999, p. 136).

5 "Passivation" is Green's (1986b, p. 247) term for the patient's capacity to hand themselves trustingly to the analyst's care. He translates Freud's phrase, the "repudiation of femininity", as the repudiation of the mother's passivating *action*, her seductive care, rendering the infant passive. Implicit in Green's analysis of the repudiation of passivation is the way in which the passivity induced by maternal care evokes passivity in the face of the drive.

6 David (1975, p. 841) recalls the etymology of the word "mediate": to cut in half. The father's function in establishing differentiated *states* rests on his capacity to cut the child from the mother.

7 See the discussions of this debate in Perelberg (1997a, 2003, 2015c), Mitchell (1982), Chasseguet-Smirgel (1964c) and Birksted-Breen (1993).

8 A Pepweb search reveals that over the last fifty years a new collocation, – "active receptivity" – has become increasingly popular, often with a comment to say that receptivity is not passivity. We can replace "passivity" by "receptivity", but still the anxiety that passivity is inertia haunts our terminology and we have to up the ante, linguistically.

9 Birksted-Breen (2005) suggests that the feminine unconscious revolves around the uneasily conjoined perspectives of the "positive" and "negative" feminine. In choosing to stay with the negative feminine in this chapter, I am merely placing to one side the notion of receptivity as an elaboration of the female body, in order to focus on receptiveness as an outcome of the renunciation of phallic bisexuality.

# 11

# ALIENATING IDENTIFICATIONS AND SEXUALITY

*Donald Campbell*

## Introduction

Mr Jones sought treatment for what he experienced as his "ambivalence". He did not know who he was and was deeply unhappy that he could not have any meaningful relationships. At the beginning of his therapy Mr Jones declared that he was gay, but he consistently tried to find out whether he could be heterosexual. Mr Jones' anxiety about his father's hostility and passivity and his mother's seductive acquisitiveness made it impossible for him to find a safe object – either man or woman – to relate to sexually. Instead, his identifications with his oedipal couple led to alienation. He could not satisfactorily express his sexuality or engage in a relationship of his choice, whether homosexual or heterosexual. He retreated into masturbatory activities, taking his own body as his sexual object.

This chapter is a clinical account of how Mr Jones' alienating identifications undermined the development of his sexuality.

## Clinical material

### First six months

Mr Jones, who was 27 and single, told me that he was gay at the outset of his analysis. He also told me that he needed help because of his "ambivalence". He said, "I can never make up my mind. I can never decide who I want to be with, and what I want to do.

I really can't have any meaningful relationships." Mr Jones told me that masturbating was the only way he got any sexual pleasure. He had never had intercourse with a woman but had numerous girl-friends when he was an adolescent (13–18 years old), with a lot of violent fantasies. He had a frequent phantasy of women tying him up with ropes. He would break the ropes and aggressively "screw" the women. It was the "switch" that startled them, and their sur-prised look excited him. This sequence of Mr Jones' associations points to his fear of being taken over by women and his use of sad-omasochism to control them. In the first month it became clear that he was ambivalent about his sexual orientation. As he said, "I can't decide whether to go to a gay massage place or a straight one."

Mr Jones worked as a graphic designer and came to his once-a-week psychoanalytic–psychotherapeutic sessions dressed in jeans, sweater and trainers. However, his tense movements and his alert expression undercut his casual appearance. His flat affect persisted throughout his seven years of working with me. He used the couch throughout.

In the second month, Mr Jones came back after a weekend and said, "I don't know how to say this. (Silence.) I don't know. (Silence.) It's really embarrassing." Then very quietly and hesitantly he said, "I love you." I acknowledged his feelings with a murmur, but said nothing. This was a moment without a context, from someone who felt like a stranger, like someone he might have met in a gay massage parlour. It was unsettling, and I was filled with uncertainty. I did not know who he was in love with in the transference. At that moment, I did not know who I was for him. Also, I did not know who he was identified with, his mother or his father. I was struck by how multi-determined his remark was and how initially I could not find an object – even myself – in the communication. The moment passed, but I had a sense that I had been subjected to the projection of an active sexuality by an undifferentiated object.

Later, I thought that my initial reaction had, in part, been an attempt to defend against feelings of shock and disorientation. Mr Jones could say, "I love you" so directly and without a context pre-cisely because he did not experience me in a relationship – hence, my initial reaction of looking for and not finding who I was in the transference. Actually, I think he felt we were strangers. He could say, "I love you" *because* there was no relationship. In his mind, we were strangers. I came to understand this moment as an enactment of Mr Jones' masturbation phantasy, of his ongoing need to avoid any kind of intercourse. The therapy continued while he filled this state of limbo with sensations that disarmed me, just as he was able to do with his remark, "I love you". In this way, Mr Jones created a love object that was disoriented. This captured a feature of Mr Jones's way of relating to me that persisted throughout the time of his work with me. Although Mr Jones could occasionally report feelings and express them in sessions, there was more likely to be an absence of affect.

In the third month Mr Jones said with some relief that on a recent holiday he had been active for the first time when masturbating a man in a gay massage parlour. He added, "But I got really upset. I got sexually excited, and then couldn't do anything with it. We just pretended to ignore it, and talked about something else." His comment made me aware of how I had defended myself against Mr Jones profession of love for me by talking about other things. Did he want to have sex with me, or did he just want to be held by me?

Later, he told me that before he started coming to see me he had fallen in love with a man who became engaged to a woman. He vehemently denied that this mattered to him and brushed aside the link I made to his feelings about me. However, he felt relieved when I took up his feeling empty, his wish to be loved for himself, not just for the way he looked after this man, and his fear that he would not find anyone else apart from me. This led him to tell me about how his narcissistic mother had smothered him. He said, "She kept asking me if she was a good mother. I had to look after her all the time and make her feel good about herself." Her narcissistic love for him was her way of taking total possession of him. This retrospectively added another way of understanding his profession of love for the analyst. It was a way of narcissistically taking possession of me.

Mr Jones felt empty because he could not define himself in a relationship with another object. There was a masturbatory quality in the sessions, a lack of internal development and a sense of stasis.

### Eighteen months later

On a Monday Mr Jones told me that over the weekend he chose to go to a "heterosexual" massage parlour and was pleased that he got an erection while a woman massaged him for the first time. He had been afraid he wouldn't. In the silence that followed I wondered to myself, why now? Had he been missing me over the weekend? Was he identifying with me, or rather imitating what he thought I would do? Did my interpretations about his anxiety that I, like his mother, would smother him enable him to feel safer with a woman?

Mr Jones broke the silence to say, "Fantasies about women ... fucking angry at my boss and you." This was followed by a silence. I took up his anxiety that I would disapprove of his fantasies about women because he was leaving me for a woman. Mr Jones' associations moved from faceless women that he "just put it into" to fantasizing about lying next to a woman who would be his pregnant wife and feeling her tummy and their child inside, which led to an erection. His next association was to his father, who always disapproved of him. Mr Jones said that he felt that his sexual attraction to his mother had to be denied and kept "outside". I took up his feeling that he could only be a potent man from a distance. He agreed, then complained about a "nasal block", and left the room "to get a drink". On his return, I decided to take up how thinking about being unblocked, being a potent male with a female, led to anxiety about being with a woman, perhaps being suffocated by a "nasal block", like the one he feels with me and his mother.

During the following silence, I thought that Mr Jones' heterosexual phantasy collapsed under the weight of his anxiety about his father's disapproval and the threat of his mother's engulfment. Mr Jones did not have a third object who could support his masculinity in relation to a woman or represent an alternative to a dangerous mother. There seemed to be no room for a father and no room for an oedipal couple in the mind of his mother. She only had room for her son.

Mr Jones then told me that during the previous summer holiday, when he shared a room with a girl on a Greek island, mucus streamed from his nose, but it stopped as soon as he left the island.

Mr Jones' ambivalence about his sexual identity took the form of his thinking about his homosexuality as an attack on his heterosexuality. Sexuality – homosexual and heterosexual – was dirty, messy and out of control (his nose streaming with mucus). He said that he masturbated every day "to not get randy and keep myself asexual".

When I took up his self-castration as identification with his mother who, he thought, had neutered his father, he angrily replied, "What did she do to Dad's masculinity? Why didn't Dad fight back?" Mr Jones then became anxious about what he would do to a woman.

The following weekend Mr Jones went home. At the next session he reported his father's attacks on his masculinity, saying, by way of an example, "Dad tried to cut me off on the way from the public toilet back to mom." The phallic "race" with father from the anality of the public toilet to mother was not so much a competition as a castration.

The theme of castration anxiety being triggered by Mr Jones' move from anality to genitality persisted. Mr Jones often experienced me as an attacking father whenever his heterosexual fantasies emerged. I linked this to his father's retaliation for Mr Jones' incestuous wishes towards his mother.

Did Mr Jones unconsciously feel safer in the toilet with his father? Although he entertained sexual fantasies about his mother, he also felt smothered by her and was anxious about being violent towards women, which, in turn, made him anxious about penetrating them. Mr Jones appeared to occupy a no-man's land, a place without a secure homosexual or heterosexual identity, which was played out in the following session.

Mr Jones walked into the consulting room looking dazed and disoriented. He walked awkwardly past the couch, towards a chair behind my desk, before he realized what he was doing, turned around, went back to the couch and lay down.

After a silence, he said that he had had a dream before the last session and wondered why he had not told me about it. I wondered, too, but said nothing.

*In this dream, he is standing at a bus stop with a number of other chaps, not actually forming a queue but standing as though waiting for a bus. The men were in civilian clothes, but he knew they were members of the Territorial Army. When the bus arrived and he got on he noticed that there was one seat in the middle of the bus next to the window. A captain occupied the seat next to the empty seat. Sitting next to the captain on the aisle was his lieutenant. Mr Jones thought the empty seat was the best seat on the bus, a special seat, and asked the captain if he minded if he sat there. The captain nodded his agreement, and Mr Jones sat down, feeling quite pleased with himself.*

231

Mr Jones said, "I think this dream is about my wish to be special. Something to do with wanting to be special to you, like I always wanted to be special to my dad, but never was." He was also pleased that in the dream he was able to take some initiative and actually got what he wanted. But there was some trepidation about what he was doing.

After a brief silence, Mr Jones said that he had had another dream last night, which reminded him of the room where he has his sessions, although it was not quite like that. "*The room was about twice the size of this one*", and he extended his hand in the direction of the wall opposite the couch. He then recalled that when he moved from the previous consulting room – which was, in fact, more spacious than the room we were now in – he felt cramped in this smaller room. My own association, which I did not mention, was to wonder whether the smaller room, which reduced the distance between us, increased his anxiety about being smothered by me, his mother in the transference.

> *In his dream, there was a couch like the one he was lying on, in the same position. There was also another couch in the other half of the room opposite the analytic couch, which was more like a bed with the cover pulled back. He was standing by this bed while a man and a woman, whom he vaguely associated to being somewhat friendly, benign people at work, were standing and talking near the analytic couch. He noticed his semen on the sheets of the bed and surreptitiously pulled the cover over it, so that the couple would not see his semen. He then realized that it was his session time, and he walked past the couple to the couch. He was annoyed with the couple, especially the woman, and shouted to her as he was getting on the couch, "You don't know what this cost me." With another shout and a gesture, he got them both to leave.*

His first association was to the couple. "They were not close friends, but friendly to me at work. I feel embarrassed that I actually got rid of them." He thought this couple must have something to do with his parents and his anger at them, especially his mother, for not being better parents and, therefore, responsible for his ending up "here". He was also worried that their presence would actually interfere with his therapy, as though they were taking up his time with me. This led to his thinking about pushing women away.

I was struck by the way he came into the room as though he actually expected the room to be larger than it was. He felt awkward and hemmed-in by the reality of the size of the room, as though consciously he had not expected the wall to be where it was. And he walked right past me as I was sitting behind the couch, the first time he had done that, and walked towards my empty chair behind my desk. I confirmed that he had enacted his wish in the dream to sit next to me. I added, "I wonder if we can see another aspect of the first dream from the way you walked into the room, that is to take my seat at the desk, and in this way, feel special not just by being next to me, but by taking my place." This was followed by a thoughtful silence.

My thoughts led me back to my earlier association to his feeling cramped in this consulting room. Was that a projection of his smothering mother? I put it to him that going directly to my desk chair, which was next to me (as in the dream), seemed to represent an effort to find a safe man to be with when he felt overwhelmed by his mother. Mr Jones let out a long sigh and then, through gritted teeth, said, "Yeah."

I broke the ensuing angry silence to say, "In the second dream you not only felt shame about your masculinity, your semen on the sheets that you covered over, but also anxious." He replied, "Yes, I remember feeling ashamed and confused." I said that perhaps his confusion reflected his anxiety. After a pause I added, "I thought that you defended against your anxiety about sexual intercourse with women by getting rid of the couple, perhaps your parents, who were engaged in verbal intercourse. You then took up a passive dependent position on your back on the couch." I said that shouting at them, "You don't know what this cost me" was his way of using his passive submissive behaviour to attack his mother as though he was saying, "Look what you have done to me. Look what you've turned me into. Someone who has to hide his semen." In this way, he could blame his mother and avoid the shame and anxiety associated with his semen, the evidence of his generative masculinity. "I don't like to think about that" he said, "but I do feel shame and I do want to attack my mother." Later, I took up what it cost him to resolve the trap represented by bringing his mother and father together in the dream. However, the solution was only temporary. But why? Was the mother's genital, the repository of his semen, seen as disturbing his mind? Or, did he project his guilt onto

233

the heterosexual couple who would retaliate because he got rid of them, and then chose to return to a passive homosexual relationship with his male analyst?

My own puzzlement seemed to reflect Mr Jones' dissociated state at the beginning of the session when his perception of reality had been distorted and the boundaries of the room were blurred. I thought that the transference to his mother aroused psychotic anxieties about loss of his orientation to reality and body boundaries. In this dissociated state, Mr Jones moved towards the masculine object, me (and my chair). I said that I thought this state reflected the anxiety he felt about his sexual boundaries, and his wish for me to help him claim his masculinity, to own his semen. Mr Jones was also struck by how awkward and disoriented he felt when he walked into the room. He said, "Yeah, it was like I didn't know where I was, and the walls didn't seem to be where I expected them to be." I thought Mr Jones was trying to tell me that I had moved too close to him with my comment that he wanted me to "help him claim his masculinity". Mr Jones' reaction seemed to represent the confused state of his internal world; wondering where the boundaries between us were, the uncertain balance between his activity and passivity, the confused nature and function of his masculinity and his object choices, triggered by coming into my consulting room.

With much hesitation and shame, he returned to his masturbation. He felt so humiliated by the fact that he was still just masturbating at his age, because it showed that he did not have a sexual relationship with a woman. There's always a vicious cycle when he masturbates. As soon as he has a heterosexual phantasy, he becomes excited and then anxious about being able to act on it. As his anxiety increases, he masturbates in order to find some relief and reduce the urge to actually find a woman for himself. This produces another phantasy and more masturbation. I was now thinking about what Mr Jones had told me earlier about getting satisfaction out of insight and understanding, while he readily admitted that none of it led to any change in his behaviour. I said that I thought that he gets excited by my insights, but then feels overwhelmed by me. He is able to triumph over me by masturbating rather than engaging in what he believes will be destabilizing and dangerous sexual intercourse. He replied, "I may masturbate to fantasies of girls, but I can never ejaculate. I can only ejaculate when I switch to fantasies of men. I can't let go even when I masturbate." I linked the danger of intercourse to his experience of his mother and father as a couple. He immediately said that he saw me as this inept, useless father who would never help him become a man, who could never stand up to his mother. "My mum treated me like her private penis. We had this thing, like we were a special couple. I always felt I was better than Dad." I thought I now understood more about Mr Jones's reaction to my assumption that he wanted me to help him own his masculinity. He actually believed that I could never help him because I couldn't stand up to his mother. Mr Jones believed that identification with his father would not lead to a potent internal masculine identity. Instead he quickly associated to masturbation in order to concretely take possession of his penis.

Although I did not take this up with Mr Jones at the time, I thought, in retrospect, that the two couches in the dream represented two aspects of his analysis. The couch with the semen had the potential for creativity, but sexual intercourse was also shameful and covered up. The couple and their potential generativity are dismissed, and the semen is left as a wet dream, not deposited in a woman. In the dream, the analytic couch appears to represent Mr Jones' resolution of his anxieties about using his semen in intercourse with a woman by making a passive homosexual submission to his analyst and choosing a sterile, masturbatory analysis.

## Alienating identifications

Mr Jones' relationship with his parents was dominated by their narcissism. He was not experienced as separate and independent, but was unconsciously used as a receptacle for unacceptable aspects of the parents and then identified by the parents as such. Mr Jones' mother saw him as her "private penis". His father projected his passive masculinity into his son.

Faimberg (2005) has suggested that "acknowledging the child as a separate individual involves the parents in an active elaboration of their narcissism, in order to permit the child to work through a genuine oedipal position" (p. 9). When this does not take place, the individual is trapped in what Faimberg calls an "alienated identification" – that is, "the split or alienated part of the ego is *identified with the narcissistic logic of the parents*" (p. 10 original italics). In such situations, there is no space "for the child to develop his own identity, free from the alienating power of the parents' narcissism" (p. 11).

235

Faimberg views the kind of parents described by Mr Jones as retaining pleasure as a component of the ego, while unpleasure, the equivalent of the non-ego, is projected onto their children. This is seen as a repetition of their introjection of their parents' – the child's grandparents' – projections of unpleasurable aspects of themselves and the patient's re-projection of the parents' projections into their children.

This transgenerational process of identification is represented in a dream:

> *Mr Jones dreamt about his grandfather standing on a rickety chair as he tried to reach something. He fell, and Mr Jones broke his fall, but the grandfather collapsed in a crumpled heap. Mr Jones was shocked at his grandfather's crumpled state and felt guilty. He should have anticipated the fall, but, in the dream, Mr Jones questions why he should feel guilty. It would have been worse if he had not broken grandfather's fall. Then grandfather got up and laughed at him for being upset.*

Mr Jones' first association was that the dream was about his relationship with his father. This seemed to confirm a sense that Mr Jones' father, in some way, represented grandfather, who could generate anxieties about his survival. I thought of this as an unconscious acknowledgement that his father was too unstable to stand up to his mother and stake a claim for a relationship with Mr Jones. His father was not a masculine object with whom Mr Jones could identify because his own father – the grandfather in the dream – was an insubstantial masculine figure. I said that his anger at his own father for his weakness (the collapsed grandfather) would have destroyed the (grand)father if they had separated. So, Mr Jones avoided any murderous thoughts towards his father by not leaving him (by breaking his fall). Mr Jones was unable to separate from a father whom he saw as emasculated by his mother. As a consequence, Mr Jones was left with an alienating identification.

Perelberg (2009, 2011) has distinguished between the murdered father – when the individual cannot conceive of the father in the primal scene – and the dead, symbolic father. In the dream in which Mr Jones takes a seat next to the captain, the captain may be conceived as the "dead father" – that is, a father who can be symbolized, an object for identification. The symbolization of the father, which is necessary if one is to be able to think about one's sexual identity, appears to be fragile as Mr Jones unconsciously moves away from the symbolic towards a concrete representation of the father, the chair behind my desk.

Mr Jones had not been able to separate from his mother either. In another session before my holiday break Mr Jones said that he felt abandoned by me during my holiday. When I added that he wanted to retaliate by getting rid of me, Mr Jones associated to his Uncle Stephen, who was born crippled and put into a residential care centre very early in his life. He last saw Uncle Stephen when he was 4 years old. Uncle Stephen was never talked about or referred to, and no one in the family ever visited him. His mother always said that she did not know where he was. Uncle Stephen died last Sunday. Mr Jones found out from other family members that his mother knew where Uncle Stephen had been all the time. He was shocked that someone in his mother's family had been shut away and forgotten. Is this what Mr Jones felt I was doing to him by leaving him? Is this what his parents had done to him psychologically? I added that he feared that I was turning a blind eye to his crippled mental state. Mr Jones associated to a ruthless side of his mother and was frightened by it. He also wondered if there was a ruthless part of him. Had he shut himself away?

The train of Mr Jones' association from wanting to get rid of me to his mother wanting to erase the crippled Uncle Stephen from his memory suggested to me that underlying the castration threat that his mother posed by claiming ownership of his penis was a deeper anxiety about her murderousness. Mr Jones was not only uncertain about his sexual identity, but also anxious about his survival.

## Sexuality and the oedipal couple

Human beings are not completely masculine or feminine, but an idiosyncratic mixture of active and penetrative impulses, on the one hand, and passive and receptive ones, on the other hand. The nature of our *psychic* bisexuality – that is, our unique amalgamation – is influenced by pre-oedipal development. Although unconscious phantasies about the nature of the sexual relationship between mother and father exist throughout development, the conjunction of bisexual elements during the phallic/genital phase of development is the definitive stimulus to the Oedipus complex and informs the child's view of the parents as an oedipal couple. Identification of the masculine and the feminine in both mother and father come together in what I have referred to as the oedipal couple and usually become fixed during adolescence, when our sexual identity is commonly reflected in our choice of a sexual object. Meanwhile, an inherent bisexuality supports the psychic movement into and out of loving attachments to father and mother, and new relationships.

Freud (1905) first drew attention to the importance of the presence of both parents in making an object choice in *Three Essays on the Theory of Sexuality* (1905d, p. 146). However, the theoretical groundwork for my focus here on the vicissitudes of identification with the oedipal couple has been laid by Ferraro (2001). She emphasizes:

> [Bisexuality] predisposes the primitive psychic organisation towards triangulation ... a resource for modulating the tensions inherent in the process of separation–individuation. This basic disposition of the drive, which induces both sexes to alternate between homoerotic and heteroerotic – originally paternal and maternal – objects, allows changes in their identificatory qualities and attributes which, when laid down in the pre-Oedipal relationship, receive their definitive organisation from the overcoming of the Oedipus complex. This double movement is crucial to the constitution of identity; in particular, the negative Oedipus complex ... which arises on the basis of a temporary bisexual position, again assumes great importance as a matrix of identifications, promoting psychic integration of the subject's own homosexuality, and acting as an intermediary in the acquisition of gender identity.
>
> (p. 494)

Mr Jones was not able to make this developmental move. Although he had a sense of his male gender, he did not know what kind of a man he was. Mr Jones suffered from alienating identifications with his parents, who, in his view, were not able to function as an oedipal couple. Mr Jones was unable to replace unconscious erotic attachments to his mother and conscious denigration and rejection of his father with identifications that would allow him to make non–incestuous object choices.

As a consequence, Mr Jones was not able to resolve an inherent and essential dissonance created by a psychic bisexual interplay between the attraction to the feminine and the masculine that affects us all. Usually one's psychic bisexuality is mediated by identification with the parental couple in order to achieve a kind of internal co-habitation and/or intercourse between sexual objects and one's active/penetrative and passive/receptive impulses. When these identifications become internalized, they form the building blocks of an individual's sexual identity. This is the process that broke down in Mr Jones.

The fluidity and uncertainty of Mr Jones' sexual identity point to his failure to "organise these (by definition) conflicting identifications in order to achieve an illusion of unity" (Perelberg, 1999a, p. 32). I understood Mr Jones' dissociative state of mind in the session that I reported as both an enactment of and a defence against the fluctuation of identificatory processes that fail to distinguish between phantasy and reality and overwhelm the mind. Identification with active/penetrating and passive/receptive characteristics of both parents usually contribute to tipping the psychic balance, sometimes only temporarily, towards a preference for a sexual partner who is, on balance, more masculine or more feminine.

However, in Mr Jones' case, his identifications did not help him actualize his sexuality, but left him threatened and unsettled and unable to find a safe place to be. Although Mr Jones described himself as gay, he also said that he did not know who he was. Should he go to a gay massage parlour or a straight one? The anxiety that he felt in intercourse with a woman led him to escape into homosexual phantasies. These anxieties led Mr Jones to repress a visceral awareness of his sexuality to such an extent that it was not available to support active or passive characteristics that could be used in sexual relationships. Throughout the time he worked with me, Mr Jones was ill at ease and out of touch with his body. The flatness of his affect was a striking feature of his analysis. When his repression came under pressure in the session I reported, he became dissociated.

Both his mother and father conspired to keep alive both the negative and positive oedipal illusions. Consequently, Mr Jones could not find a safe masculine or feminine object to identify with. He still had conscious sexual fantasies about his mother and thought of himself as her "private penis". The price he paid for refusing to relinquish a positive oedipal phantasy that his mother preferred him to his father was an abiding incestuous fear and hatred of her, which he repeatedly projected onto sexually attractive women.

However, a move towards his father in turn led to rejection and disappointment. Mr Jones could never mourn the loss of what he did not get from his father: the third who never arrived, as Britton (1989) puts it, to spell the end of the positive oedipal illusion of the son on the throne surrounded by his wife/mother and his court. Mr Jones also felt rejected by his father. However, in his dream of the bus trip and his enactment in the consulting room, there seemed to be a wish to prolong the negative oedipal attachment to his father in the hope that his father would give him a seat.

Mr Jones' mother and father remained conscious incestuous objects, creating a vicious cycle that dominated his current fantasies about other men and women. His presentation of himself as primarily homosexual was not gratifying or stable. When he was with a man, he projected feelings of disgust and rejected the man. When he reacted by moving towards a woman, she could arouse him, and he would dream about being genitally potent. However, he could not risk real sexual intercourse. He overcame his fears of intercourse by imagining that the woman would tie him up, and then be shocked by his escape and "fucking" her. This was against the background of anxieties about his seductive, ruthless and smothering mother, which triggered a flight to men.

Michael Feldman (2009) proposed a link between how the oedipal situation is construed internally and the patient's capacity to think "as any real understanding is dependent on the identification with a couple capable of a creative intercourse" (p. 20). Mr Jones experienced his parents not as relating sexually in a complementary way, but, instead, as locked in a sterile, hostile stalemate, a stalemate that was reflected in his inability to allow a negative or positive Oedipus complex to dominate his sexuality. His mother was seen as castrating his submissive father.

It is not surprising that Mr Jones did not have the internalized oedipal resources to be able to think of his penis as a creative link with a vagina (Birksted-Breen, 1996). At times, he could think of his penis as penetrating a woman's vagina, but his background of anxieties about surviving as a separate, coherent self with his mother led him to withdraw aggressively from the woman with a sadomasochistic phantasy of breaking free of her bonds, and only then being able to "fuck". After seven years, I was not able to help Mr Jones resolve these anxieties, which made it impossible for him to choose a male or female sexual object. He retreated to the safety of masturbation. His masculine body became the safest sexual object of choice.

## Conclusion

The resolution of the Oedipus complex will influence each individual's adaption to the cultural norms that define masculinity and femininity. It is common to think about adult sexual identity as heterosexual, homosexual or bisexual, based on the choice of a sexual object. However, psychoanalysts tend to identify an individual's sexual orientation by the nature of the predominant *phantasy* that is attached to that object. The idiosyncratic nature of one's latent psychic bisexuality – whether one is more or less active and penetrative, passive and receptive – is activated and developed by the individual's internalization of the bisexual dynamics of his or her phantasies regarding the parents' sexual relationship.

Mr Jones had recurrent homosexual and heterosexual fantasies. However, his alienating identifications with his father and mother left him too frightened to enact his fantasies in intercourse with a man or a woman. He had become captive to the narcissistic ideas of his parents and could not find a separate path from them (Faimberg, 2005, p. 9). This stalemate was enacted in his sessions as flatness and a lack of desire and emotional connection with me.

Over the course of his treatment Mr Jones progressed in his work and became less anxious. However, he did not develop any significant relationships. Mr Jones identified with the stalemate of his parents' oedipal relationship, which he experienced as antagonistic and non-complementary. Similarly, Mr Jones was in an internal stalemate, and, as a result, he did not know who he was. This was enacted in those moments when he was disorientated in the consulting room. Mr Jones' attempt to break out of this stalemate by identifying himself as gay was never substantial enough to enable him to have a relationship with a man or engage in homosexual sex.

Mr Jones maintained both a negative and a positive oedipal illusion, which kept alive his conscious incestuous phantasies about his mother and contributed to his anxiety about choosing a man or a woman as a sexual object. The absence of a psychic bisexual resolution for Mr Jones meant that he could not choose, consciously or unconsciously, between a masculine and a feminine partner, nor bear the fluidity, uncertainty and instability of that state of mind. On the one hand, any attempt Mr Jones made to choose a woman as a sexual object aroused severe castration anxieties, which he dealt with by withdrawal into fantasies of tying the woman up. On the

241

other hand, his unconscious search for a father and the castration anxiety that accompanied his identification with his mother led him to choose heterosexual men who did not respond to his sexual advances and left him to marry women. Mr Jones withdrew from men and women as sexual objects and, instead, he chose to identify himself as homosexual to the extent that he chose his own penis as his sexual object, and masturbation as his primary means of sexual gratification in order to avoid the terrifying prospect of relating sexually to another person.

Kohon (1999) asks a fundamental question that is germane to any attempt to think about sexuality. "What if there exists a radical antagonism between human sexuality and the task of making any sense of it?" (pp. 21–22). If our sexuality begins with the co-existence of opposing impulses – active and penetrative; passive and receptive – that are inherent in our bisexuality, it is not surprising that occasionally we find dissonance at our sexual core. However, there is a contradiction. The opposing impulses of bisexuality also create the possibility for complementarity. Usually the integration of one's psychic bisexuality is achieved, even if only temporarily, in a kind of co-habitation or intercourse between one's active/penetrative and passive/receptive impulses through identifications with the oedipal couple. Complementarity is evidence of bisexuality. Freud reminded us that we could also find evidence for bisexuality in the woman's resistance to abandoning her wish for a penis, or in the man's resistance to accepting "that a passive attitude to men does not always signify castration" (1937c, p. 252). The male "refuses to subject himself to a father-substitute, or to feel indebted to him for anything, and consequently he refuses to accept his recovery from the doctor" (p. 252). Freud acknowledged that this resistance in men produced one of "the strongest transference-resistances" (p. 252). This was true of Mr Jones. He attended his sessions with me regularly, free-associated and reflected on my interpretations. However, when I interpreted positive and negative aspects of his relationship with me, he responded as though I did not exist. On one occasion Mr Jones said that he loved me, but this sudden expression of affection was expressed without any sense that I was a differentiated other.

——————————— 12 ———————————

# THE NEUTER GENDER[1]

*André Green*

Although, for psychoanalysis, *difference* is sexual, the question of bisexuality is related to psychoanalytic theory as a whole. What is the position as far as abolishing – or as far as the phantasy of abolishing – this difference is concerned? And how are we to situate this particular problem if the reference points needed to localise it have not been defined? So two stages are involved. First, we shall have to establish the theoretical framework for our project; then, within this framework, we will attempt to elucidate the object of our study which is called the *neuter gender*.

## Reference points for psychical bisexuality

### *The point of departure: sexuality between biology and psychoanalysis*

No other question is better suited to demonstrate the relations between the biological roots of the drive and *psycho*-sexual life than that of sexuality. This privileged domain is well suited for examining Freud's hypotheses in the light of the scientific facts of biology, and for comparing medical clinical experience with the findings of clinical psychoanalysis in order to highlight their similarities and differences. Now, so far, this confrontation has revealed profound discrepancies which often confirm, and sometimes undermine, Freud's metapsychological postulates. The contributions of post–Freudian authors are not exempt from this new examination.

## Point 1. Biological sexuality and psycho-sexuality

Biological sexuality involves a series of relays spread out in time, each of which plays its role in determining sexual identity (chromosomal, gonadal, hormonal sexual identity, internal genitals, external genitals, secondary sexual characteristics). The main fact is that masculinity is the result of an active process (through the intervention of a testicle provoking masculine characteristics), femininity being the outcome of a passive process (obtained either as a result of pathological defect or by the normal absence of a testicle provoking masculine characteristics). One can therefore speak of a development of biological sexuality, from conception to puberty, which is characterised by a discontinuous and differentiated process. However, in the human species a new mutative relay (Organiser I) appears which is superimposed on biological development. This relay is at the origin of an autonomous psychological development which is different from biological development and responsible for psycho-sexuality. The human relay is the fundamental determinant of an individual's sexuality. (cf. Money, Hampson, & Hampson, 1955).

## Point 2. Parental wishes and infantile sexuality

This mutative relay is constituted by labelling the child with a sexual gender, which may conform more or less to the individual's morphological sexuality (cf. the clinical data on intersexual states with genital ambiguity: pseudo-hermaphroditism [Kreisler, 1970]). This labelling is closely connected with parental wishes. Its mode of action finds expression in the mother–child relationship from birth on until the child is about 2½ years old. At this point, the individual experiences and sees himself as clearly monosexual (Money, Hampson, & Hampson, 1955).

## Point 3. Freud

The Freudian theory of bisexuality has had the merit of distinguishing psychical bisexuality from biological bisexuality. Nevertheless, when he comes up against difficult questions, at many points in his work, Freud maintains that the solution to the mystery is to be found in biology, something which does not seem to be confirmed by science today. Moreover, the Freudian theory of libido development may nowadays seem to be too exclusively based on an individual evolution underestimating the parent–child relationship, or not related to it.

### Point 4. Melanie Klein and Winnicott

By playing down the problem of castration and the difference between the sexes, Melanie Klein's theory neglects bisexuality and, more generally, the problematics of sexuality in favour of the problematics of aggression. On the other hand, Winnicott's theory puts the emphasis on the parent–child relationship and takes into account the inter-relationships between processes of maturation and the maternal environment, but perhaps underestimates the father's role and that of parental sexuality. The role of maternal care can be interpreted in a more metapsychological way than it was by Winnicott. Of course, I am not talking about an external influence. Rather, one might conceive of it as the necessary connection of two drive apparatuses linked to each other by the difference of potential owing to their unequal development (the coverage of the child's id-ego by the mother's ego–id). This first connection would in turn be linked up with the father's drive apparatus, in a metaphorical position (Lacan). Each of these three apparatuses would initially be able to have a mediating function between the two others. This first stage would be followed by a reorganisation once monosexuality had been established.

### Point 5. The "imprint" of desire: the parental phantasy

It seems probable that when a parent labels his or her child with a sexual gender, it acts like a psychical *imprint* which, however, cannot be likened to the mechanism as it is described in animals. This *imprint* is constituted following the perception of the child's body as a sexual form, which is strengthened or weakened thereafter by the parent. The parental phantasy, in particular the mother's, therefore has to be seen as playing a powerful inductive role in establishing individual monosexuality. All eventualities are possible: ignoring sexual ambiguity (hermaphroditism or pseudo-hermaphroditism); rejecting a biological sex without ambiguity (boy brought up as a girl, and vice versa); unconsciously valuing

245

the sex which the child does not have; showing more or less total intolerance of an individual's psychical bisexuality by means of repression and by making the individual feel guilty for attitudes and tendencies which do not belong to his or her biological sex, etc. One should bear in mind that this psychical impregnation is tied up with other factors such as perpetuating a fusional relationship with the child beyond the period when this should cease, the attitude vis-à-vis aggressivity, attempting to block the transition of investment from the mother to the father and so on. What needs to be emphasised here is that this impregnation is subject to the influence of a parent who is himself (or herself) caught in a conflict with respect to psychical bisexuality.

### Point 6. Psychical bisexuality and personal phantasy

There is reason to suppose, therefore, that an individual's psychosexuality is dominated by the mother's phantasy. The latter is constituted on the basis of various parameters: an infantile desire to have a child from her father or mother; the sex of this imaginary child; the mother's acceptance of her own sex; the role the husband's (i.e. the child's father's) desire has in her own desire; desire for this desire, etc. On the other hand, the individual's psychical bisexuality is constituted by means of personal phantasy (more or less related to the parental phantasy). It is through constituting the phantasy of the other sex – the one we do not have but which we could have through imagination, in the oedipal triangle – that psychical bisexuality is organised, as Freud recognised.

### Point 7. Psychical conflict and the phantasy of the primal scene

Psychical conflict occurs on several levels which are interconnected. The individual's sex depends, then, on the way he is experienced and perceived by his mother and father, on their convergent and divergent desires for him, and on the way in which he experiences and perceives himself in his convergent and divergent desires towards them. This conflict is intimately tied up with the individual's narcissism as well as his destructive drives. It culminates in the phantasy of the primal scene (Organiser 2), which brings into play contradictory desires and identifications.

## Point 8. The neuter gender

Although this conflict ordinarily contributes to the organisation of psychical bisexuality, another possible outcome can be found in destroying sexual desire and therefore sexual identification. The counterpart and complement of psychical bisexuality, whether manifest or latent, thus seems to be the phantasy of the *neuter gender*, neither masculine nor feminine, and dominated by *absolute primary narcissism*. This crushing of drive activity leads the subject's idealising and megalomaniac inclinations not towards the fulfilment of sexual desire but towards a longing for a state of psychical nothingness in which *being nothing* seems to be the ideal condition of self-sufficiency. This tendency towards zero never, of course, attains its goal and finds expression in self-restrictive behaviour of suicidal significance.

## Point 9. The oedipal complex and the castration complex

Another mutative relay will organise all the earlier data during the oedipal complex (Organiser 3) when bisexuality is put to the test. The oedipal complex, always dual – positive and negative – culminates in a double identification, masculine and feminine. These two identifications are not, however, of equal form; they are complementary and contradictory, one dominating the other and concealing it, more or less. The castration complex, as Freud describes it, possesses an indisputable heuristic value. It is a time of reorganisation. Before it, the exchange of places and roles in phantasy did not involve any vectorisation of desire. Thereafter, maternal and paternal identifications, governed by the castration complex, obey a law governing the flow of exchanges. Bisexuality is the retroactive effect of this vectorisation. The castration complex is only operative – in the strict and specific sense denoted by the term "castration" – when the significance of the sexual gender to which the individual belongs has been acquired. It is not contemporaneous with the discovery of the difference between the sexes, but with the moment when this discovery acquires an organising significance. Overcoming the castration complex depends on earlier stages which are reinterpreted *après coup* as precursors of castration (loss of the breast and weaning, the gift of faeces, and sphincteral training). On the other hand, it is important that the pre-oedipal stages have not

247

been too conflictual, to the extent of blocking development, so that the castration complex can be elaborated. The *two phases* of libidinal development are of capital importance; the period of latency, marked by repression, creating a major discontinuity between infantile sexuality and adult sexuality.

### Point 10. Sexual reality and psychical reality

At the time of the oedipal complex, the conflict takes on the form of an opposition between the individual's *sexual reality* and his psychical reality. Sexual reality concerns the sex which is determined and fixed before the third year; psychical reality concerns the fantasies which are convergent or divergent with sexual reality. This conflict depends to a large extent on the position adopted by the ego. Depending on the case in question, the ego may completely deny reality (transsexual psychosis) or accept sexual reality by splitting it off from psychical reality, endeavouring to satisfy its fantasies by adhering to them and acting them out (perversion); or, lastly, it may reject that part of psychical reality which contradicts sexual reality (neurosis).

The ego's options are dependent on the pre-oedipal period and the more or less mobilisable marks it has made on it. The vicissitudes of biological and psychical development present us with a range of structures (real hermaphroditism, pseudo-hermaphroditism, transvestism, homosexuality, fetishism), each of which lays claim to a distinct pathogeny and different therapeutic responses, commensurate with the individual's demand (cf. Stoller, 1968).

### Point 11. Primal femininity and the repudiation of femininity

The determining role of factors stemming from the maternal environment gives us reason to assume, along with Winnicott, that, because it is intricately tied up with the new-born child's biological and psychological state of dependency, and in view of the latter's prematurity, the feminine element of maternal origin should be *accepted and integrated in both sexes* (Winnicott, 1971a, 1971b). This *primal passivation* may be the object of a primordial repression which would account for Freud's opinion that it is femininity that both sexes find most difficult to accept. It goes without saying that, in boys, the acceptance of femininity should

248

not result in making the acceptance of masculinity as the individual's real sex more onerous. Conversely, in girls, this primal femininity is real and different from secondary femininity, which is only constituted after the phallic phase and gives way to secondary maternal identification.

### Point 12. The difference between the sexual developments of boys and girls

It cannot be emphasised enough that the sexual destiny of boys and girls differs considerably. While both are attached to the feminine, maternal, primordial object, when a boy's psycho-sexual development is completed, he is able, by means of a single displacement, to find an object of the same sex as the primordial object, whereas a girl will have to find an object of a different sex to her mother's. Her evolution destines her to object-change (the first displacement-reversal, by means of substitution, is from the mother to the father), followed by a definitive object-choice (the second displacement is from the father to his substitute). This specificity of feminine development accounts for the specific difficulties of feminine sexuality.

### Point 13. The limits of psychoanalytic intervention

Cultural codes and ideology inevitably influence sexual destiny through the parents' valuing or devaluing of their child's bisexuality, a process in which collective ideas of masculinity and femininity play their part. The fact remains that these variations are integrated in individual conflicts at the parental level and that the basic induction occurs in the parents', and particularly the mother's, matrix exchanges with the child. The analytic situation certainly does not constitute a mere repetition of this situation but, through transference, it creates an analogical model. Nonetheless, the deeply inscribed character of certain marks sets limits to the changes that are likely to occur through psychoanalysis.

## Bisexuality and primary narcissism: the neuter gender

More often than not the analyst has to deal with psychical bisexuality in the form of a latent conflict which is uncovered during analysis. Indeed, this is one of the difficulties of psychoanalysis and

249

is manifested by the analyst's limited capacity to tolerate, to allow to develop, to interpret with precision, the transference concerning the imago of the sex which is not his own. So the problem analytic theory has today resides in the fact that each of its two dominant figures met with this stumbling block in their own respective ways. Freud was undoubtedly – he admitted as much himself – troubled in his analyses of feminine sexuality by his embarrassment at feeling he was the object of a maternal transference. And in spite of going "deeper" than Freud, Melanie Klein does not seem, for her part, to have learnt much from analysing the paternal transference of her patients. Nonetheless, if there is a problem, it is because the conflict here is unconscious.

In other cases, the analyst may have the opportunity of seeing other structures where bisexuality is displayed or even actualised. (In this case both heterosexual and homosexual activity can be observed. It is nonetheless exceptional that both types are equally invested. The neurotic nature of these cases is highly questionable. The perverse structure falls a long way short of providing an adequate explanation for the psychopathology of patients who present such characteristics. In certain extreme cases of transvestism, bisexuality can even be brought about through hormonal impregnation by injecting oestrogen.) I cannot go into all the details here concerning the observation of a patient I saw in 1959 at the Paris Centre for Psychoanalytic Consultations and Treatment.[2] I shall just give the main outlines which will serve to illustrate the ideas I have put forward.

The subject in question was a female, somewhat stout, of sturdy build, and even athletic in appearance. As soon as she was seated, she[3] produced a photocopy of a document from the French Ministry of Employment certifying that she presented feminine and masculine attributes with a feminine dominance and informed me that she had undertaken steps to have her identity changed.

The case history is probably worth telling, not only because of the sometimes fantastic turns in the singular destiny of this person – so fantastic that one even wondered at times whether mythomania did not enter into the clinical picture – but also because, as one listened to her account, one got a glimpse of a maternal image to which she was deeply bound. *"My mother hated me before I was born; she told me so..."* was one of the first things she said at the beginning of two consultations. The mother's feminine induction was reported in an allusion to the child who had just told her of her success in obtaining her school leaving certificate: "Which teacher did you sleep with to get through this exam?" As is usual in these cases the child was brought up and dressed as a girl until she started school. Her public transvestite practices began around the age of 16 or 17 (disguising herself as a girl so as to be able to attend the neighbouring village balls). As is also often the case, homosexuality was deeply repressed. Not the least paradoxical aspect of the case – and this was verified – was that the patient was living together with an older woman with whom she participated in minor sadomasochistic practices of a completely puerile and infantile character. Thus, on Sundays, she sometimes wanted to go out "to have some fun" but found she was prohibited from doing so by her friend, who chained her to a stove to make her finish her washing and ironing first! The patient accepted this treatment: she had the key of the padlock on her but declined to use it. Anality pervaded the clinical picture and the aspect of dirtiness was striking. The inside of the apartment was reported to be repulsively dirty. The domination she herself was subjected to was converted into her own dominating approach at work where, apparently, she worked wonders re-educating physically disabled people.

The search for contradictory satisfactions was evident: her attitude towards any form of authority, public authorities, for example, was one of rejection, and her need to be kept under tight rein, to be bullied and dominated meant she longed to be in a passive position. The quest here for a powerful maternal character is patently clear. On the other hand, the poverty of sexual satisfactions is remarkable. The fondling of her breasts – which had apparently developed as a result of oestrogen injections given by the Germans during the war – was the only pleasure she procured: "*It is as if my body were divided in two; as if below the belt I didn't exist, or was another person.*"

During our second meeting, the patient spoke of the periods she had every 28 days "*through rectal porosity*", and once again produced certificates. "*A few days before my period, I am absolutely impossible, irritable, nervous, etc. I have never accepted being a complete woman.*" At this point I said to her: "In fact you don't want to be either a man or a woman", and, before I had time to add anything else, she went on as if she had just understood something important: "*I think you're the first person to get to the heart of the matter; I don't want to give up any of the advantages of the two sexes.*"

251

In the rest of this meeting, we discussed the problem of a surgical operation, for it was difficult to differentiate between transsexualism, which involves a pressing demand for a sex change, and transvestism, in which perverse practices seem to suffice for obtaining satisfaction. The patient's reply is worth citing:

> *"You're telling me, Doctor, that when I leave this room, I will have the choice between two solutions:*
>
> On the right, is an operating theatre with all the equipment needed for giving me a vagina, a uterus, etc. But once I had been operated on, I would be an emasculated individual who would lose all his shape, put on weight, find himself stripped of all his will and energy, who would be unable any longer to make a living and would just be good for walking the streets and getting screwed; well, in that case, I would refuse, and I'm sure you can't guarantee me that that is not what would happen if I had an operation.
>
> On the left, there is a well-equipped laboratory which could give me back my virility and make my breasts disappear with the help of hormonal injections. There again, I would not believe you. I think there will always be something feminine in me: I don't want to live as a man."

This development led me to point out that the image which she was trying to give of herself was not that of a woman but of a *masculine woman*. The patient agreed that this was, indeed, the impression she gave. At this point a new stage of the story began – phantasy or reality? – in which the patient talked about a situation in which he claimed he felt he was "entirely female". This account concerns events in which she served as a partner for a perverse burglar who would break into apartments and then introduce our patient into them saying, "This is my place. Everything here belongs to me. Lie down on the bed." The partner would then throw himself on the patient, having an orgasm almost immediately, and then order his partner to take off "her" clothes (a woman's clothing) and to take others from the wardrobe of the burgled apartment, which they would then leave as soon as the stolen clothes had been put on.

A notable fact here was that the theft never assumed proportions other than symbolic. The ritual sometimes became more complex. For instance, in each apartment that was burgled, the thief was capable of requiring the patient to undress and remain naked. Finally, this complicity came to an end since the perverse practices took a sadistic turn which frightened the patient: he feared, it seems, there was a real danger of being castrated. At any rate, during the time they were living together, this was the only time that the feminine identification was complete: "*I had become his victim and I did whatever he told me to do.*"

This observation speaks for itself: the image of the phallic mother stands out in this tragi-comic fresco with the eclipsing of the father as its shadow, so to speak. The patient appeals to the fantasmatic imago of a father *really castrating* the woman with a penis. The structure of the case is dominated by the phantasy of the primal scene. It will thus come as no surprise to learn that the subject's first sexual relationship was with a young girl, at his home, in his parents' bed – a short-lived experience, during which they both lost their virginity, and which ended in their separating for good.

We will leave this patient recalling a family "story" to which it is tempting to attach great importance: "My grandmother used to tell me an anecdote in which I took extreme pleasure and which I would ask her to tell again, even though I knew it by heart: it took place during an outing in the country which my parents had made with some friends of theirs. While the women were conversing on the grass, the men were fishing for trout in the river. My father lost his footing, falling into the water and was completely soaked. He took off his wet clothes and then had to make do with whatever was at hand. Most likely out of fun, more than necessity, each of the women divested themselves of a piece of their clothing in order to cover my father who ended up being dressed entirely as a woman."

This, then, was the story of someone who was given three first names by his parents: Pierre (like his father), Marie (like his mother) and André. His application for a change of civil status contained a deletion, that of his paternal first name, and, an addition, a mute *e* to feminise his personal first name, a symbol of masculinity. So he came to be called "Marie-Andrée". When I pointed out to him how he had thereby excluded his "father's name", he denied ferociously that this could be anything other than a coincidence; although normally he very readily confessed his perverse desires.

In a long footnote at the end of the fourth chapter of *Civilization and Its Discontents* Freud develops his views on bisexuality:

253

...if we assume it as a fact that each individual seeks to satisfy both male and female wishes in his sexual life, we are prepared for the possibility that those [two sets of] demands are not fulfilled by the same object, and that they interfere with each other unless they can be kept apart and each impulse guided into a particular channel that is suited to it.

(Freud, 1930a, p. 106 n.3)

Here, then, is a remark confirming that human sexuality is, indeed, as the word used by R. Lewinter (1969) suggests, "*sexion*". Moreover, etymology backs this up. The word sex is thought to originate from *secare*: to cut, separate. Here the biological metaphor supports the phantasy, since each of the two sexes separates in order to unite with the missing half provided by the other sex. Psychical bisexuality takes its revenge for this *sexion—cession* and recuperates through phantasy the *jouissance* conceded to the sex one does not have. Bisexuality is thus closely linked to the difference between the sexes. Where there is bisexuality, there is also difference. Where there is difference, there is a cut, a caesura, a castration of the potentialities for *jouissance* of the complementary sex: inverse and symmetrical. *Claiming real bisexuality means refusing sexual difference insofar as the latter implies the lack of the other sex*. If, by definition, each sex lacks the other, putting both sexes, so to speak, on the same level, castration, the phantasy of castration, i.e. the absence or the loss of the virile member, *symbolises* and *subsumes* this lack, *whichever sex one may have*. It is possible for a boy to lose the sex he has, or, for a girl to materialise the lack of the sex she does not have. Admittedly, a girl has *something else*: a vagina, a womb that can be fertilised, as well as numerous and varied enticements. It remains true that she does not have a penis. True enough, a boy also lacks what a woman has; which he does not have. But these assets are not visible at the level of the sexual organs. The nature of *imaginary capture* is such that what can be represented is this additional or missing feature of the penis; an imaginary feature to be symbolised. And there is good reason for thinking that penis envy is not envy for this piece of flesh, but for what is fantasised about the powers it confers, and which are conferred on it by parental desire.

Continuing to study this problem from this point of view is to assume that certain problems have been resolved and affirms that the male–female dilemma implicitly admits of their difference or, at the very least, admits that the subject is a sexual being.

The patient I was speaking about earlier came to see me because of his anxieties – anxieties, he said, which gripped him every morning on waking, so that he wondered if that day would not be the day of his death. The consultation revealed that this anxious state reflected the time when he was a prisoner of the Germans, who were said to have carried out feminising experiments on him. Each time he woke up he wondered whether he would survive. Here death anxiety and castration anxiety are connected.

The problem is not a simple one.

In *La logique du vivant* (1971), François Jacob writes, "But the two most important inventions [of evolution] are sex and death." A fruit of coincidence, perhaps, but united, in any case, by necessity. Jacob speaks of death "imposed from within like a prescribed necessity". I will not let myself be tempted here by the sirens of "metabiology", and will stay in the realm of clinical experience which is closely akin to myth.

In certain psychopathological structures in which sexuality as a whole is rejected outright, without qualification or distinction, the subject builds and constantly nourishes the phantasy of *a-sexuality*. The subject claims to be neither masculine nor feminine but *neuter*. Neither one nor the other, *ne uter*. He sees to it that any form of hetero- or homosexual aspiration is expunged from his behaviour, as from his desire. These cases are rare but they do exist. Of course, it is a defensive position which can be overcome with analysis. This phantasy of neutrality, constructed with the help of all the resources of intemperate narcissism, bears the marks of the absolute despotism of a tyrannical and megalomaniac ego ideal. For where desire is concerned, everything is settled in an all-or-nothing mode: "Since I cannot have and be everything, I will have and be *nothing*."

This phantasy could easily be elaborated in relation to the perception of the maternal phantasy which wishes her child to be neither sexual nor alive. But the quest for maternal love goes hand in hand with an inextinguishable thirst for love and an exaggerated sensibility towards any manifestation of rejection by the loved object, whether it be a maternal or paternal substitute. Consequently, salvation is only to be found in the phantasy of the neuter gender, in its states of undifferentiated sexuality; a sign both of obedience to the mother's desire as well as vengeance on her, through the violent rejection of her.

It is remarkable, then, that the aspiration for Nothing is in keeping with ascetic behaviour of reducing needs, just as primary narcissism endeavours to reduce tensions to the level zero. Here I mean absolute primary narcissism in the strongest sense of the term; that is, I am not speaking of primary narcissism as it is used to describe the subject's unification into a singular entity, but, on the contrary, of negative narcissism which ardently seeks a return to the quiescent state. The latter finds expression in suicidal behaviour which is more or less disguised or acted out. In Chapters 2 and 4 [of *Life Narcissism, Death Narcissism* (Green, 1973/2001)], I showed that primary narcissism should not be confused with primary masochism, precisely because the concealing of *jouissance* by means of masochistic manoeuvres is absent here, the final goal being the extinction of all excitation, of all desire, whether it is agreeable or disagreeable. This fascination with death underlies a phantasy of immortality; for, being nothing is simply a way of abolishing the possibility of no longer existing, of one day lacking something, even if it is only the breath of life.

The phantasy of the neuter gender is closely akin to the myth studied by Marie Delcourt (1958). The complete human being, i.e. the union of the Father's spirit and maternal nature, is linked with the symbol of the androgynous, self-begetting and immortal Phoenix. There is nonetheless a further need for a baptism of fire which reduces everything to ashes. The Gnostic idea puts the finishing touch to this link between androgyny and deliverance from the flesh.

Totality is safeguarded and lack is denied. It is not in the positivity of actual complementarity that sexual difference is abolished, where Hermes and Aphrodite are but one, but in the even more radical movement of a negative process in which the nothing is incarnated and desire results in the death of desire and triumphs over the death of desire. The One proves to be an impossible concept to think about. Because it is made up of two different halves, which cannot be called one because they are lacking something they need to be complete, and because it is caught between the double and the half, only the Zero seems safe. But in order for the zero to exist, it has to be named, put into writing. But in so doing the One, which cannot be eliminated, re-emerges beneath it.

Similarly, designating negative hallucination or castration inevitably involves positivising them. Thus Freud attributed the id with the neuter gender. But the id comprises all the clamour for life of Eros, and also the silence of the destructive drives – the silence one never hears. To be heard, it needs to be expressed with the help of sounds or signs, which are inevitably too noisy and too garish to represent it.

## Notes

1 This chapter was originally published in English in André Green, *Life Narcissism, Death Narcissism*. London: Free Association Books, 2001, pp. 15–169. Reprinted and translated by kind permission of Free Association Books. The chapter was translated by Andrew Weller.
2 Centre de Consultations et de Traitements Psychanalytiques de Paris. [transl. note].
3 The alternate use of masculine and feminine to refer to the subject is inevitable in view of the extent to which the analyst, the misled spectator of this hybridisation, was alternately caught between illusion and reality.

———————————— 13 ————————————

# BYE-BYE, SEXUALITY

*Gregorio Kohon*

The psychoanalytic concept of sexuality continues to be misunderstood and confused as something else. For Freud, sexuality does not offer any firm ground where the subject can stand up, walk steadily, move forward easily and travel comfortably to a given destination. It does not ever represent some "thing" that men and women can conquer and/or possess. As a concept, it cannot be compared to gender, which offers culturally and socially reassuring explanations. In contrast, Freudian sexuality, bisexuality and sexual difference cannot be fitted into any model; they do not constitute a guide or a map full of recognizable signs to follow, like heavenly bodies in the firmament. Just the opposite: they produce confusion, anxieties, uncertainty. Sexuality is problematic and conflicting; unconscious desires will never be fully realized. If anything could be said about sexuality, it would be to characterize it as infantile and polymorphous; perverse and not gender-specific. It is also, in part, an unconsciously remembered event: it belongs to a previous moment in the subject's infantile life, now repeated, never forgotten: ... *once upon a time.* ... Suckling at the breast or playing and experimenting with different orifices of the body, for example, reappear in the foreplay of adult sexuality. This link is necessarily unconscious; paradoxically, the knowledge of this connection is not accepted by our consciousness, because it never existed in the first place – except, rather ironically, *nachträglich*. This irony can also be understood as a tragic joke: sexual pleasure is possible because the connection was, from the beginning, only there in the negative – completely unknown to the subject.[1]

In 1999, I wrote:

There are many jokes in the history of psychoanalysis, but none compares to the fact that Freud discovered psychoanalysis through his transference relationship with Fliess. The first, original analysis was a perverse scene of seduction between a very tense, mad scientist, who played the grand seer (in reality, he did not have any status in the scientific community of the time), and a questing and ambitious young doctor eager to discover the great secrets of sexuality (and) the neuroses. ... The disciple of Brücke, von Fleischl-Marxow, Helmholtz, Charcot, and Breuer, turned a truly crazy trickster (and a rather dangerous one – given certain operations on patients' noses) into his master and friend. What an amazing comedy!

(Kohon, 1999, p. 163)

The bond between the two friends was not necessarily based on a genuinely mutual respect for each other's individual scientific capacities and specific knowledge: it was an idealized "love" relationship with each enamoured by what was projected onto the other.

Freud believed Fliess to be a genius, at one point even referring to him as a "Messiah" (Letter 10 July 1893, in Masson, 1985)! Freud confessed that he was writing, not so much *to* Fliess (although he sent Fliess plenty of letters) as *for* him (Letter 23 September 1895, in Masson, 1985). True, they shared a common "scientific" interest in sexuality, each believing that sexuality was both the origin and the cause of the complaints brought by their patients, and from 1887 onwards they discussed and exchanged views on the concept of bisexuality.

In 1896, after reading Fliess's manuscript on *The Relation between the Nose and the Female Sex Organs, Presented in Their Biological Significance* (published the following year), Freud declared it to be brilliant; there was not a critical word or a negative comment about Fliess's ideas for a universal theory of life and nature. For Fliess, the ear-nose-and-throat specialist, there were links between the nose and the genital organs: he believed that he had found similar morphological characteristics between the nasal cavity, on the one hand, and the clitoris, nipples and penis, on the other; noses were considered erectile bodies that changed during menstruation; when congested, their sensitivity increased, and their tendency to bleed proved them to be "equivalent" to female genitals. According to Fliess, menstruation was a fundamental process that regulated the changing rhythm of life and death; childbirth was a prolonged menstrual period when blood was discharged after nine months; labour pains were just reflections of menstrual cramps easily controlled by dosages of cocaine to be taken through the nose – and by cauterization (see André, 1999, pp. 27–41).

Crowning this magnificently delirious pseudo-scientific edifice, Fliess developed his grandiose idea of periodicity: he believed that the equivalence between pregnancy and menstruation meant that labour would always start on a date representing a multiple of 28 days – that is, a multiple of the duration of the menstrual period. For Fliess, menstruation was everywhere and in everybody: it was linked to neuralgic pains, anxiety, asthma, urticaria, diabetes, strokes, migraines, teething – and the development of language. In his theoretical construction, menstruation was not exclusive to women: men also had traces of it, shown by the apparently frequent nosebleeds they suffered during intercourse. The masculine cycle he deemed to last 23 days, although there were exceptions: Goethe's life was calculated in a ratio of feminine cycles of 28 days, dying in his 1077th feminine menstruation (Gherovici, 2010, p. 66).

In referring to "male menstrual periods", Fliess announced his plans for a future monograph where he would prove that menstruation was manifest throughout the whole of nature, its universal influence made possible by his very idea of periodicity. Periodicity came to dominate his vision of the world: everything that showed signs of being "periodic" would became, in his understanding, "menstrual". Freud's idealized "scientist" argued that Napoleon "lost the battles of Dresden and Borodino because he in effect had his period that day" (quoted in André, 1999, p. 32).

Complementing his theory of periodicity, Fliess proposed the existence of a "sexual toxin", the sole principle of life and death, a substance that through its periodic discharges created life, only then to destroy all living organisms. This toxin was supposedly produced by the thyroid, but it existed also in a diversity of organs: nose, tonsils, and so on, all of them controlled by "menstrual radiation".

In developing this idea of the existence of parallel menstrual periods between females (28 days) and males (23 days), Fliess came to his misguided conclusion that the imaginary parallel "demonstrated" that human beings are basically bisexual – an idea that was to become part of psychoanalytic dogma.

Freud's concept of bisexuality, and its theoretical and clinical implementation, appeared to share or at least be inspired by Fliess's idea of a primary bisexuality, common to all humans.[2] In their *Language of Psychoanalysis*, Laplanche and Pontalis described bisexuality thus:

> Notion introduced into psycho-analysis by Freud, under the influence of Wilhelm Fliess, according to which every human being is endowed constitutionally with both masculine and feminine sexual dispositions...
>
> (1967, p. 52)

There is no doubt about Fliess's influence. Freud firmly wanted to believe that the concept could eventually be given a biological foundation; however, from the start this created enormous theoretical difficulties for him. The correlation, if there was one, between the biological, the sociological and the psychological meanings of the concept was never properly worked out by Freud and, in the end, he remained ambivalent and equivocal. In reality, of course, he could not find any scientific evidence that would indicate or confirm some kind of a "vestigial presence" of characteristics of the opposite sex in a particular sex.[3] But this did not stop bisexuality from becoming an important concept in psychoanalysis.

Although Freud repudiated Fliess's understanding of bisexuality in "A Child Is Being Beaten" (1919e), many years after his rupture with Fliess, Freud declared:

> The theory of bisexuality is still surrounded by many obscurities and we cannot but feel it as a serious impediment in psychoanalysis that it has not yet found any link with the theory of the instincts.
>
> (1930a, p. 105)

"surrounded by many obscurities..." Indeed. And yet ... Freud seemed to be expressing a wish that the "serious impediment..." could eventually be overcome, that a link with his own theory of the instincts could be found. Freud's ambivalence and the difficulties he encountered in giving an adequate psychoanalytic description of the concept were not helped by his reference to the

261

binary opposition present in the concept as the opposition between "masculine" and "feminine" (Freud, 1905d, p. 219, n.1).

A few years later, there was still a profound ambiguity in his attitude to the concept. He stated that bisexuality "is the attitude proper to the opposite sex which has succumbed to repression". This statement was made as late as 1937, in "Analysis Terminable and Interminable" (1937c, p. 251); it was a description that could have fitted well with Fliess's own suggestions that there is a universal repression of the other sex, hidden from the subject's manifest sexual characteristics and identity, an idea originally criticized by Freud.

"Bisexuality" was not, therefore, the self-evident concept that would have helped to elucidate the "mystery" of sexuality; if anything, it helped to point out and confirm the complexity of sexuality.[4] In time, it became clear that the contrast between Fliess's and Freud's different understandings was significant: for each of them, bisexuality and the concept of sexuality were different things. One might wish now that Freud had stuck to his early, rather provocative and well-known suggestion that every sexual act was an event that involved four individuals (Letter, 1 August 1899, in Masson, 1985).[5] Perhaps this would have helped him to describe more precisely the notion of a universal, psychic, human bisexual disposition, comprising unconscious male and female identifications and the potential to experience sexual desire towards both sexes. After all, Freud's statement, in the letter mentioned above, denoted a specifically psychoanalytical point of view. It referred, by implication, to the notion of unconscious phantasies and his understanding (not fully elaborated at that point in time) of the psychic structure of an individual, independent of conscious experience and behaviour.

At this point, it is worth summarizing Serge André's review of the contrast between Fliess's and Freud's views on sexuality and bisexuality (André, 1999, pp. 35–38):

1   While for Fliess, sexual difference was a given, biological phenomenon, Freud maintained that this difference could not be inscribed at the level of the unconscious.
2   For Fliess, there was a symmetrical relationship, a bisexual complementarity between the two sexes, each containing the other by way of repression: if a woman, the "male" was repressed; if a man, the "female" was repressed. Freud, in contrast, came to

the conclusion that there was an essential asymmetry between the boy and the girl, as well as separate sexual destinies; no complementarity here, only a divide – at most, with luck, a fragile bridge between a man and a woman (Kohon, 1999, p. 22; see also Kohon, 2005a, 2005b).

3   Fliess considered both sexes, albeit different and separated, as united through the natural law of periodic menstruation. For Freud, there was no such a thing as a "natural" union between the sexes; there was only one libido – but this did not make the two sexes one.

4   For Fliess, sexuality is notably guided not by the vicissitudes of individual desire, but by the preservation of the species; in this way, sexuality went hand in hand with reproduction. In this context, his notion of bisexuality is imbued with a sense of harmony, offering an illusion of totality; he even suggested that asexual reproduction was possible – "possible", that is, through self-generation. Freud's understanding of sexuality, while at times contradictory and controversial, does not suggest any kind of harmony created by a given biological bisexuality. Just the opposite: sexuality would always be uncertain, traumatic and difficult. As stated above, psychic bisexuality, a universal human mental *disposition*, would comprise unconsciously male and female identifications, the potential capacity to experience sexual desire towards both sexes.

## Theoretical legacy

Although Fliess was not Schreber, it would be tempting to make a link between the psychotic quality common to the structure of their ideas. In the case of Fliess, motivated by his rivalry with Freud and possibly incensed by feeling that he had been plagiarized, a certain malignant anti-psychoanalytic obtuseness emerges in his "scientific" constructions. Freud, on his part, was never fully satisfied with the concept: given his own unresolved mixed feelings towards his friend, he remained simultaneously attached to and yet intensely ambivalent about the concept of bisexuality, perhaps reflecting his feelings towards Fliess.

In view of the challenging complexity of the subject, Freud's disciples remained attached to the notion of bisexuality and continued to use it in all its confusion. As a result of Freud's indecisive stance,

263

Fliess's central idea that one sex contained the other through repression permeated psychoanalytic theoretical and clinical developments. It frequently appeared as an unquestioned concept in many writings by important authors, perhaps because bisexuality offered an apparently "easy" solution to the question of the differentiation of the sexes.

Although Fliess was very rarely quoted, he was constantly referred to through the use that Freud had made of the concept of bisexuality. Unquestioned as it was, it took a prominent place in the psychoanalytic theory as an accepted, generalized and universal phenomenon, becoming integral to clinical and theoretical discussions. To my mind, this represents a genuine piece of resistance, a pseudo-explanation of common, familiar, and yet misunderstood and difficult clinical facts. In approaching these discussions and as an attempt to offer a resolution, one still hears statements like, "we are bisexual, after all" or "we naturally contain both sexes in our individual self".

My purpose here is not to trace back in the psychoanalytic literature the influence of this un-Freudian way of understanding. Nevertheless, Groddeck's early work (1931), while constituting an extreme case, could be taken as exemplary and paradigmatic. Although the reaction of psychoanalysts to the writings of Georg Groddeck has mostly been characterized by a certain caution, it has also included admiration and praise (Grotjahn, 1945).

Taking as the point of departure Fliess's idea of bisexuality, Groddeck considered that the distinction between a man and a woman was only circumstantial: a human being is "masculine–feminine", that is, bisexual. Everything pertaining to human beings should be considered as influenced by bisexuality which, in Groddeck's opinion, was mostly neglected by psychoanalysts. He was convinced that the following "truth" was systematically repressed by Freud's colleagues: that no man or woman can be separated, that human beings are all woman–man and man–woman in one. For him, bisexuality is everywhere, not only in instinctual life but also in mental life, as much as in the anatomical, physiological and pathological fields. In his view, this was not just a matter of a "symbolic" interpretation of reality: for example, the mouth is really female but, since it is used for talking or for breathing, this "shows", Groddeck argued, its bisexual character. Conceiving and accepting that breathing is bisexual, new ways would then be open for the study of all psychic, physical, and pathological processes. According to Groddeck, we must acknowledge the bisexuality of the heart, of the kidneys, of the digestive organs, of the digestive processes – and its influence in the development of language. This would necessarily include new ways of viewing organic complaints, like tumours.

There is more to say about Groddeck's short article on the bisexuality of human beings (1931), but my point is a rather limited one: while psychoanalysts might not have regarded his contributions as "scientific" (see Grotjahn, 1945), he would occasionally be found in the literature as a considered reference. In an early contribution,[6] Christian David, in referring to psychosexual dimorphism (as real and equally important as biological dimorphism), states:

> More than stressing the difference between the sexes it may be more revealing to consider the similarities, by studying their source in bisexuality. Thus, Groddeck said that we are bisexual through our life and therefore in each man there is a woman and in each woman a man.
>
> (1964, p. 67)

"Groddeck said", as if he were a reliable authority in this matter.

Another author worth mentioning in this context was Carl Gustav Jung, whose relationship with Freud had finally broken up in 1913. One way or another, Jung's influence was considerable and continued to be so in many parts of the world. His notion of bisexuality was also, like Fliess's and Groddeck's, imbued with a sense of harmony, offering an illusion of totality, a unified Self. As part of his misunderstanding of the Freudian concept of sexuality, Jung postulated, in a parallel and yet dissimilar manner to Groddeck, that each individual has both masculine and feminine complementary components of the psyche. For a male, the feminine component is the *anima*, and for a female it is the *animus*. Jung identified the anima as being the unconscious feminine component of men, and the animus as the unconscious masculine component in women. For him, human biological and psychological developments are informed by this mixture of masculine and feminine energies, both symbolic and archetypal – in other words, transpersonal. Jung believed that the anima and animus act as guides to the unification and completion of the unconscious Self. This particular bisexual combination of the anima and the animus was very important in his theories: it included its presence in myths, either as godly figures that were hermaphrodites and/or as an explanation for

265

the separation of one into two complementary things. According to Jung, the gods in most religions have an androgynous nature ascribed to them in some form or other.[7]

## A conundrum?

A conundrum: the word is usually understood as a reference to a difficult question and/or a puzzling problem; also, it can be something laborious to name: "what-d-ye-call-it?" (*Oxford English Dictionary*). Alternatively, it can also be understood as a humorous trick – for example, "a riddle in the form of a question the answer to which involves a pun or play on words" or "a word-play depending on similarity of sound in words of different meaning" (*Oxford English Dictionary*). It can be argued that we are confronted by a conundrum (a problem? or a joke?) that has been created through the collapse of two concepts into one: "gender" and "sexual difference" – as if they share a comparable, interchangeable meaning.

In the late 1970s and mid-1980s, the psychoanalytic concept of sexual difference was challenged and eventually displaced by a theory of a social construction of gender. In 1990, Judith Butler criticized feminist, psychoanalytic and philosophical authors like Simone de Beauvoir and Luce Irigaray, Sigmund Freud and Jacques Lacan, Julia Kristeva and Jacques Derrida. As a result of her engagement with the ideas of Michel Foucault, Butler challenged the apparent coherence of the categories of sex and gender, arguing that genders were culturally constructed. They were established through repetition in time, as "ontological" forms of being; in fact, she suggested, they could only be considered as performative (Butler, 1990). Thus, sexual identity could not be defined by reference to a given "natural" essence, not could it be constrained to a normative sexuality dictated by social norms. If identity were to be constructed, this opened up the potential for alternative constructions; identities could not be fixed, nor easily categorized or labelled. Three years later, faced with critical responses to her early work, Butler published *Bodies That Matter: On the Discursive Limits of "Sex"* (1993), where she further elaborated some of her ideas from her first book, which she herself described as having produced some confusion.

I have previously referred to what had been described as the original philosophical behaviourism of Judith Butler's first book (Kohon, 1999, p. 9). Butler had explicitly challenged biological

accounts of binary sex, considering the sexed body as itself culturally constructed by regulative discourse: since identity is constructed
as far as it is not naturally defined, there is no such a thing as an
essential, given or inherent identity. In Butler's account, it was on
the basis of the construction of natural binary sex that binary gender
and heterosexuality would likewise be constructed as natural.

A few years earlier, the questioning of sexuality and sexual difference, which had initially brought political feminism (on the one
hand) and theoretical and clinical psychoanalysis (on the other)
closer together, was transformed and turned into a feminist theory
of gender that conceived the subject "as multiple, rather than
divided" (de Lauretis, 1987, p. x).[8] In the 1990s, ideas characteriz-
ing sexual identity as free, flexible, and multiple and gender as a
performance became very influential; in turn, they served as one of
the foundations of queer theory.

In fact, subjectivity is precarious: each individual faces an unavoid-
ably long and difficult struggle to establish an identity, but at the same
time, as Perelberg reminds us, there is a simultaneous and parallel
resistance to identity at the very core of psychic life (Perelberg, 1999a,
1999b, 2011). Feminist theory, Butler's ideas and queer theory all
have an affinity with psychoanalysis in their acknowledgement of this
struggle and the recognition of "the division and precariousness of
human subjectivity itself" (Rose, 1982, p. 27). However, let us take
note: Rose spoke of "division" not "multiplicity", a truly crucial distinction between human subjectivity as divided (as in psychoanalysis),
rather than multiple (as in queer theory).

At present, people may be referred to as non-binary, gender-
queer, third-gender, bi-gender, tri-gender, a-gender, inter-gender,
gender-fluid, genderless, pan-gender, neutrois, androgyne, two-
spirit, self-coined, girl and boy, girl in boy, boy as girl, girl who is a
boy dressed as a girl, girl who has to be a boy so as to be a girl, pan-
sexual, cis-gender, cis-sexual, queer, *Hijra*, heterosexual, third sex,
poly-sexual, demi-boy, demi-girl, trans man, trans woman, as well
as be spoken in terms of androphilia, synophilia, etc. We seem to
end up producing labels, and the list could grow and extend further
because, if it is only a matter of a social construction, there are then
as many ways of experiencing and expressing one's gender as there
are people. This is clearly a form of reductionism; it represents a
form of social and political voluntarism, as if everything were just a
matter of will (Phillips, 1997, p. 157).

## What to make of it all?

We moved from Fliess' and Groddeck's concept of bisexuality (the "yin and yang" of sexuality) to a "well-meaning", politically correct form of social constructionism, which has led to an abundant glossary of gender identities, a plethora of existential options.

In the move from sexual difference to the construction of gender and the consequent displacement of meaning that ensued, something was lost. Most significantly, for a number of feminist authors, queer theory desexualized identity – which is truly ironic, as the issue to be addressed *is* sexual identity (Jagose, 1996). Sexual difference, a concept specific to psychoanalytic theory, was expelled from theoretical discourse and reduced to a biological distinction (see Kohon, 1999; Matthis, 2011; Mitchell, 2011). In this process, the sex of sexual difference dropped out: gender theory "removed sex from sex" and the gender theorists "ceased to question the sexual" (Copjec, 2016, p. 108). This constitutes a relevant critique and raises important theoretical objections.

At the same time, if queer theory was supposed to unsettle a certain complacency in gay and lesbian studies, that very theory has itself become a rather popular academic subject, widely accepted and at times openly promoted by the Western academic world. In fact, it has become conventional, almost culturally "trendy", part of a "liberal" ideology. In parts of the United States, it is not uncommon nowadays to hear of parents who, influenced by the deconstructive project of queer theory, make the effort to bring their children up without reference to gender. Some of these parents apparently expect their children to arrive at a point when they will declare their own chosen gender; in the meantime, they may prefer to use "they" when referring to an individual, avoiding the use of a defined gender, "he" or "she".

It was Foucault who usefully suggested that concepts within a discourse must be understood as a function of power, linked ultimately to the law and the state. This has been used to validate queer theory, celebrating theoretical perspectives that oppose the idea of so-called "normal heterosexuality". Unfortunately, this has also somewhat clouded the significance of gay and lesbian studies in universities, which have contributed important ideas to the theoretical and clinical debates on human *sexuality*. As a consequence of its commitment to deconstruction, queer theory makes it nearly impossible to speak of lesbian or gay individuals: it cannot, by definition, offer a framework for examining their selves, their subjectivities and/or their sexuality.

The establishment in the NHS of gender services for young people as well as for adults, while marking a significant and progressive social and political step, has not necessarily provided an adequate framework for the consideration of these issues. If "normality" involves a narrowing, inhibiting and rather useless concept, transgressive practices, once a challenge to the "straight" establishment, are themselves becoming rapidly "normalized" ways of choosing a gender identity or creating a family. In the end, queer theory came to restrict its analytic focus to discourse; the questioning of sexuality has been dropped. (See also Kohon, 2012.)

We appear to be faced with a sterile, ideological, pendular movement that moved from *"there are no distinctions, we are all the same"*, to *"we can all be as different as we like and choose to be whatever we fancy"*. While social constructionism addressed the impossibility of making absolute judgements about reality, it ran the risk of itself becoming an absolute judgement. The post-modern suggestion that, since the very notion of the subject has been de-centred, the entire world is purely fictionalized, comes to mind. Post-modernism has rightly questioned and criticized binary oppositions and the logic of political, philosophical or psychological Manichaeism. Nevertheless, the acceptance of such criticisms does not imply that we should forget and thus accept the breakdown of all distinctions (Kohon, 2016). Unfortunately, political good intentions are never enough, and most societies have a serious and chronic problem of discrimination against different expressions of sexual identities. This needs to be identified, critically addressed and politically fought against. Nevertheless, the idea that we can reduce the complex question of sexuality to a simplified predicament of supposedly being free to "choose your gender" can only appease our troubled souls for a little while.

The precariousness of subjectivity, the resistance to identity and the question of transgression are all crucial when considering the nature of subjective experience. Butler admitted in her "Melancholy Gender/Refused Identification" (1997) that there was no "position beyond exclusion – or difference, or separateness', and no "world in which leaving and being left out disappears" (p. 164). She acknowledged that to question the notion of binary sex does not, could not, would not create the possibility of a "third sex" to be "found" somewhere in the theory or "pursued" in reality. In the end, constructed or not, alternative or straight, there are only two sexes. While it may be considered unfair, discriminatory, unjust, unreasonable, a bore or a challenge, we cannot but accept this reality. As Toril Moi has explicitly, almost mournfully, stated, "we need to acknowledge our sexual finitude, to understand that we can't be more than one sex" (2004, p. 872). In other words, we need to take responsibility for not being more than what we are, to recognize our finitude and give up omnipotence, accepting that our desires can never be fulfilled.

A baby is born: is it a boy or a girl? There are only two sexes, and the marker is there. It is definitely there, and undeniably … *phallic* – most definitely, a clearly loaded word, the seat of numerous misunderstandings. This marker is not an arbitrary decision made by the parents, the midwife or any other adult around at the time of birth. It is not a given choice, the subject cannot choose, it is something that cannot be avoided. Even if we do not accept the theoretical naivety of biological essentialism, how can we imagine that the *anatomical* difference present at birth would not have, one way or another, profound psychic consequences for the subject? If the consequences are traumatic, how then does the human psyche deal with such a discovery: that we can only be born *one* sex and not the other? Confronted with the possible existence of such a potentially aggressive, chauvinistic, offensive marker, we can always choose to deny and/or ignore the phallic reference – and proceed to invent explanatory stories where sexual difference is eradicated. This will not change reality, but it may temporarily satisfy children all over the world: babies will be brought by storks, grow under cabbages in city allotments and/or be expelled into existence through the mother's (or even the father's) anus.[9]

However, there are further ironies: from a psychoanalytic point of view, contrary to a common misunderstanding, the marker of sexual difference does not mean very much. It does *not* offer an identity to the subject. Most importantly, it does not represent any guarantee of security or happiness for the boy, nor does it mean an unjust or punitive sentence for the girl; it is a signifier of difference that cannot be reduced to the phallic difference, even though the latter establishes it in the first place. It does not prescribe reality, although it helps the subject to construct it. It is what it is, and nothing will change it.

Things are never simple. The symbolic order and the generational difference contribute to determine the subject's destiny from the beginning of conception. The baby will arrive in an already signifying world, which was there well before delivery: parents' phantasies, wishes, anxieties and dreams; names chosen, the name finally given, and so on. If, later in life, as the result of the vicissitudes of the subject's history, there is a decision to change his/her sex, to modify the original body by mutilating it or adding something to it, to choose a different gender identity, such changes take place in the present, but *they never were nor could become a past.*

How can we understand this paradox? Sexual difference, being a difference, cannot be reduced to any "usual" difference (Dolar, 2016).

In sexual difference, there is always something missing. There are two sexes, each offering the other what the other has not got: a "penis", a "baby". Nevertheless, as Irène Matthis points out (following Juliet Mitchell's paper on "The difference between gender and sexual difference"), this is "an illusory exchange, doomed to miscarry, as we can never become 'whole'" (2011, p. 11). In contrast, since difference becomes irrelevant, there is nothing "missing" in the concept of gender; it is the same and it is the other, at one and the same time; it is an economy of narcissism, in which "the other is the self" (Mitchell, 2004, p. 67).

Together with the phallic reference, we might also consider reproduction as another reference for the question of sexual difference: the presence of a womb inevitably implies and implicates difference. Nevertheless, while contemporary reproductive technologies involve issues of gender, they are not necessarily determined by sex; equally, nor are they imbued with sexuality. Such technologies are simply disconnected from anything *sexual.*[10]

## Where do we go from here?

Freud's fundamental idea was that we cannot easily distinguish between what one may think of as "normal" sexuality and what may be considered pathological or perverse. This idea has been, is, and will continue to be Freudian; it is not the result of any contemporary theory or discovery: we owe to Freud the understanding that the notion of a sexuality already defined in nature is not sustainable.

271

Sexuality cannot be confined to any one scientific discipline, nor can it be defined by any cultural law. Freud famously refused to account for the existence of sex by "giving way to anatomy or to convention" (Freud, 1933a, p. 114). In this respect, Freud was clear: since the sexual is not explained or determined by biology, it cannot be reduced to genitality: *Trieb* does not have a natural object. This alone, by itself, would justify the existence of the concept of *Trieb, pulsion, drive*. Sexual difference seems to be the result of a division that is essential and yet precarious; necessary yet alienating. On the other hand, and in disagreement with Freud's own suggestion, sexual difference cannot be described in the conventional terms of masculine and feminine. By its very nature, sexual desire itself tends to dissolve (rather than confirm or accept) the opposition between biological and social, nature and nurture, subject and object, sex and gender, inside and outside, masculine and feminine.

Christian David suggested the notion of a *bisexualization process*: this would describe the integration of masculine and feminine aspects of the sexuality present in both men and women; it would enable the acquisition of the capacity "to fantasise, understand and share the sexual and psychosexual experience of someone of the other sex" (David, 1975, p. 836; also Chapter 1, in this volume). Furthermore, David proposed the notion of a "bisexual mediation", the presence of a psychic bisexuality in inter-subjective as well as in intra-subjective relationships; he believes that there could be a "virtual complementarity" between the opposite sexualities – a complementary defined as a capacity for each sex to identify with the psychosexuality of the other sex. Furthermore, and most importantly, the proposed bisexual mediation entails an articulation through "the methaphorisation of bodily experience in terms of the wish to penetrate and the wish to be penetrated" (Gibeault, 2010, p. 559). From the point of view of the theory of the drives, the drives would normally oscillate between female and male objects; in terms of the drive's attempts to achieve satisfaction, the choice of an object varies in extraordinary ways. And as Freud clearly argued in *Three Essays on the Theory of Sexuality*, attachments to people of the same sex play no less a part, as factors in normal mental life, as do similar attachments to the opposite sex (1905d).

Is this too optimistic; wishful thinking? We should tentatively ask: what if sexual difference cannot be negotiated, deconstructed, complemented (Kohon, 1999)? What if it cannot be fully understood?

In contrast to David, Elizabeth Grosz suggested that sexual difference entails a "certain failure of knowledge". Perhaps it is impossible to cross that great divide, to bridge the gap between a man and a woman: "There remains something ungraspable, something outside, unpredictable, and uncontainable about the other sex for each sex" (1994, p. 208; see also Kohon, 1999, p. 22). The same failure of knowledge might exist between heterosexuals and homosexuals, between cis and trans. The divide comes to represent a rupture of meaning.

In 1999, I wrote:

What if there exists a radical antagonism between human sexuality and the task of making any sense of it? What if we cannot ever fully account for our sexual phantasies, which are outrageous, enjoyable, perverse, wonderful, horrific, and sometimes totally politically incorrect? ... How are we to include the body (stubbornly sexual), which, while it might be a social construction, is not irrelevant to gender identification? What if sexual desire and jouissance, while not pre-linguistic, still remain beyond language?

(Kohon, 1999, pp. 21–22)

The richness of Freud's original concept of *Trieb* has always resided in the fact that it distinguishes itself from the instinct, because *Trieb*, in its very constitution, is always, intrinsically, inevitably bound to representation; it is always "constructed". It is not just heterosexuality that is an "inevitable comedy" (as argued by Butler, 1990). All sexuality is a constant parody of itself. The human sexual drive, so full of complexity and complications, of displacements and distortions, so unnatural, so threatened in its accomplishments, is a wretched parody of the sexual instinct of animals.

Juliet Mitchell wrote, "because human subjectivity cannot ultimately exist outside a division into one of the two sexes, then it is castration that finally comes to symbolize this split" (1984, p. 307). From a psychoanalytic point of view, castration conveys, above all, something about the uniqueness of each sex; if it represents a lack, it is a unique lack for both sexes (Moi, 2004); it is a trauma shared by both sexes. Castration here should perhaps be understood not as a noun but rather, as Heidegger argues about being, a verb, a place in movement; thus, the lack does not constitute a given entity, a

273

thing that can be identified. However, it can be imagined, considered and understood as a primary and fundamental determinant of the subjectivity of an individual, without being the only and exclusive determinant factor. The phallus is a function, and it cannot be represented. In fact, the very idea of a body, from the point of view of psychoanalysis, cannot be represented either. The psychoanalytic body is constructed through the imaginary existence of erotogenic zones and the special and specific role that the orifices, for example, play in the history of a subject. In this respect, psychoanalysis created a different kind of anatomy: Picasso's paintings may help us to imagine it while the illustrations and descriptions from a book of anatomy would prove to be useless.

Can we understand the one-sexedness of each sex without resorting to the concept of castration? This remains a theoretical and clinical challenge. The acceptance of the one-sexedness of each sex does not deny the complex and at times surprising ways in which people live their lives, nor does it intend to deny the vagaries of social change, nor to suggest that we should desperately cling onto an existing reactionary or prejudiced order of things. There are many different and alternative narratives, both individual and social, that account for the way in which people live. They all give testimony to the challenging discontinuities, the constant transformations of the dynamics of human relationships. Sexuality exists (and can be imagined only as existing) at the impossible frontier between the (only) two sexes; neither sex can possess it, be the proud owner of it or believe itself to be blessed with it. Moreover, even the enjoyment of it will always be in question. The phallic reference creates a difference that is both sexual and primary; it defines, from the very beginning, the one-sexedness of one as well as the one-sexedness of the other. But since the phallus does not exist in reality, and it belongs neither to one sex nor to the other, the illusion of its existence creates, for each one-sex, a particular way of relating to it. How could we consider sex without understanding the different relationships that each one-sexed unconscious subject has to the phallic function? And, above all, how can we accept the different relationships to the otherness that this implies?

Psychoanalysis inhabits the ambiguity of multiple paradoxes in need of explanation, which is something that psychoanalysis has struggled to do from its beginning.

Perhaps this is as much as psychoanalysis can say.

# Notes

1 See Alenka Zupančič (2016).

2 In the context of the relationship between Fliess and Freud, the history of the concept of bisexuality is, as one would expect, rather complicated; it involves issues of plagiarism (allegedly perpetrated by Otto Weininger, in *Sex and Character*, 1903/1906), and the inevitable involvement of other people and authors of the time (see Gherovici, 2010, pp. 68–71).

3 Darwin was the first to use the word "bisexuality" in *The Variations of Animals and Plants Under Domestication* (1868). For Darwin and his contemporaries, bisexuality was an exclusive biological notion, synonymous with hermaphroditism; it described the presence of female and male characteristics within one organism, whether fauna or flora. In fact, for many centuries, it was believed that there was a "bisexual primitive developmental stage" in the foetus. At present, we are aware that, after the sixth week of the foetus' development, sexual differentiation in humans emerges from neutral embryonic structures. In normal circumstances, the human foetus has the potential to develop either female or male organs, *one or the other*, depending on genetic and hormonal influences. This makes the use of "female" and "male" indispensable descriptive categories in biology: they describe specific and undeniable material differences, the result of an embryonic process. This is different to the belief in, and to the notion, of an original, complementary, "primary bisexuality".

4 In a rather simplified way, it is used at times to describe the sexual tendency of subjects who are attracted to both women and men.

5 Following Freud's trans-generational formula of the symbolic internalization of each of the parent's parental figures in the dissolution of the Oedipus complex, and its resolution through the development of the superego, Gherovici humorously calculated that "the sexual act of any 2 partners should involve 14 people at least" (2010, p. 77).

6 In the following years, Christian David, whom I quote again further below, wrote on sexuality and bisexuality from a critical, insightful and innovative point of view (1973, 1975).

7 Jung referred to Christ's "bi-sexuality", describing him as an "androgynous" figure, a mixture of man and woman. Christ's representation is the source of many historical and religious debates. Nevertheless, following Georg Koepgen (*Die Gnosis des Christentums*, 1939), Freud argued that Christ's voluntary acceptance of his sacrificial death was "feminine"; through his sacrifice, male and female became an unbroken androgynous unity in him. Furthermore, Koepgen argued that the Catholic Church, as the mystical body of Christ, would also

be considered as "androgynous" – and this would be manifested in the celibacy of the clergy. Jung seemed to go along with Koepgen's argument that celibacy should not be considered as "mere bachelor virginity" but as the androgynous unity of the soul achieved by Christ, a genuine reconciliation of the opposites (see Jung 1959, paras. 292–294). For some, the concept of bisexuality seemed to have been intoxicating.

8  The concept of gender was introduced by John Money in his study of the human hermaphroditism (Money, Hampson, & Hampson, 1955).

9  For the relevance of the phallic reference, see also Kohon (1999, pp. 8–16).

10  In Freudian theory, on the other hand, reproduction is understood as conceived by, and impregnated with sexuality because of the explosiveness of the oedipal drama.

# Glossary

*Après-coup* **(descriptive and dynamic)** I have suggested a differentiation between the notions of descriptive *après-coup* and dynamic *après-coup*. Descriptive *après-coup*, as used in colloquial psychoanalysis, simply means retrospective signification. Dynamic *après-coup*, on the other hand, includes various notions of temporality, such as fixation, regression, repetition compulsion and the return of the repressed. These different notions of time refer to the heterochrony in psychoanalysis (Green, 2002). Furthermore, dynamic *après-coup* is connected to a network of concepts such as trauma, castration and infantile sexuality, giving a specific meaning to the whole body of Freud's theory (Perelberg, 2006). It is the linkage of *après-coup* to this network of concepts that gives it a meta-psychological dimension. It is *après-coup* that meaning can be comprehended 'in the last instance' (2006, p. 120). *The temporality of the après-coup, establishing the links between the here and now and there and then*, marks the passage from a dyadic to a triadic structure in an analysis (Perelberg, 2013a, p. 581).

**Bisexuality, psychic** Freud progressively elaborated his views on psychic bisexuality, starting in his correspondence with Fliess. In "Psychogenesis of a Case of Homosexuality in a Woman", he suggested that the aim of an analytic process should be to restore "full bisexual functions" (Freud, 1920a, p. 171). "The economy of each person's sexuality (to give the word the full wealth of meaning that psychoanalysis confers on it) is based on an ever-fragile relationship between the assertion of bisexuality and the assertion of sexual specificity. Reckoning with the oscillation between femininity and masculinity − a constant in our psychic life − with the highly composite nature of the concept of sexual difference, and with the fact that the individual psychosexual position − I mean each

277

person's position on the infinitely varied spectrum of concrete sexualities – is the result of a long and hazardous drive-related and personal evolution, it becomes evident that "psychic participation" has transformed human sexuality into an extremely plastic and polymorphous reality (David, Chapter 1, in this volume).

**Bisexualization process** This is the integration of masculine and feminine aspects of the sexuality present in both men and women: it enables the acquisition of the capacity "to fantasise, understand and share the sexual and psychosexual experience of someone of the other sex" (David, Chapter 1, this volume). David also suggests that:

> The differential integration of sexuality, far from excluding an active psychic bisexuality, and far from necessarily requiring its entirely successful repression in accordance with prevailing norms, can (in some cases even should) go hand in hand with an authentic bisexual fulfilment.

**Black pact** Described by Godfrind, is the unconscious pact that is transmitted between mother and daughter. This pact relates to the transmission of a non-subjectivized part of the maternal unconscious that alienates the girl's unconscious. Its unconscious content relates to a shared hatred of the feminine. It masks a boundless, incestuous, fusional love between mother and daughter, sealing a shared denial of otherness and the third.

**Castration complex** The castration complex is closely linked to the oedipal complex. It refers to infantile sexual theories that stress the belief that both boys and girls possess a penis. Freud's suggested that the discovery of the differences between the sexes is traumatic for the child. Castration becomes the fundamental organizer of sexual difference. The fear of castration requires the renunciation of the incestuous desires and marks the inauguration of culture.

**Crypt** According to Godfrind, the crypt contains the part of the relation with the mother that constitutes a "black pact":

> Behind the sometimes deadly hate that exists between daughter and mother, suddenly there appears a bewildered love for the mother, a fascination that rivets the daughter to the mother, appealing to an encounter "*de trou à trou*" – "hole to hole" – the daughter being totally attached to the mother, bewitched, a link I call "*primary homosexuality*".
>
> (Godfrind, Chapter 5, in this volume)

278

**Divalence**   The term was originally used by Pichon-Riviere (1970, 1971) to convey the dual aspect of good and bad in each subject. It was then used by Lacan in order to indicate that the hysterical woman is caught up between the identification between mother and father. The hysteric question is: "Am I a man or a woman?" Gregorio Kohon has suggested that this is a stage that develops together with the constitution of whole objects, father and mother, and it defines a specific moment in the development of the individual in which the subject is confronted with the choice between these two objects:

> It is an hysterical stage, present in every woman, probably throughout her life. It characterizes, within the context of the oedipal drama, something specifically female. It would take place at that precise moment at which the subject, after the full recognition of sexual differences, has to make the change from mother to father.
>
> (1984, p. 81)

**Foreclosure**   Lacan (2006a) introduced this term as equivalent to Freud's "*Verwerfung*" (repudiation). Although several meanings may be identified in Freud's use of this term (Laplanche & Pontalis, 1967), the most significant for Lacan is present in the Wolf Man text:

> We are already acquainted with the attitude which our patient first adopted to the problem of castration. He rejected castration, and held to his theory of intercourse by the anus. When I speak of his having rejected it, the first meaning of the phrase is that he would have nothing to do with it, in the sense of having repressed it. This really involved no judgement upon the question of its existence, but it was the same as if it did not exist.
>
> (Freud, 1918b, p. 83)

Lacan suggests that foreclosure means "not symbolizing what ought to have been symbolized (castration): it is a 'symbolic abolition'" (Laplanche & Pontalis, 1988, p. 168).

**Gender**   Gender differences are culturally selected from among biological characteristics and are turned into "natural differences" between the sexes (La Fontaine, 1985). Robert J. Stoller (1968) coined the term "core gender identity" (Laplanche, 2007).

***Jouissance*** "can designate the excess of pleasure, a satisfaction that the subject finds too intense, as well as the suffering which can result from the prolonged state of internal excitation which can upset the equilibrium required by the pleasure principle" (Morel, 2011, p. 10). Freud offered several examples of this state in his book, *Beyond the Pleasure Principle*: the *fort-da* game, the dreams of traumatic neurosis, the compulsion to repeat, the negative therapeutic reaction. Men and women are placed differently in terms of their *jouissance*.

**Narcissistic contract** Aulagnier (2001) has suggested the term "narcissistic contract", which links the child and the social group to which he belongs. It defines the place of the subject in the chain of generations, his unconscious missions, in exchange for the care given and the parental and collective narcissistic cathexis. The *"statements of certainty"* are the words that convey to the child the meanings, identificatory processes, cultural bearings and taboos shared by the group. These statements also help to define the alien, the stranger and the enemy to be excluded from the group.

**Negative pact** According to R. Kaës, in Hirsch, Chapter 8, p. 187, in this volume:

> The negative pact accounts for the transmission between the subjects of a group or the transgenerational transmission inside a family. The negative pact is also a "meta-defence" because it creates, on the whole and in each one, areas of silence that keep the subject as a foreigner to its own history. These imply shared mechanisms of repression, denial or foreclosure shared by each individual, so that some representations remain unconscious in each of the related subjects.

**Oedipus 1 and 2** Kristeva suggests a two-sided Oedipus phase for the girl: "Oedipus 1" relates to both boys and girls, where the desire for the mother is dominant, before there is a change of the object for the girl towards the father:

> Masturbation, incestuous desire for the mother: here is the first aspect of the Oedipus complex (I will call it Oedipus 1) that structurally defines the girl, as well as the boy, before she arrives at Oedipus 2, which causes her to change objects (the father instead of the mother). Yet, starting with this structuring (Oedipus 1), there are differences between the girl's phallicism and the boy's.
>
> (Kristeva, 2000, p. 99)

**Passivation** is a term coined by André Green that refers to patients' capacity to entrust themselves to analytic care. He interprets Freud's concept of the "repudiation of femininity" as the repudiation of the mother's passivating action, her seductive care, rendering the infant passive. This also refers to the individual's passivity in the face of the drives (1986b, p. 247).

**Phallus** The distinction between penis and phallus is an important reference in the psychoanalytic understanding of bisexuality and sexual difference. It refers to the differentiation between biological and psychic reality. Penis designates the anatomical and physiological reality (Laplanche & Pontalis, 1967, p. 56); phallus, on the other hand, exists outside anatomical reality. Lacan suggests that it is the signifier of the mother's desire. The central question of the Oedipus complex thus becomes to be or not to be the phallus – that is, to be or not to be the object of the mother's desire (Dor, 1985, p. 102). The role of the father also becomes symbolic: he represents the impossibility of being the object of the mother's desire.

**Primary homosexuality** The term "primary homosexuality" was first formulated by Fenichel, who introduced it in connection with female homosexuality: "The first object of every human being is the mother: all women, in contradistinction to men, have had a primary homosexual attachment, which may later be revived if normal heterosexuality is blocked" (Fenichel, 1946, p. 338). It concerns the primordial relationship, mainly undifferentiated, at the heart of which the baby encounters the mother as "similar to him". The mother agrees to merge into her baby's emotional states and to respond in a specular way to his needs. She establishes the foundations of primary narcissism. Denis views this "primary homosexual" cathexis as having a transitional function, in that it opens a path towards the acceptance of otherness and the recognition of sexual difference. Godfrind uses this terminology to describe a fascination that rivets the daughter to the mother, appealing to an encounter "*de trou à trou*" – "hole to hole" – the daughter being totally attached to and bewitched by the mother. See *black pact*.

**Psychosexuality** The object of psychoanalysis is not gender but psychosexuality that establishes a link between sexuality and the unconscious. The latter is permanently challenging our apparent unity as subjects. This unity is a specular construction that enables the individual to enter into the realm of symbolic exchanges.

**Repudiation of femininity**  In 1937 Freud concluded that both sexes "repudiate femininity" – a phenomenon that is an essential element of the asymmetry between the sexes. This repudiation is, Freud suggests, the bedrock of psychoanalysis and part of the great riddle of sex (1937c, p. 252). It is part of the domain of what is unanalysable for Freud.

**Secondary homosexuality**  relates back to the oedipal genital attraction to the parent of the same sex. It concerns the homosexual identifications of the inverted Oedipus complex.

**Sexuation**  Lacan has suggested the concept of sexuation to underline the object of psychoanalysis in relation to sexuality. Sexuation, as distinct from biological differences between the sexes, designates the way in which the subject is inscribed in the difference between the sexes, specifically in terms of the unconscious and castration, that is, as "inhabiting language" (Lacan, 1998, p. 80).

# References

Abensour, L. (2010). L'ombre du maternel [The shadow of the maternal]. *Bulletin de la SPP*, Nov/Dec.

Abraham, N., & Torok, M. (1994). *The Shell and the Kernel*. Chicago, IL: University of Chicago Press.

Aisenstein, M. (2005). Le non-désir d'enfant. In R. Frydman & M. Trèves (Eds.), *Rêves de femmes*. Paris: Odile Jacob.

Aisenstein, M. (2012). A particular form of paternal identification in women. *Psychoanalytic Quarterly*, 81: 17–37.

Ambrosio, G. (Ed.) (2009). *Transvestism, Transsexualism in the Psychoanalytic Dimension*. London: Karnac.

André, J. (1995). *Aux origines féminines de la sexualité* [The feminine origins of sexuality]. Paris: Presses Universitaires de France.

André, S. (1999). *What Does a Woman Want?*, trans. S. Fairfield. New York: Other Press.

Anzieu, D. (1986). *Freud's Self-Analysis*. New York: International Universities Press.

Appignanesi, L., & Forrester, J. (2000). *Freud's Women*. London: Weidenfeld & Nicolson.

Aulagnier, P. (2001). *The Violence of Interpretation: From Pictogram to Statement*, trans. A. Sheridan. London: Routledge.

Bailly, L. (2009). *Lacan: A Beginner's Guide*. London: One World Publications.

Balint, E. (1973). Technical problems found in the analysis of women by a woman analyst. *International Journal of Psychoanalysis*, 54: 195–201.

Balint, E. (1997). The analysis of women by a woman analyst: What does a woman want? In J. Raphael-Leff & R. J. Perelberg (Eds.), *Female Experience: Four Generations of Women on Work with Women*, new edition. London: Anna Freud Centre, 2008, pp. 36–45.

Barthes, R. (1978). *A Lover's Discourse: Fragments*, trans. R. Howard. New York: Farrar, Straus and Giroux.

283

Bateson, G. (1958 [1936]). *Naven*. Redwood City, CA: Stanford University Press.

Bauduin, A. (2007). *Psychanalyse de l'imposture* [Psychoanalysis of deception]. Paris: Éditions du Seuil.

Bergler, E. (1956). *Homosexuality: Disease or Way of Life?* New York: Hill & Wang.

Birksted-Breen, D. (1989). Working with an anorexic patient. *International Journal of Psychoanalysis*, 70: 29–40. Also in J. Raphael-Leff & R. J. Perelberg (Eds.), *Female Experience: Four Generations of Women on Work with Women*, new edition. London: Anna Freud Centre, 2008, pp. 104–122.

Birksted-Breen, D. (1993). General introduction. In *The Gender Conundrum: Contemporary Psychoanalytic Perspectives on Femininity and Masculinity*. London: Routledge & The Institute of Psychoanalysis.

Birksted-Breen, D. (1996). Phallus, penis and mental space. *International Journal of Psychoanalysis*, 77: 649–657.

Birksted-Breen, D. (2005). The feminine. In S. Budd & R. Rusbridger (Eds.), *Introducing Psychoanalysis: Essential Themes and Topics*. Hove: Routledge.

Birksted-Breen, D., Flanders, S., & Gibeault, A. (2010). *Reading French Psychoanalysis*. London: Routledge.

Bleger, J. (1985). *Symbiose et ambiguïté. Etude psychanalytique* [Symbiosis and ambiguity: A psychoanalytic study]. Paris: Presses Universitaires de France.

Blum, H. P. (1971). On the conception and development of the transference neurosis. *Journal of the American Psychoanalytic Association*, 19: 41–53.

Bokanowski, T. (2010). Rêve, transferts et scène primitive chez l'Homme aux loups. *Revue Française de Psychanalyse*, 4 (74): 969–980.

Bollas, C. (2000). *Hysteria*. London: Routledge.

Boris, H. (1984). The problem of anorexia nervosa. *International Journal of Psychoanalysis*, 65: 315–322.

Braunschweig, D., & Fain, M. (1975). *La nuit, le jour. Essai psychanalytique sur le fonctionnement mental* [Night, day: A psychoanalytic essay on mental functioning]. Paris: Presses Universitaires de France.

Brenman, E. (1985). Hysteria. *International Journal of Psychoanalysis*, 66: 423–432.

Brierley, M. (1932). Some problems of integration in women. *International Journal of Psychoanalysis*, 13: 433–448.

Britton, R. (1989). The missing link: Parental sexuality in the Oedipus complex. In *The Oedipus Complex Today: Clinical Implications*. London: Karnac, pp. 83–101.

Britton, R. (1998). *Belief and Imagination*. London: Routledge.

Britton, R. (1999). Getting in on the act: The hysterical solution. *International Journal of Psychoanalysis*, 80 (1): 1–14.

Budd, S. (2005). The psychogenesis of a case of female homosexuality. In R. J. Perelberg (Ed.), *Freud: A Modern Reader*. London: Wiley, pp. 234–250.

Burgner, M. (1997). Analytic treatment of an adolescent with bulimia nervosa. In J. Raphael-Leff & R. J. Perelberg (Eds.), *Female Experience: Four Generations of Women on Work with Women*, new edition. London: Anna Freud Centre, 2008, pp. 93–103.

Butler, J. (1990). *Gender Trouble: Feminism and the Subversion of Identity*. London: Routledge.

Butler, J. (1993). *Bodies That Matter: On the Discursive Limits of "Sex"*. London: Routledge.

Butler, J. (1997). Melancholy gender/refused identification. In J. Butler, *The Psychic Life of Power*. Stanford, CA: Stanford University Press, pp. 132–150.

Butler, J. (2015). Ideologies of the super-ego: Psychoanalysis and feminism revisited. In R. Duschinsky & S. Walker (Eds.), *Juliet Mitchell and the Lateral Axis*. New York: Palgrave, pp. 57–76.

Campbell, D. (2018). *The Core Complex, Violence and Perverse Solutions: Mervin Glasser's Contributions to Psychoanalysis*. London: Routledge.

Chabert, C. (2003). *Féminin mélancolique* [The melancholic feminine]. Paris: Presses Universitaires de France.

Chabert, C. (2005). Clinical and metapsychological reflections on "A Child Is Being Beaten". In R. J. Perelberg (Ed.), *Freud: A Modern Reader*. London: Wiley, pp. 224–233.

Chasseguet-Smirgel, J. (1964a). La culpabilité féminine [Feminine guilt]. In J. Chasseguet-Smirgel (Ed.), *La vie sexuelle*. Paris: Payot.

Chasseguet-Smirgel, J. (1964b). *Female Sexuality: New Psychoanalytic Views*. Ann Arbor, MI: University of Michigan Press, 1970; reprinted London: Karnac, 1991.

Chasseguet-Smirgel, J. (1964c). Feminine guilt and the Oedipus complex. In J. Chasseguet-Smirgel (Ed.), *Female Sexuality: New Psychoanalytic Views*. Ann Arbor, MI: University of Michigan Press, 1970; reprinted London: Karnac, 1991.

Chasseguet-Smirgel, J. (1976). Freud and female sexuality: The consideration of some blind spots in the exploration of the "dark continent". *International Journal of Psychoanalysis*, 57: 275–286.

Chasseguet-Smirgel, J. (1985). *Creativity and Perversion*. London: Free Association Books.

Chasseguet-Smirgel, J. (1986). *Sexuality and Mind*. New York: New York University Press.

Chervet, B. (2009). L'après-coup. La tentative d'inscrire ce qui tend à disparaître. *Revue Française de Psychanalyse*, 73: 1361–1442.

Chevalier, M. (1893) *L'inversion sexuelle*, Lyon (141,143,n.)

Chiland, C (2005). *Exploring transsexualism*, trans. D. Alcorn. London: Karnac.

Ciccone, A. (2012). *La transmission psychique inconsciente* [Unconscious psychic transmission]. Paris: Dunod.

Cixous, H. (1981). Castration or decapitation? *Signs: Journal of Women in Culture and Society*, 7 (1): 36–55.

Copjec, J. (2016). The sexual compact. In A. Cerda-Rueda (Ed.), *Sex and Nothing: Bridges from Psychoanalysis to Philosophy*. London: Karnac.

Cournut-Janin, M. (1998a). *Féminin et féminité*. Paris: Presses Universitaires de France.

Cournut-Janin, M. (1998b). The feminine and femininity. In D. Birksted-Breen, S. Flanders, & A. Gibeault (Eds.), *Reading French Psychoanalysis*. London: Routledge, 2010, pp. 623–640.

Cournut-Janin, M. (2005). Dora: Fragment of an analysis of hysteria. In R. J. Perelberg (Ed.), *Freud: A Modern Reader*. London: Wiley, pp. 47–60.

Cournut-Janin, M., & Cournut, J. (1993). La castration et le féminin dans les deux sexes. *Revue Française de Psychanalyse*, 5: 1353–1558.

Darwin, C. (1868). *The Variations of Animals and Plants Under Domestication*. London: John Murray.

David, C. (1964). A masculine mythology of femininity. In J. Chasseguet-Smirgel, *Female Sexuality: New Psychoanalytic Views*. Ann Arbor, MI: University of Michigan Press, 1970; reprinted London: Karnac, 1991.

David, C. (1973). Les belles différences. *Nouvelle Revue de Psychanalyse*, 7: 21–45. Also in *La bisexualité psychique*. Paris: Payot, 1992. [The beautiful differences. In D. Birksted-Breen, S. Flanders, & A. Gibeault (Eds.), *Reading French Psychoanalysis*. London: Routledge, 2010, pp. 649–667.].

David, C. (1975). La médiation sexuelle. *Revue Française de Psychanalyse*, 39 (5–6): 824–845. Also in *La bisexualité psychique*. Paris: Payot, 1992.

David, C. (1992). *La bisexualité psychique*. Paris: Payot.

Davies, R. (2012). Anxiety: The importunate companion: Psychoanalytic theory of castration and separation anxiety and implications for clinical technique. *International Journal of Psychoanalysis*, 93: 1101–1114.

de Lauretis, T. (1987). *Technologies of Gender*. Bloomington, IN: Indiana University Press.

Delcourt, M. (1958). *Hermaphrodite*. Paris: Presses Universitaires de France.

Denis, P. (1982). Primary homosexuality: A foundation of contradictions. In D. Birksted-Breen, S. Flanders, & A. Gibeault (Eds.), *Reading French Psychoanalysis*. London: Routledge, 2010, pp. 641–648.

Denis, P. (1997). *Emprise et satisfaction. Les deux formants de la pulsion*. Paris: Presses Universitaires de France.

Dolar, M. (2016). Officers, maids, and chimneysweepers. In A. Cerda-Rueda (Ed.), *Sex and Nothing: Bridges from Psychoanalysis to Philosophy*. London: Karnac, pp. 107–137.

Dor, J. (1985). *Introduction à la lecture de Lacan*. Paris: Denoël.

Dor, J. (1998). *Introduction to the Reading of Lacan*. New York: Other Press.

Faimberg, H. (1995). Le temps de la construction. Répétition et surprise [The time of construction: Repetition and surprise]. *Revue Française de Psychanalyse*, 4 (59): 1159–1171.

Faimberg, H. (2005). *The Telescoping of Generations: Listening to the Narcissistic Links between Generations*. London: Karnac.

Fain, M. (1982). *Le désir de l'interprète*. Paris: Aubier Montaigne.

Fairbairn, W. R. D. (1931). Features in the analysis of a patient with a physical genital abnormality. In *Psychoanalytical Studies of the Personality*. London: Routledge & Kegan Paul, 1981, pp. 197–222.

Feldman, M. (2009). The Oedipus complex: Manifestations in the inner world and the therapeutic situation, In *Doubt, Conviction and the Analytic Process*. London: Routledge, pp. 1–20.

Fenichel, O. (1946). *The Psychoanalytic Theory of Neurosis*. London: Routledge & Kegan Paul.

Ferraro, F. (2001). Vicissitudes of bisexuality: Crucial points and clinical implications. *International Journal of Psychoanalysis*, 82: 485–499.

Fliess, W. (1897). *Die Beziehungen zwischen Nase und weiblichen Geschlechtsorganen in ihren biologischen Bedeutung dargestellt*. Leipzig and Vienna: Franz Deuticke. [*Les relations entre le nez et les organes génitaux de la femme: Présentées selon leurs signification biologique*. Paris: Éditions du Seuil, 1977.]

Freud, E. L. (Ed.). (1960). *Letters of Sigmund Freud 1873–1939*. London: Hogarth Press.

Freud, S. (1895b). On the grounds for detaching a particular syndrome from neurasthenia under the description "anxiety neurosis". *Standard Edition*, 3: 85–115.

Freud, S. (1895d) (with Breuer, J.). *Studies on Hysteria. Standard Edition*, 2.

Freud, S. (1900a). *The Interpretation of Dreams. Standard Edition*, 4–5.

Freud, S. (1905d). *Three Essays on the Theory of Sexuality. Standard Edition*, 7: 123–245.

Freud, S. (1905e). Fragment of an analysis of a case of hysteria. *Standard Edition*, 7: 1–122.

Freud, S. (1908a). Hysterical phantasies and their relation to bisexuality. *Standard Edition*, 9: 157–166.

Freud, S. (1908c). On the sexual theories of children. *Standard Edition*, 9: 209–226.

Freud, S. (1909b). Analysis of a phobia in a five-year-old boy. *Standard Edition*, 9: 1–150.

Freud, S. (1909d). Notes upon a case of obsessional neurosis. *Standard Edition*, 10: 153–320.

Freud, S. (1910c). *Leonardo da Vinci and a Memory of His Childhood*. *Standard Edition*, 11: 51–137.

Freud, S. (1911c). Psycho-analytic notes on an autobiographical account of a case of paranoia (Dementia paranoides). *Standard Edition*, 12: 3–82.

Freud, S. (1912b). The dynamics of transference. *Standard Edition*, 12: 99–108.

Freud, S. (1912d). On the universal tendency to debasement in the sphere of love. *Standard Edition*, 11: 177–190.

Freud, S. (1912–13). *Totem and Taboo*. *Standard Edition*, 13: 1–161.

Freud, S. (1913c). On beginning the treatment. *Standard Edition*, 12: 123–144.

Freud, S. (1913j). The claims of psycho-analysis to scientific interest. *Standard Edition*, 13: 165–192.

Freud, S. (1914c). On narcissism: An introduction. *Standard Edition*, 14: 73–102.

Freud, S. (1914g). Remembering, repeating and working-through [Further recommendations on the technique of psycho-analysis]. *Standard Edition*, 12: 147–156.

Freud, S. (1915a). Observations on transference-love [Further recommendations on the technique of psycho-analysis]. *Standard Edition*, 12: 159–171.

Freud, S. (1915f). A case of paranoia running counter to the psycho-analytic theory of disease. *Standard Edition*, 14: 261–272.

Freud, S. (1917c). On transformations of instinct as exemplified in anal erotism. *Standard Edition*, 17: 127–133.

Freud, S. (1917e). Mourning and melancholia. *Standard Edition*, 14: 237–258.

Freud, S. (1918b). From the history of an infantile neurosis. *Standard Edition*, 17: 3–123.

Freud, S. (1919e). "A child is being beaten": A contribution to the study of the genesis of sexual perversions. *Standard Edition*, 17: 195–204.

Freud, S. (1919h). The "Uncanny". *Standard Edition*, 17: 217–256.

Freud, S. (1920a). The psychogenesis of a case of homosexuality in a woman. *Standard Edition*, 18: 147–172.

Freud, S. (1920g). *Beyond the Pleasure Principle*. *Standard Edition*, 18: 7–64.

Freud, S. (1921c). *Group Psychology and the Analysis of the Ego*. *Standard Edition*, 18: 65–143.

Freud, S. (1923b). *The Ego and the Id*. *Standard Edition*, 19: 12–66.

Freud, S. (1923e). The infantile genital organization. *Standard Edition*, 19: 141–148.

Freud, S. (1924c). The economic problem of masochism. *Standard Edition*, 19: 159–170.

Freud, S. (1924d). The dissolution of the Oedipus complex. *Standard Edition*, 19: 173–179.

Freud, S. (1925j). Some psychical consequences of the anatomical distinction between the sexes. *Standard Edition*, 19: 248–258.

Freud, S. (1926d). *Inhibitions, Symptoms and Anxiety. Standard Edition*, 20: 77–175.

Freud, S. (1926e). *The Question of Lay Analysis. Standard Edition*, 20: 183–250.

Freud, S. (1927c). *The Future of an Illusion. Standard Edition*, 21: 1–56.

Freud, S. (1927e). Fetishism. *Standard Edition*, 21: 152–157.

Freud, S. (1928b). Dostoevsky and parricide. *Standard Edition*, 21: 177–196.

Freud, S. (1930a). *Civilization and Its Discontents. Standard Edition*, 21.

Freud, S. (1931b). Female sexuality. *Standard Edition,* 21: 223–246.

Freud, S. (1933a). *New Introductory Lectures on Psycho-Analysis. Standard Edition*, 22: 1–184.

Freud, S. (1935). Freud and female sexuality: A previously unpublished letter [Letter to Carl Müller-Braunschweig]. *Psychiatry*, 34 (No. 3, 1971): 328–329.

Freud, S. (1937c). Analysis terminable and interminable. *Standard Edition*, 23: 209–253.

Freud, S. (1939a). *Moses and Monotheism. Standard Edition*, 23: 7–140.

Freud, S. (1940a). *An Outline of Psycho-Analysis. Standard Edition*, 23: 141–208.

Freud, S. (1940e). Splitting of the ego in the process of defence. *Standard Edition*, 23: 275–278.

Freud, S. (1941f [1938]). Findings, ideas, problems. *Standard Edition*, 23: 299–300.

Freud, S. (1950 [1892–99]). Extracts from the Fliess Papers. *Standard Edition*, 1: 173–280.

Freud, S., & Bullitt, W. (1967). *Woodrow Wilson: A Psychological Study*. Boston, MA: Mifflin.

Gallop, J. (1982). *Feminism and Psychoanalysis: The Daughter's Seduction*. London: Macmillan.

Gary, R. (1962). *Promise at Dawn*, trans. J. M. Beach. London: Michael Joseph. [*La promesse de l'aube*. Paris: Gallimard, 1960.]

Gary, R. [Ajar, E.] (1974). *Pseudo*. Paris: Gallimard.

Gary, R. (1981). *Vie et mort d'Émile Ajar* [Life and death of Émile Ajar]. Paris: Gallimard.

Gherovici, P. (2010). *Please Select Your Gender: From the Invention of Hysteria to the Democratizing of Transgenderism*. New York: Routledge.

Gibeault, A. (2010). Masculine and feminine sexuality: Introduction. In D. Birksted-Breen, S. Flanders, & A. Gibeault (Eds.), *Reading French Psychoanalysis*. London: Routledge, pp. 554–562.

Glasser, M. (1979a). From the analysis of a transvestite. *International Review of Psycho-Analysis*, 6: 163–173.

Glasser, M. (1979b). Some aspects of the role of aggression in the perversions. In I. Rosen (Ed.), *Sexual Deviation*. Oxford: Oxford University Press, pp. 278–305.

Glover, E. (1955). *The Technique of Psychoanalysis*. New York: International Universities Press.

Godfrind, J. (1994). Le pacte noir [The black pact]. *Revue Française de Psychanalyse*, 1.

Godfrind, J. (1997). La bisexualité psychique. Guerre et paix des sexes. In A. Fine, D. Le Boeuf, & A. Le Guen (Eds.), *Bisexualité*. Monographie de la Revue Française de Psychanalyse. Paris: Presses Universitaires de France, pp. 131–146.

Godfrind, J. (2001). *Comment la féminité vient aux femmes*. Paris: Presses Universitaires de France.

Gozlan, O. (2015). *Transsexuality and the Art of Transitioning: A Lacanian Approach*. London: Routledge.

Green, A. (1972). Aggression, femininity, paranoia and reality. *International Journal of Psychoanalysis*, 53 (2).

Green, A. (1973). Le genre neutre. In *Bisexualité et la différence des sexes*. Nouvelle Revue de Psychanalyse, No. 7. Paris: Gallimard. Also in *Narcissisme de vie. Narcissism de mort*. Paris: Minuit, 1983, pp. 208–221. [The neuter gender. In: *Life Narcissism, Death Narcissism*, trans. A. Weller. London: Free Association Books, 2001, pp. 158–169.]

Green, A. (1983). The dead mother. In *Life Narcissism, Death Narcissism*, trans. A. Weller. London: Free Association Books, 2001, pp. 170–200.

Green, A. (1986a). The dead mother. In *On Private Madness*. London: Hogarth Press, pp. 142–173.

Green, A. (1986b). Passions and their vicissitudes. In *On Private Madness*. London: Hogarth Press, pp. 214–253.

Green, A. (1986c [1977]). The borderline concept: A conceptual framework for understanding of borderline patients. In *On Private Madness*. London: Hogarth Press and The Institute of Psychoanalysis, pp. 60–83.

Green, A. (1999). *The Work of the Negative*, trans. A. Weller. London: Free Association Books.

Green, A. (2002). The construction of heterochrony. In A. Green, *Time in Psychoanalysis: Some Contradictory Aspects*. London: Free Association Books, pp. 9–27.

Groddeck, G. (1931). La bisexualidad del ser humano. *Revista de la Asociación Española de Neuropsiquiatría*, 21 (No. 79, 2001): 83–87. Traducción de Angel Cagigas. [Das Zwiegeschlecht des Menschen. *Psychoanalytische Bewegung*, 3 (1931): 166–172.]

Grosz, E. (1994). *Volatile Bodies: Towards a Corporeal Feminism*. St Leonards, New South Wales: Allen & Unwin.

Grotjahn, M. (1945). Georg Groddeck and his teachings about man's innate need for symbolization: A contribution to the history of early psychoanalytic psychosomatic medicine. *Psychoanalytic Review*, 32: 9–24.

Harris, A. (1991). Gender as contradiction. *Psychoanalytic Dialogues*, 1 (2): 197–224.

Héritier, F. (2002). *Masculin/féminin, II. Dissoudre la hiérarchie*. Paris: Odile Jacob.

Héritier, F. (2012). *Masculin/féminin, I*. Paris: Odile Jacob.

Hirsch, D. (2009). Du futur antérieur au passé re-composé. Construction et interprétation à l'adolescence [From the future perfect to the new present perfect. Construction and interpretation in adolescence]. *Revue Adolescence*, 27 (4): 1027–1037.

Hirsch, D. (2014). Position dépressive et après-coup, situation oedipienne et complexe d'Oedipe [The depressive position and deferred action, the oedipal situation and the Oedipus complex]. Discussion of R. Britton's paper "Rupture et Œdipe". *Psychanalyse en Europe*, 68: 73–76.

House of Commons (2016). House of Commons Women & Equalities Committee. Transgender Equality: First report of Session 2015–16, 8 December 2015. www.publications.parliament.uk/pa/cm201516/cmselect/cmwomeq/390/390.pdf.

Houzel, D. (2003). Archaïque et bisexualité psychique. *Journal de Psychanalyse de l'Enfant*, 32: 75–96.

Irigaray, L. (1989). The gesture in psychoanalysis. In T. Brenman (Ed.), *Between Feminism and Psychoanalysis*. London: Routledge.

Jacob, F. (1971). *La logique du vivant*. Paris: Gallimard.

Jagose, A. (1996). *Queer Theory: An Introduction*. New York: New York Universities Press.

Jones, E. (1974). *Sigmund Freud: Life and Work*. London: Hogarth Press.

Jung, C. G. (1959). *The Collected Works of C. G. Jung, Vol. 9, Part 1: The Archetypes and the Collective Unconscious*. Hove: Routledge, 2014.

Kaës, R. (2002). *La polyphonie du rêve* [The polyphony of dreams]. Paris: Dunod.

Kaës, R. (2009). *Les alliances inconscientes* [Unconscious alliances]. Paris: Dunod.

Kaës, R. (2010). *L'appareil psychique groupal* [The psychic apparatus of the group]. Paris: Dunod.

Kamel, F. (1997). Quelques données fondamentales sur le concept de bisexualité psychique dans l'œuvre de Freud. In A. Fine, D. Le Beuf, & A. Le Guen (Eds.), *Bisexualité*. Monographies de la Revue Française de Psychanalyse. Paris: Presses Universitaires de France, pp. 11–20.

Kestemberg, E. (1984). "Astrid" ou homosexualité, identité, adolescence. Quelques propositions hypothétiques. In *Adolescence à vif*. Paris: Presses Universitaires de France, 1999, pp. 239–265.

Kestenberg, J. (1968). Outside and inside, male and female. *Journal of the American Psychoanalytic Association*, 16: 457–520.

Kiernan, J. G. (1888). Sexual perversion and the Whitechapel Murders. *Medical Standard, Chicago*, 4: 170.

Klein, M. (1928). Early stages of the Oedipus complex. *International Journal of Psychoanalysis*, 9: 167–180.

Koepgen, G. (1939). *Die Gnosis des Christentums*. Salzburg.

Kohon, G. (1984). Reflections on Dora: The case of hysteria. *International Journal of Psychoanalysis*, 65: 73–84.

Kohon, G. (1986a). *The British School of Psychoanalysis: The Independent Tradition*. London: Free Association Books.

Kohon, G. (1986b). Reflections on Dora: The case of hysteria. In *The British School of Psychoanalysis: The Independent Tradition*. London: Free Association Books.

Kohon, G. (1987). Fetishism revisited. *International Journal of Psychoanalysis*, 68: 213–229.

Kohon, G. (1999). *No Lost Certainties to Be Recovered*. London: Karnac.

Kohon, G. (2005a). Love in a time of madness. In A. Green & G. Kohon, *Love and Its Vicissitudes*. London: Routledge.

Kohon, G. (2005b). The Oedipus complex. In S. Budd & R. Rusbridger (Eds.), *Introducing Psychoanalysis: Essential Themes and Topics*. Hove: Routledge. Also in P. Williams, J. Keene, & S. Dermen (Eds.), *Independent Psychoanalysis Today*. London: Karnac, 2012.

Kohon, G. (2012). On Peter Fonagy and Elizabeth Allison's scientific theory of homosexuality. (A response to "A Scientific Theory of Homosexuality for Psychoanalysis" by Peter Fonagy and Elizabeth Allison. Paper given at the Scientific Meeting of the British Psycho-analytical Society on 17th October, 2012). *Bulletin of the British Psychoanalytical Society*, 48 (No. 7, September).

Kohon, G. (2016). *Reflections on the Aesthetic Experience: Psychoanalysis and the Uncanny*. London: Routledge.

Kreisler, L. (1970). Les intersexuels avec ambiguïté génitale. *La Psychiatrie de l'Enfant*, 13: 5–127.

Kristeva, J. (1995). *New Maladies of the Soul*. New York: Columbia University Press.

Kristeva, J. (2000). *The Sense and Non-Sense of Revolt*. New York: Columbia University Press.

Kristeva, J. (2012). Fatigue in the feminine. In *Hatred and Forgiveness*. New York: Columbia University Press, pp. 114–126.

Lacan, J. (1958). *Le séminaire, livre V. Les formations de l'inconscient.* Paris: Éditions du Seuil, 1998.

Lacan, J. (1968). The phallic phase and the subjective import of the castration complex. In J. Mitchell & J. Rose (Eds.), *Jacques Lacan and the École Freudienne: Feminine Sexuality.* London: Penguin, 1982, pp. 99–122.

Lacan, J. (1973). *Le séminaire, Livre XI. Les quatre concepts fondamentaux de la psychanalyse.* Paris: Éditions du Seuil.

Lacan, J. (1978). *Le séminaire, Livre II. Le moi dans la théorie de Freud et dans la technique de la psychanalyse.* Paris: Éditions du Seuil.

Lacan, J. (1981). *Le séminaire, Livre III. Les psychoses (1955–56).* Paris: Éditions du Seuil.

Lacan, J. (1991). *The Seminar of Jaques Lacan, Book II. The Ego in Freud's Theory and in the Technique of Psychoanalysis, 1954–1955,* trans S. Tomaselli. New York: W. W. Norton.

Lacan, J. (1993). *The Seminar of Jaques Lacan, Book III. The Psychosis, 1955–56,* trans R. Grigg. London: Routledge.

Lacan, J. (1994). *Le séminaire, Livre IV. La relation d'objet.* Paris: Éditions du Seuil.

Lacan, J. (1998). *The Seminar of Jacques Lacan, Book XX. On Feminine Sexuality: The Limits of Love and Knowledge, Encore,* trans. B. Fink. New York: W.W. Norton.

Lacan, J. (2006a). *Écrits,* trans. B. Fink. New York: W.W. Norton.

Lacan, J. (2006b). The mirror stage as formative of the I function as revealed in psychoanalytic experience. In *Écrits,* trans B. Fink. New York: W.W. Norton, pp. 75–81.

La Fontaine, J. S. (1981). The domestication of the savage male. *Man,* 16: 333–349.

La Fontaine, J. S. (1985). Anthropological perspectives on the family and social change. *Quarterly Journal of Social Affairs,* 1 (1): 29–56.

Lane, E. W. (Trans.). (1883). *The Thousand and One Nights: Commonly Called, in England, the Arabian Nights' Entertainments, Vol. 2,* ed. E. S. Poole. London: Chatto & Windus.

Laplanche, J. (Reporter). (1973). Panel on "Hysteria Today". *International Journal of Psychoanalysis,* 55 (1974): 459–469.

Laplanche, J. (1976). *Life and Death in Psychoanalysis,* trans. J. Mehlman. Baltimore, MD: Johns Hopkins University Press.

Laplanche, J. (1987). *Nouveaux fondements pour la psychanalyse.* Paris: Presses Universitaires de France.

Laplanche, J. (1989). *New Foundations for Psychoanalysis,* trans. D. Macey. Oxford: Blackwell.

Laplanche, J. (1992). Interpretation between determinism and hermeneutics: A restatement of the problem. *International Journal of Psychoanalysis,* 73: 429–445.

Laplanche, J. (1999). *Essays on Otherness*. London: Routledge.

Laplanche, J. (2007). Gender, sex, and the sexual. *Studies in Gender and Sexuality*, 8: 201–219.

Laplanche, J., & Pontalis, J.-B. (1967). *The Language of Psychoanalysis*. London: Hogarth Press, 1973; reprinted London: Karnac, 1988.

Laufer, M. E. (1993). The female Oedipus complex and the relationship to the body. In D. Birksted-Breen (Ed.), *The Gender Conundrum*. London: Routledge, pp. 67–81.

Leclaire, S. (1975). *On tue un enfant*. Paris: Éditions du Seuil.

Leclaire, S. (1980). Jerome, or death in the life of the obsessional. In S. Schneiderman (Ed.), *Returning to Freud: Clinical Psychoanalysis in the School of Lacan*. New Haven, CT: Yale University Press.

Lemma, A. (2013). The body one has and the body one is: The transsexual's need to be seen. *International Journal of Psychoanalysis*, 94 (2): 277–292.

Lemma, A. (2016). The black mirror: Identity, body, technology. Unpublished paper presented to UCL Conference, December.

Lévi-Strauss, C. (1969 [1967]). *The Elementary Structures of Kinship and Marriage*. Boston, MA: Beacon Press.

Lewinter, R. (1969). Preface. In G. Groddeck, *La maladie, l'art et le symbole* [Illness, art and the symbol]. Paris: Gallimard, pp. 290–309.

Luquet-Parat, C. (1962). Réflexions sur le transfert homosexuel dans le cas particulier d'un homme analysé par une femme [Reflections on the homosexual transference in the particular case of a man analysed by a woman]. *Revue Française de Psychanalyse*, 5.

Lydston, G. F. (1889). A lecture on sexual perversion, satyriasis and nymphomania. *Medical Surgical Reporter, Philadelphia, 61* (7 September).

Magid, B. (1993). A young woman's homosexuality reconsidered. *Journal of the American Academy of Psychoanalysis and Dynamic Psychiatry*, 21: 421–432.

Mardrus, J. C. (Trans.). (1990). *Mille et une Nuits* [A thousand and one nights]. Paris: Ed. de la Revue Blanche.

Masson, J. M. (Ed.). (1985). *The Complete Letters of Sigmund Freud to Wilhelm Fliess, 1887–1904*. Cambridge, MA: Belknap Press.

Matthis, I. (Ed.). (2011). *Dialogues on Sexuality, Gender and Psychoanalysis*. London: Karnac.

McDougall, J. (1980). *A Plea for a Measure of Abnormality*. New York: International Universities Press.

McDougall, J. (1989). The dead father: On early psychic trauma and its relation to disturbance in sexual identity and in creative activity. *International Journal of Psychoanalysis*, 70: 205–219.

McDougall, J. (1995). *The Many Faces of Eros*. London: Free Association Books.

McGuire, W. (Ed.). (1974). *The Freud/Jung Letters: The Correspondence between Sigmund Freud and C. G. Jung.* Princeton, NJ: Princeton University Press.

Mead, M. (1935). *Sex and Temperament in Three Primitive Societies.* London: Routledge & Kegan Paul.

Miller, A. (1984). *Le drame de l'enfant doué.* Paris: Payot.

Millot, C. (1990). *Horsexe: Essays on transsexuality,* trans. K. Hylton. Brooklyn, NY: Automedia.

Mitchell, J. (1974). *Psychoanalysis and Feminism: A Radical Reassessment of Freudian Psychoanalysis.* London: Allen Lane.

Mitchell, J. (1982). Introduction – I. In *Feminine Sexuality: Jacques Lacan and the École Freudienne,* J. Mitchell & J. Rose (Eds.). London: Macmillan, pp. 1–26.

Mitchell, J. (1984). The question of femininity and the theory of psychoanalysis. In J. Mitchell, *Women: The Longest Revolution. Essays in Feminism, Literature and Psychoanalysis.* London: Virago Press. Also in G. Kohon (Ed.), *The British School of Psychoanalysis: The Independent Tradition.* London: Free Association Books, 1986, pp. 381–398.

Mitchell, J. (1999). Introduction. In *Psychoanalysis and Feminism.* Harmondsworth: Penguin, pp. xv–xxxviii.

Mitchell, J. (2000). *Mad Men and Medusas: Reclaiming Hysteria and the Effects of Sibling Relations on the Human Condition.* London: Penguin.

Mitchell, J. (2004). The difference between gender and sexual difference. In I. Matthis (Ed.), *Dialogues on Sexuality, Gender and Psychoanalysis.* London: Karnac.

Mitchell, J. (2015). Debating sexual difference, politics and the unconscious: With discussant section by Jacqueline Rose. In R. Duschinsky & S. Walker (Eds.), *Juliet Mitchell and the Lateral Axis.* New York: Palgrave Macmillan, pp. 77–100.

Mitchell, J. (2016). Sibling, body-minds. Unpublished paper delivered to New York Psychoanalytic Society.

Mitchell, J., & Rose, J. (Eds.). (1982). *Jacques Lacan and the École Freudienne: Feminine Sexuality.* London: Penguin.

Moi, T. (2004). From femininity to finitude: Freud, Lacan, and feminism, again. *Signs: Journal of Women in Culture and Society,* 29 (3): 841–878. Also in I. Matthis (Ed.), *Dialogues on Sexuality, Gender and Psychoanalysis.* London: Karnac, 2004.

Money, J., Hampson, J. G., & Hampson, J. L. (1955). Hermaphroditism: Recommendations concerning assignment of sex, change of sex, and psychological management. *Bulletin of the Johns Hopkins Hospital,* 97: 284–300.

Morel, G. (2011). *Sexual Ambiguities.* London: Karnac.

Nasio, J.-D. (1998). *Hysteria from Freud to Lacan: The Splendid Child of Psychoanalysis*, New York: Other Press.

Oliver, K. (2012). Kristeva's maternal passions. *Journal of French and Francophone Philosophy*, 7 (1): 1–8.

Parat, C. (1995). *L'affect partagé*. Paris: Presses Universitaires de France.

Parsons, M. (2014). *Living Psychoanalysis*. London: Routledge.

Perelberg, R. J. (1981). Umbanda and psychoanalysis as different ways of interpreting mental illness. *British Journal of Medical Psychology*, 53: 323–332.

Perelberg, R. J. (1990a). Equality, asymmetry, and diversity: On conceptualizations of gender. In R. J. Perelberg & A. Miller, *Gender and Power in Families*. London: Karnac, 2012.

Perelberg, R. J. (1990b). Introduction – I. In R. J. Perelberg & A. Miller, *Gender and Power in Families*. London: Karnac, 2012.

Perelberg, R. J. (1996). "To be or not to be here: that is the question." Ce qu'une femme croit d'elle-même, de ses objets et de ces accidents. *Revue Francaise de Psychosomatique*, 10: 59–80. Reprinted as "To be – or not to be – here": A woman's denial of time and memory. In J. Raphael-Leff & R. J. Perelberg (Eds.), *Female Experience: Four Generations of Women on Work with Women*, new edition. London: Anna Freud Centre, 2008, pp. 60–76.

Perelberg, R. J. (1997a). Introduction to Part I. In J. Raphael-Leff & R. J. Perelberg (Eds.), *Female Experience: Four Generations of British Women Psychoanalysts on Work with Women*, new edition. London: Anna Freud Centre, 2008, pp. 21–35.

Perelberg, R. J. (1997b). Introduction to Part III. In J. Raphael-Leff & R. J. Perelberg (Eds.), *Female Experience: Four Generations of Women Psychoanalysts on Work with Women*, new edition. London: Anna Freud Centre, 2008, pp. 218–227.

Perelberg, R. J. (1997c). "To be – or not to be – here": A woman's denial of time and memory. In J. Raphael-Leff & R. J. Perelberg (Eds.), *Female Experience: Three Generations of Women Psychoanalysts on Work with Women*. London: Routledge. New edition: *Female Experience: Four Generations of Women Psychoanalysts on Work with Women*. London: Anna Freud Centre, 2008, pp. 60–76.

Perelberg, R. J. (1999a). The interplay between identifications and identity in the analysis of a violent young man. *International Journal of Psychoanalysis*, 80: 31–45. Also in *Time, Space and Phantasy*. London: Routledge, 2008, pp. 66–86.

Perelberg, R. J. (1999b). The interplay of identifications: Violence, hysteria and the repudiation of femininity. In G. Kohon (Ed.), *The Dead Mother: The Work of André Green*. London: Routledge, pp. 173–192.

Perelberg, R. J. (2003). Full and empty spaces in the analytic process. *International Journal of Psychoanalysis*, 84: 579–592.

Perelberg, R. J. (2005). Unconscious phantasy and après coup: From the history of an infantile neurosis. In R. J. Perelberg (Ed.), *Freud: A Modern Reader*. London: Wiley, pp. 206–223.

Perelberg, R. J. (2006). Controversial discussions and après-coup. *International Journal of Psychoanalysis*, 87: 1199–1220. Also in *Time, Space and Phantasy*. London: Routledge, 2008, pp. 106–130.

Perelberg, R. J. (2007). Space and time in psychoanalytic listening. *International Journal of Psychoanalysis*, 88: 1473–1490. Also in *Time, Space and Phantasy*. London: Routledge, 2008, pp. 131–149.

Perelberg, R. J. (2008). *Time, Space and Phantasy*. London: Routledge.

Perelberg, R. J. (2009). Murdered father, dead father: Revisiting the Oedipus complex. *International Journal of Psychoanalysis*, 90: 713–732.

Perelberg, R. J. (2011). "A father is being beaten": Constructions in the analysis of some male patients. *International Journal of Psychoanalysis*, 92: 97–116.

Perelberg, R. J. (2013a). Paternal function and thirdness in psychoanalysis and legend: Has the future been foretold? *Psychoanalytic Quarterly*, 82 (3): 557–585.

Perelberg, R. J. (2013b). Revue Française de Psychanalyse, 2011, Vols. 1–5: On some of the current themes in French psychoanalysis [Review]. *International Journal of Psychoanalysis*, 94: 589–617.

Perelberg, R. J. (2015a). On excess, trauma and helplessness: Repetition and transformations. *International Journal of Psychoanalysis*, 96: 1453–1476.

Perelberg, R. J. (2015b). *Murdered Father, Dead Father: Revisiting the Oedipus Complex*. London: Routledge.

Perelberg, R. J. (2015c). The structuring function of the Oedipus complex. In *Murdered Father, Dead Father: Revisiting the Oedipus Complex*. London: Routledge, pp. 125–160.

Perelberg, R. J. (2016). Negative hallucinations, dreams and hallucinations: The framing structure and its representation in the analytic setting. *International Journal of Psychoanalysis*, 97 (6): 1575–1590.

Perelberg, R. J. (2017). Love and melancholia in the analysis of women by women. *International Journal of Psychoanalysis*, 98 (6): 1533–1549.

Phillips, A. (1997). Keeping it moving: Commentary on Judith Butler. In J. Butler, *The Psychic Life of Power*. Stanford, CA: Stanford University Press, pp. 151–159.

Pichon-Riviere, E. (1970). *Del psicoanalisis a la psicología social, Tomo 1*. Buenos Aires: Editorial Galerna.

Pichon-Riviere, E. (1971). *Del psicoanalisis a la psicologia social, Tomo I1*. Buenos Aires: Editorial Galerna.

Pines, D. (1993). Skin communication: Early skin disorders and their effect on transference and countertransference. In *A Woman's Unconscious Use of Her Body: A Psychoanalytical Perspective*. London: Virago Press, pp. 8–24.

Pollock, G. H. (1968). The possible significance of childhood object loss in the Josef Breuer–Bertha Pappenheim (Anna O.)–Sigmund Freud relationship. *Journal of the American Psychoanalytic Association*, 16: 711–739.

Pontalis, J.-B. (1974). L'insaisissable entre-deux. In *Bisexualité et différence des sexes*. Paris: Gallimard.

Pontalis, J.-B. (1977). *Entre le rêve et la douleur*. Paris: Gallimard.

Pontalis, J.-B. (1999). *La force d'attraction. Trois essais de psychanalyse* [The force of attraction: Three essays on psychoanalysis]. Paris: Points Essais.

Preciado, P. B. (2013). *Testo Junkie: Sex, Drugs and Biopolitics in the Pharmacopornographic Era*. New York: The Feminist Press.

Racker, H. A. (1953). Contribution to the problem of countertransference. *International Journal of Psychoanalysis*, 34: 313–324.

Rado, S. (1940). A critical examination of the concept of bisexuality. *Psychosomatic Medicine*, 2 (4): 459–467.

Raphael-Leff, J., & Perelberg, R. J. (Eds.). (1997). *Female Experience: Four Generations of Women on Work with Women*, new edition. London: Anna Freud Centre, 2008.

Riviere, J. (1936). A contribution to the analysis of the negative therapeutic reaction, 1. *International Journal of Psychoanalysis*, 17: 304–320.

Rolland, J.-C. (2007). On the relevance of the borderline situation. In A. Green (Ed.), *Resonance of Suffering*. London: International Psychoanalytical Association, pp. 195–202.

Rosaldo, M. Z., & Lamphere, L. (Eds.) (1974). *Women, Culture and Society*. Stanford, CA: Stanford University Press.

Rose, J. (1982). Introduction – II. In J. Mitchell & J. Rose (Eds.), *Feminine Sexuality: Jacques Lacan and the École Freudienne*. London: Macmillan, pp. 27–57.

Rose, J. (2016). Who do you think you are? *London Review of Books*, 38 (9): 3–13.

Rosenberg, B. (1988). *Masochisme mortifère et masochisme gardien de la vie* [Deadly masochism and life-preserving masochism]. Paris: Presses Universitaires de France.

Roth, P. (2002). *The Dying Animal*. London: Vintage.

Salomé, L. A. (1916). *Anal and Sexual*. Oxford: Mimesis.

Sandler, J. (1976). Counter-transference and role-responsiveness. *International Review of Psycho-Analysis*, 3: 43–47.

Scarfone, D. (2010). In the hollow of transference: The analyst's position between activity and passivity. *Sitegeist*, 4.

Schaeffer, J. (1986). Le rubis a horreur du rouge. Relation et contre-investissement hystérique. *Revue Française de Psychanalyse*, 50: 923–944.

Schaeffer, J. (1994). "La belle au bois dormant". Comment le féminin vient aux filles? ["Sleeping beauty": How do girls encounter the feminine?]. *Revue Française de Psychanalyse*, Tome LVIII: 83–120.

Schaeffer, J. (1997). *Le refus du féminin*. Paris: Presses Universitaires de France.

Sherfey, M. J. (1972). *The Nature and Evolution of Female Sexuality*. New York: Random House.

Showalter, E. (1997). *Hystories*. London: Picador.

Smith, A. (2014). *How to Be Both*. London: Hamish Hamilton.

Sodré, I. (1994). Obsessional certainty versus obsessional doubt: From two to three. *Psychoanalytic Inquiry*, 14: 379–392.

Steiner, J. (2005). Gaze, dominance and humiliation in the Schreber case. In R. J. Perelberg (Ed.), *Freud: A Modern Reader*. London: Wiley, pp. 189–205.

Stoller, R. J. (1968). *Sex and Gender*. London: Karnac, 1984.

Temperley, J. (2005). The analysis of a phobia in a five-year-old boy. In R. J. Perelberg (Ed.), *Freud: A Modern Reader*. London: Wiley, pp. 61–71.

Torok, M. (1964). The meaning of penis-envy in women. In N. Abraham & M. Torok, *The Shell and the Kernel*, trans. N. Rand. Chicago, IL: University of Chicago Press, 1994.

Torok, M. (1994). The illness of mourning and the phantasy of the exquisite corpse. In N. Abraham & M. Torok, *The Shell and the Kernel*, trans. N. Rand. Chicago, IL: University of Chicago Press.

United Nations (1995). *Human Development Report*. Oxford: Oxford University Press.

Verhaeghe, P. (2009). *New Studies of Old Villains: A Radical Reconsideration of the Oedipus Complex*. New York: Other Press.

Weininger, O. (1903). *Geschlecht und Charakter*. Vienna. [*Sex and Character*. London, 1906.]

Williams, P. (2005). Notes upon a case of obsessional neuroses. In R. J. Perelberg (Ed.), *Freud: A Modern Reader*. London: Wiley, pp. 177–188.

Winnicott, D. W. (1959). Nothing at the centre. In *Psycho-Analytic Explorations*, pp. 49–52. London: Karnac, 1989.

Winnicott, D. W. (1966). The split-off male and female elements to be found clinically in men and women. [Paper read to the British Psychoanalytical Society.] In *Playing and Reality*. London: Tavistock Publications, 1971, pp. 72–79.

Winnicott, D. W. (1971a). Creativity and its origins. In *Playing and Reality*. London: Tavistock Publications, pp. 65–85.

Winnicott, D. W. (1971b). The use of an object and relating through identifications. In *Playing and Reality*. London: Tavistock Publications, pp. 86–94.

Wolf-Bernstein, J. (2011). A matter of choice (Review of book *Please select your gender*). DIVISION/Review, 3: 4–5.

Woolf, V. (2000). *A Room of One's Own*. London: Penguin.

Yarom, N. (1997). A matrix of hysteria. *International Journal of Psychoanalysis*, 78: 1119–1134.

Zilkha, N. (2013). Un héritage et une conquête au féminin. In G. Cabrol, M. Emmanuelli, & F. Nayrou (Eds.), *La sexualité féminine. Monographies et débats de la psychanalyse*. Paris: Presses Universitaires de France, pp. 181–201.

Zupančič, A. (2016). Sexuality within the limits of reason alone. In A. Cerda-Rueda (Ed.), *Sex and Nothing: Bridges from Psychoanalysis to Philosophy*. London: Karnac.

# Index

Abensour, L. 182
aboulia 156
Abraham, N. xvii, 115
active receptivity 226
adhesive love 123
Adler, A. 21
aesthetics, and psychoanalysis 57
affective perversion, innate perverse
  sexuality as 65
Aisenstein, M. 46; bisexuality,
  concept of 133–50
alienated identification 235
alienating alliances 172–3
alienating identification(s) 39; and
  sexuality 227–42; with parents
  238
alienating pact: between mother
  and daughter 178, 179;
  narcissistic 174–5; unconscious,
  acted-out transference of 181
amalgamating drives, theory of xv
ambisexuality 70
Ambrosio, G. 56
amenorrhoea 156, 157
anal eroticism 12
anal regression 12
anal zone 101
anality 15, 44, 52, 101, 158, 231, 251

analysand, active interpretation of
  183
analysis(es): bodily symptoms in
  105–7, 112, 156; dyadic structure
  in 277; flight from 95; psychic
  bisexuality unfolding in 151;
  sadomasochistic relationship in
  104; triadic structure in 277; of
  women, irrepresentable in 104
analyst(s): bisexualisation process of
  51, 224; bisexual listening of 46,
  134; female [analysis of women
  by 45, 49, 66–7, 103–21; gender
  of, relevance of 45, 64–71, 107,
  148, 153; male [analysis of
  female patient by 48, 49;
  sadomasochistic relationship with
  104; sleepiness of 207–9;
  thinking of, attacks on 184;
  transference to 107]
analytic session, articulation of
  psychic bisexuality within
  207–26
analytic situation, oedipal
  configuration of 107
analytic treatment, inherent
  restrictive conditions in, as
  experimental reproduction 65

Index

universal theory of life and
nature 259
foreclosure 14, 172; definition 279;
shared mechanism of 280; of
signifier of phallus 39; as
symbolic abolition 279
Forrester, J. 199
fort-da game 280
Foucault, M. 266, 268
fractured sexual subject 201
free associations, analysis of 7
French psychoanalysis 30, 33, 48,
49, 191
Freud, E.L. 4, 58
Freud, M. 91, 102
Freud, S. (*passim*): analyst's gender,
relevance of 107; articulation of
psyche 89; bisexual functions,
full restoration of, as aim of
analytic process 277; bisexuality
(of all human beings 1, 42, 86,
190, 207; as biological concept
59; and drive theory, search for
link between xvi; incontestable
ambiguity about 59–64;
universality of 50); case of
18-year-old woman homosexual
17–19; "A Child Is Being
Beaten" 19–21; difference
between sexes 89; Dora 4, 39,
197, 204 (masculine and
feminine identifications in
relation to primal scene implicit
or explicit in 7–9); drive theory
xv; ego, instigator of repression
to advantage of one sexual
orientations 62; Elizabeth Von
R 4; feminine, bedrock of 100;
femininity, repudiation of 21–2,
50, 209, 223, 282; and Fliess

90–1; fort-da game 280; full
bisexual function 42, 71;
hysteria, and bisexuality, link
between 3–6; hysterical
symptoms, sexual origins of 7;
identificatory processes, fluidity
of 37; infantile sexuality xvi;
Irma 119; Katharina 3; Little
Hans 7, 27, 98, 278 (masculine
and feminine identifications in
relation to primal scene implicit
or explicit in 9–10); Lucy R 4;
metapsychology xv; Minoan–
Mycenean period 144; "mono-
sex" theory 126; penis envy as
centre of gravity of femininity
126; pre-oedipal relationship to
mother 103; primal scene, and
anxiety, link between 4;
psychoanalytic treatment of
homosexuality 41, 64; "The
Psychogenesis of a Case of
Homosexuality in a Woman"
17–19; Rat Man 7, 42, 51, 84,
85 (masculine and feminine
identifications in relation to
primal scene implicit or explicit
in 10–12); repetition
compulsion 29, 280;
repression, and bisexuality, link
between 6; Schreber case 7,
169, 263 (masculine and
feminine identifications in
relation to primal scene implicit
or explicit in 13–14); self-
analysis 92, 98, 102, 198;
sexual difference, incontestable
ambiguity about 59–64;
splitting of ego, concept of 14;
traumatic neurosis, dreams

307